INSIGHT GUIDES

The world's largest collection of visual travel guides

Texas

Edited by Diana Ackland and Janie Freeburg
Updated by John Wilcock
Managing Editor: Martha Ellen Zenfell

Editorial Director: Brian Bell

APA PUBLICATIONS **L**

Part of the Langenscheidt Publishing Group

INSIGHT GUIDES

Texas

CONTACTING THE EDITORS: Although every effort
is made to provide accurate information in this
publication, we live in a fast-changing world and would
appreciate it if readers would call our attention to any
errors or outdated information that may occur by
writing to us at Apa Publications,
P.O. Box 7910, London SE1 8ZB, England.
Fax: (44) 171-620-1074.
e-mail: insight@apaguide.demon.co.uk.

First Edition 1986
Second Edition 1998

Distributed in the United States by
Langenscheidt Publishers Inc.
46–35 54th Road
Maspeth
NY 11378
Tel: (718) 784 0055
Fax: (718) 784 0640

Distributed in the UK & Ireland by
GeoCenter International Ltd
The Viables Centre, Harrow Way
Basingstoke, Hampshire RG22 4BJ
Fax: (44 1256) 817988

Worldwide distribution enquiries:
APA Publications GmbH & Co. Verlag KG
(Singapore branch)
38 Joo Koon Road
Singapore 628990
Tel: 65-8651600
Fax: 65-8616438

Printed in Singapore by
Insight Print Services (Pte) Ltd
38 Joo Koon Road
Singapore 628990
Fax: 65-8616438

Texas is one of those American
place names that always conjures up
immediate images: cowboys, cattle,
horses, Dallas, the Rio Grande. But it also
has a fascinating history and culture which
made it briefly an independent country and
gave the state a personality that has hardly changed since frontier days.

Ackland

These are the ideal ingredients for the
Insight Guide series, which is directed at the
serious traveler who wants to know more than
the routine tourist information. The formula
calls for each book to be well-written, illustrated with fine photographs, filled with frank,
clear journalism and detailed information at
the back. To tackle the task, Apa named as
project editors two experienced women who,
between them, had already coordinated several Insight Guides.

Freeburg

Diana Ackland has been an editor of *Good
Housekeeping* and a promotion manager for
the Los Angeles *Times* Syndicate. She and
her husband, Donald Ackland, run Sequoia
Communications, a Santa Barbara company.
Diana Ackland studied art history and English at Pine Manor and Dickinson colleges.

Janie Freeburg, Sequoia Communications'
managing editor, has planned, designed and
edited a number of publications in her years
as a public relations consultant, and has a
degree in comparative cultures from the University of California.

Smith

Together, Ackland and Freeburg assembled a team of fine Texas talent they
claimed rivaled the group behind the
publicly funded WPA Writers' Program Guide
to Texas, first published in 1940.

A freelance writer and editor who is especially knowledgeable about "Texana" is **John
Smith**, who gained a BFA in art history from
the University of Texas at Austin, then worked
for Southwestern Bell in the lovely Central Texas towns he writes about ("Waxahachie to
Waco" and "Waco to Austin").

Greene

Great-grandson of a Colorado gold rush-
er, and son of a West Texas sheriff, **Paul Pow-
ell** has traveled widely and his work has been
published in several journals ranging from *Na-*

Taylor

ture (London) to the *Tropical Root and Tuber Crop Newsletter*. **Mel McCombie**, who wrote about Houston, is a freelance writer specializing in art history and criticism, and divides her time between Austin and Houston.

The writer of the introductory sections is **A.C. Greene**, a past president of the Texas Institute of Letters and has worked as a "Texas Sketches" historical columnist for the well-known *Dallas Morning News*.

Jantzen

T he author John Steinbeck, in his book *Travels with Charley*, observed: "Once you are in Texas it seems to take forever to get out, and some people never make it." This is certainly true for most writers on the *Insight Guide: Texas* team, and few have complained about it.

Lisa Jones, who wrote about Tex-Mex food, was born at Fort Hood in Central Texas, and has worked in the manuscript collection of the Humanities Research Center.

For many years **Sue Winton Moss**, who was born in Mineral Wells, has traveled all over Texas as a historian and planner for the Texas Parks and Wildlife Department.

Folklorist **Winston Derdon**, who wrote the article "Don't Fence Me In," comes from Georgia. After moving to Texas he freelanced for publications such as *Western Folklore*.

Dubose

Another folklorist, **John Minton**, wrote the feature called "Musical Traditions." A guitarist from Kansas who likes to play country blues, he is working on a PhD in anthropology, with a concentration in folklore. "East Texas" and "The Gulf Coast" are based on reports filed by **Gary Taylor** of Houston, an emigré newspaperman from St Louis. Taylor has been a crime reporter in both Houston and Michigan.

Michael Murphy, who writes about Dallas and Fort Worth, and **Pamela Jantzen** who writes about Amarillo, Lubbock and penned the feature on Buddy Holly, are both based in Lubbock. Jantzen now works for an oil company. Murphy is a painter and a banker.

Wilcock

Fernando de Luna runs his well-known wine shop, Vintages, in Austin. He learned about fine wines and sherries from his grandfather and continued to major in wine while

Hara

at work on degrees in French and English from the University of Texas in Austin and St Edward's University.

The feature article, "Contemporary Texas Architecture," was written by **Lisa Germany** while putting together an exhibition and catalogue for the University of Texas School of Architecture. She is known for her architectural criticism in *Texas Monthly*.

Louis Dubose, who wrote "El Paso to the Desert," "Del Rio to Laredo," and "Rio Grande Valley," has lived all over Texas and has written for Austin's *Texas Observer*.

A travel guide is only as good as its most recent update. The text for this edition has been thoroughly scrutinized by Apa stalwart **John Wilcock**, who also wrote a completely new set of Travel Tips and the one-page feature on Neiman-Marcus.

J ohn Steinbeck, warming to his theme in *Travels with Charley*, continued: "Texas is a state of mind, Texas is an obsession," and this is certainly true of the photographers who traveled in all weathers and worked in all conditions to come up with the images reproduced here.

The excellent work of New York-based **Joe Viesti** has appeared in a number of *Insight Guides* as well as in publications such as *Geo, Stern* and *Pacific*. **Hara**, who gave us some pointed photo tips, is herself a Texan and a graduate of the Brooks Institute. She has worked for the National Park Service and the Smithsonian Institution in Washington.

Other contributing photographers include **Ruben Guzman**, born in Raymondville; **Kenneth Breisch**, who works for the Texas Historical Commission's National Register Department and **Richard Reynolds** and **Michael Murphy**, who traveled around the state shooting for the Texas Tourist Development Agency.

John Pezlak, a professor of chemistry at Hardin Simmons University in Abilene, allowed usage of several of his slides from his collection of over 1,500 transparencies; and **Linda Fink** of the Texas Highway Department made her archives available.

CONTENTS

Preceding pages: cattle brands; cowboy in contemplation; Dallas at dusk.

Maps

TRAVEL TIPS

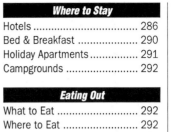

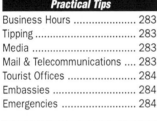

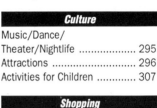

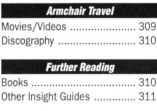

WELCOME TO TEXAS

There's one word people use more than any other to describe Texas. **BIG**. Big ranches, big cities, big money, big sky, big smiles, big mountains, big fun, and above all, big hearts. Plain and simple, Texas is a big place, and its image in the American mind has always been larger than life. It's been said that the United States is a frontier nation and that distinctly American notions like "rugged individualism" were shaped by the vast wilderness that beckoned at the country's western border. Possibly more than any other state, Texas epitomizes this frontier ethic. And, as some people see it, the American spirit has blossomed here more fully than anywhere else.

In fact, for many people, Texas is America. It's the one place where the American dream is still alive – where the values and traditions that helped build the nation are still a viable part of the culture. Think, for example, of all the American icons that come from Texas: the cowboy, the sheriff, the six-shooter, the 10-gallon hat, the maverick, the oil baron, the longhorn and the open range, just to name a few. And how many times have you seen the big-hearted, drawling Texan used to represent Americans as a whole, slapping the world on the back and inviting it in for a barbecue. These are all distortions, of course, but they immediately evoke an image of America that is recognized around the world.

Getting to know a place that is as broadly mythologized as Texas can be difficult. All too often we mistake the myth for reality. We prefer to see stereotypes or caricatures rather than develop an understanding of people and events. That's why it's important for travelers to strip away their preconceptions and try to pry the real Texas away from the "Texas image." Sometimes they are the same thing, but you'll find that they are often quite different.

The best way to approach the state is to forget about "Big Texas" and concentrate on something smaller. Texas isn't a single place, after all, and Texans aren't a single people. There is as much diversity here as there is anywhere else in the country. In fact, when you begin to focus on specific people, towns or places, you'll be surprised at how quickly the stereotypes begin to fall away. Yes, there are cowboys and wealthy oilmen. There are ranchers, Native Americans, Hispanics and plenty of horse traders, too. But there are also things that you never expected: a Vietnamese fishing community along the Gulf Coast, a Czech farming town out on the plains or a community of artists in a dusty border town.

In the world at large, this land will always be thought of as "Big Texas". But there is a "small Texas" too – a magnificent diversity of hopes, dreams, faiths and traditions that will reward any traveler willing to find them.

Preceding pages: cowgirl in good cheer; rodeo parade, Wichita Falls; cheerleaders at Southern football games have been a mainstay for decades; Tom Landry as legendary coach of the Dallas Cowboys; as easy as falling off a horse; Amarillo steakhouse. **Left**, flying fingers at Luckenbach, Hill Country.

Texas is a world in itself. To understand this, one starts with size. Texas, with 267,300 sq. miles (692,300 sq. km) in land area, is larger than many nations of the world, including all those of Europe. Size creates space, space makes for distance and distance creates differences. These are the basic ingredients that have contributed to making Texas and Texans outstanding in the eyes of the civilized world. Although often treated as a kind of international joke, the inescapable truth is that Texas is enormous, and its inhabitants are inordinately proud of it.

This explains not only the wide geographic choices for the visitor but the diversity of its people and their cultures. For in reality there is no such thing as "a Texas" or "a Texan." There are several different things which go under the collective name of "Texas" and several types of residents who share the common designation of "Texan."

Because of its size, traveling the entire state takes a good deal of time. There are 938 miles (1,509 km) of highway between Texline on the northern border of the Texas Panhandle, and Brownsville at the mouth of the Rio Grande across from Mexico. From Texarkana in the northeast corner beside the Arkansas border to El Paso at the extreme western tip of Texas is 813 miles (1,308 km). Even in the swiftest automobile, bus or train, most people cannot hope to cross the state in one day.

Distance and difference: As one crosses this vast surface, everything changes: the configuration of the earth, the economy, time zones, and often as not, the very seasons. It is quite possible, for example, to be snowbound in Amarillo and the next day be sunbathing on South Padre Island, on the lower Gulf Coast. And the torrid Texas summer that prevails in most of the state is pleasantly tempered by altitude in the vast mountain areas of the Big Bend and around Fort Davis in the Trans-Pecos region. After traveling a while, the visitor begins to understand why Texans never think of their province as one place, one thing or one society.

Preceding pages: the Amarillo Hotel. **Left,** downtown Fort Worth.

Size in Texas creates an amazing diversity of landscape, ranging from the beaches of the Gulf Coast to the Guadalupe Mountains, which tower over West Texas and Southern New Mexico as high as 8,750 feet (2,670 meters). On the eastern side of Texas it's easy to find dense forests, humid swamps and wide, slow-moving rivers, while at its western edges, some 500 miles (800 km) away, there are arid deserts, barren mountains and streams that, although furious when full, are often bone dry.

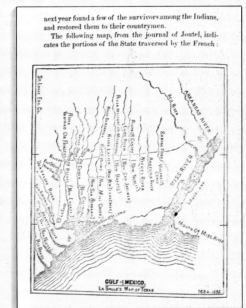

Its size also means that diverse natural resources and agricultural products are to be found in Texas. Oil and gas, of course, are almost everywhere in the state. Only 34 of Texas' 254 counties have not found oil or natural gas within their boundaries. Texas is the largest petroleum-producing state in the United States, and it has been estimated by economists that if Texas were an independent nation, it would rank as the world's fifth largest petroleum-producing country. The diminishing oil, however, is getting more and more expensive to pump out of the ground and no major new wells have been discovered for half a century or more.

In Texas, where forests and grasses clothe the land, one's sense of the past comes from human works – the buildings, roads and other monuments remaining from centuries of creative efforts. In Texas, what is under the land has often been more important than what is on top of it. Faults, folds, intrusions and other geologic movements, beginning 250 million years ago, formed the hidden reservoirs and basins that contain the great supplies of petroleum, natural gas, coal, salt and other minerals that bless Texas.

Not only has Texas increased in wealth and importance because of its subsurface minerals, but in its most important agricultural regions, the High Plains, where water around the many small conical hills, standing in pastures like the islands they once were. At its exposed southern end and along a 300-mile (480-km) northeastern jag, these upthrusts become the Edwards Plateau with its rolling hills and flowing springs.

The five states: The geographic magnitude of Texas and its topographical differences combine to produce not just separate, easily distinguishable natural regions, but corresponding cultures and societies almost as easily identified. It is interesting to note that the old Republic of Texas, when it joined the United States in 1845, retained by treaty the right to divide itself into as many as five states, should it so decide. And although this

pumped to the surface from underground aquafers has transformed a "desert" into one of the world's great cotton- and food-producing areas.

Nowhere is geology more interesting and dramatic than in western Texas, where the life of the gaunt, eroded landscape is measured in aeons. Submerged mountain ranges criss-cross great portions of the state, creating under West Texas the huge, shallow Permian Basin of petroleum fame, which emerges to form the dramatic canyons and cliffs of the Trans-Pecos and Big Bend regions. This country looks as if the waters of its ancient seas had dried up only recently option has so far been eschewed, it is still at the back of some minds. Despite the general uniformity of American culture brought on by the media and the concentration of political power in Washington, DC, a surprising variety of Texans exists. The so-called "Five States of Texas" are recognizable by the manner in which the inhabitants earn their living, the crops they farm, their attitude toward their own and other people's customs, religions and traditions.

The exact boundaries of North, South, West and East Texas may vary but the inhabitants of each seem to accept public definitions. Each major region contains its subregions, which are also recognizable to most Texans, such as the Gulf Coast, the Rio Grande Valley, the Panhandle and the High Plains. But these subregions have not acquired their own unique cultural patterns in the way the larger "states" have. For example, when a Texan mentions "West Texas," it is not just the western portion of the state that is being described. It is also a collection of traditions associated with that part of Texas and attached to its residents.

West Texans are considered highly individualistic, quick to react but free with their purse and time. In West Texas one is seldom told, "I don't have time to see you now." Because so many of the region's leaders

nomic survival. But all over Texas, the sight of the "horsehead" pump is common, some towering as high as a three-story building, pulling oil from those ancient reefs and seabeds many meters below the surface. One is bound to see more pump jacks than cowboys even in West Texas, informally known as "Big Ranch Country".

Place of legends: East Texas natives, especially old timers, are held by the rest of Texas to be shrewder, more Southern-rural, often gifted with a special kind of earthy humour and wisdom. Or, as one may still hear in certain parts of East Texas, they're "coonier," a tribute to the clever tactics of the raccoon, an animal quite prevalent in the region. This

have associated themselves with ranching and the oil business, West Texans are seen as people willing to gamble – forced to gamble by the nature of their enterprises. Ranching, whether cattle or sheep and goats, is a very cyclic undertaking, dependent on the fluctuations of both the weather and the market.

Oil is famous for not always being where the oil-man drills, but it can also reward its finder, and the landowner, with instant wealth. Most West Texas ranches today depend on oil and gas from their vast acres for eco-

was the part of Texas most like the Old South, with cotton plantations and slow, unhurried ways back in the time of its agricultural dominance.

Even today, East Texas is a region of mostly smaller towns and many rural communities of the crossroads variety, consisting of a general store, a service station, a couple of churches (usually Protestant) and maybe a schoolhouse left empty when the country schools were consolidated years ago. East Texas, incidentally, has produced some of Texas' better known writers and other artists, many of them working from the strong sense of tradition that seems to come with the

Left, cattle and oil in West Texas. <u>Above</u>, Sam Houston Park in Houston.

land. The late William Goyen's writings were filled with East Texas imagery. Alvin Ailey, the renowned choreographer, was born in East Texas. And sculptor James Surls, whose work can be seen in major Texas art museums, is based in East Texas and uses various woods found in the area as his main medium.

South Texas starts (in the Texas mind) at San Antonio and continues southward to the Rio Grande. Along its edges it supports two separate cultures; the long, well-populated curve of the Gulf Coast and that other world of mostly Hispanic Texans along the river border with Mexico. South Texas was the birthplace of the Texas cowboy, who began

as a Mexican *vaquero* (which is where the western term "buckaroo" came from) and of the 19th-century trail drives made famous in story, film and song, which began in the brush country. It remains a spread out, sparse land containing several of the state's major ranches, including the famous 800,000-acre (324,000-hectare) King Ranch, one of the largest series of ranching operations found in the world.

Owing to the centuries-old Hispanic influence (some land deeds in South Texas go back to the Spanish kings), South Texans have the reputation of being easy-going and are passionate and fiercely loyal to their

families and political leaders. The lower Rio Grande Valley, called simply "The Valley" by Texans, furnishes a large percentage of the citrus fruit and vegetables for sale in the United States.

North Texas shares fewer traditional traits, probably because of the region's long-time role as merchant to all the rest of Texas and the Southwest. Storekeepers have always had to learn to be all things to all customers, and North Texas has found customers all over the world for everything from clothing to electronics. Because Dallas and Fort Worth are its key metropolises – their combined areas going by the name "The Metroplex" – North Texas assumes more sophistication than other parts of Texas, although the statement meets fierce and determined resentment if repeated too often.

An atmosphere of promotion and display has influenced an unusual number of film and theatrical figures to come out of North Texas, including two Dallas playwrights, the late Preston Jones with his *Texas Trilogy*, and Don Coburn, whose *Gin Game* won a Pulitzer Prize in 1978. There is also writer Robert Benton, from Waxahachie, and Academy Award-winning film actress Sissy Spacek from Quitman.

Central Texas is not as well-defined geographically as the other sections, often overlapping them. But the folklore of its people is strong. Central Texas, perhaps from the fact that it contains Austin, the state capital, or because it has had to learn political compromise with its bordering regions, has contributed a large proportion of political figures to the lore of the Lone Star state.

The foremost example, of course, is the late US President Lyndon Johnson, who was born in the Hill Country, to the north and west of the capital, and who never attempted to pull up those roots throughout his lengthy career. The Hill Country, a southerly extension of the Edwards Plateau, with its clean rivers, lovely valleys and hilltop views – not to mention the best deer and wild turkey hunting in the state each fall – serves as a country retreat for thousands of Texans. Central Texas holds large German and Czech populations remaining from 19th-century colonization.

Left, stained glass of oil well. Right, page from an album of cattlemen.

Jared L. Brush.

Charles Lux.

R. G. Head.

John H. Iliff.

Thos. H. Lawrence.

John W. Snyder.

John T. Lytle.

A Texan's love of, and zeal for, Texas is stronger and more important than any regional affiliation. And the thing that binds Texans tightest is history. Pass through a few Texas towns large enough to have an independent school system, and the names on the schools will begin to take on a familiar sound: Austin, Crockett, Fannin, Bonham, Travis, Houston. Every town will have buildings or streets carrying one or more of those names, too. Schoolchildren, taught Texas history by legislative decree, grow up on

TRADING WITH THE INDIANS.

stories about its legendary heroes. Today, with thousands of Hispanic and black students, schools are beginning to be called by the names of ethnic heroes such as Benito Juárez, Emiliano Zapáta or Martin Luther King. Historical mythology is strong in all ethnic groups.

Unlike New England or the Atlantic seaboard states, Texas had no single source of settlement. White men came quite early to some parts of the state and arrived 350 years later to the others. The famous "Six Flags Over Texas" theme was quite real. Each flag – those of Spain, Mexico, France, the Republic of Texas, the Confederacy, the United States – represented a separate, if brief, period of the state's history.

The Texan coast may have been sighted by Amerigo Vespucci as early as 1497, but there is evidence of much earlier inhabitants – some possibly as far back as 37,000 years. Archaeological studies have revealed no grand past civilizations in Texas such as were found in Mexico and Central and South America. There were interesting cliff dwellers in the Texas Panhandle, and cave dwellers left traces of their fascinating paintings throughout western Texas for us to ponder. The Caddo confederations encountered in eastern Texas by the first Europeans were an agricultural people.

Natives: Along the Gulf Coast lived the nomadic Karankawas, who used simple farming methods and were not given to nomadic movement. Said to have been quite tall – and cannibals – they were wiped out by the white man's diseases and bullets before the 1850s. The Native Americans whom the Texas settlers battled were Plains tribes who rode in from the north on horses descended from those brought to the New World by early Spanish explorers.

One of these, Alvar Núñez Cabeza de Vaca, was cast ashore on what is believed to be Galveston Island, working his way across Texas for eight years before finally reaching Spanish Mexico in 1536. He and three other shipwrecked survivors of the Narvaez expedition were enslaved by the Karankawas, but after escaping gained such reputations as medicine men that when they approached a strange tribe, everyone turned out to welcome them. Cabeza de Vaca is said to have performed the first surgical operation in Texas, when he cut an embedded flint from a tribesman's shoulder.

When Cabeza de Vaca returned to civilization, he told tales of cities of gold and pearl "to the north" and the myth of the Seven Cities of Cibola became the motive for several Spanish expeditions to Arizona, New Mexico and Texas. The golden cities of Cibola and the equally mythical Gran Quivira were never found, of course, but the search for them led to Spanish colonization of the Southwest.

It was the French who caused the Spanish to begin settling Texas. In 1685, French explorer René Robert Cavelier, Sieur de La Salle, landed on the Texas coast in the area of Matagorda Bay and built a fort, claiming the surrounding area for France. By the time Spanish authorities in Mexico heard of the French intrusion, La Salle had been murdered by his own men and what was left of the colony was wiped out or captured by Native Americans in 1689. Nevertheless, the Spanish proceeded to build missions on the border separating French Louisiana and Spanish Texas.

In East Texas they met Native Americans who greeted them with the cry, "Tejas!"

for protection against the French and the Native Americans. Even San Antonio, the major Spanish settlement, was more important as a mission and military center than as a commercial center. But Spain's mark is still strong in Texas. Most of the outstanding geographical features and all major rivers bear Spanish names.

Spanish missions, today at least partly restored, are found in many Spanish settlements and a number of Spanish legal terms and property laws survive as Texas statutes. Perhaps the most important Spanish inheritance passed to cattle ranching. Almost every practice and piece of equipment used by ranchers has a Spanish name and origin. The

SAM. HOUSTON.

DAVID CROCKETT.

Thinking this was the name of a large tribe, the Spanish explorers called the area Tejas, or Texas. Later, settlers realized the word was a widely used greeting meaning "friend." Unsurprisingly, the Texas state motto is "Friendship."

Spanish heritage: Spain owned Texas for nearly three centuries but settled it only in narrow strips along the coast and the rivers

Preceding pages: the Alamo; storming of the Alamo. Left, trading with the natives. Above: heroes of the Texas Revolution: left, Sam Houston, Governor and Senator of Tennessee; and right, David Crockett, Congressman.

old regions of greatest Spanish colonization, from San Antonio and Laredo south, especially along the Rio Grande, show evidence of this influence in their architecture, language, religion and everyday customs.

In 1821, Mexico gained its independence from Spain and took control of Texas. During that same year Spain, then Mexico, granted Moses Austin permission to settle 300 Anglo-American families in Texas. Moses Austin died just as the permit was issued, but his son Stephen F. Austin carried on and is today known as the "Father of Texas." Those first colonists are to Anglo-Texas what the passengers of the *Mayflower* are to

Massachusetts; the proudest blood lines go back to "The Old 300." Eventually, hundreds more settlers joined the Austin colonists – many of them from other nations.

The Texas nation: "Texians" (as they were then called) never learned to get along well with the Latin laws, religion and political practices of Mexico. The inevitable break came in 1835 when the Anglo-American majority in Texas led a rebellion against what were considered despotic governmental practices – although, in reality, the despotism was mainly created by Mexican dictator Santa Ana.

The Texas Revolution lasted only eight months, but it gave Texas the myth and heroes such as Presidents Mirabeau B. Lamar and Anson Jones. This period was the seedbed for the feelings of loyalty that Texans are so famous for. And no matter how diverse their lives, or how far from Texas they may wander, all Texans hold the Alamo in common ownership.

For nearly a decade, from 1836 to 1845, the Republic of Texas was an independent nation with its own flag, its own ambassadors, its own President and Congress, and after some moving around, its own specifically designed national capital at Austin. It is true that millions of Texans today may recall the Republic only occasionally, but they have never forgotten it.

image which Texans are exhorted to live up to. It was this short but successful period of rebellion that created the Texas Valhalla with such heroes as Ben Milam, James Fannin, Jim Bowie, William B. Travis, James Bonham, Davy Crockett and General Sam Houston.

From the Texas Revolution came the stories of the Alamo, the massacre at Goliad, and the victory at San Jacinto, April 21, 1836, when a handful of Texans defeated the larger Mexican army commanded by Santa Ana and effectively ended Mexican control. After that eight-month period came the Republic of Texas with its own pageant of

Their self-reliance and fierce loyalty (which has not always endeared Texans to their fellow American citizens) comes from that decade of independence. The Lone Star flag, which is displayed as frequently as the national banner, and the state seal remain from that independent government; and according to the terms of the annexation treaty, Texas is one of the few states which refused to surrender its public lands to the federal government.

During this period of revolution, resettlement and republic, thousands of people came to Texas to get away from whatever their life had been "back home." They weren't always fleeing from the law. More often, the new Texans came west to escape failure or some sort of unhappiness that could be left behind. This is very much a continuing tradition.

Even today Texas becomes home for thousands who leave other parts of the nation every month to seek new opportunities in the Lone Star state. When one recalls that a high percentage of the dead at the Alamo, and a majority of the unfortunates who were slaughtered at Goliad, were recent arrivals in Texas, and that even Davy Crockett, the superhero of the Alamo, had only been in Texas for a few weeks, the tradition of the newcomer hero becomes more understandable. Of course, some of the natives grumble about

the modern "instant Texans" who move to Houstan or Dallas, buy themselves a pair of cowboy boots and immediately start "talkin' Texan," but most people don't care, just so long as Texas loyalty is pledged.

The Texas "style": The tradition of independence has had a direct influence on both the business climate and the political philosophy of modern Texas, creating a sense of self-sufficiency which, critics say, amounts

Left, Texas' only extant battle flag, displayed in the State Capitol in Austin. <u>Above</u>, General Ignazio Zaragoza, who defeated the French at Pueblo (Mexico), May 5, 1862.

at times to the conviction of Divine Destiny in the minds of some residents. Ownership of its public lands means that Texas controls its internal affairs with almost as much autonomy as in the days of the Republic. Rather than Texas going to Washington every time someone wants to create a park or cut a stand of timber, Washington has to come to Texas to ask permission to do such things – although today the federal government owns and controls several thousand acres of national forest in Texas.

The opportunity frontier: At the time of the Civil War, most Texas settlers were from the agricultural South. A plantation economy, with its accompanying slavery, controlled East Texas and the Coastal Plains, where cotton was a profitable crop.

Thus, Texas was overwhelmingly drawn into the Civil War on the side of the Confederacy. It was never torn by any major battles, and after the war sectional wounds healed quicker in Texas than in any other Southern state. Within a decade, newcomers from the Northern states were not only arriving in great numbers but were assuming positions of business and economic leadership.

Texas went through relatively little of the sorrow and desperation of the Reconstruction period. And because it was the only ex-Confederate state that offered its Southern sister states hope of a new beginning, Southerners flocked there too. The 15 years after Appomattox saw Texas emerge as the opportunity frontier of the whole nation, north and south alike. It has held that position and reputation in the following century.

Families from every social level picked up and moved to Texas, bursting the old frontier boundaries until, like a flooding river, they swept out on to the prairies and battled with Native Americans for the wealth of grass and soil which was once thought to be the "Great American Desert."

This movement to the frontier created two new Texas myths: one was the frontiersman and his sturdy pioneer wife, and the other was the cowboy. The cowboy survives, although a visitor will seldom see one mounted on his horse along the highways. Back on the ranches, cowboys still rope, brand and ride. Sometimes they use a pickup truck or even a helicopter, but horse and rider are still the best (and sometimes the only) way to work range cattle.

Although at least a dozen western states contributed to the cowboy legend, Texas has done more than its share to make the cowboy an American icon. Several thousand cowboys can still be found doing all the traditional cowboy chores except fighting Native Americans – which was never a cowboy chore in the first place. The traditional garb of the cowboy is also seen in hundreds of Texas cities, towns and villages, although not everyone wearing high-heeled boots and a cowboy hat will be a cowboy.

citizen, openness, mutual trust and a sense of sharing by people living under the same pressures. A lot of Texas business, including big business deals, is conducted on the basis of a handshake or a telephone conversation. That is rare in any part of the globe and, unfortunately, is rapidly becoming rarer even in Texas.

But the frontier was a mutually dependent society. If someone was lazy, weak or careless, everyone might be hurt, and thus all were expected to shoulder their share of

Boots, oversized belt buckles, denims and rodeo shirts are everyday wear for millions of Texans – not a costume – and a visitor who wishes to dress in the same manner should feel perfectly free to do so. Unlike some areas of the world where the traditional national dress is held sacred, Texans not only accept but encourage visitors to wear traditional clothes.

In a sense, the frontiersman and his mate survive, although the conditions and the times that made them have long since passed. It is the frontier that still provides so much of the motivation for today's Texas: self-sufficiency, a sense of obligation to one's fellow

community work and duty. Hard work and shrewdness were valued over the creative arts and purely intellectual pursuits. Today, most Texans are still deeply influenced by these values, although by now they are far more receptive to intellectual and artistic accomplishment.

The great oil rush: The greatest change in the way Texas lived and viewed itself began in 1901, when the Spindletop oil field near Beaumont, in the southeastern corner of the state, blew in with billions of barrels of oil each year. Spindletop is where the world's modern petroleum industry was born. No field like it had been dreamed of before, and the dramatic flow of its initial producer, the Lucas gusher, guaranteed that Texas, and the world, would never be the same.

With Spindletop the state jumped from an agricultural economy to a financial-industrial economy. At first, Texans were slow to recognize the change. In fact, they still haven't fully accepted it. To this day, the struggle between rural and urban values continues to divide the state. In the decades since Spindletop, Texas has never failed to lead the United States in petroleum production. In many of the early days, it led the world. This added to the tendency of Texas to measure itself not against sister states but against the world – the universe!

Texas facts and figures are seldom expressed as "*One* of the biggest... *One* of the best." Everything tends to be carried to the highest power: *The* biggest, *The* best. And Texas planners tend to think along the same lines. That's one of the reason why such a high percentage of recent US building and real estate development has taken place in cities such as Dallas, Houston and Austin: bigger is better! Of course, this is not always the case, and some Texas cities have experi-

Left, mosaic in Gonzales, southeast of Austin, commemorates the first shot fired in the Texas Revolution. **Above**, not-so-lonesome cowboy.

enced the disadvantages of uncontrolled growth. But this fact has not discouraged Texas developers.

Today, the oil industry is more than an important part of the economy. It unites the state. Even in the 34 non-producing counties, oil plays a vital part in local business. Dallas is a perfect example: it is a city legendary the world over for its involvement in the oil business, but it is located in a section of Texas that has never produced any of it.

But Texas' rich oil resources are a double-edged sword. On the one hand, oil has brought immeasurable wealth to the state, especially now that domestic sources of energy are so highly valued. But Texans' reliance on oil has also made the state vulnerable. The crash in world oil prices has caused a great deal of hardship in Texas over the last few years, and now more than ever state leaders have finally recognized the importance of economic diversification.

Everything from the fashion industry to electronics is currently taking root in Texas, and together they are challenging the oil industry's long tenure at the head of the economic pyramid. The new economy is based on a more generalized and sounder combination of manufacturing and finance.

Texas has taken over national leadership in many phases of the chemical industry (not just petrochemicals), has remained an important aerospace center, and is attracting more and more technological manufacturing and development firms. But still a major farm and ranch center, it contains the most farmland of any American state and ranks third within the United States in total agricultural income. It is first in the production of cotton, cattle, sheep and goats and, in most years, rice.

Sunbelt advantages: Its location in the US "Sunbelt" is also slowly but steadily drawing the national headquarters of all sorts of corporations, which are shifting thousands of employees to the Lone Star state not just for its more favourable year-round climate but also because of its access to world markets, its central location and its eagerness to acquire fiscal and industrial families. Major international corporations have been opening branches in Dallas and Houston.

Despite their strong sense of history, Texans have always been receptive to new ideas, never holding on to some outdated asset for sentimental or historical reasons. Although they quite clearly appreciate tradition, they are also a pragmatic people, and they are willing to make changes in the name of progress. Even the Alamo, the sacred shrine of Texas liberty, had to be rescued from commercial development as late as 1905. In most cases, historical and sentimental concerns take a back seat when they involve anything less than the biggest and the best. This attitude might strike some observers as rather hard-hearted or mercenary but Texans are so frank about it that most people find it somewhat endearing.

So now we have looked at Texas as it was, as it is, and as it is mythologized. Its history

multilingual they have great patience with anyone who has difficulty with English.

Most Texans show a great deal of public respect for the elderly and for women. Even street urchins use such terms as "ma'am" (madam) and "sir" to adults. Many Texans see themselves as the highest expression of the American character. To them, Texas is the epitome of the American dream, valid in every way. They believe in Texas in a way more often found in older, more chauvinistic cultures. But Texas is also maturing, taking on an international viewpoint as more of its young people travel outside its borders.

Texas is growing swiftly and coming of age socially and artistically with a speed to

has remained an important factor in creating and maintaining the Texas of mythology and the enthusiastic Texas of today – but history has not restrained the state at any stage of its journey.

Friendliness and hospitality are Texan traditions that are quickly adopted by new residents. Visitors will find Texans, in general, helpful and gracious. They are never too busy to answer questions, give directions or help out people in need. The smaller the town, the more likely you will receive this personal attention, but even the big cities of Texas have more public heart than most other big cities. Although few Texans are

match its technology. Although artists are not yet given the respect and support they receive in other societies, Texas is beginning to accept more responsibility for supporting the arts in their many and varied forms. And there are few visitors who will not find some expression of their native or national tradition honored and admired in one of the Texas museums, galleries or parks.

Texas plays a lot and is dedicated to sports, particularly baseball and American football, although soccer has become popular with millions of younger Texans, more and more of whom are playing the game. Texas athletes of both sexes have established them-

42

selves as stars and record-holders in track and field, swimming, gymnastics, golf, baseball, basketball, tennis, racing (both motor and horse racing), sailing and polo. There is scarcely a town that cannot volunteer the name of some native son or daughter who has gone on to receive national or international acclaim in some sport. And visitors who participate in such activities as golf or tennis will find doors open to them throughout the state.

Challenging changes: Although in the eyes of the United States, as well as the rest of the world, the prevailing image of Texas remains rural, it is solidly urbanized by a ratio of 10 to one. Life today in the larger Texas

rior rural values. Regardless of their value as background in television series or films, to depict sophisticated shopping centers and cosmopolitan boutiques as typical of Texas violates some of the world's most precious conceptions (or misconceptions). Yet the urbanity is all true, and in the major cities one can find virtually every famous retail name and designer fashion label offered in the capitals of Europe and Asia, or in New York or Los Angeles.

As a matter of fact, many Europeans and glamorous figures from the rest of the United States come to Texas to shop in such exclusive stores as the world-renowned Neiman-Marcus. Few people realize that Dallas ranks

cities has scant connection with the Texas of history and romance. Nevertheless, these metropolitan people were fascinated, along with everybody else, by the television drama *Dallas*, which – despite the cast working in high-rise offices and partying at various night clubs – pictured the ranch as the center of Texas family life, even if the Ewings were not exactly an average family.

Films like *Tender Mercies* not only have a rural setting but celebrate supposedly supe-

Left, dressing as a frontiersman and his mate at a charity ball. **Above**, Southfork Ranch where the exteriors for TV's *Dallas* were shot.

as the second or third largest fashion marketing center in the United States. But of course, as Texas has grown, it inevitably acquired the vices and problems it long scorned as "foreign" or "big city." It has three of the dozen largest US cities within its borders, so slums, smog, pollution and traffic are a part of the urban scene.

Texas is said to be modern America in microcosm, bowing to changes while proclaiming rugged individualism. Perhaps this is the best way for personal independence in the United States to survive – honoring rigid traditions while at the same time regarding them with a flexible state of mind.

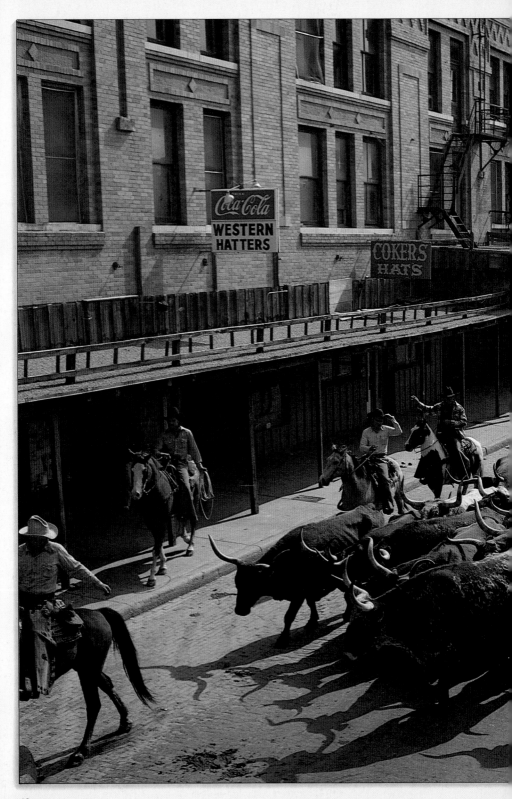

One of the saddest sights in New Orleans or Galveston is the daily arrival of hundreds of refugees from the older Southern states, seeking homes on the Texan prairies. The flood of emigration from South Carolina, Alabama and Georgia is formidable... Old men and little children, youths and maidens clad in homespun, crowd the railway cars, looking forward eagerly to the land of promise. The ignorance of these people with regard to the geography of the country in general, is dense. "I never travelled so much befo'," is a common phrase; "is Texas a mighty long ways off yet?"

—Edward King, 1874

Anglos established the overall trends of the state's cultural development when they wrested the area from Mexico a century and a half ago. But there have been other constant cultural influences: Texas is crosshatched with a complicated pattern of regional and ethnic divisions. Anglos who settled in Texas before annexation were mainly from the American South, although, even within this group, there were significant cultural differences. Immigrants from the deep South – where slavery was most deeply rooted – tended to settle to the east of San Antonio. Those from the upper South – where slavery was less pervasive – tended to settle to the west. Like Southerners today, these settlers held a wide range of political, religious and moral views, some of them in direct opposition to each other. And yet, despite their differences, early settlers established the powerful Anglo-Southern or Anglo-Celtic-Southern culture in contrast to, and usually at odds with, those of other immigrants.

The cowboy image: For a long time the Anglos east of San Antonio set the tone for the whole state. Texas was not just Southern – it was an extension of the Deep South. In the oil-rich 20th century their influence waned while the West, with its powerful icons, became more influential. Denim overalls

and cotton growing gave way to cowboy boots and cattle raising as essential elements in Texas' international image. Non-Southern dishes like chicken-fried steak, chili and tortillas have by and large replaced grits, greens and cornbread on the Anglo table.

Today, Texas is identified much more readily with the American West than with the South, and recent immigrants seem to prefer the state's "cowboy image" to its connection with the Confederacy. Even long-time Texans seem to be giving up their claim

to the Old South and their nostalgic attachments to the heyday of Southern culture. Although, for the most part, cowboys are a thing of the past, the "cowboy image" seems more in keeping with the state's vitality than the cultivation of Southern memories. And because cowboying was never an exclusively Anglo experience, it tends to cross Texas' many ethnic boundaries.

Anglo-Southerners are not just being westernized, they are disappearing as such. Whites of Old Southern descent definitely make up less than half the population. And due to the large number of Mexican-Americans living in Texas, white non-Hispanics form a smaller percentage of the population here than in the country as a whole.

The composition usually called "Anglo" is likely to consist of several European and possibly some non-European elements. Texas was the location of the earliest Polish community in the United States and some of the first Irish ones. The largest group of immigrants to come directly from Europe were Germans. Intermarriage between Anglo-Southerners and recently arrived continental colonists and between these groups and Hispanics occurred as soon as they began to live within sight of each other. The taboo against Anglo-black marriages is rarely broken even today, but if the 32 great-great-

dently wanted an Irish Catholic buffer between the areas of increasing Protestant-born Anglo settlement and the Spanish-speaking Catholics.

After the Republic of Texas was declared in 1836, the Europeans viewed the area as more stable politically than when it was part of Mexico. Leaders of the Republic encouraged immigration more actively than had the Mexican government. Whether Texas would be annexed by the United States was then unknown, but these factors combined to open Texas up to a flood of Europeans whose imagination had been captured by the Texas Revolution. From the beginning, the Texas government saw to it that new settlers re-

grandparents of typical Texas blacks could be assembled, some of them would be black and some of them would be white.

An O'Conner becomes Oconór: The Irish were among the first Europeans in Texas. In fact, Hugo Oconór was a Spanish governor of Texas in the late 18th century. Where this Oconór came from and how he ended up in the employ of the Spanish are questions to which the answers are lost. He was called the "Red Captain" for the color of his hair. More Irish arrived in Texas in the 1820s, when the Spaniards granted what are now the counties of Refugio and San Patricio (Saint Patrick) to Irish settlers. The Mexican government evi-

ceived land. Immigrant aid groups like the Adelsverein organized migration to Texas but it was not well-administered and ran short of badly needed relief funds.

Germans: *One of the party said to me: "I think if one or two of the German tyrants I could mention could look in upon us now, they would display some chagrin at our enjoyment, for there is hardly a gentleman in this company whom they have not condemned to death, or to imprisonment for life." … Laboring like slaves (I have seen them working side by side, in adjoining fields), their wealth gone; deprived of the enjoyment of art, and, in a great degree, of literature;*

removed from their friends, and their great hopeful designs so sadly prostrated. I have been assured, I doubt not, with sincerity, by several of them, that never in Europe had they had so much satisfaction – so much intellectual enjoyment of life, as here.
　　　　　　　—Frederick Law Olmsted, 1857

The Germans' first permanent settlement was Industry in Austin County west of Houston, so-called for its cigar factory. Many Germans settled in the port cities of Galveston and Indianola. Typically, they wrote home an "America letter" that described – often with exaggerated if not downright false hopefulness – the human happiness, fertility and

found their bearings, they proceeded to establish daughter communities. Constrained by the settlement patterns of previous groups and the threat of Comanche raids farther west, most Germans made their homes in a 10-county strip to the north of San Antonio. In fact, San Antonio became the center of German influence in the state.

The German immigrants came from all walks of life. Some were simple peasant farmers, others had never tended the land but were quite well-educated. They brought their libraries with them – extensive for the time and place – and belonged to such learned organizations as the Goethe Society. Men of science such as Nikolas Zink, an engineer;

wonderful climate of Texas. Their letters were shared by a village or other group from which more brave Germans, despite the danger, set out. German immigrants tried to bring along an entire support group, motivated in varying degrees by wanderlust, political idealism and the desire for social and economic improvement. Those who did not stay in the relatively urban ports usually settled for a while in the interior where there were friends and relatives. After they had

Left, cadet and date at Texas Air Museum, Harlingen. **Above**, German Texans at Auslander Restaurant, Fredericksburg.

Dr Ernst Kapp, a geography professor; and Duke Paul of Württenberg, an explorer, were important influential members of their settlements.

In *Journey Through Texas,* Frederick Law Olmsted, who traveled throughout the South from 1850 to 1859, wrote with surprise and admiration about the intellectual attainments of the German colonists in Texas. He described their primitive but neat log cabins, plastered and stuccoed, and their books, musical instruments and paintings. Olmsted hoped their liberal influence would move Texas out of the Old Southern sisterhood of slave states.

Most of the Germans disliked slavery. Neither did they wish to annihilate the Native American, who considered Germans – when it was possible to differentiate – a distinct tribe, superior to the loathsome Spaniards, Mexicans and Anglo-Americans. Today Germany is the origin of most non-Hispanic whites in Texas, after Britain.

The Latin colonies: In the German agricultural villages of Sisterdale, Bettina and Comfort, Latin was spoken in everyday life. They are remembered as "Latin colonies," and they mystified their Anglo neighbors. It is just as well the neighbors understood little of what the Germans had to say, for their beliefs were generally very different from those of

the Anglo-Southerners. Not only were many of them opposed to slavery, as Olmsted the Abolitionist noted, but several communities – Sisterdale and its daughter village of Comfort, in particular – were the centers of free thought and agnosticism. Many of the German settlers were Lutheran and a few Catholic, but their free-thinking may have been unique on the frontier.

German settlers often gathered on market days and holidays to sell their produce or celebrate. On these occasions, whether revisiting a large market city such as San Antonio or just celebrating at one of their farms or villages, they roasted a calf, sheep

or goat. Some people regard this custom as the origin of that typically Texan food, the barbecue. There are also people who believe another unique Texas preparation, chicken-fried steak, is of German derivation. They point to its obvious similarities with the German schnitzels, which are also breaded and pan-fried cuts of meat. To make chicken-fried steak, a cream-style gravy is added.

Whether or not the Germans gave these two entrées to Texas cooking, broad German influence continues to this day in certain parts of Texas. Until the 1950s, the Tex-Deutsch dialect, an amalgam of English and German, was spoken in many settlements of San Antonio. Today it has almost disappeared, and the Germans of the Texas Hill Country are becoming more like the Anglo majority and less like a true minority group.

Deliberate attempts to preserve German festivals have resulted in the regular celebration of the Fredericksburg Easter Fires and the *Wurstfest* in New Braunfels. The Easter Fires are lighted on the hills surrounding Fredericksburg on the Saturday before Easter. While local legend holds these fires were originally set by Comanche Indians, scholars such as the University of Texas geographer Terry Jordan have demonstrated that they were probably a custom brought from southern Germany which can be traced to pagan roots.

The *Wurstfest* in New Braunfels usually comes in fall at more or less the same time as the German *Oktoberfest*. Sausage and beer consumption, and a *gemütlich* sociability, link this New World celebration to the beer halls and *kellers* of Munich.

Slavs: *Trilingual (Wendish-German-English) community founded in 1854 by 588 Wends under the leadership of the Rev. John Kilian. The Rev. Kilian (Evangelical Lutheran) named the place Serbin because the Wends were descendants of Serbs.*

A thriving town 1865–1890; had grocery, dry goods, jewelry, drug and music stores, shops of wagon maker, blacksmith, saddler, post office, three doctors, two dentists.

On Smithville-Houston Oxcart Road – sending out cotton, other produce, and hauling in staples.

Decline began about 1890 as railroads bypassed settlement by several miles.

—Texas State Historical Marker at Serbin, Texas

Just as German communities have adapted more and more to the dominant Anglo culture except for the occasional fête, other small groups have been similarly absorbed. A group of Polish Catholics followed their priest southeast of San Antonio in 1854 to set up the first Polish colony in the United States, Panna Maria. Later, several more Polish towns were established in Texas. Two other major Slavic groups in the state are the Czechs and Wends.

Together, several central and eastern counties still have the largest rural populations of Czechs in the United States. Czech settlements are generally agricultural, and most Texas Czechs have made their names and

tin to eat sausage and sauerkraut and dance the polka. Wends are a German-speaking group who left their homes in Prussia in the 1840s. Those in Texas settled in two counties east of Austin, Lee and Fayette. The church and farm were the centers of Wendish life. Today most Wends have left the smaller towns for the city, but their colony in Texas was the only such community located in North America.

Cajuns and others: French colonization of Texas was sporadic. While La Salle and other French explorers were among the early visitors to Texas, and Jean Lafitte and his pirate band established an early enclave in Galveston, the present French influence on

fortunes as farmers. Not as numerous as the Germans, the Czechs have nevertheless preserved their culinary traditions. Their jam-filled rolls called *kolaches* are especially popular and are a special treat at the Institute of Texan Cultures' Folk Fest in San Antonio each August.

Several Czech communities hold special celebrations to honor their heritage. Annual festivals in West, Taylor and Ennis draw city-dwellers from Dallas, Houston and Aus-

Left, Treue der Union Monument in Comfort honors German Texans murdered by Confederate soldiers in 1862. Above, German Texans.

the state has mainly come from a group of French-American settlers. The Cajuns are descendants of the Acadians, who were removed from their Canadian homeland in the 19th century. After resettling in French-owned Louisiana, they developed their own culture combining French, Spanish, Indian and black elements.

In the early 20th century, the discovery of oil in East Texas lured Cajuns to the area. The Texas Cajuns tend to blend into other ethnic groups and be considered either Anglo or black, but their Gallic love of good food and good times lends a distinctive flavor to the East Texas areas where they have settled.

Jambalaya, gumbo, and crawfish *étouffé* are eaten throughout the bayou country of East Texas. Cajun music is also enjoying renewed popularity in the state. Usually played on accordions and guitars and sung in the Cajun French *patois*, this music brings many an East Texas dance hall high kicking and alive on Saturday nights.

Other even smaller groups have blended into the Anglo culture. A substantial Scandinavian population immigrated to the hot climate of Texas. Greeks settled along the coast, with Galveston as their most important community. A small Italian contingent lived in larger cities but had several agricultural settlements in the Brazos Valley.

Spanish cathedral where swarthy penitents, muffled in shawls, crouch on the stone floor and tell their beads. Here are spacious stores, filled with as costly goods as can be found in Eastern cities, daily newspapers, banks, water works, gas works, telegraph offices, a club and a theatre; and there are quaint and dirty little Mexican shops, adobe buildings with loop-holed battlements, scarred with bullet marks, alongside wagon trains from Chihuahua and Monterrey bringing silver and taking back cotton, soldiers, priests, nuns, negroes, greasers, half-breed Comanches, dirt, dogs and fleas.
—Description of San Antonio in
New York Tribune, 1879

The Jews' principal migration took place in the 19th century when German and Eastern European Jews came to Texas. Today Jews are an urban group in Texas, but synagogues in small towns like Brenham and Corsicana are reminders that they have been here as long as many other Europeans.

Hispanics: *Here are fine stone mansions that would not be out of place in the loveliest suburbs of Philadelphia, and here are Mexican huts thatched with cornstalks, beside which the dwellings Stanley saw in Uganda were models of comfort. Fine modern churches, with carpeted aisles and cushioned pews, stand in sight of a venerable*

In his book of essays, *In a Narrow Grave*, Larry McMurtry says that Texas cities are always improved when the Hispanic influences the Anglo. If this is true, Texas cities must be improving: their Hispanic populations are increasing steadily. In the 1980 census, San Antonio, Houston and El Paso were among the top eight US metropolitan areas in total Hispanic population. Texas follows only California in number of Hispanics; people with Spanish surnames make up more than a quarter of its population. In cities like Dallas and Houston, where blacks used to be the largest minority, Hispanics are gaining on or surpassing them.

At some point in the late 1940s they overtook blacks as the dominant minority group in the state. Spanish-speaking peoples are re-Hispanicizing the state, following much the same immigration patterns as Anglos.

This is ironic, as it was the inability of the Mexican government to induce Spanish speakers to move to Texas that was one of the reasons Mexico could not hold on to the area. They are no longer confined behind the imaginary boundary that kept them west and south of the San Antonio River. There are *barrios* in Dallas and Fort Worth and even the Panhandle, bringing Mexican-American customs, traditions and color as far as the windswept High Plains.

speaking Texans have made their cuisine part of the mainstream of Texas life and, increasingly, that of the rest of the nation. *Tacos, enchiladas, fajitas* and all the rest of the Tex-Mex menu are found as often on the Texas table as chuck roast and ice-tea.

While chili may be an Englishman's attempt to reproduce curry in Texas, and the barbecue may have originated with German Texans, neither of these staples of Texas cooking would taste the way they do without their Hispanic spices.

Blacks: *But the more he read and learned about the blues, the more he discovered why the secret was so well-kept. "The Rollin' Stones, Eric Clapton and Cream – who I*

The Hispanics were the first non-Native American Texans, or *Tejanos*, and descendants of these original settlers form a small, stable and often wealthy core of the Spanish-speaking population of Texas. Sometimes intermarrying with wealthy Anglos, these *Tejanos* have preserved a culture distinct even from the rest of the Spanish-speakers.

Hispanic influence is strongly felt at the dinner tables and snack bars of Texas. More than any other minority group, Spanish-

Left, lively Mexican-Americans in traditional costume are a common sight during festivals. **Above,** compadres at the Brownsville City Hall.

used to love – all my idols fell apart before my very eyes. They were nothing but low-down, dirty thieves! They steal the music from these cats and then carry on like they are something. They can't admit that they stole it! They can't be big enough to stand up there and say, "Hey, if you like me, you should check out the masters, the men who made this music first."
—Austin nightclub-owner Clifford Antone (Antone's) to Ed Ward in the *Austin American-Statesman*, 1980

The other major minority group, blacks, have not been absorbed by the Anglo culture as the Germans and Czechs have, but they have lived in Texas as long as the Spaniards themselves. When Cabeza de Vaca was shipwrecked on the Gulf Coast in 1528, Esteban, or Black Stephen, was a guide for the Coronado Expedition. He was eventually killed by Native Americans, probably in Sonora, Mexico. Blacks, enslaved or free, were found in subsequent Spanish settlements, and intermarriage resulted in a significant mulatto population in Spanish Texas.

Many Texas blacks count Spanish names among their forebears. The first large infusion of blacks came after the Republic of Texas was established. The Mexican stand against slavery had made owners reluctant to

responsible for the decline in the share of the general population that is Afro-American: Hispanics have now overtaken blacks as the largest minority group. Geographer Terry Jordan believes that Texas' transition from a Southern to a Western self-image is linked to this shift in the most visible minority. Blacks are part of the Southern tradition, while Hispanics seem to belong to later 19th-century frontier history.

The popularly accepted idea that blacks were not an important part of western frontier life ignores some significant black history. Many runaway slaves and free blacks joined the Native Americans and lived with them, not just on the frontier but beyond it.

import their human chattels. The absence of slavery had created a haven for free blacks, but after independence it became legal and former Deep Southerners began to bring in slaves at an increasing rate. Slavery tended to be concentrated east of the Texarkana-San Antonio line, where the Anglo "masters" were settled.

Following Emancipation, and into the 20th century, blacks often lived a rural life on scattered farms or in small black communities. Today, as they move to cities within Texas and elsewhere, the rural communities that preserved black culture are dying out. Black migration to cities outside the state is

The black soldiers of the ninth and 10th Cavalry and the 24th and 25th Infantries who fought the Native Americans were called "buffalo soldiers" by the tribes. The 10th Cavalry adopted the buffalo as its coat of arms. Despite the role played by black soldiers in the Indian wars, most Texans continue to associate blacks only with the Southern strands of Texas' history. Blacks themselves are more often urban now, so that their political and cultural influence is most strongly felt in the cities.

Native Americans: Texans tend to think their Native American population was killed off or dispersed to other states. In fact, many

Texas tribes were totally destroyed, including the Tejas who gave the state its name. For many years, it was commonly believed that the only unassimilated Native Americans in the state were the Alabama and Coushatta, Southern tribes who migrated to East Texas where they lived on one of the state's three reservations.

Other important groups include the Tiguas, who preserved their culture almost in secret in the *barrio indio* of El Paso, and the Kickapoos, who migrate annually from Mexico to Eagle Pass in South Texas. Recently, Native Americans have been staging a comeback in Texas.

Oklahoman and New Mexican Indians,

especially Cherokee and Navajo, have moved to the larger cities. In Dallas and Houston, which have the largest Native American populations, they live in distinct communities, but not along tribal lines. When this new wave of immigration is added to the sum of all the Texans who have at least some Indian blood, Native Americans in Texas may turn out to be a better represented group than had been thought.

Left to right: black Texan serving barbecue at Buffalo Gap, Abilene; Native American at a Texan ranch; Asian Texan at Pantex Assembly Plant, Amarillo.

Asians: Asians were the last large group to be added to the Texas mix, although they first came to the state on their eastward trek after the California gold rush. Chinese laborers worked on the railroad, but rail companies frequently abandoned them when tracks were finished. Isolated in a strange world, the Chinese were often hired as cheap labor to undercut emancipated blacks.

The first wave of Chinese immigrants did not have much lasting impact on Texas since US immigration laws banned most Chinese women from the United States. Some agricultural laborers in Robertson County intermarried with local women, producing the "Black Chinese" of Calvert. Chinatowns were formed in El Paso, and later in San Antonio, but restrictive immigration policies kept the Asian population to a low level in Texas until fairly recent times.

In the early 20th century, Japanese settlers were brought in to start experimental rice-farming communities along the coast while Chinese and Japanese merchants established small businesses in San Antonio and other cities. Until recently Asian groceries served the black community, but another influx of Southeast Asians has made selling Asian products more profitable.

The latest Asian migration, the result of the Vietnam War, has included Vietnamese, Cambodians and other Asians. Many have settled on the Texas Gulf Coast where they fish in areas traditionally harvested by other groups, particularly Anglos. Misunderstandings and prejudice resulted in several killings and other ugly incidents that involved the influence of the Ku Klux Klan. The coast is now fairly calm, and Texas seems ready to add another piece to its mosaic of cultures.

While a distinctive Vietnamese culture might seem most likely to thrive in fishing settlements along the coast, not all Vietnamese live in these areas nor do they all earn a living by fishing. Many of the latest group of immigrants are technicians and other highly trained people who have settled in Texas' urban areas. Vietnamese and Cambodians are also found in rural communities as professional workers, farmers and ranchers. The Southeast Asians are reminiscent of other Texas immigrant groups – that is, most Texans – in the value many of them place on family life and hard work.

American and European humorists had been getting a laugh out of the rough-and-tumble American frontiersmen long before the frontier reached the plains of Texas. When Texas became the frontier, the larger than life characteristics of Daniel Boone, Davy Crockett, and Mike Fink (the riverboat man) were grafted on to the cowboy.

In the popular imagination he became the Tall Texan, who could outshoot, outdrink, outeat and outlive any living creature. Because he lived on the last American frontier – in a country that revered its wild frontier experience – the Texas cowboy has captured more attention than any other pioneer from Italy's hills to Argentina's pampas to Canada's prairies.

The cowboy as he is known best is primarily a creation of movie-makers and novelists. The real working cowboy inspired writers like Ned Buntline (*The Black Avenger, The Comanche's Dream*) and Owen Wister (*The Virginian*), who immortalized him in the dime novels written in the 1880s and 1890s. They made the cowboy into something of a romantic hero at about the time the frontier was being closed by the progress of civilization. Other novelists, like Zane Grey (*The Riders of the Purple Sage*) and Louis L'Amour (*Hondo*), have kept the cowboy hero alive for later generations.

Cowboy stars: Movie directors, among them John Ford *(Stagecoach, Fort Apache)* and Sam Peckinpah (*Ride the High Country, The Wild Bunch*) put a heroic version of the West on film, helping to make stars of such actors as John Wayne, Gary Cooper and Jimmy Stewart. "Serious" western stars shared the screen in the pre-television era with singing cowboys like Roy Rogers and Gene Autry, who starred in western serials.

Underneath all the storybook and movie glitter there was always a real working cowboy, and there still is today. The working cowboy did not fight nearly as many brawls or shoot as many Indians as we see him doing in the movies. Most of the Native Americans

Left, much of the Big Ranch Country experiences a heavy winter. **Right**, raising longhorns for meat is making a comeback.

were gone when the cowboy arrived. Like the Indian, the cowboy came to be seen as a noble hero.

The cowboy lived out under the stars. He supplied his own strong code of frontier ethics in a land with no established law, and he enforced it with a gun. And he did all his work on horseback. The cowboy's closeness to nature, his strong defense of his honor, and his horse made him the image of the modern knight. Of course this heroic image has always appealed to the popular imagination.

Texas vs Spanish cowboys: The history of the working cowboy begins with the introduction of cattle into the New World by Spanish explorers as early as the 16th century. Most of the details of cattle ranching had been worked out by the Spaniards in northern Mexico and southern Texas by the time the first Anglos came into the area in the 1820s. The Spanish cattle ranching vocabulary was assimilated by the early Texas cattlemen along with the rest of Spanish cattle culture. Words like *lariat* (rope), *remuda* (string of riding horses) and *corral* (holding pen for cattle) are still in use today. Words for unique western land forms like *mesa*

(high plateau) and *arroyo* (dry wash) were also adopted.

Cowboy costume: Much of the Texas cowboy's costume came from the *vaquero*, as the Spanish cowboy was called. High-heeled boots helped to keep a cowboy's feet in the stirrups when he was riding his horse. The narrow toes of the boots were designed to slide easily into the stirrup. The boot tops were 12–16 inches (30–40 cm) high and perfectly plain in design. His leather was good quality and durable. The boot was one of the cowboy's tools: he had no need of the exotic leathers and elaborately stitched tops seen on today's fashionably *macho* and extremely expensive footwear.

chaps, when he rode through brushy country. "Chaps" is a corruption of the Spanish word *chapparal*, meaning heavy brush.

The bandana, an oversized neckerchief, was invaluable to cowboy and *vaquero* alike. It kept the hot sun off the back of their necks and mopped the sweat from their faces. It could be a sling for a broken arm or a mask to filter the acrid dust of the trail. Wrapped around a couple of biscuits, a bandana could serve as a lunchpail for a cowboy riding night watch on his herd.

The tall-crowned, wide-brimmed *sombrero* worn by the *vaquero* was never favored by the Texas cowboy. The fabled ten-gallon hat was worn by no one but the movie

The Texas cowboy was generally concerned with the well-being of his animals. He replaced the sharp, roweled spurs favored by the *vaquero* with larger blunt wheels in order to protect his horse's flanks. The jingle of spurs was "saddle music" to the cowboy. While the *vaquero* usually wore spurs only when working, many a Texas cowboy felt naked if he had to take them off.

For a long time, cowboys wore a very characteristic pair of striped breeches. These gave way in the 1870s to the blue denims manufactured by the Levi-Strauss Company of San Francisco. A cowboy covered his breeches with heavy leather leggings, called

cowboys. There was a wide variety of headwear among cowboys, from the cavalry-style fedora to the shapeless farmboy's hat. By the 1870s, though, the hats made by John B. Stetson of Philadelphia were standard western wear. Cowboys who worked for a dollar a day would pay $10–$20 for a good hat and $20–$30 for a good pair of boots. They were that important to his job.

Shirts were widely varied, some no more than homemade flour sack affairs. As likely as not, they were covered with a vest. The sleeveless vest gave warmth and protection, but did not bind the cowboy's arms while he worked. For cold weather, cowboys wore blue jean jackets or fleece-lined leather shortcoats. Oilcloth slickers kept off the rain. A cowboy rarely carried more than one change of clothes, which he packed into a bedroll with his other apparel.

Trail driving days: The cowboy's life was a hard one. As many a "greenhorn" quickly learned, a cowboy had to have plenty of common sense and a head for survival. The heyday of Texas cowboying were the trail drive years from the mid-1860s through the 1880s, prior to which the cattle business in Texas was rather low-key. It centered on Spanish-style ranches that were loosely run and generally unfenced – prime conditions for creating "mavericks" in the rich South

The black cowboys: Although it is a little known fact, some of the best young cowboys to come into Texas were black Americans leaving the war-ravaged South. Blacks in the West often met the same prejudice they faced elsewhere. Few acquired property or social distinction. But to a cowboy, a man was as much a man as he could prove himself to be. A black drover who could show his dependability to the outfit was accepted with little regard for his color.

A cowboy's work began in spring with the cattle roundups or "cow hunts," as old-time cowboys called them. Nursing calves followed their mothers as the cattle were herded into holding pens. There the animals were

Texas grasslands where longhorn cattle could easily survive on their own.

After the Civil War, a flood of immigrants from the South entered Texas, many of them young single men looking for a new life. They found it as cowboys. The price of cattle in the big cities of the North was up to $40 a head, whereas in South Texas, longhorn range cattle could be bought for $4, thus there was plenty of work for cowboys driving cattle from Texas to the railheads in Kansas where beef was then shipped to city markets.

Left, saddling up. **Above**, an artist's concept of calf-roping.

separated by brands and claimed by their owners. Young calves had the same brand as their mother's burned into their left flank with a branding-iron heated in an open fire. The calves came to be known on the trail as "dogies" from the short rope that tethered the newborn calk to its mother.

As herds became larger and cattle thieves began to alter brands, some ranchers cut notches in the ears of their cattle as a secondary form of identification.

Brands were not widely used by Spanish and Mexican ranchers because their *ranchos* operated on the *patron* system. The *patron*, in the manner of a feudal lord, owned all the cattle and land within his *rancho*, so there was little need to establish his ownership by branding. Cattle on his land were his. Each ranch had its own distinctive brand, which was registered with the Cattleman's Association. Established brands were known by their pattern everywhere on the range.

Before the Civil War, it was not uncommon for a South Texas rancher to start a herd by rounding up unbranded cattle and giving them his brand. "Mavericks," or unbranded cattle, are said to have gotten their name from Sam Maverick, a Matagorda County entrepreneur of the 1840s. Maverick was reputed to be exceptionally adept at building herds from unbranded cattle.

Trail ballads: After the roundup and branding, the trail drive began. Herds of cattle numbering in the thousands of head were driven from the grazing ranges of Texas to the railroad centers in Kansas – a journey of 1,200–1,500 miles (1,900–2,400 km). Many a cowboy ballad was composed on the open trail as the cowboys sang to comfort the cattle and keep them from stampeding. Cowboy ballads were usually laments about loneliness, lost love, and life on the trail. Movie cowboys like Gene Autry and Roy Rogers capitalized on this aspect of cowboy life, making their careers as "singing cowboys." Historians are scornful about this excess of

song, pointing out that a hard day's drive more usually ended with conversation around the first or a game of poker. Few had room in their saddlebags for musical instruments of any kind, much less something as bulky as a guitar or banjo.

To start a drive, small herds of cattle were rounded up in South Texas by a crew of four or five cowboys, who could handle up to about a thousand head. Then the various small herds were driven toward a pre-arranged point. As groups of cowboys drove them together, a trail herd was formed. Small operators with only 10 or 12 cowboys went up the same trails used by big outfits with 50 or more cowhands.

The trail drives followed well-known routes that were determined more by general directions involving designated passes or river fords than by specific paths. The Chisholm Trail, for example, began below San Antonio and headed due north to Abilene. At the railheads the cattle were sold for shipment to the packing houses in Chicago, St Louis and Kansas City.

With the sale of the cattle in Abilene, the cowboys were paid for the first time on their long ride from Texas. For many of them all the long nights of sleeping on the ground and long days of herding cattle over the open plains were erased in wild drinking and carousing in houses of ill-repute. When the last dust of the trail drive had been washed away, the cowboys mounted up for the long ride home. Some were broke, some were hungover, and a few who had been indiscreet with their revolvers were shot.

Not all cowboys wasted their money in the saloon and the bordello. Often as not, the wages of the trail drive were used to buy cattle back in South Texas or in Mexico. A cowboy might also take his pay in cattle when he returned home, driving them north as part of a larger herd the following summer. In this way some cowboys became ranchers. They invested their profits in land and cattle, building up small spreads of their own. Some land was also available through homesteading, but cowboys were cattle workers and not much for farming.

The fenced range: By the 1890s most of the open rangeland between Texas and Kansas had been claimed by private owners – ranchers as well as farmers – and fenced with barbed wire. Its strands of wire twisted into sharp metal barbs were designed to cut the hides of cattle.

This fencing effectively prevented driving cattle to the railheads. At the same time, the railroad was expanding. In Texas, Fort Worth became the major railhead. Slaughter houses and packing companies were built in Fort Worth and San Antonio, making it unnecessary to drive cattle to Kansas. Amarillo and Abilene became active cattle markets in northwest Texas.

With the closing of the open range, cowboys settled down to work on ranches throughout all but the wooded eastern third of Texas. Some became ranch owners by working up from small holdings or by mar-

Hard work was still a major part of life for the ranch cowboy. In addition to the spring roundup and branding, the ranch cowboy had to look after his cattle year-round. Cowboys gave up sleeping under the stars for the bunkhouse. The trail drive chuckwagon was replaced by the ranch kitchen. Cowboys still practiced riding and roping, but now worked in the corral or inside the ranch fences. In fall and winter, cowboys rode the fencelines in order to mend them, even though fences were the ultimate insult to a range-bred cowboy. Winter was also a time for repairing saddles and other ranch equipment.

Gigantic spreads: It was in the era of the open range that the great ranches of Texas

rying into cattle ranching families. Others signed on as hired hands with larger outfits.

It was not uncommon for a rancher to marry a woman much younger than himself, his own younger years being given to building up a ranch that would support a family. This practice left many women widowed and in charge of ranches since their husbands generally passed away first. Some women, who would not be confined to hearth and home, took an active part in the management of Texas ranches and still do so today.

Left, cowboy and cowgirl. **Above**, riding in the sophisticated eastern style.

began to form. King Ranch in South Texas is the state's largest. Texans measure the ranch's current size as 1.23 RIs (Rhode Islands) or about 800,000 acres (324,000 hectares). Founded in 1853 by a former Rio Grande steamboat captain, Richard King, King Ranch was modeled closely on the Spanish *rancho*; King even led an entire village out of Mexico in order to work on his ranch. The original boundaries of the ranch are no longer the same, but it is substantially intact and still family-owned. Although there are no longer organized tours of King Ranch, visitors can take a free self-guided tour along a 12-mile (19-km) loop of it.

The XIT Ranch in the Texas Panhandle is celebrated in the history and fiction of the West. It was started, not by Texans, but by northeastern land and cattle syndicates. In the 1870s and 1880s the state sold the land to the syndicates to finance the present State Capitol in Austin, completed in 1888. Originally a monstrous 4.54 RIs (about 3 million acres or 1.2 million hectares), the XIT was split up in later years as the out-of-state investors went their separate ways. As times have changed, ranches have become more mechanized. The only contemporary ranch of any size doing business in the traditional way is the Kokernot 06 between Fort Davis and Balmorhea in Jeff Davis County. Exotic

breeds of heavy beef cattle like the Hereford, the Angus, and the Charolais have replaced the stringy old longhorns of trail drive days.

Longhorns, though, are making a comeback with some modern breeders because of their resistance to disease, longevity, and high calf yield. Today, veterinarians freeze semen from championship bulls and artificially inseminate prize cows. Some breeders even transplant the embryos of artificial matings into surrogate mothers. Breeders in recent years have bid as much as a million dollars for breeding rights to championship bulls. The cattle ranch has become scientific and mechanized like the rest of the world.

Cowboy spectaculars: Rodeo is the sport of cowboys. It grew out of their skills and tasks as they worked with livestock. Early rodeos were informal gatherings of locals who all pitched in to provide livestock, riders and entertainment. Today rodeo is sanctioned by the Professional Rodeo Cowboys Association (PRCA). The events are bull riding, bareback bronco riding, calf roping, steer wrestling, saddle bronco riding and, for women, barrel racing.

In the 1930s and 1940s there was an extensive women's rodeo circuit. Women competed in the same events as men and added gymnastic trick-riding as well. During World War II, women's rodeo was discontinued and never regained popularity.

The PRCA sanctions over 650 rodeos each year all over the United States – even in New York City. The National Finals Rodeo is held each year in mid-December in Oklahoma City. Top rodeo cowboys make six-digit salaries competing in as many as 125 rodeos a year.

Rodeos can be held indoors or outdoors, but the basic requirement is a large dirt-floored corral or arena with chutes along one side and escape gates for the livestock opposite them. The arena is surrounded by stands. Behind the stands are barns and holding pens where the stock is kept before entering the arena. Bull and bronco riders mount up in small pens that open directly into the arena.

When the gate swings open, a rider tries to stay on the bucking animal for 8 seconds. Half of the points scored in a ride come from the total time the rider stays mounted; the other half are awarded for style and daring.

Like bullfighting, rodeo can be a very dangerous sport. The animals are wild, and often attempt to trample or gore dismounted riders. The rodeo cowboy's best friend is the clown, who runs into the arena to distract the mount while the rider is on the ground. Whether local, regional or national, modern rodeo almost always awards prize money to the top riders. Elaborately inscribed belt buckles displaying the cowboy's name and the event he won are presented as trophies.

Cowboy culture and heritage: The world of the cowboy and the Wild West has been preserved in several modern museums dedicated to its memory. One of the finest collections is in the Panhandle-Plains Museum in Canyon, Texas. The T-Anchor Ranch Headquarters, built in 1877 and still intact, is on the museum grounds. Another fine collection is in the Longhorn Museum in Pleasanton, which claims to be "the birthplace of the American cowboy." Exhibits in this museum document the American cowboy and his Indian and Spanish antecedents.

San Antonio not only has The Trail Drivers Association and Texas Ranger Museum, but the Institute of Texan Cultures. Each has a good collection of cowboy – and cowgirl – memorabilia. The XIT Museum in Dalhart chronicles the history of that famous old ranch. The collection of the National Cowgirl Hall of Fame and Heritage Center in Hereford celebrates women in rodeo.

Mexico. Almost any county historical museum in any town in cattle country (South and West Texas) preserves some artifacts from the trail drive and cowboy era.

Lost cowboy skills: The visitor looking for working cowboys today is at something of a loss. Modern equipment has made many of the cowboy's traditional jobs obsolete. Contemporary cowboys still using traditional methods, like those on the Kokernot 06, operate in isolation on the back pastures of large ranches. The best ranch to visit is the YO Ranch near Kerrville. Dude ranches in the Bandera area also offer a taste of ranch life. All in all, a rodeo is the most accessible form of cowboy life available today.

The Ranching Heritage Center on the campus of Texas Tech University in Lubbock is the home of 20 buildings representing ranch housing from the Spanish days to the large family ranch houses of 1890s cattle barons.

The Texas Ranger Hall of Fame in Waco is dedicated to the 150-year history of the Texas Rangers. An intricate multimedia presentation and life-size wax figures in natural settings tell the story of the legendary lawmen who first brought law and order to Texas in the early days after independence from

Left, rip-roarin' rodeo at Huntsville. **Above,** bulldogging a calf.

Not all the folks you see strolling around in boots and jeans are cowboys. People who *look* like cowboys may have never even been astride a horse. Cowboy hats, western-cut shirts with pearl snaps, big buckles on tooled leather belts and exotic leather boots are standard fashion for many modern Texans. Find a fellow who takes things too far by adding a swagger and some big talk to this costume and you have what's popularly referred to as a "drug store cowboy" or, more facetiously, as a "Rexall ranger".

He's the cowboy who spends more time at the drug store lunch counter than he does astride a horse.

To a Mediterranean person, vines and wine are at the center of life. The Spaniards brought the essentials of their civilization with them when they colonized the Americas. So it is not surprising that they brought vine cuttings to Texas in order to provide themselves with wine as a beverage, for medicine and to celebrate Mass. They also sent Texas wine back to Spain. There was Texas wine at least 100 years before vineyards had been planted in California.

In the 19th century, Italian, German and Slavic immigrants, in particular, planted wine grapes at Fredericksburg, New Braunfels, El Paso and elsewhere. Texas rootstock saved the vineyards of France from destruction by the root louse *phylloxera* in the 1880s when Thomas Volney Munson of Denison, a small town north of Dallas on the Oklahoma state line, sent over large amounts of it for grafting to French vines. Munson's Texas rootstock was resistant to the *phylloxera*, which destroyed millions of acres of European vineyards before it was finally brought under control. In France there are at least three statues, and a *place* in Bordeaux, dedicated to Munson. If the names of most of the grapes in Texas vineyards are French, under the ground a considerable percentage of French rootstock is Texan.

A "new dawn": The vineyards of Texas died out during the long night of Prohibition. Now, half a century after its repeal, and to the surprise of almost everyone, lush new vineyards – amid the scrub brush of the limestone belt of Central Texas, and on the high western plains – must be added to the picture the world has of Texas. Since the 1960s, the revolution in wine making and wine consumption in America has swept like a "blue norther" into Texas. It has transformed the landscape, altered the agricultural economy and often influenced Texans' choice of beverages to serve with barbecue, Tex-Mex or Mexican dinners, as well as traditional American or classic French cuisine. Refinements in the science of grape growing have enabled Texans to identify places in the state where grapes can be grown for wine.

One of the classic images of Texas is the barren land dotted with oil derricks under a scorching sun. But in the real Texas, geology and geography are as complex as in any other winegrowing region of the world. The rugged Davis Mountains in dry West Texas are in the area of the state with the highest average elevation, a mile or more (1,600 meters) above sea level; the South Plains around Lubbock are around 3,000 feet (900 meters). Although their daytime temperature is in the nineties (32°C) in summer, and can go over a hundred (38°C), radiation cooling at these altitudes causes night tem-

peratures to fall to the 50s and 60s (10–20°C). In the Hill Country, which can also be very hot in summer, one of the vineyards is cooled by its proximity to a large lake.

On the whole, the climate is comparable to that of France and California, so that *vitis vinifera*, the grape variety that produces all their great wines, also thrives in Texas. Soils in Texas are generally poor in organic matter. But this is a condition wine grapes thrive on because the vines develop a widespread root system while the production of grapes is limited – a necessity for fine wine.

Individualistic Texans: With proper climate and soil, the stage is set for the appearance of the other essential ingredient – the grape itself. Even within the very short history of modern viticulture in Texas, there has been some radical rethinking about which grapes to plant.

At first, on the advice of experts in California, most Texas vineyards were planted in French hybrids (these were a cross between hardy, native American vines and finer, more complex French ones). These hybrids produce pleasant wine, but do not scale the heights possible with vinifera grapes. The conventional wisdom dictated that the climate and soil of Texas were better suited to the vigorous, if coarser, hybrids. Fortunately, individualistic Texans planted their first small

sible for the great Médocs and red Graves of Bordeaux) is a favorite with Texas wine makers striving for world-class wine. Cabernet Sauvignon is now grown by more than seven wineries. Llano Estacado of Lubbock, just below the Texas Panhandle, has produced a rich, ripe, cedary Cabernet that can stand beside the finest Cabernets from California, establishing a Cabernet benchmark for other wine makers.

Another dictate of conventional wisdom was that Pinot Noir, the delicate, fragile grape of France's red Burgundies, simply could not survive in the Texas climate. But the Oberhellmann Vineyards near Fredericksburg, in Central Texas, have been

vineyards with both the French-American hybrids and pure vinifera grapes. They found that vinifera vines not only survived, but thoroughly outperformed their hybrid cousins. After this encouraging sign, vineyard owners began to plant an ever increasing percentage of vinifera.

The Texas grape grower has many choices of vinifera grapes to plant, but among red wine grapes, Cabernet Sauvignon (respon-

Left, outside the salesroom of Moyer Champagne Cellars on Interstate 35 in New Braunfels. **Above**, Fall Creek Vineyards is situated near Tow in the Hill Country.

so encouraged by its Pinot Noir that considerable acreage is now dedicated to it.

The other major red vinifera grapes planted thus far include Zinfandel, the unique California grape; Ruby Cabernet, a cross of Cabernet Sauvignon and Carignane; and Barbera, from the Piedmont in Italy.

Among white wine varieties, Emerald Riesling was an early favorite with growers for its light, fruity, semi-dry wine with some of the delicacy of Germany's great Rieslings. Chenin Blanc was also a popular early choice for its ability to retain a well-balanced acidity in Texas' warm growing climate. But it is with France's two greatest white grape varieties, Chardonnay and Sauvignon Blanc, that several Texas wineries have achieved unexpected success. Llano Estacado and Pheasant Ridge, both near Lubbock, are notable for their large-scaled, buttery, oaky Chardonnays. At the other end of the wine spectrum, the Oberhellmann Vineyards in Fredericksburg make a light, crisp, lemony wine that reminds one of Italian Chardonnays from the Alto Adige or Fruili.

Sauvignon Blanc, happily, is in more ample supply. This grape is grown in France along the Loire in Pouilly-Fumé and Sancerre, as well as in Bordeaux. To date, its Texas cousin aligns in style with white Graves. World-class Sauvignon Blancs appeared in

most sophisticated wineries is producing wines that are redefining what Texas can achieve. Oberhellmann Vineyards, founded by Bob Oberhellmann, a Dallas food broker, has broken new ground with its fine Chardonnay and Pinot Noir, two of the varieties that are not supposed to do well in Texas. In addition, Oberhellmann is producing a German-style Gewürztraminer and a dry, crisp Sauvignon Blanc blended with Semillon for greater complexity.

Along the granitic northeastern shores of Lake Buchanan, Fall Creek Vineyards, begun by Ed and Susan Auler, is one of Texas' leaders in high quality vinifera wines. While in France in 1973, the Aulers noted the

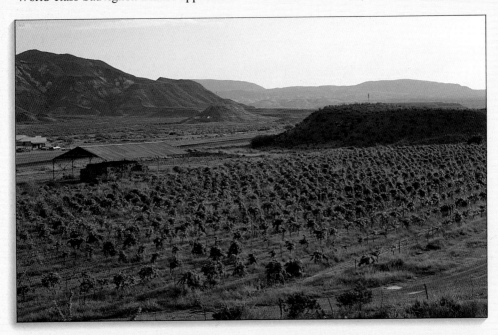

the 1984 vintage from Cypress Valley Winery and Fall Creek Vineyards, both in the vicinity of Austin. In that year they produced complex, subtle, delicately herbaceous wines that are a delight.

Texas vineyards are concentrated in four basic areas: the limestone Hill Country to the west of Austin, the state capital; the High Plains around Lubbock; the hilly plains west of Fort Worth and Dallas; and the rugged Davis Mountains in Far West Texas. There are also a few wineries scattered around in East and Far South Texas.

Near the southwestern edge of the Hill Country, in Fredericksburg, one of the state's

similarities of climate and soil between their ranch in the Texas Hill Country and several of the French wine regions. Beginning with a 1.5-acre (half a hectare) experimental plot planted in 1975, the Aulers have seen their vineyard grow to 29 acres (12 hectares) planted almost entirely in vinifera, surrounding an elegant and comfortable house and winery. The Aulers believe that Sauvignon Blanc promises to be their premier wine. Fall Creek wines are now being sold in Britain.

Not more than 30 miles (48 km) west of Austin is the Cypress Valley Winery, located at Cypress Mill. Following a string of average Rieslings and Chenin Blancs, Dale and Penny Bettis have released more recent Ruby Cabernet and Barbera that are quite exciting. Even more exciting still is the Bettis' Sauvignon Blanc, which is perhaps the finest example of this wine yet made in the good 'ole state of Texas.

Wimberly Valley, southwest of Austin in Driftwood, buys most of its grapes from Blue Mountain Vineyards in the Davis Mountains of Far West Texas, some of the oldest and finest vinifera plantings in the state. The Blue Mountain Vineyards were planted by Gretchen Glasscock on her family's West Texas ranch after extensive research in the early 1970s.

Halfway between Austin and San Antonio

is the only sparkling wine producer in Texas, the Moyer Champagne Cellars. The first sparkling wines they produced were made from still wines purchased in California and Ohio. However, in late 1984, Ken Moyer released a *méthode champenoise* sparkling wine which was made from 100 percent Texas-grown *chenin blanc*. It was an impressive debut: clean, crisp and delicate, with the finesse and interest of a *vin mousseux* from Vouvray.

Guadalupe Valley Winery in Gruene near

Left, vineyards at Lajitas in far West Texas. **Above**, Texas wine.

New Braunfels is like a traditional European wine *négociant*: owning no vineyards themselves, Larry and Donna Lehr buy grapes from around the state, make them into wine, and sell it under their own label. To help promote their wines as well as others from across the state, the Lehrs have opened the Winery Restaurant and Gift Shop. Most of the wineries in Texas have tasting rooms and are happy to give visitors a tour. But it is best to call first to check visiting hours.

Northeast of the Hill Country, the Messina Hof Vineyards in Bryan, near Texas A&M University in College Station, make wines from their own grapes as well as others from around the state.

Fine wines of West Texas: The high, open plains in which the Lubbock wineries are located are quite different from the rolling Hill Country, but like Central Texas they have vineyards that produce some of the finest Texas wines. Llano Estacado and Pheasant Ridge are making promising Gewürztraminer, Johannisberg Riesling, Barbera and Sauvignon Blanc, in addition to world class Cabernet and Chardonnay.

In the Parker County ranchland west of Fort Worth are the Sanchez Creek Winery in Weatherford (the home of Larry Hagman's mother, Mary Martin, where he studied locals for inspiration into his J.R. Ewing character on TV's *Dallas*), the Château Montgolfier Vineyards in Aledo (with the Montgolfier balloon on the label), La Buena Vida Vineyards in Springtown and the Ivanhoe Winery in Ivanhoe.

One of the most exciting developments in the Texas wine industry is the entry of the University of Texas, the owner of over 2 million acres (800,000 hectares), into partnership with the world-renowned Bordeaux-based Cordier wine *négociant*, Richter S.A., France's leading viticulture company, and Dick Gill, a San Antonio and Chicago-based entrepreneur.

With hundreds of acres already planted, and thousands more to be planted in the coming years, the UT/Gill/Richter Cordier consortium will undoubtedly seek out more international markets for their estimated 5 million cases per year. Their ultimate goal is to produce only the finest varietal wines from their good-quality plantings of Sauvignon Blanc, Cabernet Sauvignon, Chenin Blanc and Petit Sirah.

While Texas is associated in most people's minds with country music – especially cowboy songs – the state has a rich and varied musical tradition to which most of the state's important immigrant groups, notably the Anglo-Irish, blacks, Hispanics and Czechs, have contributed. None of these groups existed in a vacuum. The constant cross-fertilization of distinct ethnic sources accounts for both the diversity and the similarity of traditional Texas music.

The tendency to think of Texas as the

Texans also developed distinctive instrumental styles, like the highly ornamented and fluid Texas fiddle style that can be heard at the many annual fiddle contests. Held throughout the state during the spring and summer, particularly in East Texas where the popular annual gatherings at Crockett and Athens take place, these contests allow both young and old fiddlers to display their skills and compete. One of the Texas fiddle style's earliest practitioners, the legendary A.C. "Eck" Robertson, was also one of the

home of country-and-western and cowboy music is understandable; Texans have made some of the most important contributions to the development of country music, from its beginnings in the late 19th century to the present. When they came to the South, the early Anglo-Irish settlers brought with them a vigorous heritage of folksongs, ballads and fiddle music. In Texas and the surrounding region unique Southwestern forms soon developed, like the cowboy songs that were documented extensively in the first part of the 20th century by the Texan John A. Lomax, one of America's earliest and most prodigious folksong collectors.

first country musicians to record. In the 1920s he waxed such classics as *Sally Gooden* and *Brilliancy*.

The continued vitality of country music in Texas is seen in the ongoing popularity of small country-and-western dance halls that are dotted throughout the state and, of course, in the ever-increasing popularity of larger nightclubs such as Gilley's in Houston and Billy Bob's in Fort Worth. The 1970s saw the emergence of the "Outlaws" – led by native Texans Willie Nelson and Waylon Jennings – from Nashville to Austin. The capital of Texas continues to threaten to supplant, or at least supplement, Nashville as the country music capital of the United States. There is a wide audience for the television series *Austin City Limits*, filmed on the University of Texas campus and aired since 1974 by PBS stations across America. During this time the widely popular show has featured more than 300 musicians including Ray Charles, Roy Orbison, Emmylou Harris, Tammy Wynette and Bonnie Raitt.

Western swing: Perhaps Texas' most original contribution to country music is the musical style known as "Western Swing". It was originally developed by Bob Wills and His Texas Playboys, whose career stretched from the 1920s right to the 1970s, and their contemporaries, Milton Brown and His

Tex-Mex and Czech music and is still in the repertoire of contemporary groups like the Austin-based band, Asleep At the Wheel.

The blues: "Blues came to Texas, lopin' like a mule," sang the famous Texas bluesman Blind Lemon Jefferson. The line has caused some scholars to speculate that the blues may even have originated in Texas. While it is now recognized that the blues developed gradually throughout the southern United States, Texans were certainly indispensable to the style's development. The blues put the freely structured melodic wail of the field holler (the song of a person laboring alone in the fields) into the densely structured, rhythmic polyphony of the work

Musical Brownies, who might have achieved the stature of Wills and the Playboys had it not been for Brown's untimely death in a car wreck at the beginning of his career in 1936.

While Western Swing drew heavily on the Anglo-American repertoire of folksongs and fiddle music, most groups used an instrumental lineup similar to the big bands of Benny Goodman and Duke Ellington, including brass. Western Swing shares important cross-influences with Afro-American,

Left, music after mass, San José Mission in San Antonio. **Above**, Kris Kristofferson and Willie Nelson helped put Texas music on the map.

songs that coordinated the movements of convict gangs and the religious songs that united church congregations. All of these influences can be heard in the work of important early Texas bluesmen like Blind Lemon Jefferson, Alger "Texas" Alexander, and Blind Willie Johnson, who all began recording in the 1920s. Aaron "T Bone" Walker, whose recording career also began in the 1920s and who went on to become one of the first performers to play blues in a "modern" style – on the electric guitar – also hailed from Texas.

Even after national labels began issuing large numbers of "race" records (the industry term for records by blacks) in the 1920s, most performers were unable to make a living from their music. Still others, particularly the "songsters" like "Ragtime" Henry Thomas, another recording artist from the 1920s, made a specialty of playing at country dances, picnics and suppers for both blacks and whites. The songsters featured some blues, but they also sang and played folksongs, ballads, dance pieces and even the popular "Tin Pan Alley" songs, all of which were the common heritage of black and white Texans. The Texas songster tradition persisted into the 1960s and 1970s, when young whites "rediscovered" the blues. Mance Lipscomb, who died at the age of 80

stardom ended in a tragic death – through to current popular products of Austin's very respected music scene.

"Conjunto" or "Tex-Mex": Like their Anglo-American counterparts, the settlers who emigrated from Mexico brought with them a vast store of folksongs and ballads, or *corridos*, which have been documented largely through the efforts of the distinguished Texas folklorist, Professor Americo Paredes. Texas-Mexicans were also innovators and helped develop a distinctive Mexican-American dance music called *conjunto*. While *conjunto*'s distinguishing feature, the accordion, may have been introduced to Texas-Mexicans by the Germans who arrived in the

in 1976, was one of these rediscovered black songsters. The country blues were also being performed by Sam "Lightnin'" Hopkins (died 1982), a cousin of "Texas" Alexander, and Weldon "Juke Boy" Bonner. Today, Texas' next generation of players, like Albert Collins – another cousin of Lightnin' Hopkins – and Clarence "Gatemouth" Brown, continues to produce exciting blues.

Texas has also been home to the younger white artists who draw their inspiration from the blues. A trend which stretches from the late Janis Joplin – who was part of Austin's folk revival scene in the 1960s before moving on to California, where her rapid rise to

1840s, by the late 19th century they had developed a unique accordion style that they could call their own.

Conjunto was not insulated from other ethnic traditions. The early performer Narciso Martínez, whose first recording was released in 1935 and who is sometimes called the "Father of *Conjunto* Music," even recorded a version of the Bob Wills standard *San Antonio Rose*. *Conjunto* is drifting farther from its working-class roots, and contemporary artists like Flaco Jimenez enjoy a wide following. *Conjunto* has also had an interesting influence on Texas rock 'n' roll, which can be heard in the Brave Combo's "new wave polka," the "border wave" of the Sir Douglas Quintet, or the "nuevo wavo" of Joe King Carrasco and the Crowns.

Most visitors will be unaware of Texas' long tradition of Czech dance music. Like the *conjunto* bands, Czech brass bands, such as the famous Baca family who recorded in the 1920s and 1930s, predominantly played polkas, the two types of music – *conjunto* and polka – being mutually reinforcing. Some Czech bands, like violinist Adolph Hofner's, played Czech dance music along with Western Swing. Czech music in Texas has not received as much attention as it deserves, but it's to be hoped it will receive further study.

If you happen to be in Texas, there are tion of the local newspapers. The annual fiddle contests and other musical events are usually well-advertised. There is a great deal more live music heard in Texas than in most other states. The Texas Folklife Festival, sponsored every August by the University of Texas Institute of Texan Cultures at San Antonio, offers a fairly comprehensive sampling of authentic traditional Texas music as well as revival forms.

An essay can hardly exhaust the many musical components of Texas culture. The southeastern Gulf Coast, for example, shares a tradition of Cajun (French-Acadian) music with neighboring Louisiana. Other ethnic populations have equally intriguing musical

clubs throughout the state that offer fine live music; however, the club scene is fairly volatile, with clubs opening and closing and changing ownership, name or location continuously. An Austin club, Antone's, is a good example. It has been at its third location, just north of the University of Texas campus, since the early 1980s. Antone's, which seems likely to endure, offers fine blues by both local acts and nationally touring ones. The best strategy is to read the ads and music reviews in the entertainment sec-

histories. Recordings by most of the artists mentioned here, especially the country-and-western, blues and rock musicians, are readily available. Most record dealers should have them in stock, or will be able to order them. The Folklyric label has issued an excellent 16-album series of Texas-Mexican border music.

The Library of Congress has issued a 15-record series, *Folk Music in America*, that is especially rich in Texas music and contains examples of all types of ethnic music discussed here. In addition, the influences of the Austin music scene continue to be felt in both the US and international record charts.

Left, *mariachi* band at San Juan. **Above**, fiddle and guitar, the basis of most Texas music.

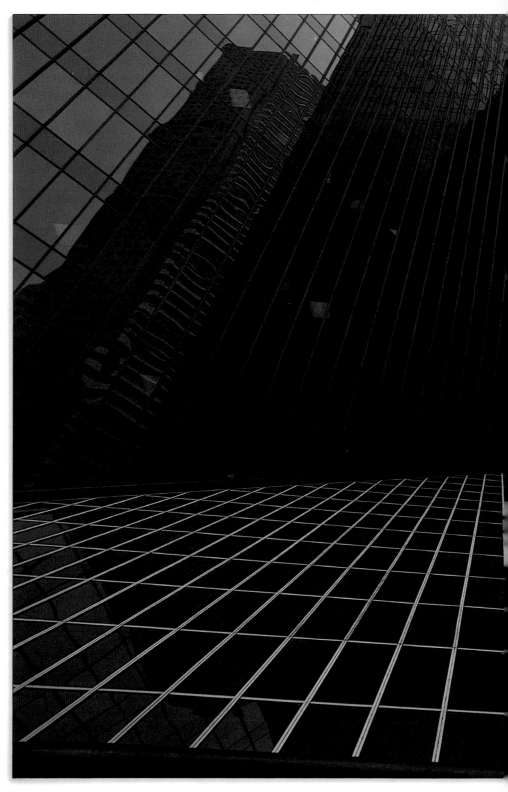

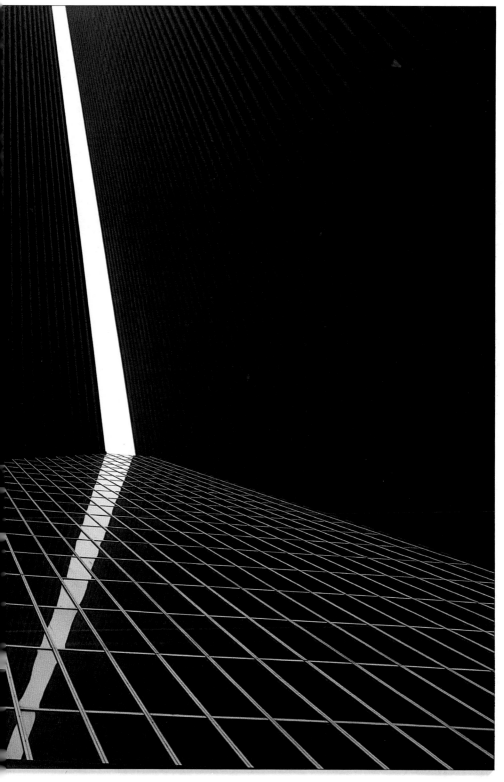

In Texas today the words "Remember the Alamo" also have a special relevance to Texas architecture. During most of the 20th century, but especially in recent years, a battle has been waged between people who want new Texas architecture to reflect native values and styles and those who want to move beyond regionalism to the very cutting edge of international design.

It's an issue that is not likely to be resolved soon, because at a deeper level it is a struggle over the image of Texas itself. The conflict between regional design and international design isn't just about architecture. It's part of an ongoing struggle between rural and urban Texas, between native architects and outsiders, and between the mythical Lone Star state and the real, contradictory, contemporary Texas.

Adobe – the practical solution: To remember the Alamo in San Antonio is, of course, to remember the Spaniards – Texas' first European settlers. The Spaniards gave architectural life to the creamy white limestone of Central Texas, and introduced skill and efficiency to the simple adobe technique of the Native Americans. Although the late 19th-century Spanish architect, Antoni Gaudí, would have approved of the tribes' method of globbing one handful of mud on top of another to make a wall, the 18th-century Spanish friars taught them to mold heavy, regular adobe bricks in wooden frames.

Adobe, together with wood and stone, was used by the Native Americans, and later the Spaniards, all along the lower Rio Grande River. It was easier to make adobe bricks than to quarry stone, even the soft limestone from a creek bed, and an adobe wall several feet thick protected the interior of a house or church from the intense Texas heat just as well as stone did.

Not only is adobe sturdy and well-suited to the hot, dry Southwestern climate, it is a remarkably sensuous material that affords all sorts of gratuitous stylistic features. For

instance, because the walls are so thick, all windows have window seats; and because steps and oven hoods are also made of adobe and plastered over, in the same manner as the walls, the interiors have a sculpted all-of-a-piece quality. The beams and wooden shelves seem to be sunk in surfaces as soft as wet clay – which they once were.

Remember the Alamo: The Spanish missionaries in Texas, used to the Renaissance churches of their homeland, took pains to create an architecture that went beyond func-

tion. They wanted their buildings to express beauty in the wilderness. Their work was modest, but graceful. The Alamo is remembered as the bloody place where early Texans sacrificed their lives for freedom, but the building itself, in the heart of downtown San Antonio, is the image of quiet repose. The stone arches and carved niches suggest that the Alamo deserved a quite different kind of fame. The bell tower and "rose window" of the San José Mission in San Antonio are proof that the Spaniards intended not merely to survive, but to glorify as well.

Such a claim can hardly be made for the early Anglo-American settlers of the 1820s

Preceding pages: Houston style. Left, early 1970s bank tower in Fort Worth. Right, welcome whimsical details are reappearing on many postmodern buildings.

and 1830s. When farmers from Tennessee, Kentucky, Mississippi and Alabama rolled into Texas, they brought with them the only architecture they knew – the plain log house and its cousin, the frame house of roughly hewn boards. There was nothing extra in these houses, nothing to make life on the Texas frontier a little sweeter or softer. They were the most functional sort of shelters.

And yet, as is often the case with architecture, function led people to design structures that were, if not beautiful, still natural and comfortable in the landscape. The deep porch offered protection against the sun, the dog or possum "trot" (an open breezeway between two essential rooms or cabins) was used for

a verandah, with a sign hanging before it, 'Guadalupe Hotel, J. Schmitz'."

Gentility: Before the Civil War, most people in Texas did not live in houses as snug and pleasant as those of the Germans in Central Texas. They were only too glad to leave behind their relatively crude houses when life grew easier, and when the classic Greek Revival and later Victorian styles were brought into the eastern, central and southern parts of the state.

The Greek Revival put classical columns on the porches of even the simplest log houses, and gave a touch of Southern formality and grace to larger buildings. Greek Revival is found in Austin (for instance, in the

such things as curing meat and for sleeping outdoors, and the steeply pitched gable roof protected the house from the pounding rain. These features not only eased the hardships of frontier life, they created a style whose simplicity and grace is appealing to this day.

Even the Germans who emigrated to Texas from the 1840s onwards modified their age-old method of building stone and timber (*Fachwerk*) houses in order to incorporate elements of the Anglo farmhouse. In the mid-1850s, Frederick Law Olmsted, traveling to San Antonio from East Texas, slept in New Braunfels in a "small cottage of a single story, having the roof extended so as to form

Governor's Mansion), but it flowered in East Texas. Crockett, Jefferson, Marshall, Tyler and Houston all have charming and varied examples of the Greek Revival, which remained popular into the 1870s when Victoriana became all the rage. The Victorian buildings of Nicholas Clayton of Galveston, and the Richardson-Romanesque courthouses of James Riley Gordon in many of the county seats (look for his buildings in San Antonio, Waxahachie, La Grange, Stephenville, Sulphur Springs, Giddings, New Braunfels and other cities across the state) are evidence of the growing influence of gentility. When Texans began to concern themselves with porticoes and turrets, high culture had clearly arrived.

Modern Texas: Beaux-arts eclecticism held sway in Texas briefly, long enough to influence some public and university buildings. The trickledown popularity of Britain's Arts and Crafts Movement found expression in thousands of bungalows. During the Great Depression, courthouses and other public buildings were built by government labor. Their blocky, repetitive shapes and flat reliefs in the Art Moderne style make it easy to date such monumental buildings as the Fort Worth City Hall and the courthouses of Travis, Brazoria and Eastland Counties to this period. Not many skyscrapers were built

set for the 1950s movie *Giant* (about a Texas rancher and oilman) captured this spirit of brashness, while the Second Empire mansion silhouetted against endless West Texas ranchland carried it to the most absurd limits.

Some of the houses in Houston's River Oaks section are only a little less self-conscious. Even when the stylistic adaptations are imaginatively and tastefully handled, and local stone, such as pink granite, was used, there is often a feeling of insecurity about the homes of newly rich Texans. Sometimes those who made it felt the need to rise above their architectural roots – sullied as they were by poverty, struggle and, not infrequently, illiteracy.

in Texas in the 1920s and 1930s. The few that did go up, like the Esperson Building in Houston, were in the then-popular eclectic skyscraper style.

Within a period of about 50 years, roughly between 1870 and 1920, domestic architecture in Texas matured. Indeed, wealthy Texans systematically demonstrated that what was fashionable in Paris or London was fashionable in Houston or on the ranch. The

Left, unrestored Mission Concepción San Antonio. **Above left**, ornate column capital at Rice University, Houston; and **right**, Victorian house in Old City Park, Dallas.

In the 1920s and 1930s, small groups of architects – in California, New York and Spring Green, Wisconsin (at Frank Lloyd Wright's Taliesin compound) – formulated new ideas that would eventually make it acceptable for Texans to look upon their architectural heritage without shame. These ideas ranged from Wright's "organic naturalism" to the "machines for living" of the Frenchman Le Corbusier; but all of them respected function in architecture – and opposed what was merely applied and decorative. In this light, the functional and formal aspects of missions and ranch houses were re-evaluated. If early Texans had allowed form to "follow" function out of necessity, a later generation made a conscious choice to do so. The result was the flowering of Texas architecture in the mid-20th century.

It was at this time that Texas buildings began to show not contempt, but deference to their older neighbors. The San Antonio architect O'Neil Ford, who, along with others, became interested in the accurate restoration of Spanish colonial architecture, taught Texans to respect the scale and character of indigenous buildings, and to appreciate the native materials used in them. Ford's own Trinity University campus in San Antonio (begun in 1949), a group of brick buildings that beg comparison with Italian hillside

Boxes: Ironically, the Modern emphasis on function, which prepared the way for a new appreciation of Texas' early buildings, was also responsible for giving birth to the attitude that the architecture of the past did not stack up well against the box. When the German Bauhaus architects sold Americans on their philosophy after World War II, cities like New York and San Francisco began to build boxy skyscrapers alongside their Chrysler Buildings and Coit Towers.

Texas cities were still young in the 1940s and 1950s, and possessed a few charming old buildings and virtually no tradition of urban architecture. Thus, when cities like Houston and Dallas began to expand, much

villages, is conscious of, and faithful to, the nature of the hilly Texas landscape. His Johnson City Post Office (1970), commissioned by Lady Bird Johnson, is a modified ranch house of limestone blocks with a wide front porch and a sloping metal roof. His Cowboy Artists of America Museum in Kerrville (1983) is at the same time a fortress built of creamy limestone and a gallery of almost forgotten building techniques. Its brick bovedo domes were constructed by Mexican craftsmen. Throughout his life (he died in 1982) Ford had a widespread influence on Texas architects. His teachings still form the basis of the regionalist school of thought.

of their growth took the logical and appropriate form of the Modern glass box. Their new urban buildings delivered a message as honest and flat-footed as that conveyed by the early settlers' houses: unadorned simplicity was still at home in Texas.

Early Texas structures were admired for their utility and for their rural beauty, but they certainly didn't influence high-rise architecture in the heyday of the box. A golden sunset reflected by the limestone facades of Central Texas could evoke the memory of Coronado and his search for the Seven Golden Cities; or a lonely wind whistling through a broken windmill near an isolated ranch house could conjure up romantic images of the hard frontier life. But what, after all, did rough-cut limestone blocks or pitched roofs have to do with multi-story, steel-framed buildings?

During the years in which the glass box seemed to be the end of the line, Houston architecture in particular came into its own. Buildings like the Tenneco skyscraper of 1963, with its exposed steel frame, or One Shell Plaza of 1965, with its clean white facades, were as sophisticated and current as buildings being built anywhere at the time.

Later, by breaking up the rigidity of the Bauhaus box with the trapezoidal towers of his Pennzoil Place (1976) and his round-cornered, horizontally striped Post Oak Cen-

edge, sent cantilevered floors of offices precariously out over a plaza.

Skyscrapers of the era: Although the situation of the Dallas office workers only seemed precarious, O'Neil Ford was outspokenly annoyed by the City Hall because he believed its effectiveness depended on playing tricks with the viewer's expectations. It was intentionally unnerving. Ford and his opinions are relevant to the shift in taste that began to be noticeable in skyscraper design in the early 1980s.

Once again, with his Houston skyscrapers, Philip Johnson (with his partner John Burgee) led the way for developer Gerald Hines, but this time he did more than just break out

tral buildings (also 1976), Philip Johnson focused international attention on Texas architecture. The state that was famous for its rugged individualism at last had a Modern architecture that expressed it. Even the more conservative Dallas received oddly-shaped, shimmering, reflective glass buildings (as viewers of the program *Dallas* saw) and a controversial City Hall (dedicated 1978), which broke out of the box completely. I.M. Pei's design, which took the form of an immense wedge or triangle balancing on one

Left, curving box in Amarillo. Above, the Kimbell Art Museum in Fort Worth.

of the box. His designs now referred openly to the architectural styles of the past. Johnson's lighthouse-like Transco Tower, with art deco setbacks, and his Gothic Republic Bank tower were the world's first Postmodern skyscrapers.

And that wasn't all. By sheathing Republic Bank in red granite, Johnson made an oblique reference to the many granite public buildings in Texas. His 1983 plan for The Crescent in Dallas (a mixed-use development with a hotel and shopping court in addition to offices) was said to draw its inspiration from early Texas architecture. Suddenly, the regional architecture that pragmatists like O'Neil Ford and his followers had championed became popular with Postmodern architects who were interested in its romantic connotations.

Regionalism versus internationalism: A thin sheath of limestone or granite on a steel-framed skyscraper does not, however, make a regionalist building. If anything, it only serves to muddy the water between the opposing regional and international camps. For the most part, regionalist architecture is still practiced by Texas architects on a small scale in rural areas. Large urban commissions still go to outsiders. In the past several years, for instance, the green glass Allied Bank Building by Skidmore, Owings and

Merrill, the steel and glass Four Leaf Towers designed by Yale architecture dean Cesar Pelli, and the silvery granite needle of I.M. Pei's Texas Commerce Bank have been added to Houston's skyline. A scheme for a new Bank of the Southwest by Chicago architect Helmut Jahn is a nostalgic throwback to the Chrysler Building in Manhattan.

Dallas, meanwhile, is becoming somewhat more daring. The designs for new office towers have not been innovative – most go no farther than the now-clichéd sawtooth edge – but things are changing. I.M. Pei has designed two 60-story rockets of glass docked in a water garden downtown, and the inde-

fatigable Philip Johnson plans a Postmodern building whose arches allude to the work of the Italian architect Palladio.

As Texas keeps growing, its architecture will continue to change. Houston has attracted attention as a center of new architecture by the country's best-known architects. But in the days ahead, the cities to watch may be San Antonio and Austin. (The controversial library in San Antonio is particularly noticeable.) Since their growth has been lately compared with Dallas' and Houston's, an architectural character is already established, more demanding of respect. Moreover, local architects are being given important commissions instead of "imported" talent.

Already, in Austin – a town that incidentally is especially rich in Victorian structures – one of the new office buildings on Congress Avenue, which leads to the pink granite Capitol, is made of granite from the same quarry and has a gable roof. Another, a few blocks down, is faced in limestone and has three setbacks. Several other buildings with early-Texas pretensions are in progress or in the planning stages. The challenge for architects is to keep these new buildings honest and original – learning from Texas' past, but anticipating a new Texas.

A building that meets these requirements already exists in Fort Worth – the much-admired Kimbell Museum, opened in 1972. The Kimbell draws from the past in subtle ways. Many people believe that its barrel vaults, which allow light to stream down along interior walls, are references to the silos or grain elevators the architect, Louis Kahn, admired in the Texas landscape. But these associations are, at best, conjecture. What makes the Kimbell appropriate to Texas – and beloved by Texans – is its strength and tranquility, its quiet confidence. In this way, it looks back to the years before Texas dressed its buildings up in the styles of the East, beyond the Victorian and Greek Revival periods to the simple, functional early Texas buildings.

The Kimbell is therefore regional in the finest sense of the word. If it is imperative for Texans to remember the Alamo, it should also be imperative that neither they, nor visitors to Texas, forget the Kimbell.

Left, Victorian houses in Galveston. **Right**, Fair Park in Dallas.

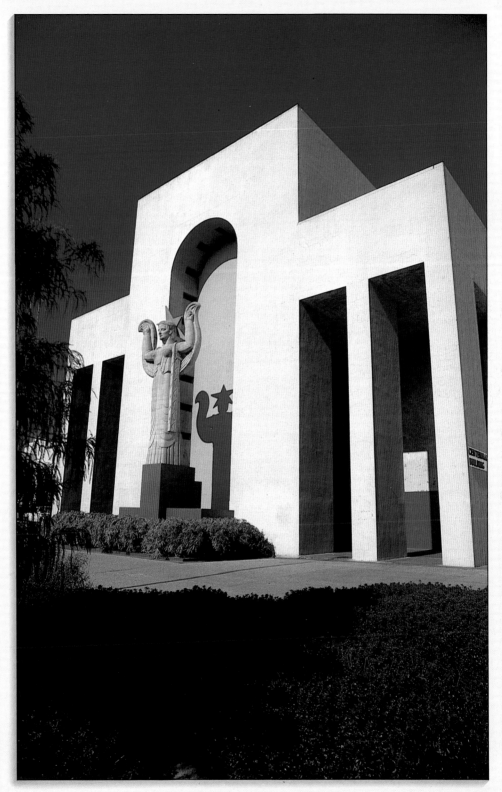

If you are like most travelers, you enjoy the memories and evocative images photos of your trip can bring to mind. Taking good photographs can be most rewarding and is a way of reliving your trip when you are back home. But photography is an expensive hobby and it is disappointing when you find that your shots have all failed to capture the true essence of the place and people or, because the light or exposure was wrong, haven't captured anything at all.

Texas offers endless possibilities for cap-

looking at the sun through the camera lens; it can cause eye damage.

Wildlife: Keep your camera ready. Stay at a safe, unobtrusive distance; a fixed telephoto or zoom lens is ideal. In your car, a small bean-bag over the door frame (window open) makes a good lens support.

Best light: At dawn and dusk, when most animals feed.

Exposure: Set ahead of time; use a higher shutter speed (1/250th) and wider aperture (F-8) to concentrate on your subject.

turing on film scenery, wildlife, western flavor and even "tall Texans." Be prepared for this region of contrasts, use your imagination, and keep the following photo tips in mind when shooting in the Lone Star state:

Landscapes: Decide whether your shot will be wide angle or telephoto, or both. Choose a center of interest and compose the shot to accent that subject. (Avoid always centering horizons and subjects.)

Best light: Sunrise, late afternoon and sunset. Desert scenes and dramatic rock formations "warm up" with the golden glow of afternoon light. Side lighting is an excellent way to maximize drama. Be careful to avoid

Wild flowers: Focus is critical when photographing wild flowers, and depth of field gets shallower as you get closer. Use a macro lens for extreme close-ups. A tripod isn't necessary if wind is calm and light adequate.

Best light: Early morning, late afternoon and shade. Remember, you can make your own shade.

People and events: For candid and action shoots, pre-set exposure and approximate focus on your telephoto lens. Then browse, ready to catch an interesting face unaware. For a studied pose, window-light and shade provide good portrait lighting. Inside or outside, use a portable flash when possible to ensure an adequate amount of lighting for your subject.

Architecture: Tilting up will cause distortion; when photographing monuments or buildings try to keep your camera parallel to the ground. When possible, find a spot which is higher than the base of the building, and shoot from there.

Best light: Afternoon or morning. Accent the facade by throwing one side in shade if possible.

Overcast: This is a great solution to portraits when you don't have a flash. Many subjects that don't photograph well in sunlight make good subjects under cloudy skies that create their own mood and atmosphere.

Night shots: To photograph night events, rodeos, or flood-lit buildings, bracket from ½ second to 1/125 second exposure at a widest possible aperture (F-4.5). Cities are best photographed just after sunset. When shooting landscapes lit by the full moon, use a tripod and 30-second, one-minute, two-minute and four-minute exposures.

Aerial: If you're fearless, a small plane or helicopter, with the door removed or window opened, is a successful way to photograph. If you plan to shoot through windows, however, be sure to clean them before leaving the ground, and shoot out of the shady side of the plane. Use a high shutter speed (1/250 or 1/500) and focus on infinity. Slower

Rain: You can capture raindrops during the daylight when the background is dark, or illustrate the reflecting neon signs in wet city streets at night. In rainy weather, always carry an umbrella to protect your equipment, or put the camera in a loose plastic bag, with an open hole around the filter, with the lens poking through.

Fog: Take advantage of this weather condition. For some cities and landscapes, fog is an essential part of the local flavor. Coastal and boat scenes take on a new dimension in fog.

Left, shooting at the YO Ranch. **Above,** cactus.

films (ASA 64 or 100) give best results. Use your body to absorb any vibrations and under all circumstances, be sure to keep your horizon straight!

Underwater: Along streams, freshwater springs or pools, photograph subjects 10 feet (3 meters) in depth or closer. Try placing your camera lens down in a dive mask in calm water and carefully lower the mask an inch below the water's surface.

Best light: Midday. Some light loss will occur when photographing underwater; compensate a stop per 10 feet (3 meters) of depth, or rely on the automatic setting. Knee pads come in handy on rocky shores.

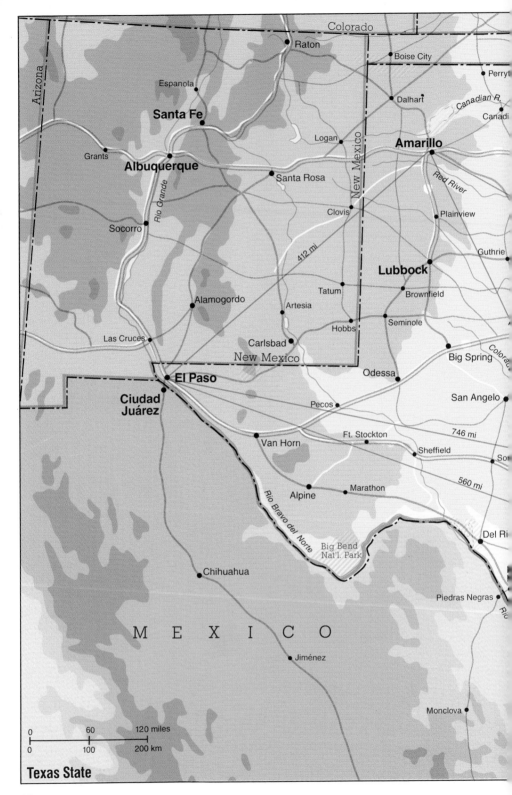

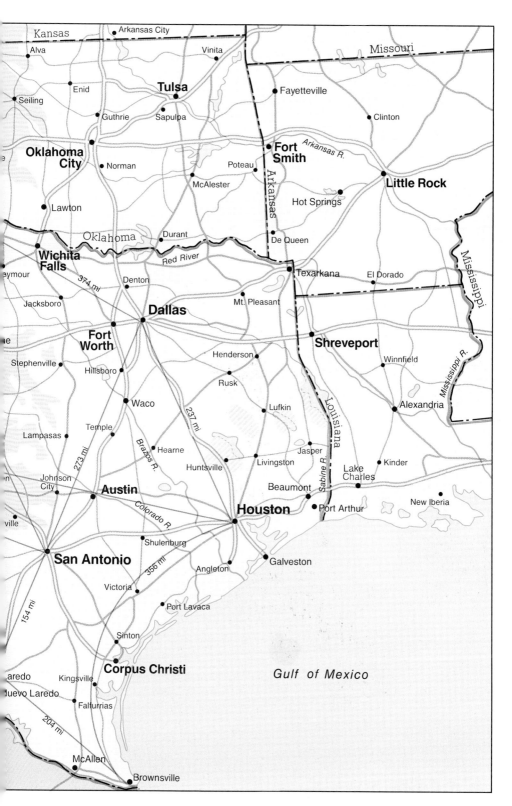

PLACES

Texas has it all: sophisticated cities, beautiful beaches, colorful deserts, sleepy border towns, wide open plains and dramatic mountains. In both geography and culture, it is a microcosm of the entire country. Texas contains as much diversity and internal contradictions as any other part of the United States. You'll find wild rodeos and honky-tonks, but also fine museums and elegant restaurants. Towering glass skyscrapers and bustling sidewalks, but also quaint Victorian homes and old-time country fairs.

Texas is a place where all sorts of social, economic and geographic boundaries intersect, and each part of the state has a distinct character. You'll notice the influence of the Old South in East Texas, and the vital mix of Mexican and American cultures along the Rio Grande. You'll find that Texans are still struggling with the conflict between rural and urban values, and that there are more "cowboys" walking the streets of Houston or Dallas than there are on the range.

Tours of Texas generally start in the Dallas-Fort Worth Metroplex, two cities that have grown into a single bustling metropolitan area. The Metroplex has been a major business center for years, but recently the cities have also made strides in the cultural arena as well. Fort Worth's museum district houses some of the finest collections in the state and the new Dallas Arts District is quickly becoming a hub of culture and entertainment.

To the east, Houston is Texas' largest city, and with its rich ethnic mix, great wealth, exciting architecture and thriving arts community, it is also one of the liveliest. People don't often think of Texas as a coastal state, but Texans have been enjoying the warm breezes, glorious sunshine and brilliant blue waters of the Gulf of Mexico from the early 1900s. America's "Third Coast" boasts over 300 miles (500 km) of white, powdery beaches, quaint Victorian villages, modern resorts, bustling fishing towns and major ports.

As you travel south, toward the Rio Grande, Texas' Hispanic roots become apparent. San Antonio is the urban capital of Hispanic politics and culture in Texas – as well as the home of the Alamo – but it is in the small towns along the Rio Grande that the Tex-Mex blend of *la frontera* is most distinct.

The scene changes dramatically as you travel west. In Central Texas, the land begins to open up and the towns grow farther apart. In the state's westernmost corner, the plains give way to desert. El Paso, this region's largest city, has more in common with its New Mexican neighbors than it does with her sister cities to the east.

Wherever you go in Texas, this vast, intriguing land will undoubtedly surprise and delight you.

Preceding pages: Hill Country southwest of Austin; Guadalupe Mountains; Lajitas in far West Texas; two-lane highway in West Texas; the Cadillac Ranch near Amarillo, a long-standing contemporary monument. Left, "Big Tex," for years a big Texan fixture.

FORT WORTH AND DALLAS

Fort Worth and Dallas are nearly one city now, although from the middle of one to the middle of the other is a distance of 30 miles (48 km). Dallas, the eighth largest city in the United States, is grander and larger, but Fort Worth, population 500,000, has found a certain equilibrium that Dallas still does not possess. For many years, Dallas monopolized the news of Texas north of Houston, both good and bad. The only news that managed to creep out of Fort Worth in the old days tended to refer to the city's rather shocking murder rate, but in the past few years Fort Worth's crime rate has dropped substantially and the city has approved an increased sales tax to further beef up law enforcement. The average visitor will be more likely to comment upon the city's generally clean and quiet appearance.

The lives of the earliest settlers of Fort Worth were ordered by the constraints of frontier life and consisted of resisting the Native Americans, praying together, and sharing strong drink. Some of the first arrivals, who built a church named Lonesome Dove near present-day **Grapevine** (by the Dallas-Fort Worth Airport), came from Missouri as early as 1846.

Major Ripley J. Arnold and his soldiers were sent to join their fight against the Comanche in 1849 and stayed for four years. Most of the Native Americans left the area long before Arnold's arrival, and in all that time they never did any fighting. After the soldiers left, the fort itself became the village of Fort Worth, slipped into a decline and did not rally until it beat the nearby town of Birdville in the contest for county seat.

By 1860, the national argument over slavery had pushed aside all other questions in Fort Worth, and when three white men were accused of "tampering" with slaves, a mob was raised and the men were hanged outside of town. When war began, the soldiers of the Republic who had been keeping order in the countryside were sent east to the front.

With its ranks depleted by the war, Texas' Confederate Frontier Regiment was scattered too thinly across the hinterlands to discharge effectively its peace-keeping duties. Outlaws were quick to take advantage of the lawless situation, and the area became a well-known haven for bandits and military deserters. In fact, Fort Worth became the site of a neighborhood famous for its notorious residents. It was known as Hell's Half Acre, and before its destruction in the early 1900s, it was a temporary home for a host of infamous characters including Butch Cassidy and the Sundance Kid, The Hole in the Wall Gang, and Bonnie and Clyde.

Today, the site of Hell's Half Acre is occupied by the **Fort Worth/Tarrant County Convention Center**, downtown between Houston and Commerce. For some years after the neighborhood's destruction, the city's criminal element moved out to the string of rough-and-tumble roadhouses on **Jacksboro Highway** (State Highway 199), which took up where Hell's Half Acre left off.

Preceding pages: Cowboys vs. Washington Redskins; Dallas buildings. Left, Fort Worth. Right, Dallas Cowboys' cheerleader.

Fort Worth had another source of demand for rowdy amusements. By 1870, large numbers of cowboys had begun to take their rest and pleasure in Fort Worth as they drove great herds of longhorn cattle along the Chisholm Trail from the large Texas ranches to railheads in Kansas. In Fort Worth they bathed, drank, gambled and whored to forget their arduous, lonely and monotonous trail-driving. After resting and having provisioned themselves, the cowboys went on their way with thousands of bawling cattle, through dust or mud.

With the arrival of the Texas and Pacific Railroad in 1876, several hundred miles were cut off the cattle drives. Eight lines eventually connected Fort Worth with the northern markets. The cattle were, of course, the worse for wear for every mile they traveled, and thinner, thus cattle freighted from Fort Worth were in much better condition than they would have been had they struggled all the way to Kansas. Acres of pens were built to receive the herds, where they fattened idly before being transported.

Attendant industries such as meat-packing developed rapidly and the cattle industry remained Fort Worth's most important source of income through the 1920s. Just as improvements in transportation had brought the cattle business to Fort Worth, further improvements began to take part of it away. Larger trucks and better highways made centralized marketing and fattening of cattle unnecessary. Cattlemen could fatten their herds in local feedlots and auction locally for truck delivery. **The Cattleman's Museum,** 1301 West Seventh Street downtown, deals with this fascinating phase of Texas history.

By the time the cattle business began to dwindle, however, Fort Worth had begun to profit from the West Texas oil boom and to serve as headquarters for many oil companies.

The museums district: Several of Fort Worth's museums – the Amon Carter Museum of Western Art, the Modern Art Museum of Fort Worth, the Kimbell Art Museum and the Fort Worth Museum of Science and History – are near

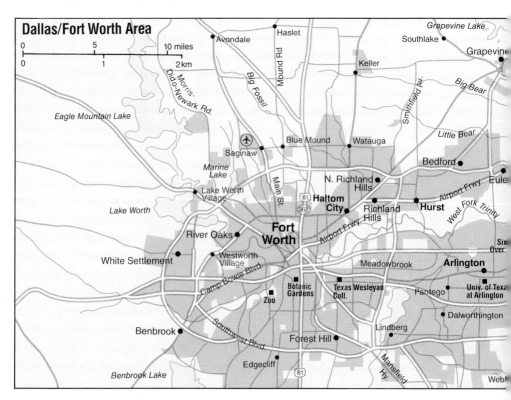

Dallas/Fort Worth Area

each other, where Lancaster Avenue meets Camp Bowie Boulevard. The much-celebrated **Kimbell Art Museum**, designed by the late Louis Kahn and considered by critics to be his most perfect work, combines concrete, marble, glass and vegetation with subtle modulations of natural light in a simple, exquisitely detailed whole. Even people who do not like museums ought to visit this one. It is not large, but its collection is wide and is constantly being expanded. There are objects which would, on their own, justify a visit: a Duccio, a Giovanni Bellini, Vuillards, a Cézanne, a David, a Rembrandt and a spectacular Oriental collection.

Near the Kimbell is the **Amon Carter Museum of Western Art**, the work of another American architect who was influenced by the work of Louis Kahn, Philip Johnson. The museum is best known for collections of works by Frederic Remington and Charles Russell, who specialized in depicting life on the range and along the cattle trails. One additional surprise the mu-

seum offers is a collection of significant paintings by such revered American artists as Thomas Eakins, Winslow Homer and Jasper Cropsey.

The Carter Museum also has a considerable collection of 19th- and 20th-century photographs and great amounts of genealogical and other information about the American West in its well-known library.

The **Modern Art Museum of Fort Worth** has a permanent collection that includes works by such 20th-century favorites as Clyfford Still, Frank Stella, Mark Rothko, Morris Louis, Joseph Cornell and Pablo Picasso, with contemporary sculpture dotting the adjoining garden.

The **Fort Worth Museum of Science and History** is acclaimed for its imaginative interactive special exhibits on subjects from dinosaurs to computers, which help to pull in one million visitors each year. Its additional attractions are an IMAX theater with an 80-foot (24-meter) screen, and daily shows at the Noble Planetarium.

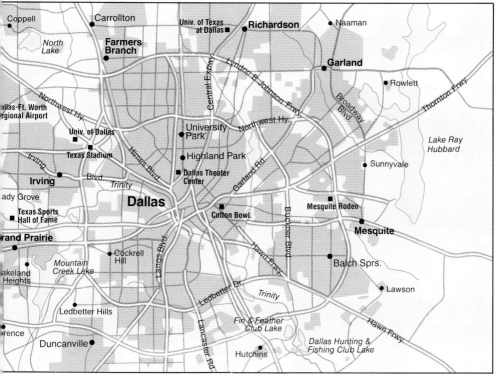

Casa Mañana on West Lancaster at University Drive was one of Fort Worth's tributes to the Texas Centennial Celebration of 1936. This intriguing theater-in-the-round is roofed with R. Buckminster Fuller's invention of a modified geodesic dome, a later example of which forms the top of Reunion Tower in Dallas. Based on the triangle and requiring no internal support, the geodesic dome grows stronger as it grows larger, can withstand hurricanes and, unlike domes in general, has good acoustics.

Fort Worth's **Water Gardens**, Commerce and 15th streets, has been imitated in other cities all over the country. Philip Johnson and his associate John Burgee created a city garden featuring the region's scarcest resource: water. Xylophoning aggregate slabs are tipped at delicate angles to carry, direct or stop water that is swirling, falling, sprinkling or lying still. Some effects at the Water Garden may be mildly disturbing to the non-swimmer: water flowing under descending stepping stones, or the "quiet garden" where the visitor seems to be standing at the bottom of a swimming pool with water flowing in over the sides behind some frail trees, and just beginning to collect. There are many places for sitting in fine weather and there are hundreds of steps for children to scramble up and down.

Although few are to be seen at the Water Gardens, Fort Worth has made a point of collecting animals and plants. The **Fort Worth Zoo** in Forest Park contains one of the largest collections of reptiles and amphibians to be seen anywhere. Among them is a large sampling of the many kinds of lizards and snakes that inhabit all parts of Texas. This zoo is unusual in permitting visitors to view baby birds and mammals in the zoo nursery where they live until old enough to rejoin their fellows. Also interesting is the zoo's wildlife art gallery, which is said to be a first for any zoo in the US. It contains 28 enormous paintings by the German artist Wilhelm Kuhnert, who went into the East African bush to work from life.

Left, American buffalo. Right, prairie dog.

Several American buffalo live here, on a 3,400-acre (1,375-hectare) range of their own. There is a prairie dog "town" where small burrowing owls may be seen creeping in and out of the abandoned prairie dog holes. Trails abound: some intended for ordinary walkers, some for horseriders and others – paved – for those in wheelchairs or propelling baby carriages.

Not far from the zoo is **Log Cabin Village**, a re-creation of pioneer life.

Off Interstate Highway 30, just west of University Drive, is the **Botanic Garden**, a 114-acre (46-hectare) park watered by natural springs containing more than 50 species of trees, all sorts of roses, and a Japanese Garden. One plot has been planted particularly for the strength and variety of its scent in anticipation of blind visitors.

Midway between the museum area and downtown, to the west, is **Thistle Hill**, at 1509 Pennsylvania Avenue, an imposing example of a cattle baron's mansion dating to the turn of the century. The landscaped gardens are as interesting as the house restoration, which contains period furnishings and original pieces.

Leonardo da Vinci's mural painting of the Last Supper is a ruin, but remains famous, nevertheless. In the **Lord's Supper Display**, at 250 Ridgmar Plaza, and the **Palace of Wax and Ripley's Believe It or Not**, at Beltline Road in Grand Prairie, are wax renderings of the painting as it might appear life-size and in three dimensions. There are also life-size Kennedy assassination tableaux.

Rigs, cattle and big business: There were more than 60 stores sitting empty in downtown Fort Worth during much of the 1960s. The oil boom had definitely subsided. Today, however, the old **Stockyard District,** cobbled and gaslit to suggest the past, is very much a part of the commercial present. There are studios, restaurants and shops, and, on Rodeo Plaza, **Billy Bob's**, billed as the "world's largest honky-tonk."

A **Wild West theme park** now occupies the site of the old Stockyard Station on Exchange Avenue, where you can

ort Worth
t night.

also find the colorful **Stockyards Museum** and the legendary **Cowboy Coliseum**, built in 1907 to accommodate some of the earliest indoor rodeos. Two century-old attractions are the **White Elephant Saloon**, with its bullet-splintered floorboards, and **Tarantula**, a still-operating steam railroad.

Antique shoppers and those with a nostalgia for the past will enjoy a side trip to **Granbury**, 20 miles southwest on US-377 with its scores of stores. Granbury's historic town center is dominated by several 19th-century buildings, including a courthouse, jail and 1896 opera house which is still in use. Trips on the lake can be taken in the Morgan, a replica of a Mississippi paddle-wheeler.

The livestock business, in its present form, is doing very well in Fort Worth, as are the aerospace industry, banking and insurance. But for all its renewed success in comparatively impersonal lines, Fort Worth retains a specifically Texas earthiness that Dallas has always tried hard to shake.

DALLAS: There is no visible reason why a city of more than a million should be located where Dallas is. John Neely Bryan, the original settler – whose reconstructed log cabin can still be visited – chose the site in 1841, mistakenly believing the Trinity River to be navigable for trade all the way to the Gulf of Mexico. But the river ran thin or swelled and overflowed its banks.

Bryan began a ferry, for the high seasons, of scooped out logs floored over and hauled across the water on a rope of buffalo hide. This is as far as river commerce ever got. Rather, the place turned out to lie at the crossing point for routes connecting the great North American cities of Los Angeles, Mexico City, Chicago and New York.

Dallas' early years were uneventful. Only one resident of what is now greater Dallas was scalped by the Native Americans, a Dr Calder, in 1843, and he took one of the scalpers with him. Fifteen years later, about 100 of the 300 peaceable Europeans who had formed the Fourierist socialist colony of La Reun-

Preceding pages: the Dallas skyline is constantly changing. Below, Kimbell Museum.

ion settled in nearby Dallas after the colony's three-year experiment failed, largely because the colonists had been artisans in Europe, not farmers.

The original site of the settlers is now marked by the 50-story **Reunion Tower** with its revolving restaurant and nearby sporting arena and hotel complex just off I-35 at the southwest edge of downtown. A DART train – the light rail network that loops around three sides of the city – connects the complex to other parts of Dallas.

Early history: On a summer Sunday in 1860, every hotel and store in Dallas was burned in a fire. An informal jury, or mob, tried and convicted three blacks accused of setting the blaze and hanged them. Nevertheless, during and after the Civil War, many blacks moved to Dallas, settling at first in freedmen's towns outside the town margins and later in all-black neighborhoods in the city such as **Deep Ellum**, at Elm and Oakland east of today's US-45. It was there that world-famous Texan bluesmen like Blind Lemon Jefferson and Huddie

"Leadbelly" Leadbetter began their careers, and it is here today amidst old warehouses and small commercial buildings that a multitude of clubs and restaurants provide much of the city's liveliest nightlife.

In the 1960s, Dallas was one of the few large American cities to integrate its school system without any major controversy. Although a lot has been done to break down social, economic and political barriers in the city, there is still a long way to go.

Among the VIPs on hand to welcome the first passengers arriving on the Houston and Texas Central Railroad in 1872 was Dallas' founder, John Neely Bryan. In true western style, the party dined on barbecued buffalo meat. By the time the Texas and Pacific line reached the city in 1873, a nationwide financial panic had begun to slow rail expansion, fixing Dallas as a railhead of the utmost importance. By the mid-1870s, three mulecar lines were transporting the locals over gaslit streets under which lay wooden water lines.

egasus,
Iobil Oil's
ying horse,
s a symbol of
allas.

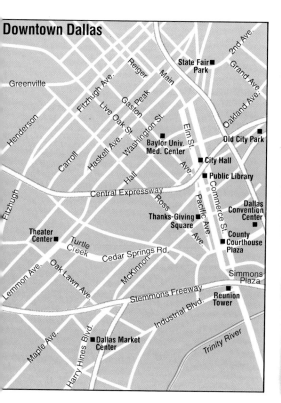

Downtown Dallas

Between 1880 and 1890, Dallas' population tripled to 38,000, the mule-cars were replaced by electric trams, the *Dallas Morning News* began publication, and the fair that became the State Fair of Texas was being held annually. The city also boasted a professional baseball team and a very bloody chicken fighting tournament.

Financial district: In 1907, the Dallas Cotton Exchange was organized and the specialty store of **Neiman-Marcus**, which would soon become world famous, opened its doors at Elm and Murphy streets. Dallas became, and for many years remained, the world's largest inland cotton market, and all the farmers of North Texas did their banking there. According to a Texas law of 1908, every insurance company doing business in the state was required to keep a substantial part of its assets in Texas. Many of them set up headquarters in Dallas. Insurance remains essential to the city's economy, along with banking, merchandising, and, most recently, high technology.

Dallas' passion for business should come as no surprise. It is, after all, a marketplace, one of the largest in the United States. And if its penchant for self-promotion seems to have more in common with, say, New York than with the "old West," that should come as no surprise either. Like New York, Dallas has earned its place among the nation's leading financial centers.

By the beginning of World War I, Dallas had become city enough to be added to the itinerary of touring theater and opera companies employing talents such as Alla Nazimova, Sir Edward Forbes-Robertson, and, on the occasion of her quarrel with a theater syndicate, Sarah Bernhardt, who happened to perform in a tent.

It was after World War II that Dallas began its most accelerated growth. Two large aircraft factories were built in the suburbs, and for a time in the 1950s Dallas was headquarters for more than 450 oil companies. The outsiders who settled in Dallas for business reasons are given credit for a certain broadening of cultural interests and offerings. The

Dallas Civic Opera (Fort Worth had had a resident company for 10 years) staged its first production in 1957 and has since given American audiences their first hearing of such world-class talents as Joan Sutherland, Teresa Berganza, Montserrat Caballe and Jon Vickers.

Assassination: Dallas' darkest stain, an association it seemed the city would never lose, is the assassination of John F. Kennedy, President of the United States, on November 22, 1963. His accused assassin, Lee Harvey Oswald, fired his rifle from the **Texas School Book Depository** as the president rode past in an open car. Two days later, while still in police custody, Oswald was murdered by Jack Ruby, the owner of a strip-joint in Dallas. To the horror of viewers across the country, the event was broadcast on live television. There is a marker at the site of the assassination, and 200 yards (180 meters) away there is another memorial, the **Cenotaph** designed by architect Philip Johnson. Doubt and controversy concerning the assassination has never stopped.

ft, cabin aimed to be at of John ely Bryan. ght, the site the nnedy sassination.

The Depository, which is located at 411 Elm Street, was later bought by Dallas County to house government offices. It has now been converted into the **Sixth Floor Museum**, a memorial to the late president who was fatally shot from a sixth floor window.

The museum's exhibits examine John F. Kennedy's life through photographs, original interviews and documentary film, with special emphasis on the events of that fatal weekend. Beside a realistic re-creation of the southeast window from which the shots were fired is the radio teletype that first announced the shocking news of the assassination, and in one of the building's two theaters a 10-minute film, narrated by Walter Cronkite, deals with the long-term consequences of the assassination.

Despite the conclusions of four major investigations into the crime, almost four out of five Americans believe that the killing was the result of a conspiracy, and an exhibit discusses alleged conspirators and their possible motives. The museum, which gets an average of 1,000 visitors each day, is open daily except Christmas Day, 9am–6pm, and audio guides are available in several languages, as well as one for children.

Nostalgia: The arched entryway at Market and Elm streets is the beginning of the city's **West End Historic District**, an area filled with many of the city's oldest buildings restored as shops and cafés and filled with arts and crafts, pushcart traders, clubs, boutiques and even a brewery. Visitors can stroll or take horse-drawn carriage rides around the area. John Neely Bryan's 1841 cabin and the Old Red Courthouse are here on **Dallas County Historical Plaza**.

A few blocks south, opposite the 50-story Reunion Tower, is the restored **Union Station** (1914), from which the DART train heads back east to the Convention Center. Dallas is the nation's second most popular venue for conventions, and its modern convention center, at Young and Griffin streets, is situated right at the spot where, in 1854, the northbound Shawnee Trail began. In 4-acre (1.6-hectare) **Pioneer Park**, be-

Thanksgiving Square.

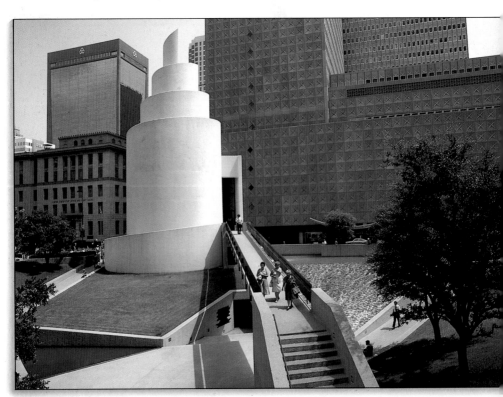

side the center, a herd of larger-than-life longhorn steers descend down a rocky bluff watched by cowboy riders in what has become the world's largest display of bronze sculpture. Created by Robert Somers, the sculpture is enhanced by native plants and a stream that cascades over a miniature limestone cliff.

Another nostalgic trip into the past can be made in **Old City Park**, Gano and Ervay streets, with its log cabins, turn-of-the-century shops, a colonial mansion or two and a Victorian bandstand on the village green. Nearby at Cadiz and Harwood is the huge **Farmers' Market**, open daily 5am to 7pm.

Thanksgiving Square, bounded by Pacific Avenue, Bryan and Ervay, counterbalances lugubrious monuments and unhappy memories. It is intended to symbolize and stimulate thanksgiving for life. This square is also Dallas' answer to a highly successful work by the Cenotaph architects, Philip Johnson and John Burgee, in Fort Worth: the Water Gardens. When called upon to surpass themselves, they produced a zany miniature golf course: a twisting chapel with French stained glass, a reflecting pool, waterfalls, a copse of sweet gum trees, a red granite slab supporting a column of white marble, and a tower with bells that ring. In the square is one of the entrances to the **underground city** – three miles of subterranean shops and restaurants – and also a DART station. Barely a block away is the mother store of **Neiman-Marcus**, at Commerce and Ervay streets.

The streets adjoining Thanksgiving Square are lined with the steel and glass high-rises that reflect the prosperity of late-20th-century Dallas. The **Magnolia Building**, topped with its landmark red-neon Pegasus, dates back to 1921, but further west on Main street is the more recent **Nations Bank Building**, a 72-story giant outlined with two miles of green neon.

Sign of the south: Those who maintain that Dallas is not a particularly southern city ought to consider the number and importance of Southern Baptists in Dallas. The **First Baptist Church**, only

Reunion Complex.

one of many Baptist churches, takes up six blocks on the north side of downtown Dallas. This denomination, with its history of reactionary political sentiment and ingrained anti-intellectualism, has represented biases not easily distinguishable from Dallas' own. It is a sociological truism that southern culture exists wherever there are Southern Baptists. When people begin to climb socially in Dallas, they frequently climb out of the Southern Baptist church and into the Episcopal, the religion of the eastern urban establishment.

The arts: The citizens of Dallas are young, median age 28.7 years, and in the large cities of the US only the people of Houston are richer. In their youth and their prosperity, they abandon downtown Dallas at night as abruptly as a prairie wind. Partly to counter this phenomenon, Dallas developed its **Arts District**, northeast of the Financial Center, in hopes of luring people out of their after-dinner sleep or away from clubs along Greenville Avenue with the blandishments of culture. The city set aside 20 blocks for the district, beginning at Harwood and Ross where the **Dallas Museum of Art** opened its new quarters in 1984 after leaving its pokey old building in Fair Park. The new museum quickly became one of the city's main tourist attractions. Nearby is the I.M.Pei-designed **Morton H. Meyerson Concert Hall**, the home of the Dallas Symphony Orchestra, and between them is the sculpture garden of the **Trammel Crow Center**, with 22 bronze sculptures, including several beauties by Rodin.

The Arts District also hosts several free outdoor festivals held throughout the year. Visitors can enjoy the Gospel Festival in February, the Imagination Celebration (a children's arts festival) in April, the Jazz Concert Series in May, the Latin Jazz Festival in June and the Dallas Dance Festival in September.

One building of historical importance in the Arts District is **Belo Mansion** at Olive and Ross, although it is no longer the funeral home it was in 1932 when it was the scene of the funeral of Clyde Barrow, the famous bank robber and partner of Bonnie Parker. (For years, relatives campaigned to have Bonnie and Clyde buried together; in 1997 they were successful).

Nowadays there is always shopping to be done in Dallas (even on Sunday) at the famous mother store of the Neiman-Marcus chain and at other old downtown stores. In North Dallas the shopping is equally enticing, with its 20 million sq. feet (1.8 million sq. meters) of retail space comprising several large malls: **North Park Center**, the **Galleria** and the **Valley View**.

North Dallas' Park Cities, as they are known, are mainly for living and are very desirable. **Highland Park Village** was designed by William David Cook, who also designed Beverly Hills. The only theater ever built to a design by Frank Lloyd Wright, the **Dallas Theater Center**, is on Turtle Creek Road.

In this part of Dallas, appropriately, is Texas' most expensive institution of higher learning, **Southern Methodist University**. One of the school's benefactors was the late Algur H. Mead-

Below, Meadows Museum. Right, marvelous Nieman-Marcus

NEIMAN-MARCUS

The Dallas-based Neiman-Marcus department store – world-renowned for its Christmas Book offering such "His and Her" gift suggestions as $1,600 mummy cases or pairs of matched camels ($16,000) – prides itself on unstinting service. At the request of one customer, for example, the store discreetly investigated Queen Elizabeth's stocking size so that she could be sent a pair of nylons. On another occasion the store hired a limousine to deliver a pair of ducks to a customer because Railway Express wouldn't deliver livestock.

Customers were made and kept, Stanley Marcus once explained "by [the] ability to remember small details; such as anniversary dates or birthdays, a promise to get a certain evening bag for a specific social occasion... a promise that the dress bought for a girlfriend would be billed to the Mr and not the Mrs account... it's what specialty store retailing is all about."

Stanley, one of the sons of co-founder Carrie Marcus, has been probably the most responsible for the store's modern image, but Neiman-Marcus – now a chain with a dozen branches – was a success from its start in 1907 when Nebraska-born Abraham Lincoln Neiman teamed up (and married) Kentucky-born Carrie Marcus who, aged 21, had already proved herself to be the most successful saleswoman at the Dallas department store A. Harris & Co.

Together with Carrie's brother Herbert, the trio set up a sales promotion business in Atlanta which was so successful that they sold the company for $25,000 instead of accepting an offer of the Missouri franchise for a new bottled drink, Coca Cola. It became a family joke down through the years that Neiman-Marcus was founded on a bad business judgment.

They soon set up their store at Elm and Murphy streets. Neiman, the flamboyant and egotistical buyer, traveled constantly between New York City and Dallas acquiring clothes, constantly clashing with his partners over style and design. In the 1920s, Herbert bought him out for $250,000 and the Neiman marriage broke up at the same time.

At first the store's wealthier clientele was to a large extent the state's cotton aristocracy, but just after the Great Depression began oil was discovered in east Texas. This produced a new group of millionaires who became Neiman-Marcus customers.

In a 1979 history of American department stores, author Robert Hendrickson wrote that Neiman-Marcus operated on the premise that "if we can please the 5 percent of our customers who are the most discriminating we will never have any difficulty in satisfying the other 95 percent who are less critical."

Certainly the three million recipients of the store's Christmas Book seem satisfied. Eight of them, for example, bought the $11,200 Chinese junks offered one year. One page of the catalogue is devoted to "How to Spend a Million Dollars at Neiman-Marcus," but other pages offer gifts for $25 and under. ■

ows, whose gift was the **Meadows Collection** and the building that holds it. Having begun in middle age to use his large oil fortune for art collecting, Mr Meadows was understandably grieved to discover that he was the owner of Spanish School paintings wrongly attributed to masters and that many of his early 20th-century Braques, Picassos and Modiglianis were in fact counterfeits by the Hungarian master forger Elmyr de Hory. Mr Meadows righted his collection with the help of the art historian William Jordan, and the hundred or so Spanish paintings now at SMU, by such masters as Murillo, Velázquez, Goya and Miró, are all of unquestioned quality and authenticity.

Although most of it is not open to the public, the 150-acre (60-hectare) **Dallas Market Center** (DMC) on Stemmons Freeway encloses 10 million sq. feet (920,000 sq. metres) of clothing, computers, toys and furniture.

Two DMC buildings open to the public are the **Trade Mart Court**, designed by architect Harwell Hamilton Harris,

which was the first atrium in America, and the **Infomart**, a high-tech center designed by Martin Growald. Almost every major computer company has rented space in the Infomart, modeled after London's iron and glass Crystal Palace to house the 1851 Exhibition and later destroyed by fire.

Sometimes known as "Silicon Prairie", Dallas takes pride in the fact that in 1958 the integrated circuit computer chip was invented in the city. (It also claims to have originated the chicken fajita and the frozen margarita.)

Religion on display: North Dallas is also where Mattie Carruth Byrd founded the **Biblical Arts Center** at 8909 Boedeker. It is filled with exhibits having primarily to do with the Day of Pentecost, a Biblical event. The Center building is intended to resemble the buildings of the early Christians. It shelters the **Miracle at Pentecost Museum**, a replica of Christ's garden tomb, a collection of art gathered from distant places by Mattie C. Byrd herself, and most impressively, a 30-minute light

Good Luck Service Station.

and sound presentation of the *Miracle at Pentecost* mural, which is 124 feet (38 meters) long and 20 feet (6.5 meters) tall.

The State Fair: The 227-acre (92-hectare) **Fair Park**, east of town via US-30, was the site of the 1936 Texas Centennial Exposition, which celebrated the battle at which Texas had won its fight of independence against Mexico 100 years before. Every autumn the largest talking dummy in existence, Big Tex, greets visitors to the State Fair of Texas at Fair Park, which is home to one of the largest collections of Art Deco buildings in the country. Fair Park includes the **Texas Hall of State** with its mammoth murals and statues of heroes; the **Dallas Aquarium**; the 72,000-seat **Cotton Bowl Stadium**; an amusement park dominated by an enormous ferris wheel; several theaters and seven museums, including the fine **African-American Museum**, the **Dallas Museum of Natural History**, the **Science Place** and the **Age of Steam Railroad Museum**.

In 1996, the world-renowned Texas Instruments company opened an **IMAX theater** at the Science Place with a six-minute signature film about Dallas.

TV fame: The television series *Dallas*, which first ran from 1978 to 1990, probably did more to spread the city's fame than anything else – even if the image of greedy oilmen and disfunctional families was not exactly what the city fathers might have chosen. No matter, it made the **Southfork Ranch**, which is half an hour's drive north of downtown via US-75 (take the Renner Road exit), and where the Ewing clan supposedly lived, familiar to viewers in almost one hundred countries. And today, years after the series ended – it is still in reruns all over the world – Southfork remains the area's major tourist attraction.

The family who originally lived there were forced to move out by the hordes of tourists, and soon the ranch became a popular location for events from weddings to conventions and private rodeos. Tours starting from J.R.'s den are conducted daily throughout the year – book by phoning (800) 989-7800.

Old City Park.

HOUSTON

Houston is without a doubt the weirdest, most entertaining city in Texas, consisting as it does of subtropical funk, life in the fast lane, a layer of oil, cowboys and spacemen. "Houston" was the first word spoken by a man from the moon when the astronauts made contact with home base. With its population of over four million, making it the largest city in Texas and the fourth largest in the United States, it is not only huge but it is mostly new. One must really search in Houston to find buildings earlier than 1960. Houston, in fact, is a success in spite of itself. The freeway traffic is as thick as Tokyo's; the hot humid summers are as bad as Calcutta's. The lack of initial planning has allowed a Texas-sized sprawl: an unchecked, wide open city overlaid with intersecting highways.

Surreal scale and proportion result from the lack of zoning: a small boutique may stand next to a 60-story office building adjoining a house next to a heliport. Houston, more than anywhere else in Texas, operates according to the wildcatter's philosophy: "Dig a little deeper where others have given up, and maybe you'll bring something in." Its economy is based on black gold, on an oil and gas industry notorious for the eccentrics and risk-takers it spawns. Because of the oil price fluctuation in the 1970s, Houston's fortunes rose more quickly than those of any other Texas city. After the drop in world oil prices and the demand for energy supplies, its growth slowed to merely brisk. However, a boom that is now in its third decade continues to shape Houston.

Another legacy of the 1970s is the diversity of Houston's ethnic mix. There are large communities of Hispanics, blacks, Native Americans, Indians, Iranians and Vietnamese. Many came here to work in energy-related industries.

Ethnic diversity is part of the reason Houston is so tolerant of individuality – and eccentricity. There is plenty of room here for personal and professional growth. The entrepreneurial spirit is expressed in everything from Vietnamese corner restaurants to the apartment empire of California "Valley Boy" Michael Pollock, who touts his real estate with cheesy local commercials. Diversity goes beyond demography. No sane person would call the terrain around Houston scenic in any conventional way, but it is varied.

Near this utterly flat city are low hills and pine forests, salt marshes and swamps and steamy "bayous" (marshy inlets), some of which are infested with alligators. Far to the west, but no more than a day's drive, are real hills, then cactus and the desert. And it is only an hour's drive to the Gulf of Mexico beaches, the most restful of which are about 10 miles (16 km) west of Galveston.

Freeway life: The only logical way to tour Houston is by car. Because of its size, most Houstonians spend a great deal of time in cars. Many of them spend more time in their cars than at home, and more on car payments than on rent. The downtown area is enclosed by I-45 on

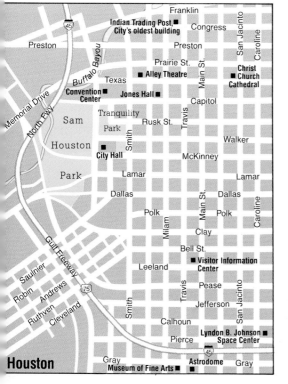

the west and, some way to the east, US-59, with two other much visited areas – the Museum District and the Texas Medical Center – southwest of downtown. The city positively sprawls between a vast network of busy highways, as a result of which buildings are consciously designed as "freeway architecture." Since there are no changes whatever in elevation, tall buildings usually function as the only local landmarks for the driver. Perhaps the best known is Philip Johnson's **Pennzoil Place**, with its two towers that appear to separate and then come together as one drives around the city. A block away from Pennzoil Place is I.M. Pei's distinctive **Texas Commerce Bank Tower**, a cool gray slab whose nickname, the "Texas Tombstone," sets it apart from its towering neighbors.

When Houston is broken into neighborhoods, one finds wild diversity. To the east of town, on the other side of US-59, is **Chinatown**, where the **Tien-Hou Temple** can be found at Leeland and Delano. Here visitors can determine their fortune by shaking out numbered reeds. Be sure to visit the nearby **Kim Son**, 2001 Jefferson, a Vietnamese landmark that is the largest Oriental restaurant in the state. There's a burgeoning Vietnamese community with other restaurants on Milam Street just south of downtown. And if those aren't to your taste, don't worry – there are an estimated 6,000 restaurants in the city from which to choose. Houstonians are said to eat out more than the residents of any other community in America.

Also located east of downtown is the **Pasadena-Baytown Industrial Corridor**, a region rife with every kind of petrochemical processing plant imaginable. The air, which smells like floor cleaner, plays havoc with the sinuses, although at night the industrial landscape takes on a beautiful otherworldly quality. The plants light up, spewing flames and smoke that seem to stretch into infinity. Pasadena, however, does have a couple of landmarks worth mentioning: the vast **Armand Bayou Nature Center** and **Gilley's**, the country

Mechanical bull at Gilley's.

and western honky-tonk with the mechanical bull made famous by the movie *Urban Cowboy.*

San Jacinto monument: Appropriately, one of Texas' major civic monuments is located practically in the middle of an oil refinery. The art deco **San Jacinto Monument** commemorates the Battle of San Jacinto in 1836, which freed Texas from Mexico. Open daily 10am–5.30pm, the tower offers an elevator ride 570 feet (174 meters) to the top for a view of downtown Houston on one side and a spaghetti bowl of pipelines on the other. There is a museum and a 35-minute presentation of Texas history.

What made Houston the rich city it is today was not only the oil discovered elsewhere, but the 50-mile (80-km) **Ship Channel** that turned it into an inland port, stealing the glory (and the wealth) from coastal Galveston. Ferociously competitive late 19th-century Houston businessmen banded together, lobbied in Washington and Austin, and persuaded the government to pay for the channel to the sea, turning their city into what has become one of the three busiest ports in the United States.

The Ship Channel's turning basin, off US-90A near Navigation Boulevard, is listed as a tourist attraction and is the site of free harbor tours – for reservations call (713) 670-2416 – but a more rewarding trip is to visit the other end of the Channel where it enters **Burnett Bay** and the final part of its journey to the sea.

Needless to say, there are numerous rough-and-ready bars along the Ship Channel that are favorites of the sailors and stevedores who work in the area. Some have belly dancing and most have strong drinks and mediocre food. They can be rowdily entertaining but are not recommended for women on their own.

Colorful community: Southwest of downtown is **Montrose**, one of the main entertainment areas. One way to get to Montrose is to drive from downtown along Gray Street through the old Fourth Ward, a tough neighborhood of poor blacks and single-corridor houses. The Montrose district has derived its charac-

Houston from Ship Channel.

ter from two major arteries, Westheimer and Montrose, intersecting at its center.

Montrose is the home of the largest gay community in Texas, as well as various artists, designers, museum personnel and trendy young singles. In its back streets are gay bars catering to every taste; on Westheimer, the main drag, entertainment is directed to a broader spectrum. Here boutiques with improbable names display vintage clothing, erotic birthday cakes, neon hair ornaments and punk garb (spiked collars and hobnailed boots). For a change of pace, in the 5000–6000 blocks are some of the city's most expensive and upscale shops.

East of the intersection of Montrose and Westheimer is a string of restaurants and bars. Tex-Mex cuisine and the sort of dance clubs that feature lasers, videos and neon are prevalent around here. Grab a drink at a café and watch a colorful parade of punks, college kids, trendy singles, footloose couples and transvestites cruise by on foot, on motorcycles and in cars.

Art and architecture: As Montrose Boulevard heads south it becomes more elegant preparatory to crossing US-59 and heading into the grassy realms of the **Museum District**. A few blocks west at 1515 Sulross in a specially designed building is the **de Menil collection** (open Wednesday–Sunday) ranging from medieval and Byzantine art to contemporary works. Facing it at the corner of Yupon is the **Rothko Chapel**, commissioned by John and Dominique de Menil to house 14 paintings by the abstract expressionist, Mark Rothko. This interfaith chapel, entrance flanked by Broken Obelisk – a memorial to Dr Martin Luther King – is open every day, 10am–6pm.

The stretch of Richmond Avenue between Chimney Rock and Hillcroft emulates a Parisian-style boulevard lined with art galleries and sidewalk cafés. Many of the city's best restaurants are found in this neighborhood.

There are more museums and art galleries in Houston than in any other Texas city, and at Montrose Boulevard and

Left, Dr Denton Cooley, Texas Medical Center. Right, Houston Museum of Fine Arts.

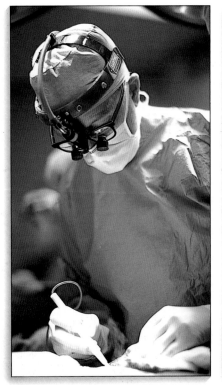

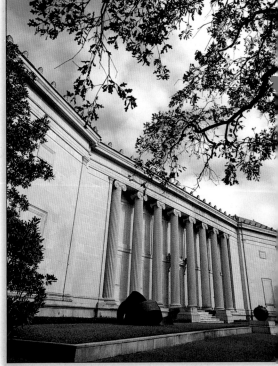

Bissonet Road, the heavy culture really sets in: the **Museum of Fine Arts** (MFA) and the **Contemporary Arts Museum** (CAM), both closed on Monday, sit across from each other.

The MFA houses a large permanent collection from all periods with strong holdings of French Impressionists and 20th-century Americans. The modern additions to the museum are by Ludwig Mies Van der Rohe. Across the street, the museum's **Cullen Sculpture Garden** is open until 10pm.

The museum also owns **Bayou Bend**, 1 Westcot Street, just before Memorial Park. This stunning 24-room mansion designed by Houston architect John F. Staub is filled with exquisite examples of American decorative arts left to the museum by the well-known philanthropist Ima Hogg (it was her real name), the daughter of Governor James Stephen Hogg (1891–95). Bayou Bend – which can be visited Tuesday–Friday afternoons and Saturday mornings – has paintings by American artists such as Gilbert Stuart, Charles Willson Peale and John Singleton Copley. The 14 acres (6 hectares) of beautifully landscaped grounds surrounding the house overlook the bend in Buffalo Bayou and are open to the public 10am–5pm Tuesday–Saturday and 1–5pm Sunday. The CAM does not have a permanent collection, but stages nine exhibitions each year featuring the latest wrinkles in new art.

Oak-shaded campus: The gentle Victorian Romanesque campus of **Rice University**, surrounded by giant live oaks, is just south of the MFA and the CAM. Beyond Rice is the immense and highly regarded **Texas Medical Center**, home of celebrity surgeons like Denton Cooley and Michael Debakey. Rice, a pleasant retreat from the sterile towers of the Med Center, has set up a monumental sculpture by Michael Heizer – three 70-ton blocks of pink Texas granite. The two art museums at Rice, the **Rice Museum** and the **Sewall Art Gallery**, are open to the public.

Other galleries and museums of note in the city include the **Blaffer Gallery** at the University of Houston, the **Mu-**

Houston
Museum of
Natural
History.

seum of **American Architecture and Decorative Arts** at Houston Baptist University, and the **Center for Photography** at 1440 Harold. Echoes of the old West are preserved in the **American Cowboy Museum**, 11822 Almeda, while the **American Funeral Service Museum**, 415 Barren Springs Drive, has a peculiar appeal.

Rice Village, Kirby and University, was Houston's first upscale shopping center and its 325 stores are still a major attraction today. The area around Rice is the most beautiful in Houston. Behind Georgian Revival facades live the old moneyed classes of Houston eccentricity, as is evident by a totally pink house at the corner of Hazard and Sunset streets. Everything, including the fence and garage, is painted tropical flamingo pink. A comprehensive tour of Houston architecture should also include the unbelievable house made of 50,000 beer cans at 222 Malone, off Memorial Drive.

Equally unbelievable is the **Orange Show** at 2402 Munger Street, tel: (713) 932-6368. This is a bizarre structure made up of tunnels, theaters, didactic murals, whirligigs and a tiny museum. The life's work of a local eccentric who built it over 26 years out of junkyard scraps, it promotes the life-giving qualities of the orange. "Be smart; eat oranges" is spelled out in mosaic tiles.

In the southern part of the city are **Six Flags AstroWorld** (Loop 610 at Kirby Drive) with its plethora of rollercoasters and other rides, and the nearby **Astrodome Convention Center**, tel: (713) 799-9954, which has to be seen to be believed. It is enormous – large enough to fit an 18-story building inside – and everything that takes place here is a Texas-sized spectacle, especially the not-to-be-missed annual **Livestock Show & Rodeo**, which daily fills the thousands of seats to watch the bronco-busting and chuck wagon racing for 17 days every February. Almost every kind of sporting event takes place under the 218-foot (66-meter) high roof of the Astrodome, which can be toured every day at 11am, 1pm and 3pm, when a movie is shown about its construction. **The Space Center.**

The Fiesta Market: Exit the Southwest Freeway at Hillcroft and head south toward the Bellaire intersection to visit the **Fiesta Market**, the ultimate ethnic grocery store. Advertising is in Spanish, Vietnamese, Chinese, Hindi and English. Fiesta sells everything from cowboy boots to goat's milk. It is always jammed with shoppers, and the interior is ablaze with huge neon signs and other images that identify each section. It is an astonishing and amusing store.

Farther along the freeway are the famous giant neon cockroach at 5617 Southwest Freeway and the giant neon grand piano at 3133 Southwest Freeway. Lots of young working people live out in this direction, usually in huge apartment complexes. There are a plethora of bars, restaurants, discos and movie theaters in Southwest Houston ("**Sin Alley**"). Just north of the center of the city and slightly west is a mixed residential and industrial neighborhood called **The Heights**. The houses are older and charming, but one of the highlights is the grave of Texas billionaire Howard Hughes in **Glenwood Cemetery** off Washington Boulevard.

Satellites and space ships: Also not to be missed is the "Owner Has Brain Damage" sign in bright red letters at **Deluxe Auto Sales** on I-45 North near the Parker Street exit. This pop monument was destroyed by Hurricane Alicia in 1983 but was rebuilt by popular demand. Interstate 45 takes one to the Inter-continental Airport and what seems to be another downtown.

Actually it is a satellite "downtown" typical of the outlying cluster developments that the combination of no-zoning and infinite growth engender. At last count, at least 19 satellite commercial centers had cropped up. One of them – a haven for shoppers marked by glamorous buildings designed by Cesar Pelli and Johnson and Burgee – is the **Galleria-Post Oak** area on Westheimer near Loop 610. The Galleria, an enclosed shopping mall, is modeled on Milan's Galleria but blown up to immense size. Every luxury store under the sun has been fitted under its roof, as well as an ice-skating rink and a jogging track around the roof. In this area are many more stores, hotels and topflight restaurants.

Although everyone seems to shop at the famous Houston Galleria now, in its early years it was supported by the well-heeled from sections like River Oaks, west of downtown. **Kirby Drive** and **River Oaks Boulevard** are the main streets of River Oaks, Houston's Monument Valley of money and conspicuous consumption. The mansions along streets like River Oaks Boulevard, Lazy Lane and Inwood belong to captains of industry, oil and cattle barons, their descendants and a few Arab sheiks. On weekends in March there are garden tours sponsored by the **River Oaks Garden Club**. Supposedly, one goes in order to admire the azaleas and dogwood, but frankly many join the tours to see how these people live.

Space City: Houston, which has been called the Bayou City and Energy City, is also known as "Space City" – and the shining example of the city's outerspace ties is the **Lyndon B. Johnson Space Center**, which is actually located in the Clear Lake area, 20 miles (32 km) southeast of downtown (take I-45, then NASA Road 1). Its many huge buildings sit on a flat, swampy plain under a sky that looks plenty big enough, with its low horizon, to shoot space rockets into. On self-guided tours one can view the earliest space capsule from the Mercury mission, as well as a full-scale training version of the space shuttle. Visitors are invited to try on space helmets and touch a piece of moon rock as well as marveling at how tiny and cramped the capsules were in which crew members lived and worked while in space. The **Souvenir Center** operated here by the National Aeronautics and Space Administration (NASA) is full of fascinating innovations from computer games to freeze-dried ice cream.

Houston is a far from a perfect city. Unlike Dallas, which loves to cover up the fact that it is boring with puffery about how well-run it is, the city is careening into the future with all its eccentricities up front. Houston is everything to excess... but never dull.

EAST TEXAS

There's a whole section of the state larger than New England – and containing more trees – that's certain to confuse most newcomers with its "unTexan" topography. It's the **Piney Woods**, the timber country between Louisiana and Central Texas, the region that was the state's economic launching pad. It was here that industrial interests first wrestled with Mother Nature, raking timber off the land and squeezing oil from below it. A lot of scars remain, such as the sinkhole at Sour Lake, but it is known as much for its natural beauty as for its oil and timber industry.

Auto travel remains the best way to explore the scattered East Texas cities and towns. The East Texas Chamber of Commerce (Longview, Texas 75601) publishes maps with several suggested routes, and the state's *Forest Trail* map is another good self-conducted tour guide to the area.

Beaumont and Port Arthur: The economic significance of the Gulf and the salt dome geological formations along the coast mean that the region's largest metropolitan area is not to be found on the regional main street. Beaumont-Port Arthur anchors East Texas at its southeastern corner. Practically located in Louisiana, the cities of Beaumont and Port Arthur flank I-10 and together they have a metropolitan population of nearly half a million.

Founded in 1835, **Beaumont**, the state's first oil boomtown, is on a deepwater ship channel dredged from the Neches River 21 miles (32 km) up from the Gulf.

Acknowledging its debt to the oil industry, Beaumont has several museums dedicated to its past, including the reconstructed **Gladys City Boomtown** on the Lamar University campus and the **Texas Energy Museum** on Main Street. Both are closed on Monday, as is the city's oldest home, the **John Jay French Historic House Museum**, which depicts the life of the Connecticut-born trader who settled here in 1845,

and the very elegant **McFaddin-Ward House**, a 17-room mansion owned by a turn-of-the-century oilman. Among the city's other sights are the **Edison Plaza Museum**, situated appropriately in a converted power station and devoted to the life of the great inventor; the **Texas State Fire Museum**; and a memorial on I-10 to one of the state's most famous athletes, Babe Didrickson Zaharias, the Beaumont-born triple winner of track and field events at the 1932 Los Angeles Olympics.

After the Spindletop oil discovery on January 10, 1901, Texas was gradually transformed from an agriculturally dominated economy into one that could tap incredibly fast-flowing pockets of wealth. Late 19th-century geologists scoffed at the theory that oil reservoirs might be tucked inside the salt domes.

A Beaumont real estate developer, Patillo Higgins, suspected the gaseous vapors and sulfurous water at nearby Spindletop Hill indicated a pool of the valuable liquid. Along with an Austrian immigrant, Anthony F. Lucas, he drilled several unsuccessful wells in 1900 before hitting the Lucas Gusher in 1901. In the space of two years, Beaumont's population swelled from 9,000 to 50,000 as East Texas became the kind of get-rich-quick magnet the nation had seen a half century before in the California gold rush of 1849.

Oil derricks sprouted here as thick as the pines, and their furious pumping of the salt domes took their toll. At the appropriately named **Sour Lake**, about 20 miles (32 km) west of Beaumont on State Highway 105, visitors can still survey the damage in the form of a 10-acre (4-hectare) sinkhole created in 1929 by three decades of drilling.

Port Arthur, to the southeast, is Beaumont's sister city. Home of the world's largest petrochemical complex, it is noted for its seafood and lively Cajun nightclubs. The much-quoted city motto – which the tourist board never tires of pointing out – is the Cajun saying, *"Les le Bon Ton Roule!"* (Let the good times roll!). Port Arthur was the home of the late rock singer Janis Joplin, whose birthday is celebrated every January 19, and is the kind of place where tourists can attend a genuine, music-filled Cajun wedding – of two alligators (call 800-235-7822). There's also a working alligator farm not far away, southwest on the I-10 at Fannett (tel: 409-794-1995).

The Sabine-Neches Ship Channel, which flows right through the city, connects **Lake Sabine** – 9 miles (14 km) long, 7.5 miles (12 km) across and rimmed with white sandy shores – to the ocean. Nearby is **Sea Rim State Park** with its airboat tours, nature trails along 5.2 miles (8 km) of coastline and 15,109 acres (6,117 hectares) of coastal marshland. **Sabine Pass Battleground State Historical Park** commemorates a battle during the Civil War in which a Union force of 20 vessels and 5,000 men invaded Texas but was turned back by 42 men with six cannons behind a small earthwork. The little town of Sabine Pass was long ago annexed by its larger neighbor Port Arthur, but it remains famous for fishing and an excellent seafood restaurant.

"**Rainbow Bridge**" joins Port Arthur with the city of **Orange** in a high, graceful arc over the Neches River spanning 1.5 miles (2.4 km) of salt marsh and industrial river channel at a clearance height of 177 feet (56 meters). Other visitor attractions include **Pompeiian Villa** (a historical site), a house on the National Register of Historic Places built in 1900 for Isaac Ellwood, the barbed-wire inventor, and the **Museum of the Gulf Coast**, on Beaumont Avenue, where such celebrated locals as Janis Joplin, the Big Bopper, Harry James, Babe Didrickson Zaharias and artist Robert Rauschenberg are honored.

On Green Street in Orange the **Stark Museum of Art** and nearby **W.H. Stark House** are eye-popping structures from the 1890s whose exteriors are almost as interesting as the furniture and artwork that they contain. From Orange, fascinating airboat tours can be taken – tel: (409) 883-7725 – of the alligator-infested swamps, marshes and bayous that surround the area. The rice fields and marshlands, with their moss-laden trees **French trading post.**

and tropical palms, are a refuge for hundreds of thousands of migrating waterfowl, attractive alike to the birdwatcher and, alas, the hunter.

Across East Texas, in the northeastern corner of the region, is **Texarkana**, perched on the Texas-Arkansas state line and thus half in each state. Texarkana is an agribusiness center for farming, livestock and timber interests in Arkansas, Louisiana and Texas. Its slogan is "Twice as Nice," a phrase to describe the city's unique status, which is best illustrated by one of its most unusual landmarks – the **Post Office Building**, which straddles the Texas-Arkansas state line. In addition to the town's **Historical Museum** (closed Monday) depicting 19th-century life in the region, there is the multi-faceted **Ace of Clubs House**, on Pine Street, built more than a century ago by the winner of a poker game and still containing the original furnishings.

Sherman and **Denison**, on the Oklahoma border near **Lake Texoma**, the 89,000-acre (36,032-hectare) impoundment of Red River in East Texas north of Dallas, are rich from farming and livestock industries. While it's well known that Texas produced President Lyndon Johnson, another President also came from the Lone Star state and Denison takes pride in honoring that favorite son, Dwight D. Eisenhower. The **Eisenhower Birthplace** is a two-story frame house gloriously restored to its appearance in 1890, the year Ike was born: the adjoining visitor center depicts life during the years when Ike was president. **Traveler's Hotel** is another Denison landmark, built in 1893 by a German sea captain and still open for business.

Three other metropolitan centers – Tyler, Longview and Marshall – are located well within East Texas and are the most representative of purely East Texan urban life with their oil and timber economic foundations.

Tyler is the largest, with about 76,000 residents. Located some 100 miles (58 km) east of Dallas just off the I-20, Tyler has been a petroleum production

Rainbow Bridge.

center since the discovery of the great East Texas Oil Field in 1930. Also known as the "Rose Capital of America," Tyler markets more than 50 percent of the nation's rose bushes, maintaining a 22-acre (9-hectare) **Municipal Rose Garden**, which is at its best from May through October.

About 30 miles (48 km) further east on I-20 is **Longview**, which lies at the geographical center of the world's largest oil field and enjoyed explosive growth in the 1930s when oil exploration moved deeper into East Texas from Beaumont. Due to a dynamic industrialization program begun after World War II, Longview considers its location among the tall pines near several well-stocked bass lakes a magnet for industry as well as recreation.

For history buffs, the city maintains the **Caddo Indian Museum** with artifacts and exhibits from this ancient Texas tribe. The **R.G. Le Tourneau Museum** displays patents and objects related to the man who became one of the world's foremost inventors of earth-moving equipment.

Marshall, 20 miles (32 km) east of Longview, was one of the most important cities in Texas until the Civil War, serving as an administrative center for the Confederacy, for which it supplied gunpowder and ammunition. Originally a stagecoach stop, it achieved its prosperity after the Texas and Pacific Railroad arrived. Those early days are recalled in the venerable **Ginocchio Hotel**, which anchors the town's three-block historic district.

Tyler, Longview and Marshall form the urban outposts of East Texas. These are places where visitors can enjoy the pace of the city amidst the rural charm of the surrounding region. For it is the historic villages and rugged forests, scattered from Houston to Texarkana along the Eastex Freeway, which really make East Texas what it is.

The towns and sites: "Boomtown" is a much overused description, but rare is the East Texas hamlet which at one time or another couldn't answer to that name. Whether they developed as an entry point for early settlers like Nacogdoches,

as a lumber town like Lufkin or, more spectacularly, as the site of an oilfield gusher like Kilgore, the towns of East Texas share that common link.

Nacogdoches has several claims to fame. It was originally settled by Native Americans several thousand years ago and it claims to be the first incorporated town in Texas. It is reputed to be a cradle of Texan liberty and it served as one of the gateways for 19th-century pioneers who eventually made Texas an independent republic.

Now a modern city of 30,000 with a solid economic base of manufacturing, agriculture, retail trade and tourism, Nacogdoches, on US-259 almost midway between Houston and Texarkana, makes a fine base for exploring the rest of East Texas.

Nacogdoches has numerous historic sites, including the **Sterne-Hoya Home** at Pilar and Lamana streets, built in 1828 by a pioneer merchant who helped found the state, and now occupied by the **Hoya Memorial Library**. Just north of town is the interesting **Millard's** Alabama-Coushatta reservation.

140

Crossing, a group of restored 19th-century buildings furnished with pioneer memorabilia. The street on which Millard's Crossing is located, **La Calle Del Norte** (presently North Street), once linked the original Native American settlement to villages in the north and is said to be the oldest public thoroughfare in the United States. Another location of note is the **Old Stone Fort**, a 1779 Spanish trading post now reconstructed on the campus of **Stephen F. Austin State University** that marks the site of four unsuccessful rebellions.

The fort houses a museum with tribal artifacts alongside memorabilia from the eras of the eight different flags which have flown above the fort – Spain, Magee-Gutierrez Expedition, Long Republic, Fredonian Republic, Mexico, Republic of Texas, Confederacy and United States.

Nacogdoches is on one of the most historic routes in America: **El Camino Real**, blazed by the Spanish as "The King's Highway," or the Old San Antonio road. Travelers can follow that path today by taking US-21 out of Nacogdoches in either direction. El Camino Real linked colonial Mexico with Spanish settlements in Texas and Louisiana by following Native American trails, shallow fords or rivers. Incorporated into the state highway system in 1929 as Highway 21, El Camino Real joins many other historical sites.

Crockett, not far to the west, is one good example. It was founded in 1837 on the spot where Davy Crockett camped en route to martyrdom at the Alamo. Historical markers note the location of **Davy Crockett Memorial Park**, 35 wooded acres (15 hectares) for picnics and play.

East of Nacogdoches, 36 miles (57 km) along US-21, is **San Augustine**, a town where nearly *every* famous Texan walked the streets. Davy Crockett was given a feast here on the way to the Alamo. Historic sites abound, including the **Ezekiel W. Cullen Home** of 1839 (not open to the public), which belonged to a legendary Texas judge; the ruins of the 18th-century **Mission Señora de los**

ompeiian
lla.

Dolores de los Ais; and **The Old Town Well**, dug to a depth of 27 feet (8 meters) by slaves in 1860 to serve the travelers on El Camino Real.

Other notable pioneer towns are Bonham and Paris in the far north of this region, marking the early settlement of Texas just south of Oklahoma. **Bonham**, on US-82, was founded in 1837 and has more than 60 marked historical sites. The town is home to the **Fannin County Museum** with its excellent pioneer exhibits, **Fort Inglish Park** with its replicas of the blockhouse and stockade built by Bailey Inglish in 1837, and the **Sam Rayburn House and Library** (closed Monday), dedicated to Bonham's favorite and most famous son, the Texas politician who served as Speaker of the House of Representatives longer than anyone else.

Founded in 1839, **Paris** – also on US-82, even nearer to the Oklahoma border – was home to a notorious list of frontiersmen including retired outlaw Frank James (brother to Jesse James), cattle baron John Chisholm, and bandit queen Belle Starr. On weekends, visitors can tour **The Maxey House State Historic Structure**, an exquisite Victorian home built in 1868 by the Confederate general and occupied by his family and ancestors for nearly a century.

In the southeast, **Jasper** offers visitors another chance to view historic sites 50 miles (80 km) south of San Augustine on US-96, which runs part of the way alongside **Sabine National Forest**. Founded in 1824 beside the Angelina River, Jasper is the home of the **Tavern Oak**, a 250-year-old giant pine oak (connected to a tavern there in 1839); the **Dixie Baptist Church**, founded in 1850 under a grove of trees by a black slave; and several historic houses dating from around the middle of the 1800s.

Henderson, between Nacogdoches and Tyler on US-259 in the center of Rusk County, is another find for visitors in search of old houses, with 50 historic markers and seven historic medallion homes. Founded in 1843 on land owned by the Cherokee Indians, Henderson's **Sabine National Forest.**

attractions include **The Depot**, an old railroad depot restored as a museum and children's learning center.

Rusk, at the intersection of US-84 and US-69 between Lufkin and Tyler, founded in 1846, is home of the **Texas State Railroad Historical Park**, a train track that forms the nation's longest and skinniest state park. Visitors can climb aboard for a 50-mile (80-km) round-trip journey through the Piney Woods. Rusk also offers the **Jim Hogg State Historical Park**, 176 acres (71 hectares) dedicated as the birthplace of Texas' first native-born governor, the legendary Jim Hogg (1891–95). Historic **Fifth Street** in Rusk features old homes and what's claimed to be the nation's longest footbridge, a 547-foot (168-meter) span built in 1861 separating the business district from the old residential area. As an important Confederate Army conscription center, Rusk figured prominently in the Civil War. Look for the historical marker that describes the **Confederate Gun Factory.**

Liberty, on US-90 near the Trinity River between Beaumont and Houston, traces its history back to the Spanish mission erected nearby and its downtown created by the Mexican government in 1831. **Huntsville**, north of Houston on US-75 and I-45, founded in 1830 by settlers from Huntsville, Alabama, has both the state prison and **Sam Houston State University** and claims added significance as the town where Sam Houston lived his later life. The site of Houston's grave is here, 70 miles (113 km) north of Houston on the I-45, which marks the western boundary of the East Texas pioneer region.

When experts on East Texas gather to swap yarns, there's always debate about which town reigns as the best place to see old homes. San Augustine usually wins great praise, but **Jefferson** on US-59, just 58 miles (93 km) south of Texarkana, must be considered a required stop. It is a living museum of antebellum houses to which the Texas State Historical Society awarded more than 90 medallions.

Laid out in 1842 as a river landing on Big Cypress Bayou, Jefferson boomed into early Texas' primary river port as steamboats from New Orleans brought settlers westward. With them came the plantation culture and architecture of the Old South. But decline began when the city refused a rail depot. Many of the city's fine old homes are open during the Annual Historical Pilgrimage in the first weekend in May.

Highlights include the **Atkins-Lemon House** (1860), featuring a collection of fine china and Bristol stone; **The Captain's Castle** (1855), with its collection of period antiques; and **The Freeman Plantation** (1850), built in Greek Revival style and embodying the grandeur of Louisiana plantation life.

Of particular interest is Jefferson's **Excelsior House Hotel** (1850), which was one of Texas' most famous inns, a place patronized by Presidents Rutherford B. Hayes and Ulysses S. Grant as well as famous 19th-century industrialist Jay Gould and playwright Oscar Wilde. Still in operation today, it offers guests a chance to stay in Jefferson amid period furnishings, many of

am Rayburn brary in enham.

them purchased when the hotel first opened more than a century ago.

The **Atlanta**, Jay Gould's private luxury railroad car, is now stationed close to The Excelsior. **The Jefferson Historical Museum** is located in the old federal courthouse built in 1888 and its artifacts are just as impressive as the building. **McGarity's Saloon** is another restoration project.

From **Jefferson Landing**, on Big Cypress Bayou across the bridge from downtown Jefferson, visitors have the chance to take a 45-minute river tour along the old steamboat channel in 20-foot (6-meter) handcrafted river boats.

After the political turmoil of the early 1800s had been quelled, a new wave of boomtowns grew up in East Texas built on another economic base: timber. **Lufkin** on US-69, 20 miles (32 km) south of Nacogdoches, founded in 1882, is the home of the South's first paper mill and remains the center of the state's timber industry.

One main attraction in this city of 32,000 people is the **Texas Forestry**

Museum, built in a grove of Texas pines with large glass windows bringing the forest right inside, with a moonshiner's still and a blacksmith's forge among the exhibits and memorabilia. Lufkin stages an annual Forest Festival every September.

The oil boom of 1900 at Beaumont proved a harbinger of things to come for the entire region as wildcatters scattered through the Piney Woods prospecting for oil. The frenzy peaked in 1930 with the discovery of the biggest well of all in Rusk County.

This well, known as the **Great East Texas Oil Field**, was a discovery that held the state's economic spotlight until the fields of West Texas surfaced after World War II. The boomtown associated more than any other with the 1930 strike is **Kilgore**, between Longview and Henderson just off US-259, in the center of the field with more than 1,000 producing wells.

The **"World's Richest Acre"** was the description for a downtown block where 24 oil wells once produced simultaneously, and the town's **East Texas Oil Museum** tells the story with exhibits, a replica of an entire boomtown main street and a short movie.

Despite the development of East Texas – and the disregard of its ecological system – there have been some attempts at conservation, with four national forests offering visitors the opportunity to sample the Piney Woods in their most primitive form.

The **Alabama-Coushatta Indian Reservation** has existed since 1854, when Sam Houston established it as a reward to this tribe for their courageous neutrality during the war for Texan independence. And one of the state's most striking natural landmarks is the **Big Thicket National Preserve**, a dense and mysterious forest that blankets the whole southeastern section of the region. A botanist's delight, the 84,550-acre (34,230-hectare) Big Thicket is not really like a national park. Rather, it includes 12 units attracting tourists with hiking trails and museums, aimed at preserving an ecological system unique in the nation.

Left, Gladys City. Right, chili peppers

144

TEX-MEX FOOD

Visitors to Texas are guaranteed to encounter Mexican food – plenty of it! But it's not *exactly* Mexican. What you will find is a Texan version of it called Tex-Mex. These dishes are quite a bit hotter than California-Mex or Arizona-Mex, so keep a few glasses of water handy. Visitors to Texas will discover that discussing what precisely constitutes Tex-Mex is a state pastime – so don't expect to discover any definitive answers.

Most Texans would probably agree that, in its most elemental form, Tex-Mex food consists of some preparation of flat cornmeal *tortilla* breads, beans, and tomatoes, onions and chili peppers frequently chopped together in a *picante* (hot) sauce. They'd possibly also agree to include in the definition cheese and chili meat sauce, but beyond that you're likely to find riotous disagreement. Texans love to talk about Tex-Mex food almost as much as they love to eat it, and every Texan believes his favorite dish represents its quintessence.

Texans are more unified in their definition of what Tex-Mex isn't. Any part of the States with a Mexican heritage will have its own related version of "Mex" cooking, but the cuisine of Mexico is not Tex-Mex. Neither is New Mexico-Mex, with its refined green *tomatillo* sauces and blue cornmeal; neither is California-Mex, rich with sour cream and lavish produce. Tex-Mex food is not fancy. What little meat it includes is usually inexpensive and tough, chopped or marinated into submission. Tex-Mex food is home fare, the food of the common people. But most importantly, it must be understood as the supreme expression of the noble chili pepper, and as such it must be hot as the hinges of Hell's Front Door.

Where to find the best Tex-Mex is a bigger debate than what it contains. Serious devotees contend that real Tex-Mex food can't be found north of Waco (located mid-state) but all Texans agree it doesn't exist outside Texas. Expatriate Texans have been known to plan their homecomings around a pilgrimage to their favorite restaurants.

Most Tex-Mex is eaten as Mexican restaurant fare. The menu traditionally consists of the following: baskets of fried *tortilla* chips and bowls of *picante* sauce, accompanied by beer or iced tea, are offered while the order is prepared. Shortly afterwards, a hot plate of several different specialties arrives.

This might include *enchiladas, tortillas* wrapped around cheese and onions and covered with meat or a spicy tomato sauce; *tacos, tortillas* folded, fried and stuffed with ground meat, beans, cheese and the above-mentioned vegetables; a *guacamole* salad of mashed avocados; and *fajitas*, marinated and grilled bits of steak. The meal is served with rice and beans, hot *tortillas*, and, of course, several more bowls of *picante* sauce to spoon over everything.

Dessert may be a token scoop of sherbet or a praline candy purchased at the cash register counter, but dessert after this spicy and sturdy meal is quite unthinkable.

Tex-Mex cooking has recently absorbed some refinements, in the preparation of better cuts of meat than its beloved *cabrito* (roast kid) and *menudo* (tripe stew) for example; and the "Tex-Mex cuisine" gaining popularity in the eastern United States and Europe is a considerably cooled down version of it. The more accessible it becomes, the less it resembles real Tex-Mex. To a certain extent this is necessary: every ethnic food has ingredients that appeal only to those who have been raised on them, and they all undergo changes when they become more widely popular. ∎

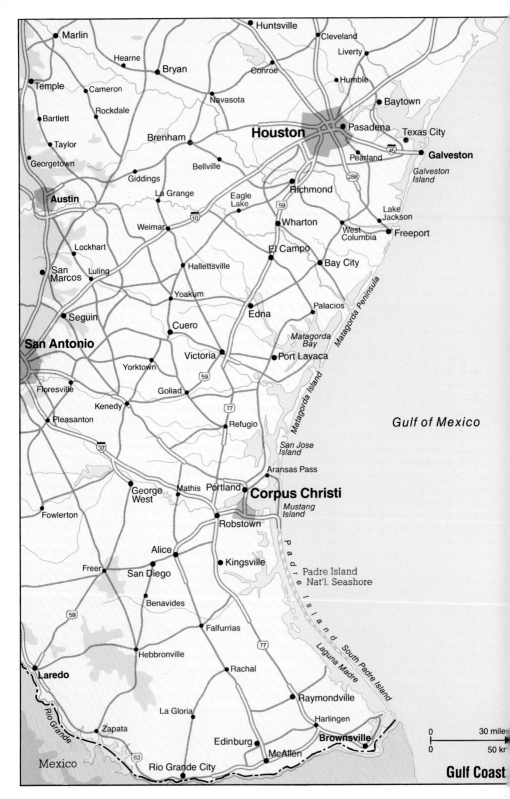

Marlin
Huntsville
Cleveland
Liverty
Hearne
Bryan
Conroe
Humble
Temple
Cameron
Navasota
Baytown
Rockdale
Houston
Pasadena
Texas City
Bartlett
Brenham
Pearland
Galveston
Taylor
Bellville
Galveston
Island
Georgetown
Giddings
La Grange
Eagle
Lake
Richmond
Lake
Jackson
Austin
Weimar
10
Wharton
West
Columbia
Freeport
Lockhart
El Campo
Bay City
San
Marcos
Luling
Hallettsville
Palacios
Seguin
Yoakum
Edna
Matagorda
Bay
Matagorda Peninsula
Cuero
Victoria
Port Lavaca
San Antonio
Yorktown
59
Floresville
Goliad
Matagorda Island
Kenedy
77
Gulf of Mexico
Pleasanton
Refugio
37
San Jose
Island
Aransas Pass
George
West
Mathis
Portland
Corpus Christi
Fowlerton
Robstown
Mustang
Island
Alice
Padre Island
Nat'l. Seashore
Freer
Kingsville
San Diego
Benavides
Falfurrias
77
Hebbronville
Rachal
Laredo
Laguna Madre
South Padre Island
La Gloria
Raymondville
59
Harlingen
Zapata
Edinburg
Brownsville
Rio Grande
Mexico
83
Rio Grande City
McAllen

0   30 mile
0   50 kr

Gulf Coast

THE GULF COAST

It's been called a lot of different things – "funky," "scruffy," oddly even "Byzantine" – but one label has rarely been pinned on the Texas Gulf Coast: "chic". It just does not fit.

Nevertheless, from South Padre Island north to the Bolivar Peninsula, the Gulf Coast ranks as one of Texas' most powerful magnets for travelers. It exudes history. When the European explorers arrived, its shores were home to Native Americans, some of them with a reputation for cannibalism.

In keeping with its faded, once rather barbaric Byzantine image, the coast actually sheltered early 19th-century pirates seeking refuge from the young United States Navy, which established strongholds on the Gulf. From such a heritage sprang a prosperous trading culture. The inheritors of that legacy are the present-day developers who have ventured cautiously on to its shores in order to build condominiums and professional buildings. They tread lightly with good reason because within that legacy lies a pattern of destruction that visits with clockwork regularity.

Mother nature's fury: Here on the Texas coast, nature has demonstrated its powers as it has nowhere else. Galveston is the site of the most celebrated catastrophe in US history – the 1900 hurricane that destroyed Galveston and killed approximately 6,000 inhabitants. Whether or not the wind and rain are pounding from above, the Gulf of Mexico is always pulling from below, eating at the shoreline and claiming the land. Engineers have predicted the eventual reclamation of beach homes situated by the sea at many points in the next century.

Still, developers take their risks and beach visitors continue to seek that special relationship with the sea. Between storms, and in spite of their fears, coastal Texans have created an enchanting domain. The Gulf of Mexico in summertime is as warm as bathwater; the hour's drive from the urban monster, Houston, to nearby tranquil Galveston provides a contrast that can literally be felt as well as seen.

Less cluttered by neon and glitz than most modern coastlines, Texas' Gulf shore functions as an escape hatch for refugees from the nearby busy cities. Visitors won't find the world's best surf, but they will find isolated beaches and sleepy villages with a lifestyle that is among the nation's most charming.

Where the land meets the sea: The Texas coastline runs 367 miles (590 km) in a great arc that forms the southeastern corner of the state. The land here does not end in the abrupt cliffs and rocky shores to be found in other parts of America. In Texas, the land gradually surrenders to the water, drifting from the region of rolling hills and pine forests known as the Coastal Plains into a grassy marshland called the Coastal Prairie, known more precisely as the Texas coast.

To the south, the coast is a playground devoted to fishing and water recreation. Starting at Bolivar Peninsula, just north of Galveston, the Texas

shore forms the world's longest chain of barrier islands as it slips towards Mexico. There are 624 miles (1,000 km) of tidewater coast when you add the bays, lagoons, and swamps between the bayou marshland in the north and coastal brush in the south. The region includes two cities – **Galveston** to the north and **Corpus Christi** to the south.

GALVESTON: Once known as the "Wall Street of the Southwest," this island city of 62,000 residents has been described as the only part of the coast you'd want to visit on a rainy day. Visitors who head directly for the beach with blinders on will miss plenty: Galveston not only beckons with its water, recreational attractions and good shopping, but with its own unique historical perspective.

But for that 1900 hurricane, Galveston might today be the industrial heavyweight instead of Houston. After a roguish beginning as a seaport haven for the pirate clan of Jean Lafitte, Galveston showed signs of becoming one of the South's most significant cities by the end of the 19th century.

The French-born Lafitte had been the inspiration of several legends in nearby New Orleans, where he and his brother Pierre created a smuggling empire in the early 1800s against a backdrop of international intrigue. In 1817, the Lafittes founded a town called Campeachy on Galveston Island. They built a fort called Maison Rouge, attracted a "navy" of over 1,000 men, and proceeded to disrupt Spanish shipping in the Gulf of Mexico. Unchecked until the United States Navy forced him out of the area in the early 1820s, Lafitte remains a romantic and puzzling figure, the last of the pirates on the Gulf. Expelled from the Texas coast, he vanished, sailing away to Mugeres Island off Yucatan.

Galveston, the one-time pirate stronghold, was developed as a seaport during the Republic, and soon became the state's largest city. Although blockaded during the Civil War for a long period, the city remained in Confederate hands except for a few months in 1862. The Union Navy entered the harbor in Octo-

Dr Cooley's renovated 1911 Hotel Galvez.

ber, landed on Christmas morning and was expelled on New Year's Day, 1863. On June 19, 1865, Galveston was taken over by the Union forces and freedom of the slaves proclaimed. "Juneteenth" has been celebrated by blacks in Texas ever since that day.

Galveston continued to grow, but San Antonio and Houston eventually overtook it in population. Much of Texas' cotton was exported through Galveston. To this day cotton warehouses and grain elevators are to be seen, and the water is still yellow in parts of the bay from the shipping of sulfur. Galveston was a hub of commercial activity between the 1870s and 1900, boasting Texas' first telegraph, electric lights, brewery and medical college. With the profits from all its commerce, some splendid mansions were erected, many with raised first floors to protect them from the constant flooding that occurred before a seawall was built.

Hurricane: Like the flipping of a switch, the 1900 hurricane dimmed Galveston's glow in a matter of hours. It swept across the island on September 8 and 9 to claim a place in US history as one of the nation's worst natural disasters. Death estimates have ranged from 5,000 to 8,000. The entire island was submerged by tides of 4–6 feet (1–2 meters), and whipped by winds sometimes in excess of 100 mph (160 kph).

There was nothing to break the hurricane's force: Galveston's highest elevation was around 8 feet (2.5 meters). It is said that at one point the water rose four feet in four seconds: 1,500 acres (600 hectares) of houses were completely destroyed. The devastation proved so complete that many voices argued to abandon the place, but the stubborn Galvestonians refused to surrender, returning to redefine forever the meaning of perseverance. They resurrected their demolished homes and constructed a 17-foot (5-meter) seawall, protection against future ravaging by the waters of the Gulf. The present seawall is 10 miles (16 km) long, 16 feet (5 meters) wide at its base and 5 feet (1.5 meters) wide at the top.

alveston
hrimp fleet.

Meanwhile, Houston seized the chance to divert attention from the previously prospering Galveston to itself. In the 1890s, the federal government had spent millions to make Galveston a deep-water port. Its big rival, Houston, had more people and better rail connections by 1900. With its federal money, Houston began dredging a ship channel in the Buffalo Bayou to the San Jacinto River and, from there, into the Gulf. So Houston became a port city while Galveston, although remaining a port, became less important and was frequently referred to as "that island city south of Houston."

Beaches and boulevards: Recent years have seen renewed development of Galveston Island and promotion of its heritage as a tourist attraction. The primary access to the island city is Interstate 45, a freeway which stretches from Dallas, through Houston, and over a bridge into Galveston. Once on the island, it becomes **Broadway**, Galveston's main street, which carries you through the oldest part of the city to

Stewart Beach. A right turn on to 61st Street before I-45 becomes Broadway bypasses the central city and takes you to the island's most popular beach district, **West Beach**, on the south shore. **Seawall Boulevard** is a broad avenue along the waterline above the city's dramatic seawall. In Galveston, all other roads seem to lead eventually to Seawall Boulevard with its array of shops, restaurants, motels, bicycle rentals, arcades and other amusements lining one side and the Gulf of Mexico pleasantly filling the horizon on the other. The tourist office, tel: (409) 763-6564, is on 21st Street.

Popular seafood restaurants on Seawall are **Gaido's**, founded in 1911, and the adjoining **Casey's**, operated by the same family. The **Flagship Hotel** is built on a pier out over the Gulf. The boulevard has several fishing piers where visitors can rent equipment and try their luck at catching redfish, trout and other Gulf game fish.

On the Galveston sea front there are also many structures of historical sig- **By the pier in Galveston.**

nificance. Visits should start with a walk on **The Strand**, which runs parallel to Broadway between 20th and 25th streets and was once part of the city's warehouse district. The solid old iron-fronted structures have been refurbished with more than 90 shops and restaurants. An old-style trolley – tel: (409) 763-4311 for schedule – operates around here.

Some area highlights include Colonel Bubbie's Surplus Store, considered by many to be the world's best army-navy surplus center with more than 10,000 items from 100 different countries; La King's Confectionary, home of old-fashioned ice-cream; Hendley Market, with its collection of everything from Victorian clothing to antique postcards; and the 400-ton *Elissa*, a restored tall ship built in 1877 in Scotland, which is docked at Pier 21. In the theater here (tel: 409-765-7834), visitors can enjoy a 27-minute documentary about The Great Storm. Three blocks away are the art galleries and shops of **Gallery Row**.

The Strand's ambiance is reminiscent of New Orleans' Bourbon Street and, like that colorful, high-steppin' Louisiana city, Galveston makes a big thing of **Mardi Gras**. In fact is has a **museum** devoted to the subject (The Strand at 23rd Street) that displays costumes and other historic memorabilia.

The **Railroad Museum**, with its collection of 35 old rail cars, also features exhibits about Galveston's commercial history at its location on Shearn Moody Plaza in the 1932 art deco Santa Fe Railroad Depot. **The Galveston County Historical Museum** at 2219 Market contains exhibits about Jean Lafitte, the 1900 hurricane and other important local events and characters. More history is on display at the **Rosenberg Library**, 23rd and Sealy, opened in 1904 as the first library in the state.

The city is rich in historical mansions, the oldest of which is the **Michael B. Menard Home**, 1605 33rd Street, built in 1838 by Galveston's founder. Even more lavish is the pink granite **Bishop's Palace**, 1402 Broadway, the only building in Texas on the American Institute of Architecture's list of 100 outstanding

◄**Purposeful porpoises.**

structures. Designed by Nicholas J. Clayton, it was completed in 1893.

On Broadway at 24th Street is **Ashton Villa** with its wide wrought-iron balcony. Built in 1859, it is now a museum containing 19th-century treasures which evoke the romance of Galveston's Victorian era.

Other historic structures include the 1839 **Williams House**, prefabricated in Maine and shipped to Galveston aboard a schooner, and the spectacular **Grand 1894 Opera House**, 2020 Post Office, where contemporary Broadway musicals perform on a stage that once hosted the likes of Sarah Bernhardt, Al Jolson and the Marx Brothers.

At the far southwest end of the island, **Galveston County Beach Pocket Park** and **Galveston Island State Park** provide beach access and parking for picnics, swimming, sunning, or just relaxing by the water.

Also out here, just south of I-45, is the 140-acre (57-hectare) **Moody Gardens**, the city's major tourist attraction, whose highlight is a 10-story Rainforest Pyra- mid packed with exotic flora and fauna in an environment complete with waterfalls, cliffs, cavers and forests. There's a Bat Cave, an IMAX theater and an authentic reproduction of an 1800s paddlewheeler that offers cruises along the bayou. Just down the coast, where the Brazos River empties into the Gulf, is the **Brazoria National Wildlife Refuge**. It was near here that Stephen F. Austin and his colonists first landed and also where the new government of the Republic of Texas held its historic, very first session.

On the other tip of the island, the east end of Seawall Boulevard, visitors can take the free ferry which links it to the remote **Bolivar Peninsula**. Extending like a long finger down the Texas Coast from Louisiana, it was named in 1815 to honor the Latin American revolutionary Simon Bolivar, during an era when the Gulf Coast and the Caribbean were aflame with anti-Spanish sentiment.

The ferry provides the only convenient access for cars and passengers to Bolivar's beaches, unless visitors relish **Tableau at the Railroad Museum.**

a long 70-mile (110-km) drive from Port Arthur. But this very remoteness has guaranteed splendid isolation for Bolivar's beach-goers.

The **Bolivar Point Lighthouse** poses for pictures alongside State 87 at Port Bolivar. Constructed in 1852, it was dismantled by Confederates in the "War Between the States" and later rebuilt.

Gilchrist is a small town about 20 miles (32 km) north on State 87 and its main attraction is **Rollover Pass**, a channel which slices through the center of town serving up some of the best bankside fishing in the state.

Between Galveston and Houston is the **Kemah-Seabrook** area, where visitors are certain to find a real mixture of Texas coastal dwellers, ranging from space scientists on their day off from NASA to old seadogs and fishermen swapping yarns at popular hangouts like **Jimmy Walker's** and **Maribelle's**.

Situated between Galveston and Corpus Christi on US-59, the **Texas Zoo** at Victoria features only animals found within the state. The 200 species on show include ocelots, armadillos, rattlesnakes, bald eagles and porcupines. Other places of interest are **Refugio**, where visitors can take haywagon rides and watch cowboys at work at the **Dos Vaqueroes** ranch – tel: (512) 543-4905 – and historic **Goliad**, at the crossroads of highways 59 and 77. Here, not far from the Fannin Battlefield, are the graves of Col. James Fannin and the 342 men who in 1836 were massacred after surrendering to the Mexican general Santa Ana. "Remember Goliad!" became a Texas Revolution battle cry.

CORPUS CHRISTI: With nearly 350,000 residents, Corpus Christi – at the other end of the coast from Galveston – is the state's seventh largest city. For many years its semitropical climate and reputation as a recreation capital have created the image of tranquility. Although it lacks the charm of historic Galveston and the picturesque quality of the smaller seaports, for fans of sparkling seaside development, Corpus suggests a young Miami Beach. For deep sea fishing, water sports or enjoying

and
armadillos
at Corpus
Christi.

the white sand of the south Texas coast, Corpus is the place to be.

In 1519, the Spanish explorer Alonzo Alvarez de Piñeda marked the feast day of Corpus Christi – "Body of Christ" – by giving its name to a bay at the mouth of the Nueces River. Until Texas joined the United States in 1845, only Henry Kinney's Trading Post marked the site. When the annexation of Texas sparked a war with Mexico, Corpus Christi came to life as a tent city and shipping point for the US Army. Growing rapidly from a town to a city and finally to a deep-water port, it has retained its military ties, with half of the US Navy's air training bases located in the area.

Driving in Corpus Christi requires a map. Because it follows the curve of the bay, few of its streets run straight. The focal point for activity is **Bayfront Plaza** at the north end of **Shoreline Drive**, which begins at the foot of **Harbor Bridge**, 250 feet (76 meters) above the water. In addition to a convention center and auditorium, the Plaza complex contains the **Art Museum of South Texas** designed by Philip Johnson, the **Corpus Christi Museum** (closed Monday) with its exhibit of shipwreck artifacts and the **Harbor Playhouse**, all built right on the water. There are a couple of floating restaurants in the marina and a boat that reputedly once belonged to Al Capone.

Corpus Christi's two-mile seawall, 14 feet (4 meters) high and 20 feet (6 meters) wide, is an attraction in itself, having been designed by the famous sculptor Gutzon Borglum, who went on to carve the presidential heads on Mount Rushmore. Steps from the seawall down to the beach are a popular resting place, while joggers, strollers and cyclists populate the top.

There are other non-recreational sites worth looking at in the city, such as the **port**, one of the nation's 10 busiest. Moored at Cargo Dock 1 here are **Las Carabelas**, authentic replicas of Columbus' ships – the *Nina*, the *Pinta* and *Santa Maria*. At the city's surprising **Museum of Oriental Cultures** is a prize collection of treasures from Japan which was acquired by a Corpus native

named Billie Trimble Chandler, during her 13 years as a teacher there.

Just across the bridge from Bayfront Plaza is **Corpus Christi Beach**, 200-400 feet (60-120 meters) wide and 1.5 miles (2 km) long. Natives call it "North Beach," and it offers the city's most challenging surf, as well as the **Texas State Aquarium** and the World War II aircraft carrier, the *USS Lexington* (open daily 10am–5pm). **McGee Beach**, also on Shoreline Drive, is about a mile south and appeals particularly to families with small children because of its calm and shallow bay waters.

Playing by the bay: Visitors essentially come to Corpus to play, and the city provides a wide range of water "toys." A visit should include a trip on a fishing boat, a number of which are available for large parties or private charter. At Corpus Christi Beach, jet skis, sailboats and catamarans can be rented, with or without instruction. There are a number of tennis courts and golf courses. Even four-wheel-drive sand buggies are available on a daily rental basis.

Taking a rest on South Padre beach.

156

These will be needed by visitors who venture south on to **North Padre Island** on the way to **Padre Island National Seashore**, the finest 80-mile (130 km) stretch of natural beach in America. The first 9 miles (14 km) are paved roadway and another 5 (8 km) can be driven by car. But the 55 rugged miles (90 km) to **Mansfield Cut** demand four-wheeling. For beachcombers and shell collectors, however, this trip is a mandatory one.

From the crook of Corpus Christi Bay, the city allows excellent access northward to Mustang Island, Port Aransas and Aransas Pass, known as the "Shrimp Capital of Texas." **Mustang Island** is a barrier between the bay and the Gulf of Mexico, protecting the city to some extent from hurricanes. Visitors will find one of the state's finest beaches located at **Mustang Island State Park**, and at the northern end of the island they'll find one of the state's best fishing ports.

A free 24-hour ferry runs across from where Highway 361 ends to **Port Aransas**, home port for hundreds of shrimp boats. One landmark is the **Tarpon Inn**, an old relic of a hotel once favored by President Franklin Roosevelt. The lobby walls are covered with tarpon scales which have been autographed by successful fishermen.

A word of warning: you may want to give Port Aransas a miss during Spring Break, when thousands of college students come to play.

This whole seashore is a big draw to bird-watchers: the Rockport–Fulton area attracts thousands of hummingbirds that rest over to gain weight for their 500-mile (805-km) flight across the Gulf of Mexico. On the **Aransas National Wildlife Refuge** at Austwell, just north of Corpus Christi – tel: (512) 286-3559 – the most famous residents are about 95 whooping cranes who migrate each November from Wood Buffalo National Park in Alberta for the winter. They can be seen through telescopes at the refuge observation tower. From a low of 16 whoopers counted in 1941, these spectacular birds have increased in number

South Padre condos.

under the protection of the government. The refuge, which has a visitors' center with exhibits, hosts a number of other Texas "critters" – such as the nine-banded armadillo and javelina.

Seashore towns: Between Corpus Christi and Galveston, along State 35 to Houston, are a number of little seashore towns, each offering a bit of new Corpus-style development mixed in with Galveston charm.

In the Lavaca and Matagorda Bays area, **Port O'Connor** is a mecca for serious fishermen and duck hunters, while **Port Lavaca** is worth a detour for travelers more interested in watching anglers than casting a line.

There are two ghost town sites and a local museum, plus the **Port Lavaca State Fishing Pier**, a 3,200-foot (975-meter) pier stretching over the bay that is open from 6am to midnight (it's lit at night). One of the ghost towns serves as another reminder of nature's awesome power. **Indianola**, now reduced to a few fishing families living among stone foundations at the water's edge, rivaled Galveston as the top Texas port until September 17, 1875, when a hurricane literally blew the place away.

Palacios is another place to look for sanctuary from city life. The **Luther Hotel**, built in 1903 when the town was founded, prides itself on an extremely loyal clientele. Telephones and televisions are not found in the rooms, which helps to make a family setting of the guests, who can watch the one television downstairs or relax around a card table in the games room.

A little farther north lie **Freeport** and **Surfside** beaches. They are hangouts for young Houstonians looking for a wilder way of life during the weekend than is available at Galveston, and are quite happy to drive a little farther in order to claim it.

Texas takes particular pride in two relatively lonely places that should appear on any beach lover's list of required visits – the Bolivar Peninsula, near Galveston, and the better known **South Padre Island**.

Corpus Christi guards the northern

tip of **Padre Island**, which is actually a 100-mile-long (160-km) white sandbar that stretches south almost to Mexico, where tiny **Port Isabel** (population 4,000) serves as sentry. For all kinds of photographers, the **Port Isabel Lighthouse** is a required stop. One of Texas' smallest state parks, it was built in 1852 on a site used by Gen Zachary Taylor in the Mexican War. It is open to visitors and deservedly remains one of the state's most photographed landmarks.

South Padre Island, a 34-mile (55-km) section at the southern tip of this long sandbar, is nowhere more than half a mile wide, yet it has become the state's premier beach resort with its windswept dunes, gorgeous beaches and balmy tropical temperatures. Only one paved road, Padre Boulevard, running up the center of the island, runs beyond the city limits but peters out after a few miles amidst blissfully undeveloped sand dunes, marshes and birdlife.

The island's **Visitor Center**, tel. (800) 343-2368, just north of the causeway from the mainland, offers brochures and information about accommodation and such attractions as fishing, water sports, windsurfing and shopping. The nearest airports are at the border town of Brownsville, 10 miles (16 km) south or Harlingen, on US-77 to the north.

Ranches and rustlers: Just inland from the Gulf Coast, along US-77 through ranch country, is **Kingsville**, from which a diversion should be made west along Highway 141 to the headquarters of the 800,000-acre (323,748-hectare) **King Ranch**, tel: (512) 592-8955. Visitors can take a free self-guided tour along a 12-mile (19-km) loop of the immense ranch, which is famous for its wealth, its stable of Kentucky Derby winners and its own breed of Santa Gertrudis cattle.

Nearby on State Road 281 is **Ben Bolt** (population 110), where the legendary Headless Horseman is buried. This phantom-like figure – who terrorized the region in the mid-1800s with a head dangling from his saddlehorn – was actually a rustler who had been killed by a Texas Ranger, the outlaw's head tied to a wild mustang as a warning to others.

Left, tourists from Mexico at Port Isabel. Right, the gulf.

SAN ANTONIO

San Antonio (population 936,000) is the most Roman Catholic, and perhaps one of the most cosmopolitan cities in America. European visitors tend to feel at home here right away, especially if they are from Mediterranean countries, in a way they rarely do in the rest of the United States.

"Of distinctive Spanish cast" was the 1893 description in *Baedeker's Guide to the United States* when, with its population of 40–50,000 "Americans, Mexicans, and Germans, with a few Coloured People," it was Texas' largest and best known city. San Antonio's 18th-century origin and reputation as the most fun-loving, hell-raising, independent-minded Wild West capital find expression in ways not always apparent to first-time visitors.

A unique ethnic mixture and sense of fun are celebrated in shops, restaurants, hotels, art collections, architecture, parks, and especially in the beautifully preserved Spanish missions.

San Antonio is sometimes called Mexico's northernmost city. Its majority Latino population is the largest of any city in the US and understandably it has the closest economic and cultural ties with its neighbor south of the border. The National Autonomous University of Mexico, the oldest institution of higher learning in this hemisphere, has maintained a campus in San Antonio since 1972.

San Antonio lies at the edge of the Mexican badlands, the unchanging flat cattle-raising "brush country" covered with mesquite and chaparral, and also at the edge of the pretty sheep and cattle-raising Central Texas Hill Country. To the east are the fertile South Central Texas plains, where the first Anglo-American colonists settled in the 1820s. Each of these areas has long considered San Antonio its principal city. It wasn't always slow-paced and charming, but today that's exactly what attracts Texans and non-Texans alike to the only city where tourism is a major industry.

"Ol' San Antone": San Antonio used to be Texas' "Tin Pan Alley." Like Austin today, the city attracted a variety of musicians, and many of them wrote songs about their new home. In many cases, the first time people outside of Texas heard about the city was through the music, and you still find tourists today who are expecting to find the "ol' San Antone" made famous in song. Although there are many wonderful tunes about the Alamo City, the most famous one is probably Bob Wills' version of "San Antonio Rose."

Crackdown: San Antonio has been compared to a neutral city in wartime, like Casablanca or Lisbon, filled with refugees of warring nations. Overall, there is not as much aggressive friendliness here as there is in other places in Texas where tourism is not a mainstay, the social and ethnic mix is less complex and life has not always been urban. In the past, San Antonio was often somewhat less than law-abiding. When President Roosevelt toured the red light district on East Commerce Street in 1936

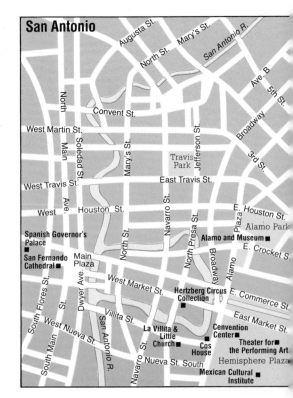

Preceding pages: San Antonio. Below, across from the Alamo.

with LBJ and the New Deal mayor Maury Maverick in tow, he exclaimed he had never seen so many taverns in one block. In fact, the taverns of San Antonio never closed; San Antonio did not observe Prohibition. Later on, Governor W. Lee (Pappy) O'Daniel – the flour salesman and radio announcer in whose first hillbilly band Bob Wills got a start as the violinist – sent Texas Rangers here to enforce the state laws by smashing bars and gambling halls.

San Antonio's first Hispanic mayor, Henry Cisneros, was elected in 1981 and overwhelmingly re-elected in 1985 as "everybody's mayor." His election was good for the self-esteem of young *Chicanos* – one of the many labels Hispanics have to choose from. In general, the Texas Hispanics are called Mexican, *Mejicano*, Mexican-American, brown, *Tejano*, Tex-Mex, Hispanic, Hispano, *Indio*, *Indio*-Hispanic and *La Raza*. Each term has a slightly different meaning; for example, *Chicano* and *Indio* acknowledge one's Native Americans heritage.

Ethnic history: Some of this early Native American history as well as natural science exhibits and local flora and fauna is documented in the art deco **Witte Memorial Museum**, tel: (21) 820-2111, in Brackenridge Park. Behind the museum is a complex of historic houses, including one owned by Francisco Ruiz, uncle of José Antonio Navarro and the second of the two native-born Texans who signed the Texas Declaration of Independence.

In the 340-acre (137-hectare) park, which adjoins Fort Sam Houston and lies between US-281 and the Austin Highway northeast of the city, can also be found the **San Antonio Zoo**, tel: (21) 734-7183, and the **Botanical Gardens**, tel: (21) 821-5115. To the west, in a redesigned old brewery on Jones Avenue, is the **San Antonio Museum of Art**, tel: (210) 978-8100, and further north, before the airport at 6000 North New Braunfels, is the **McNay Art Museum**, tel: (210) 824-5368, housing the collection of a wealthy oil heiress who donated it to the state.

Spaniards and Native Americans may have encountered one another for the first time near the Witte at the headwaters of the San Antonio River, so-named by the Spaniards for Saint Anthony of Padua. Don Martin de Alcaron and Fra Antonio de San Buenaventura Olivares arrived in the area with settlers, soldiers, Franciscans and livestock in 1718, when the Mission San Antonio de Valero (now the Alamo) and the Villa de Bejar (now Bexar), were established. Four more missions were organized along the river before 1731.

Today these are part of the San Antonio Missions National Historical Park stretching over a 6-mile (10-km) route to the south down St Mary's, beside or close to the river. They are the **Nuestra Señora de la Purisima Concepción de Acana**, Mission Road near Mitchell Street, tel: (21) 229-5732; **San Francisco de la Espada**, 10040 Espada Road, tel: (21) 627-2021; **San Juan Capistrano**, 9101 Graf Road, tel: (210) 532-5840; and **San José**, 6539 San Jose Drive, tel: (21) 229-4770. All are open daily except Christmas Day and January 1, until 6pm in summer; 5pm in winter. A free map of the Mission Trail is available at the San Antonio Visitor Information Center.

The missions vary in interest, with colonial era wall paintings on view at Concepción, an 18th-century Spanish aqueduct at Espada and a remarkable stone carving at San José.

The Alamo: The worldwide fame of the Mission San Antonio de Valero (named after the viceroy at the time) was established during 13 days of 1836 when "the Alamo" was besieged by 5,000 Mexican troops. Early in the century it had served as a garrison (and earned its name) for a cavalry unit from Alamo de Parras, but by the time General Santa Ana seized the Mexican presidency, the Anglo settlers in San Antonio were claiming the city for their own – and it was in the **Alamo** they chose to make a stand when Santa Ana came to reclaim it.

Barricading himself with his small force within the Alamo's thick stone

Spanish Governor's Palace.

walls, the commander of the "Texians" on February 24, 1836 sent out an appeal for reinforcements:

To the People of Texas and All Americans in the World –
Fellow Citizens and Compatriots:
I am besieged with a thousand or more of the Mexicans under Santa Ana. I have sustained a continual Bombardment and cannonade for 24 hours and have not lost a man. The enemy has demanded surrender at discretion, otherwise, the garrison is to be put to the sword, if the fort is taken. I have answered the demand with a cannon shot, and our flag still waves proudly from the walls. I shall never surrender or retreat. Then, I call upon you in the name of Liberty, of Patriotism, and everything dear to the American character, to come to our aid with all dispatch. The enemy is receiving reinforcements daily and will no doubt increase to three or four thousand in four or five days. If this call is neglected, I am determined to sustain myself as long as possible and die like a soldier who never forgets what is due his honor and that of his country. VICTORY or DEATH.
—William Barret Travis
Lt. Col. Comdt.

Thirty-two "Texians" from Gonzales – the Lexington of Texas where the first shot of the Revolution was fired – joined Travis after he wrote his stirring letter. They were supported in their defense by some notable Tennesseans, including Colonel James Bowie, who had disobeyed General Sam Houston's order to destroy the fortress, and Davy Crockett. Early on the morning of March 6, Santa Ana's men overran the fortress and killed all its 189 defenders.

Forty-six days later the cry "Remember the Alamo" served as the inspiration for the Texans who surrounded and decisively beat Santa Ana's men at San Jacinto on April 21, a holiday still celebrated by the city of San Antonio with an annual **Fiesta**. Thus, the Republic of Texas was born.

Mission San José.

Preserved forever: The Alamo itself, preserved as a national monument along with its library, gift shop and its pleasing grounds, as well as **Fort Sam Houston**, two miles north, are symbols of the state's stubbornly independent spirit dating from that era.

In 1883, the State of Texas bought the familiar chapel with its bullet-riddled walls; but the convent, the surrounding area around it where the beautiful **Alamo Gardens** are planted, belonged to a liquor dealer and it is said plans were being made to build a hotel. Sam Johnson, the father of President Johnson, has been called the "Savior of the Alamo" because while a State Senator in 1905 he arranged for the state to buy the Alamo convent. Clara Driscoll (owner of Laguna Gloria, the lakeside mansion in Austin that later became that city's art museum) is also known as the Savior of the Alamo since she advanced Sam Johnson $25,000 to buy it until the state was able to do so.

The San Antonio Conservation Society, organized in 1924 primarily to preserve and restore many of the Alamo buildings, later turned its attention to saving a trio of the city's art deco movie theaters. The facade is all that remains of the **Texas** (1926); the **Majestic** (1929) with "Alamo bells" in the proscenium, now a performing arts center; and the **Aztec** (1926), whose architect gained his inspiration from studying Mexico's Mayan and Aztec ruins.

Behind the Alamo, another loop of the river is flanked by the Marriott Hotel (one of the many points at which you can board a boat for a sightseeing cruise); the **Rivercenter Mall** with its 140 shops; and the city's huge **convention center**.

The story of the hallowed Alamo is told in appropriately spectacular fashion on the six-story screen of the IMAX theater – schedules and information from (210) 225-4629 – located in the mall between the 96-year-old **Crockett Hotel** and the limestone and stucco **Menger Hotel**, the city's first deluxe hostelry. In 1855, William Menger opened a brewery on the grounds of the Battle of the Alamo and, soon afterward, he and his

Mission San Juan Capistrano.

166

wife offered rooms to German farmers from Fredericksburg, Seguin, Comfort and New Braunfels.

Old German farmers gave way at the Menger to presidents, generals and writers, including Oscar Wilde and William Sydney Porter (O. Henry), Jenny Lind, Sarah Bernhardt, and consumptive poet Sidney Lanier, who came to San Antonio for his health. At the Menger, people still use the old lobby (the "rotunda") and patio. The hotel, the first in Texas to offer drive-in registration, no longer offers dinners of buffalo hump and tongue, or San Antonio River turtle.

Rough riders: In 1898, Teddy Roosevelt recruited members of the US Volunteer Cavalry ("Rough Riders") in the **Menger Bar** (now on a different side of the hotel from the original). "I need a few good men," he is supposed to have said, "who can ride a horse, shoot a gun, and want to serve their country." It is assumed that the Rough Riders were organized in San Antonio during the Spanish-American War because this was good "horse country". The elite corps of cowboys and millionaires from the East generated a great deal of attention before they went on to Cuba.

Horse trading: There is a theory that, just as San Antonio had to send to Boston for ice when the Menger was the best hotel in this part of the country, Boston sent to Spanish Texas for horses. Accordingly, the horse Paul Revere chose for his midnight ride was from a ranch where the Polish town of Cestohowa is now located.

Attractions: San Antonio's **Visitor Information Center**, tel: (210) 225-4636, is right opposite the main entrance to the Alamo. Many of the tour companies are around here, as well as such attractions as **The Texas Adventure**, tel: (210) 227-8224, a film history that, inevitably, includes yet another Alamo re-enactment; the **Plaza Theater of Wax**, tel: (210) 224-9299, which includes Ripley's Believe It or Not!; and a terrific **Cowboy Museum**, housed in an 1850 building with its reproductions of a jail, saloon and general store.

Another popular attraction, the **Hertzberg Circus Collection**, tel: (210)

207-1870, comprising thousands of items of circus memorabilia and a scale model of a five-ring circus, is at the corner of South Presa and West Market Street. On Market is the 21-story Hilton **Palacio del Rio**, built in record time in 1968 overlooking the river and said to be the world's first hotel composed of pre-constructed rooms from an "assembly line." As its honeycomb facade suggests, the nearly-500 rooms, completely furnished and ready to assign to guests, were lifted into place by a crane and nudged, nurtured and straightened by a helicopter.

The **Paseo del Alamo** links **Alamo Square** and the Paseo del Rio, or **River Walk**. The River Walk is 1.2 miles (1.9 km) long and 20 feet (6 meters) below street level. It would be quite possible, if one were not familiar with San Antonio at all, to spend a long time here and not realize that there was a river.

The story of San Antonio's bridges could fill a guidebook by themselves. There are 13 bridges in all, and each of them crosses to the River Walk. There

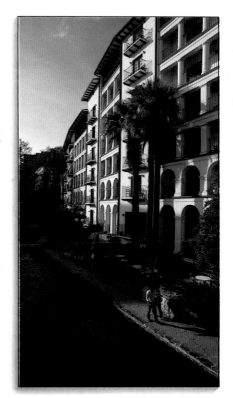

iver Walk.

are tall cottonwoods and cypresses all along the Paseo as well as shops, restaurants, galleries and night spots. There is the choice of watching flat-bottomed *chalupa* boats, with their *mariachi* musicians, drift by or boarding one of the various craft. Ask for more information at one of the shops along the way.

The River Walk is generally associated with San Antonio's colorful celebration of Fiesta in April, but it quite often looks festive. There are *luminarios*, usually votive candles in paper bags weighted with sand and cut out in pretty patterns, during the Christmas season. There is also a **Fiesta Noche del Rio** in the summer at the **Arneson Theater**, on the river at the entrance to La Villita.

After a big flood in 1921, which left the business district under 8 feet (2.4 meters) of water, a three-block-long cutoff was created joining the corners of the river where it bends around a 16-block area. It is hard to believe today, but at one time there were plans to fill in the river or run it underground so that it would, in effect, be used as a sewer.

Fortunately, the Conservation Society banded together to protect the river and its nearby landmarks. While Mayor Maverick was in office in the late 1930s, aid was sought from the Works Progress Administration (WPA) – a Federal make-work scheme to cut unemployment. The river was dredged. Dams and rock retaining walls, the pleasant cobblestone and flagstone walks, stairways from bridges and arched footbridges, designed by architect Robert Hugman, were constructed. Today, San Antonio's River Walk is considered the most successful WPA project in Texas.

Since the 19th century, the river has been the scene of social clubs, carnivals, rodeos, festivities and circuses. There were private landings and wide lawns, children swam and the whole city picnicked on it, fished in it, and were baptized under it, sometimes *en masse*, as one discovers by looking at the panoramic photographs taken by E.O. Goldbeck.

As long as San Antonio lay at the beginning of the Chisholm Trail, there

Left, blessing of the animals, January 17. Right, San Antonio River.

were murders, lynchings and gunfights by cowboys: see the memoirs of Mary Maverick, the wife of Sam Maverick who lived by the Alamo where so many of his friends died. And more than once it occurred to someone to call San Antonio a Frontier Venice.

Frederick Law Olmsted described the river in *A Journey Through Texas*: "Few cities have such a luxury. [The water] remains throughout the year without perceptible change of temperature, and never varies in height or volume. The streets are laid out in such a way that a great number of houses have a garden extending to the bank, and to a bathing-house, which is in constant use. The Mexicans seem half the time about the water. Their plump women, especially, are excellent swimmers, fond of displaying their luxurious buoyancy…"

"Hardly a day passes," he went on, "without some noise… the street affrays are numerous and characteristic … More often than otherwise, the parties meet upon the plaza by chance, and each, on catching sight of his enemy, draws a revolver, and fires away. As the actors are under more or less excitement, their aim is not apt to be of the most careful and sure, consequently it is not seldom, the passers-by who suffer. Sometimes it is a young man at a quiet dinner in a restaurant, who receives a ball in the head; sometimes an old negro woman, returning from market, who gets winged.

"After disposing of all their lead, the parties close, to try their steel, but as this species of metallic amusement is less popular, they generally contrive to be separated by friends before the wounds are mortal. If neither is seriously injured, they are brought to drink together on the following day, and the town waits for the next excitement."

Further down Alamo, past the Convention Center, is **HemisFair Park** – site of the 1968 World's Fair – dominated by the 750-foot (229-meter) **Tower of the Americas** (open till 10pm) with its glass elevators. Near also are the **Institute of Texas Culture**, tel: (210) 558-2300, and the **Mexican Cultural Institute**, tel: (210) 227-0123, both dis-

Paseo del Rio illuminated for Christmas.

playing interesting historical and contemporary exhibits.

Opposite the park is **La Villita** ("Little Town"), the old town of Béjar, now spelled "Bexar," from which Santa Ana's troops trained their cannons on the Alamo in 1836. The previous year, Santa Ana's brother-in-law, General Martin Perfecto de Cos, had stayed in a house here while in command of the Mexican forces sent to quiet the Texans. When La Villita was rehabilitated, the intention was to honor San Antonio's Spanish, German, Mexican, French, American and Texan heritage, evidence of which is found in the town's architectural styles. But today it is predominantly a reconstructed Mexican village of fake adobe, filled with the predictable craft shops and eating places.

Soon after the Republic of Texas was born, a sizeable influx of German immigrants established themselves in the historic **King William district** (named after the Prussian king) between the river and South St Mary's Street. Here in this 25-block district many refurbished Victorian homes can be admired on a walking tour conducted by the San Antonio Conservation Society, 107 King William Street. At 509 King William Street is the **Steve Homestead**, tel: (210) 225-5924, an 1876 mansion filled with period antiques. Across the river on South Alamo to the south, is the **Blue Star Arts Complex**, tel: (210) 225-6742, another restored old district now rife with shops and art galleries.

Central area: As the main river, which runs roughly north to south, makes an almost circular loop between College and Villita streets, with the vast majority of the city's attractions within or near to those perimeters, a logical walking tour would concentrate on that central section. Many visitors, however, prefer to get away from the crowds at least for a while by beginning their stroll on the quieter stretch located at 4th Street, for example, behind the **Municipal Auditorium**.

The most convenient starting point for visitors driving here from Austin is a couple of bridges nearer to the center.

Left, intersection of I-35 and I-37. **Right**, stone barn near Panna Maria.

Take the St Mary's exit from the I-35 and use the usually unfilled parking lot at Convent, opposite the former St Ursuline's convent, which is now the **Southwest Craft Center**, where artists can be seen creating pottery, calligraphy and weaving.

A major landmark along the river is at Travis Street, where the art deco **Milam Building** has been an institution since the 1920s when it housed the offices of many of the state's earliest oil companies. The next bridge is at Houston Street where, after a glance at the art deco facade of the defunct **Texas Theatre** (now absorbed into a telephone building) you might take the trolley along Houston Street to visit colorful **Market Square** which is a few blocks to the west. A network of tourist streetcars, operating on overlapping routes between Cattleman Square and St Paul Square, pass by most of the main attractions and run until late evening. Call (210) 227-2020 for specific schedules. There's music in Market Square every day, varying from occasional performances to full-scale festivals in summer and fall.

The huge **Mi Tierra** restaurant, (210) 225-1262, with its bakery – open 24 hours – is a long-established landmark here, but it's also where the *mariachis* gather, so if you want to sit outside it may be less noisy at one of the numerous other Mexican places.

Historic home: Walking back to the river along Dolorose Street you'll pass the square, stuccoed limestone **José Antonio Navarro House**, home of one of the two native-born Texans who signed the Texas Declaration of Independence; and the 18th-century **Spanish Governor's Palace**, restored between 1929 and 1930, which was never in fact the house of any governor, but served the captain of the *presidio*. Overlooking the Main Plaza is the limestone Gothic Revival **San Fernando Cathedral**, North America's first, which was rebuilt in 1872. The plaque on the front stating that the remains of the Alamo dead are located here is inaccurate, as Santa Ana burned the bodies.

At the San Fernando Cathedral,

Buckhorn Hall of Horns.

Graham Greene was reminded of Victorian albums and valentines by the *mantillas* worn by the Hispanic women. He wondered if the San Antonio River wound itself into a heart shape and, in fact, it almost does.

In 1938 the pecan "shelleries" as Greene called them, still flourished on the West Side, where impoverished pecan shellers worked for a few cents a day. He attended a rally at which the *Internationale* was sung and "pale and weak and self-conscious" Anglo girls mixed with the "dark sensual confident... half casters – who knew instinctively, you felt, all the beauty and the horror of the flesh."

The plaza fronting the cathedral is the earliest permanently settled spot (by European immigrants) in Texas and after the Revolution was the liveliest place in town with its markets and feisty, flirtatious "chili queens" who were ordered to take their chili stands away when the new City Hall and James R. Gordon's red sandstone and granite Bexar County Courthouse were completed in the 1890s.

Crowded tables: The north side of the river's loop all the way to the Alamo Plaza is lined with restaurants and big hotels, but the main **Restaurant Row** is where the loop heads south again, between Crockett and Commerce streets. The tables are always crowded with people eating and people-watching, and there's a constant new influx of sightseers coming down the fountain-fringed steps from the plaza and the glitzy shops of the Paseo del Alamo.

Another attraction can be found in the southern part of the city: the historic (1881) **Buckhorn Saloon** with its huge collection of horns, moved from downtown to the site of the Lone Star Brewery some years ago.

German heritage: Several thousand of the original German settlers to the region in the mid-1800s formed farming communities – Gruene, Comfort and New Braunfels – just northwest of San Antonio, where the German heritage survives in the form of charming *fachwerk* houses replete with gingerbread trimmings. **Gruene** is the most

interesting historically, and a free map sketching out a suggested walking tour is available at the New Braunfels Chamber of Commerce office, 390 South Seguin Street, tel: 800-572-2626.

Heading out of San Antonio along US-90 will bring you to the border at Del Rio, about 150 miles (241 km) to the west. Along the way, sightseeing stops might include the Garner Memorial Museum, tel: (210) 278-5018, at **Uvalde** and the Alamo Village Movie Location, tel: (210) 563-2580, at **Brackettville**.

Uvalde was the home of John Nance Garner, popularly known as Cactus Jack, the controversial two-term vice-president to Franklin Delano Roosevelt. **Alamo Village** on Highway 674 was the first movie location built in Texas and has been the site of hundreds of television shows and commercials, as well as such movies as *Lonesome Dove*. Its reconstruction of an early Western village, adjoining the Alamo set, includes an Indian store, saloon and John Wayne museum.

Below, Convention Center. Right, Transit Tower

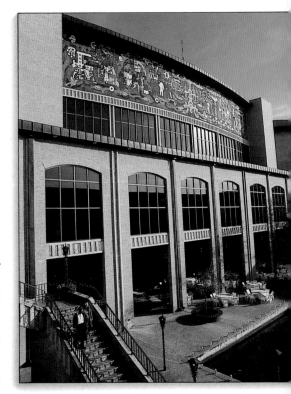

DEL RIO
TO LAREDO

Water has been the moving force in **Del Rio's** history as in the history of all the Texas border towns. Around 1870 there was considerable development of **San Felipe Springs**, whose 90 million gallons of water a day attracted farmers and ranchers, providing agricultural and drinking water for the region. Damming the Rio Grande and the Devil's and Pecos rivers has created **Lake Amistad** ("Friendship" in Spanish), an 88,000-acre (36,000-hectare) reservoir with more than 1,000 miles (1,600 km) of shoreline. Some claim this is the best lake for bass fishing in the state. The water is also clear enough for scuba diving. Hunting licenses for the game found here are also available.

Ancient caves: Native American cave paintings, some dating back 8,000 years, are also found along the shores of Lake Amistad. Many are inaccessible, but others, such as **Panther Cave**, can be reached by boat. Sadly, many of the more accessible have been defaced by vandals, but some of the better paintings are now protected by the State of Texas at **Seminole Canyon State Park**, on the northern extension of the lake. All 400 or so archaeological sites on the lakeshore are owned jointly by the United States and Mexico.

Local boosters describe Del Rio south of the lake as the wool and mohair capital of the world. There is water, wool, and also wine in this desert. San Felipe Springs has kept the Qualia family and a flock of Toulouse Weeder Geese happy, quacky and prospering at the **Val Verde Winery**, tel: (210) 775-9714, along Qualia Drive, for more than 100 years. Val Verde, Texas' oldest vintner, offers free tours almost every day except Thanksgiving, Christmas and New Year's Day.

In addition to a fine variety of 19th-century architecture in the downtown area, Del Rio (population 30,000) offers lively quarterhorse racing on the weekends. After considerable pressure by some lawmakers to introduce parimutuel gambling, their efforts were rewarded. The Del Rio racetrack was closed temporarily, but even after it reopened the issue remained a contentious one.

Across the river from Del Rio is the city named after the romantic but suicidal poet, Manuel Acuña (1849–73), one of Mexico's most widely read poets. In order to reach **Ciudad Acuña**, (population 40,000), drive out of Hudson or Las Vacas to the **International Bridge**. There is ample parking on the American side, and most of the shops offering typical *curiosidades mexicanas* are clustered together on **Hidalgo Street** near the bridge.

Doubtful authenticity: Driving late at night you may hear – even as far away as the Canadian border – the religious programming broadcast from XERF, one of the Mexican border-blaster radio stations. In the 1950s, Wolfman Jack hired on at a border-blaster and introduced a generation of Americans to rock and roll. Nowadays, the standard fare is patent medicine commercials and cassette-tape Christianity. These airwave evan-

gelists suggest that to be saved and healed (via the US Postal Service and 200,000 watts) just put your hand on the radio and a check in the mail.

The American Medical Association had its reservations about the authenticity of the "goat gland pills and elixir" marketed by an early Del Rio citizen. The proximity of the Mexican border probably made Del Rio seem a more favorable business climate to Doctor Johnny Brinkley of Kansas, who made a career of peddling exotic cures.

In 1933, Brinkley used his own border radio station – on which he cranked the power up to 500,000 watts – to sell gland extract and extended virility to thousands of Americans. He became wealthy, spent some time in jail, and built **The Dr John R. Brinkley Mansion** which still stands on **Hudson Drive**, a tribute to his entrepreneurial spirit.

The **Whitbread Memorial Museum** on Main Street is a collection of reconstructed pioneer buildings, including a replica of the famous saloon and courtroom of Judge Roy Bean who, along with his son, is buried in the grounds. Bean's original Jersey Lilly Saloon, named after Lily Langtry, the legendary English actress whom he admired from a distance, still stands in tiny **Langtry** (population 145) northwest on US-90. Proclaiming himself "Law West of the Pecos", the illiterate Judge Bean doffed his bar apron in favor of a waistcoat whenever court was in session, drafting a jury from drinkers at the bar.

Eagle Pass: Fifty-six miles (90 km) south of Del Rio is **Eagle Pass** (population 22,000) and its Mexican neighbor, **Piedras Negras** (population 33,000). Other than Mexican political unrest that closed the International Bridge on several occasions in February and March of 1985, not much has happened here since **Fort Duncan** was closed for the second and last time after World War I.

The fort had been established by the US Army in 1849, and a detachment of half-breed Native American scouts, descended from runaway black slaves, served there after the Civil War. Many of the original buildings, now restored,

Religious faith-healer at Ojinaga.

comprise the **Fort Duncan Museum**, where mighty military memorabilia and lots of relics of mid-19th-century Texas are on display.

A maverick in the herd: Eagle Pass is the seat of **Maverick County,** named after an early rancher and signer of the Texas Declaration of Independence, Samuel Maverick. Although he was considered naive because he refused to brand all his cattle, it also worked the other way: any unbranded animal that strayed from another herd in on time at all became a Maverick cow.

Piedras Negras (Black Rocks) and Eagle Pass *(Paso de Aguila)* are regular stops for Kickapoo Indians who, under a US-Mexican agreement, are free to reside in either country. Kickapoos sell handcrafted goods at the border, and at their settlement across the border in Coahuila, Yacamiento. Piedras Negras remains a stop-and-shop Mexican town with a few good restaurants.

Twin Laredos: The two Laredos – Nuevo Laredo in Mexico and **Laredo** across the border in the US – together form a city of some 200,000. Both were outposts in what was once the backwater of Spain's American colony. On the Texas side the historic downtown district has been revitalized with cobblestone streets, antique street lamps and restored buildings, although most of the culture here is commercial. Residents from each side of the border line up on the other for bargains.

Even on the Texas side, 95 percent of the residents are Hispanic. Downtown Laredo caters to Mexican shoppers buying inexpensive clothing, various electronic and electrical appliances – often made in Asia – and some processed foods. Competition for the Mexican buyer has lowered prices on portable TVs, stereos, tape players, mixers, blenders, and a variety of other items unavailable in Mexico.

About two-thirds of the US trade with Mexico crosses the border here, a volume that has only increased since the passage of the NAFTA agreements. On the US side, customs agents collect almost $250 million in duties each year.

Customs and immigration offices are open 24 hours daily. *Casas de cambio,* or currency exchanges, on both sides of the bridge usually offer a fair exchange rate for pesos and dollars, and they are convenient. Check the banks (Mexican banks are generally open weekdays from 9am to 1pm) before changing large amounts of money.

Driving into Mexico's interior requires special insurance – check with the AAA's Laredo office, tel: (512) 727-3527. Travelers who visit what's regarded as the Border Zone for less than 72 hours are exempt from obtaining the otherwise necessary tourist card. Having said that, any foreign visitor should be sure to take a passport or green card to present at the border when returning to the US, as it's impossible to predict whether it will be asked for. Better to be safe than sorry.

At present there are two international bridges crossing the border in downtown Laredo – at the foot of Convent Avenue and the southern point of I-35 – with a third bridge, Columbia-Solidarity, off FM-1472 about 18 miles (26 km) to the north. Traffic has become so heavy that there are now plans for building a fourth bridge.

Away from the bridges, the downtown area improves. **Riverdrive Mall**, on Water Street at the foot of Santa Maria, includes several outlets of national chains, as does the larger **Mall del Norte** along I-35. **San Agustín Plaza**, where the Texas city began as a Spanish settlement in the 1750s, is flanked by the century-old church, **La Posada Hotel** and the former **Capitol of the Republic of the Rio Grande**, now a museum (which is closed Mondays and major holidays).

The Republic was a short-lived revolt led by disenchanted Mexican federalists who met in convention in what was still a Mexican city in 1840. Somewhere between the rapidly expanding Manifest Destiny of the United States and the rapidly receding border of Mexico, the Republic of the Rio Grande was lost. The museum's exhibits explain some of this fascinating history.

Alamo Village located in Bracketville, South Texas.

At San Bernardo and Washington streets is **Bruni Plaza**, named after an Italian immigrant who died a politician and wealthy rancher in 1931.

Nuevo Laredo, a short walk across the old International Bridge, is something of a Texas Tijuana, with the usual plethora of tacky tourist shops along Guerro Avenue. Nuevo Laredo is old, but not charming.

There are quite a few good restaurants, many of which observe the common Mexican practice of posting menus at the entrance. The local specialty is *cabrito,* charbroiled baby goat, which can be seen cooking spread-eagled on spits in restaurant windows.

Nuevo Laredo has some interesting night spots, and there are tourists' treasures in local shops. Mexican and colonial style handcrafted furniture is a regional product. At shops located along Guerrerro, near the old bridge, there is always a vast array of clothing, jewelry, and other collectibles from Mexico and Central and South America. There is also a traditional *mercado central*, where tourists and locals can haggle over a variety of *curiosidades.*

As in the other Mexican border towns, liquor prices are low compared with the US. However, only one quart (almost a liter) of liquor or wine, or one case of beer (24-ounce containers) per person, can be brought into the US duty-free. A state excise tax must be paid on all alcoholic beverages brought into Texas. Mexico also has a one quart import limit on liquor, but usually the regulation is not strictly enforced.

The bullring in Nuevo Laredo provides a smaller and slower *Death in the Afternoon* on Sundays during the season – Easter through early September. Dogs and ponies run (on different days) at Nuevo Laredo's racetrack, **Nuevo Laredo Downs**, on Highway 85 near the airport. It caters mainly to people betting small sums, and gambling there is bilingual.

Surrounding Laredo are miles of the Texas one sees in movies. Ranches are enormous, since making a living on arid scrubland requires a "Ponderosa"-sized spread. When oil and gas were discovered, most of the region's wealth, although greatly increased, remained concentrated in the hands of just a few people. Poverty is still the norm here, unfortunately, and many of the streets of Laredo remain unpaved.

Lake Casa Blanca State Park, off Highway 59 at the eastern edge of Laredo, offers swimming, boating, fishing and camping – tel: (512) 792-1112 for reservations – and south of Laredo is **Falcon Lake**, a jointly owned American-Mexican impoundment.

The huge 87,210-acre (35,293-hectare) reservoir has an international reputation for black bass, catfish, deer and dove hunting. Downriver, the surrounding landscape gradually changes from semi-arid, scrubby hills to the lush delta of the Lower Rio Grande Valley.

Summers can be blisteringly hot on this part of the border, however, and the ideal month to visit Loredo is not during the summer but in February, when many festivals take place. The most exciting festival of all is the 10-day celebration of George Washington's birthday.

Santa Cruz Church, lying east of Rio Grande City.

EL PASO
TO THE DESERT

For some 1,200 miles (1,930 km), the Rio Grande twists and turns, widens, then roars through tight places, all the while uniting Texas with the Mexican states of Chihuahua, Coahuila, Nuevo Leon and Tamaulipas. In Spanish it is described best, as a region – *la frontera*.

The border, a place of its own, is not where you'll find the best of Texas or Mexico. Fewer than 10 international cities straddle the river. In and around them has gathered a unique mixture of Texans and Mexicans including a motley crew of international hucksters of low culture and high commerce. If you're looking for the cosmopolitan culture of Mexico City or the quiet charm of San Antonio, it's unlikely that you'll find it around here.

But wait. This place is worth a closer look. It's a pretty safe bet – check the odds at one of the half dozen or so Mexican betting parlors – that what you find here won't be found in other places: *la frontera*, if nothing else, is unique.

And much of what this border is about is people lining up on one side to cross over for something on the other side. Border regulars start this procedure before dawn. Green carders, Mexican agricultural laborers, waiting for the contractor's bus to take them to their day's work. By seven it's too late; they've missed their ride.

By eleven, the lines are on the other side. The American day trippers are here – stereotypical tourists, out for an afternoon in the market, and dinner. Almost all of them will be home before dark, with a bottle of José Cuervo tequila, crepe flowers and something for the kids. And so it goes. Dollars to pesos, pesos to dollars. You can usually spend both on either side. Money is the motor that moves this place.

Much of the recent history of this border can be read in the rate of exchange of two currencies. For some 30 years, the peso was tied to the dollar at an exchange rate of 12.5 to one. Most border towns seemed to be slouching

toward prosperity. But since the first devaluation in 1976 and then another in the early 1990s, the value of the peso has fallen precipitously, and the economic climate on both sides of the river has been, at best, cloudy.

Part of what the diminished peso means is longer lines on both sides. Mexican workers, with or without papers, find the lure of the dollar irresistible. And why shouldn't they? The federally fixed *daily* wage on the Mexican side is usually about the same as the hourly rate on the American side. For the American tourist and shopper, the lure is undervalued Mexican goods and accommodations.

First and Third Worlds: In a sense, this border is one of the few places where the First World meets the Third World. *Maquiladoras*, American-owned assembly plants in Mexico, enjoy proximity to the US border with Third World operating costs. American retail businesses, despite continuing devaluations, sell Mexicans what their country can't or won't manufacture: TVs, stereos, medi-

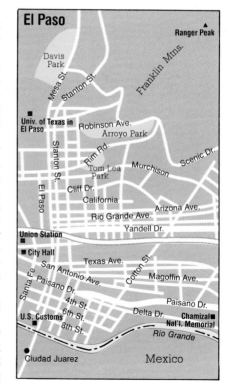

Davis Park

Franklin Mtns.

Mesa St.

Stanton St.

Univ. of Texas in El Paso

Robinson Ave.

Arroyo Park

Stanton St.

Rim Rd.

Tom Lea Park

Murchison

Scenic Dr.

El Paso

Cliff Dr.

California

Arizona Ave.

Rio Grande Ave.

Yandell Dr.

Union Station

City Hall

Texas Ave.

Cotton St.

San Antonio Ave.

Magoffin Ave.

Santa Fe

Paisano Dr.

4th St.

Paisano Dr.

U.S. Customs

6th St.

8th St.

Delta Dr.

Chamizal

Nat'l. Memorial

Rio Grande

Ciudad Juarez

Mexico

cal instruments and designer jeans. They capitalize on a widely held Mexican belief, *lo gringo es lo mejor*. American-made is best.

The differences in lifestyle and economic status are striking. Outside a Zenith assembly plant in Reynosa, a 40-year-old man scratches out an existence selling salted pumpkin seeds. *"Semillas, semillas, semillas,"* he sings to passing workers. Mostly, he is ignored.

Across the river at McAllen, a farm labor organizer with an Emiliano Zapata mustache and fierce dark eyes tells you the hatband he wears was given to him by Yasser Arafat, whom he traveled to meet in Algeria years earlier.

And strangest of all, he's telling the truth. A University of Texas-El Paso professor writes poetry describing the "trenchant sadness" of the Mexico framed in the window of his office. In the lower Rio Grande Valley, a Border Patrol officer quietly delivers three Salvadoran refugees, who have been apprehended about an hour earlier, to a church-sponsored sanctuary house. It is always an unusual mixture of people.

For the Central Americans, the Rio Grande River represents the last geographic obstacle in their struggle toward a better life, here in *el Norte*. Most are only a few weeks from a country ravaged by war and poverty. And most of them enter the country illegally. For the fortunate few who find their way to the sanctuary houses, the chances of remaining in the country usually improve. Nevertheless, many will spend their first, and last, night in *América* in one of the border detention facilities operated by the US Immigration and Naturalization Service. This is the border, *la frontera*.

The border's best: Consider **El Paso.** To get there from most Texas cities requires driving from dawn to sundown. Politicians and cartographers claim that El Paso is part of Texas. Most Texans know better. About halfway between Houston and San Diego, California, El Paso's heart belongs to New Mexico.

Sprawling across the Valley of El Paso del Norte, **El Paso-Juárez** is an

Looking down on El Paso.

international city of more than a million people. Many consider it the best city on the border. El Paso is also an interesting mix of three cultures: Tigua (or Tiwa) Indian, Norteño Mexican and Southwestern American.

The Tiguas were here first. Related to the Pueblo Indians of New Mexico, they moved to the Spanish mission of San Antonio (later San Agustín) de la Isleta del Sur in the 1680s when the Pueblos went to war with the Spanish. They claim to be the oldest continuously occupied Native American community in the country.

Today's Tiguas still reside about 12 miles (19 km) from downtown at **Ysleta** (an archaic Spanish spelling of "little island"), although most work in El Paso. This is a large agricultural community, and there is a tourist-oriented reservation – fine breads but watch out for the dangerously hot chili.

There are a few other Native American communities scattered around the city, but the major legacy of early Native Americans can be found in **Hueco**

Tanks State Historical Park, 30 miles (48 km) to the east, with its thousands of pictographs. The mission at Ysleta, built in 1682, is still in use, as are the **Socorro Mission** (1681) and **San Elizario Presidio Church** (1773). Each reflects a mixture of Spanish colonial and native architectural styles used in El Paso.

Across the border in Juárez the even older (1668) **Guadalupe Mission** is famous for the legend that its shadows point to the Lost Padre Mine in the nearby **Franklin Mountains** (a 24,000-acre/9,712-hectare park within city limits) where Spanish gold is said to be hidden. The famous El Camino Real, once a royal highway but today a quiet farm road, connects the Ysleta and Soccoro missions with the San Elizario Presidio Church.

Ever since the Spanish explorer Juan de Oñate laid claim to El Paso del Rio Grande del Norte, this city has been Hispanic. Like its history, most of its residents are Hispanic. Far removed from the events of the Texas Revolution, for more than half a century El

igua
eservation.

Paso shared a common religion, language and history with Juárez – becoming a part of Texas a full five years after Texas itself became a state.

There are a few other historic buildings, the main one being the **Magoffin Homestead**, tel: (915) 533-5147, a reconstruction of an 1875 adobe mansion containing many of the original family furnishings and paintings.

El Paso, whose 650,000 residents make it Texas' fourth largest city, nevertheless retains something of the ambience of the slap-leather town that it was in 1895 when gunman John Wesley Hardin was shot dead in the Acme Saloon. Hardin, who claimed to have killed at least 40 men, had been pardoned, reformed, and was practicing law in El Paso when a local constable ended his life. Years after his death, the city remained a convenient place for outlaws to cross the river.

Hardin, along with other notable gunslingers, is buried in the notorious Boot Hill section of **Concordia Cemetery** on the west side of town.

El Paso also has a small Chinese community, descendants of the "Chinamen" who laid the tracks for the railroad that reached here in 1881. It grew with Mexican revolutionary Pancho Villa's 1910 attacks on the Chinese living in the neighboring Mexican states of Chihuahua and Coahuila.

Tibetan revival: An unrelated Oriental feature is the Tibetan architecture on the **University of Texas at El Paso (UTEP)** campus. Katherine Worrell, the wife of the Dean when UTEP was known as the Texas State School of Mines and Metallurgy, lifted the design from *National Geographic* after a 1916 fire destroyed almost half of the campus. The three oldest buildings are pure "Bhutanese eclectic," copied from a Tibetan monastery and fortress at Grag-Gye-Jong, in the Himalayas. Most later buildings are variations on this style.

Also on the campus is the **El Paso Centennial Museum** (closed Monday), whose displays include ancient pottery, dinosaur bones and lots of other relics from the Ice Age.

UTEP building in "Bhutanese eclectic" style.

Texas-El Paso is a large state university, with a reputation for its excellent mining and civil engineering schools as well as for a successful track team built around an international recruiting program. The stadium is the site of the **Sun Bowl**, an annual football classic second only in age to Pasadena's Rose Bowl. If you can't acquire tickets for the game, usually played in late December, drag your blanket up the side of the mountain and join the locals and students.

In the same fashion El Pasoans, in 1911, gathered on the flat roofs of their houses for "battle teas" and watched the Mexican Revolution unfold in **Ciudad Juárez** across the river. For a while Pancho Villa took refuge north of the border, acquiring while there a taste for ice cream and also learning how to ride a motorcycle.

Political geography, as well as climate, shaped the character of this city, now connected to its neighbor by three bridges. It was to the Mexican city later named for him that Benito Juárez fled in 1861 when Napoleon III made the Austrian Archduke Maximilian the Emperor of Mexico. Juárez, a Zapotecan Indian, fought as President to make Mexico a secular state. In 1911, courtly Francisco Madero, the architect of Mexico's revolution, took his government to El Paso.

The vast distance from Mexico City, plus a border that is no more than a trickle of a river, have made El Paso-Juárez one of the centers of Mexican political dissent. Today, Juárez is a stronghold of the *Panistas*, partisans of Mexico's gritty conservative Party of National Action.

Although nationwide they hold less than 10 percent of elected positions, in Juárez they have made a strong fight against the Institutional Party of the Revolution (PRI). The blue and white PAN flags and posters are visible everywhere in Juárez.

Shopping: In El Paso, the fly-and-buy tourist will find the boutiques of **La Placita** conveniently located at the airport. At I-10 and Hawkins is the **Cielo Vista Mall**. Around the city are great bargains at the factory outlets for cowboy boots and western wear. On the other side of the river, in the central *mercado*, there is a variety of regionally manufactured goods – mostly leather and textiles – and the local produce. Some unprepared foods cannot be brought into the US.

Like most border towns, Juárez offers something for almost everyone. There is a government-sponsored native artisans market, **FONART**, on Lincoln Avenue (Avenida Lincoln). It is not as fecund as the *mercado central*, and there is no haggling with vendors, but is interesting nonetheless. Along Lincoln, between FONART and the intersection of Avenida de las Americas, are a number of artisans' and curio shops. A good walking tour for shoppers.

While El Paso is so sprawling that a car is almost a necessity, much of Juárez can be seen on foot and most cab drivers speak English. Agree on prices before closing the door. Spanish and English are spoken in both towns.

The atmosphere in Juárez is a little more *picante* than in El Paso. There are lots of good and bad bars, and equally

igua tribe
iembers at
e Ysleta
lission.

good and bad restaurants. Women are discouraged from visiting, and in some cases turned away from, "men's bars," the traditional *cantinas*. And there are several working-class *cantinas* in downtown Juárez that are best avoided by tourists. Size things up before you decide to stay.

Sightseeing: San Jacinto Plaza in downtown El Paso marks the original city square and is the starting point for bus lines. The El Paso Chamber of Commerce on Civic Center Plaza publishes a free guidebook that includes walking and driving tours and focuses on points of interest and border crossings. Also on the plaza are the **Visitor's Bureau** and the **Americana Museum** (closed Monday), with its dioramas depicting prehistoric life.

To the north at 1211 Montana is the **Museum of Art** (closed Monday), which in addition to its European collection and contemporary American works possesses an unusually impressive collection of Mexican colonial art. Also interesting, northeast of the city off US-54, are **Fort Bliss Replica Museum**, where history buffs can wander through the adobe pre-Civil War army outpost, and also the **Border Patrol Museum**, closed Monday, tel: (915) 759-6060.

All of El Paso can be seen from the **Ranger Peak Aerial Tramway**, which can be caught at the intersection of McKinley and Piedras Streets. Northwest of the city scenic drives across the Franklin Mountains and especially along **Trans Mountain Road** (exit off I-10 West), one of the highest roads in the state, provide spectacular views.

In Juárez, the **Museo de Arte Historia** on Avenida Lincoln exhibits Mexican art by period, from pre-Hispanic to the present. The building's design is modern and unique. Certainly worth a look. The museum is situated in a tourist-oriented commercial center that includes the FONART artisans' market. The **Chamizal Park** in Juárez, located at the foot of the **Bridge of Americas** (which is best avoided at rush hours), is a fine place for a Sunday picnic or family outing.

Crossing the border: Entry into Mexican border cities is almost unrestricted. Documents and personal identification are often only cursorily inspected by Mexican customs *(aduana)* at the international bridges. American citizens will need only proof of citizenship, such as a birth certificate or voter registration card, to apply for a 180-day Mexican Tourist Visa. Canadian citizens will be issued tourist cards upon presentation of a birth certificate. Photocopies of official documents are usually not accepted. Citizens of all other countries are required to present a current passport.

Coming back: Returning to the United States can be very difficult for non-Americans unless all travel documents are in order. Travelers can expect a thoroughly scrupulous inspection of documents by American immigration officers. To enter Mexico with a car, a vehicle title is required. Mexican automobile insurance is mandatory. It is sold, according to a daily rate fixed by the Mexican government, on both sides of the border. One American travel

Shrine on the border.

agency, **Sanborn's**, offers a couple of very good travel guides and maps with all insurance purchased through its office. Many day-trippers, however, leave their cars on the American side rather than bother with insurance and Mexican streets and highways.

Between El Paso and Big Bend: Some 280 miles (450 km) from El Paso via US-90, lies **Presidio**, an ordinary little Texas town that just happens to be on the border. The WPA guidebook to Texas, published in 1940, described it as "an old town of sunbaked adobe houses, squatting like an ancient *hombre* in the shade of giant cottonwoods." Presidio's fame is largely meteorological: on many days it is the hottest spot in the entire United States. If you visit in summer, you can expect temperatures ranging from 100–110°F (37–43°C). And it just doesn't rain here.

In Presidio (population 3,000) there is an interesting example of native adobe construction at the **Fort Leaton State Historic Site**. Fort Leaton was never a military outpost; it was a trading post operated in the mid-19th century by a Presidio trader named Ben Leaton. Leaton was among the first "Anglo" settlers to arrive in Presidio. In their fortified trading post, he and his wife outfitted and accommodated travelers who were somehow drawn to this backwater of civilization. Most of the old outpost has been restored by the State of Texas. Across the river from Presidio is **Ojinaga** (o-hee-NAH-ga). Since no one visits Presidio, Ojinaga lacks the touristy feel of most border towns. There are a few good restaurants, and at least one good hotel.

Connecting Presidio and the Big Bend National Park is **El Camino Del Rio** (FM-170), the River Road. It is 71 miles (114 km) of the most spectacular driving in Texas. This is the **Chihuahuan Desert** at its most rugged and beautiful.

Before entering the park, **Lajitas** makes an interesting stop, an old ghost town resurrected by word of mouth. Lajitas owes its existence to the Mexican revolutionary Pancho Villa. The US Army stationed troops here in 1915 in order to protect settlers against Villa's border raids. The old trading post, if no longer entirely authentic, is cool and inviting. Book raft trips on the Rio Grande here or hire a local desert guide.

The **Cavalry Post**, one of three motels in Lajitas, is built on the site of the trading post established by General Jack Pershing before he mounted his "punitive expedition" against Pancho Villa. General Pershing never caught up with Villa, but the expedition demonstrated the army's lack of experience in fighting on foreign terrain.

It was to be a dress rehearsal for the war in France in which a young lieutenant named George Patton saw his first action as a member of the expedition and killed two men and a horse.

North of Presidio, in the direction of El Paso, there is little of note. Press on through **Adobes** and **Ruidosa** for a few rougher miles to **Candelaria**, where you will find hot mineral baths and a few rustic cabins. Here's a spot for the traveler who enjoys the existential pleasure of being alone and being in the middle of nowhere.

Cow skull: a familiar border sight since frontier days.

RIO GRANDE VALLEY

Along the river from the dusty Tex-Mex town of Roma to the sultry fishing village of Port Isabel lies the Rio Grande Valley, a region backed with the history of border wars, steamboat navigation and nomadic Indians who have long since disappeared. There are 38 communities scattered along 110 miles (177 km) of alluvial plain. Most of the towns situated between Falcon Lake and lower Rio Grande Valley are nothing but caution lights and an extra lane along the highway.

Roma, founded in 1765, might be considered the beginning of the Valley. Marlon Brando came to Roma in the early 1950s to film several scenes for *Viva Zapata*, a movie about the most romantic hero of the Mexican Revolution, Emiliano Zapata. The locals there still talk about Brando and *Viva Zapata* – along with the weather and Mexican politics. Much of the movie was also filmed in the sleepy (and more picturesque) village of **San Ygnacio** further up the river. The 1830 José Trevino house here was chosen because of its typical Mexican design.

Roma is a border town in economic and architectural decline. There is a privately owned Roma **Historical Museum** – no charge to see local memorabilia – in much the same condition as the town. There is some interesting old architecture, too. But the place is so dreary that one South Texas newspaperman declared sarcastically after Falcon Dam was built that a real opportunity had been passed up when Roma wasn't relocated to its middle. The 5-mile (8-km) long dam, constructed in 1953 to control irrigation, was built jointly by the US and Mexico and bears the seals of both countries at the international border line.

Joined by a suspension bridge across the river from Roma is **Ciudad Miguel Alemán** *(ciudad* means city), a clean, modern Mexican town named after a former president. A few miles from **The Rio Grande at Laredo.**

Ciudad Alemán is the forgettable Mexican town of **Mier**. Mier was the site of the capture, in 1842, of the renegade Republic of Texas soldiers involved in the "black bean incident." After capturing Mier, the Texans had to surrender to the Mexican army. They were marched farther into Mexico to Saltillo where 17 of the 176 were executed. A lottery determined who was to die; those who drew one of the black beans from a clay pot were shot by a firing squad.

The eclectic Rio Grande: Along this stretch of the Rio Grande there are some tenuous connections with continental culture. Until the 1830s, Roma was called Garcia's Ranch. A visiting priest convinced himself, and the locals, that the hills here were like those of Rome. It still looks like Garcia's Ranch. In **Rio Grande City**, a Catholic priest built a replica of the Grotto at Lourdes in France. A nostalgic François La Borde, in 1899, commissioned a Paris architect to design the family residence, now the recently restored **La Borde Hotel** with its romantic old restaurant.

Until the arrival of the railroad the river was the Valley's principal avenue of commerce, and Rio Grande City, with its Victorian-era buildings, was an important riverboat terminal. The buildings are still there, but the river has retreated to the south, leaving the town high and dry.

On to the "Magic Valley," as it is described by local developers, where thousands of winter Texans live in their campers. They are fugitives from the midcontinental weather of Minnesota, Michigan, Wisconsin and Lubbock, who finance Airstream trailers with what they save on heating bills back home. The population here swells in winter months, when it's not uncommon to see citrus orchards doubling as seasonal trailer parks.

Rich soils: Centuries of flooding have deposited layers of rich alluvial soil along the Rio Grande's banks, helping to make Hidalgo County one of the state's richest agricultural regions with sugar cane, cotton and vegetable crops – especially onions – grown the year-

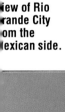

iew of Rio rande City om the lexican side.

round. But cold snaps occasionally freeze not only the winter citrus crops but many of the trees themselves. Some of the growers of the famous Texas Ruby Red grapefruit have sold out rather than replant. Since the 1970s when the peso began its protracted decline, most of the economic news here has been bad. Unemployment is higher than in any other part of the state, and a drop in price and demand for oil further crippled the once booming Mexican economy on which the Valley depended. Some argue that the only steady source of income remaining is smuggling.

If there is anything for the steady and respectable to market, it is the Valley's balmy subtropical climate. Some here are describing the Rio Grande Valley as the Florida of the future, and they are predicting an economic rebirth. This would be good news in a region where a quarter of the permanent residents live below the poverty level and directions to the home of one politician-grower often include "turn right, then look for the farm workers picketing."

Conditions may be right for its growth. Land prices are depressed, retirees are looking for something more than water and electricity hook-ups for their trailers, and the state's major condominium and mall developers are looking this way. All of this within a short drive of the best beaches on the Texas Gulf Coast at South Padre Island.

Meanwhile, like the three-car, hand-drawn ferry at **Los Ebanos** – the last of its kind – things here move slowly. The declining peso means that American merchants earn less, Mexican merchants more. The seasonal Hispanic farmworkers are usually waiting for someone to organize them.

McAllen-Reynosa: Many consider **McAllen** one of the better places in the Valley to live. It is bigger (population 84,000), tidier and a little more upbeat than most surrounding cities. There are adequate hotels and restaurants, usually full during the September white-wing dove hunting season. West of town is the ancient **Oblate Mission**, where the fathers planted the region's first citrus

Left, Ruby Red grapefruit. Right, ferry at Los Ebanos.

orchards, although the Valley's vast citrus industry began with the McAllen estate of John Shary. His estate is still privately owned.

Just east of McAllen, the little town of **Pharr** boasts **Ye Olde Clock Museum**, some of whose 1,650 exhibits are more than 200 years old. The river is eight miles south of McAllen, and here the **International Bridge** connects American **Hidalgo** – a cluster of freight-forwarding houses – with **Reynosa**, a Mexican city of 300,000. Parking is available at Hidalgo on the American side of the bridge.

Near the bridge is Reynosa's *mercado central* and an open shopping mall in the town's *zocolo*, or central plaza. The mall is a tourist market with a variety of shops and restaurants. The *zocolo* has become a focus of political protest and demonstrations. Most of the men in khaki uniforms, however, are not policemen but *cuidadores*, public parking attendants. For a reasonable fee they will watch your car for you and attend to the parking meter while you roam.

Border trouble: This muddy stretch of the Rio Grande, called the Rio Bravo in Mexico, is often shallow enough that undocumented immigrants can tie their shoes and belongings around their necks and hazard an illegal entry into the US. Sometimes they hire a "mule" who will carry passengers on his back. When the river is high, inner tubes or small boats shuttle the illegal immigrants – usually young men, hoping to find work – to the American side.

US Immigration and Naturalization Service officers, *la migra*, apprehend nearly half a million undocumented aliens in Texas each year. Most of them crossed here. What discourages illegals from crossing further north is the brutal, unforgiving desert, but from here Corpus Christi, San Antonio or Austin can be reached within days. And once in a large American community, Mexicans easily disappear into the largely Hispanic population.

American immigration policy has become a source of conflict between the church and state. Central American refu-

an Ygnacio etween aredo and oma.

gees, like Mexicans, find crossing into the US easiest here. The US government has won, and lost, cases against workers at the **Casa Romero**, a sanctuary house in **San Benito** that is funded by the Catholic Diocese.

In terms of folk culture, sometimes this section of the border is hard to define. At **San Juan**, east of McAllen on Interstate Highway 83, the rebuilt **Shrine of la Virgen de San Juan** is the home of a replica of a Mexican statue of the *Virgen de Los Lagos*. The local statue won an identity of its own when it survived a plane crash that destroyed the original shrine. *Curanderas*, or religious faith-healers, often invoke the *Virgen* to work healings, and offer some competition to the more legitimate medical practitioners here.

On the Mexican side of the river, Mexican doctors have established clinics that offer treatments the US Food and Drug Administration refuse to approve. Many alternative methods of treatment are also available here. These include weight loss – usually by injec-tion – and cancer treatment by laetrile. Some services are available through old, established clinics; others through MDs trying to compete in the seller's market created by the glut of doctors in Mexico's cities.

Maybe it's the Anglo-Saxon name, or the Confederate Air Force, or even the statue of US Marines raising the flag atop Mt Suribachi – but somehow **Harlingen** looks more like a North American city. With a population of around 55,000, the town's Valley International Airport serves as the air transport hub for the area. An interesting attraction is the **Texas Air Museum**, tel: (512) 425-1057, with its collection of World War II aircraft. Harlingen is also home to one of the 12 Texas state tourist bureaus operated by the State Highways Department, at the intersection of US Highways 77 and 83. Here information is available about every part of the state, along with maps.

Wildlife: The Rio Grande Valley is a birders' paradise. The Texas Parks and Wildlife Department publishes a list of **Snow birds.**

274 species sighted in the **Bentsen-Rio Grande Valley State Park**, 585 acres (236 hectares) of subtropical woodlands preserved as wildlife habitat. Other wildlife can be observed in the **Bentsen Park** near **Mission** and the **Santa Ana Wildlife Refuge** south of **Alamo**, which include bobcats, coyotes, ocelots and jaguarundi cats. Also open to the public is the **Laguna Atascosa National Wildlife Refuge**, 48,000 acres (14,425 hectares) of open water, marshes, coastal prairie, cropland and brushland located on the coast south of **Port Mansfield**.

The turtle lady: The most unusual wildlife "refuge" in the Valley is the home of Ila Loetscher, who has made a bayside haven for the endangered Ridley turtle. Loetscher is the founder of **Sea Turtles, Inc.**, a non-profit organization that works to find suitable nesting places for the Kemps Ridley sea turtle, a species once hunted almost to extinction. Loetscher's **Port Isabel** home is a **Turtle Museum**, usually open several afternoons a week. Mexican harvests of eggs and turtles, and the popularity of places like Port

Isabel (**Boca Chica Beach** makes it well worth a trip) threaten the turtles' existence. On FM-1419 is the **Sobal Palm Grove Wildlife Sanctuary**, an attractive preserve with self-guided trails maintained by the National Audubon Society.

To the south is **Brownsville**, the largest American city on the lower border. One attraction that draws visitors to this city, other than the nearby beach, is the **Gladys Porter Zoo**, tel: (210) 546-7187, a cageless habitat that allows visitors to wander along ingenious walkways that barely separate man from beast. There is a certain tropical charm about this city divided by *resacas* – freshwater canals that are part of the Rio Grande Delta. A twice-daily **Historic Trolley Tour**, tel: (210) 546-3721, takes visitors around the sites of the town that saw the first battle of the Mexican-American war and the last battle of the American Civil War. Photographs of some of these ancient battles can be inspected in the **Brownsville Museum**, tel: (210) 548-1313, in the 70-year-old Southern Pacific Railroad Depot.

Across the river from Brownsville in Mexico is **Matamoros**, one of the cleanest and most appealing cities on the border. Thousands of people cross backwards and forwards every day over these two borders. American citizens need only proof of identification (passports or green cards for all others) to spend up to 72 hours south of the border. Signs at the bridge direct visitors to *el centro*, the Matamoros central business district. Used clothing shops (*ropa usada*) abound and it's easy to find a bargain: haggle and perhaps even buy. The restaurants here, both at the bridge and on the square, are generally good.

The Mexican border is a political hot spot. Farm workers and growers here will continue to square off across picket lines. Mexicans and Central Americans will continue to slip across the river to work in a country where the streets may not be paved with gold but are at least paved. As the novelist and University of Texas professor Rolando Hinajosa-Smith has said, "There is no place more political than the Valley."

e turtle lady.

WACO TO AUSTIN

The impression is unavoidable: the young of Central Texas migrate to larger cities like Austin and Dallas as soon as possible. A disproportionately large percentage of the population remaining in rural areas appears to be old or very young. Past Waco, the pull of Austin, which is filled with students and ex-students, is unmistakable. Cars speed up, responding to the attraction of Texas' magnetic capital. **Temple**, with its fenced stretch of interstate that does not look as if it is supposed to be excited. **Belton**, **Killeen** and **Salado** (it rhymes with Laredo) zip by most I-35 drivers unnoticed unless they are searching out Dairy Queen or the Dixie Dog drive-in cafe; but this series of former railroad stops are more interesting than they look, and repay a visit if examined with the eye of the novelist or sociologist.

Like most towns south of Waco, Temple and Belton were originally built around loading pens and general stores about a century ago. Today, the area is known primarily for the commanding presence of **Fort Hood**, which is set on no fewer than 218,000 acres (88,223 hectares) near Lake Benton. The fort is the largest military base in the US.

The Fort Hood commandant, interviewed recently by the newspaper, admitted it had once been among the army's most dreaded assignments. Today, he says, the 37,000 soldiers do not want to leave. The main drag of nearby **Harker Heights** is lined with car dealerships, eating places and fairly rowdy nightclubs.

Life and death: There are a number of eateries in the Temple-Killeen area, and in addition to plenty of hearty Texan specialties, they offer a good opportunity to observe small-town life. In fact, Texan-watching is at its best while sawing a batter-fried "corny dog" or a chicken-fried steak, a cheap cut of hammered beef breaded like fried chicken. Chicken-fried steak is served with potatoes and gravy.

The point of bars, clubs, honky-tonks, ice-houses and beer-joints in Texas is friendliness, not fighting. But making some new friends by fighting, particularly in hole-in-the-wall joints and motel rooms, is an ongoing frontier tradition. Invitations to do so should be firmly refused. Although rare, pistol-packing is not entirely unheard of, and some of the tougher characters may carry small, inexpensive pistols known as "Saturday night specials."

In backwater towns like Temple, Belton and Killeen, there is still much pleasure to be taken in day-to-day proceedings. There are as many original characters, language tricks and private jokes as anywhere else, possibly more since the storytelling tradition remains strong in both rural and urban Texas. Temple-Killeen's Standard Metropolitan Statistical Area (SMSA) is one of the 10 fastest growing in the US. The obvious theme for the novelist, sociologist or anthropologist exploring the exploding cities of Texas is the transition from rural to urban ways of life.

Ready-to-wear: The pretty little town of Salado, once a stage halt on Salado Creek a few miles south of Killeen, is best known for its popular and picturesque **Stagecoach Inn**, a restaurant with mid-19th-century antecedents and modern motel additions. Across the street is the **Central Texas Area Museum**, where Sam Houston delivered an anti-secession speech from the balcony.

I-35 follows the railroad – the rails followed the Chisholm Trail along which cattle had been driven to rail-heads farther north – so busy Temple is a logical place to find the **Railroad and Pioneer Museum** in the Santa Fe depot at 31st Street and Avenue H. The **Slavonic Benevolent Order of the State of Texas (SPJST) Museum** at 520 N. Main Street exhibits an unusual collection, including the popular "Magic Gambling Machine," related to Czech immigration. There are SPJST, or Slovanska Podpurujci Jednota Statu Texas, halls in many Central Texas towns.

The **Bell County Museum** in Belton, on North Main Street east of the post

Hike a bike trail on Town Lake, Austin.

office, is a local history museum occupying a 1905 Carnegie Library building. Another form of humanitarianism, on a smaller scale than the donation of libraries, was practiced by the late owner of the nice **Bell County Zoo** on US-190 on the way to Killeen, where hurt or unwanted wild and exotic animals were cared for.

Unfortunately, the zoo has now closed. Restaurants, hotels, museums, wildlife refuges and zoos are likely to change their names and hours, if not disappear completely, in booming Texas. Where distances are great, telephone ahead or inquire at a Chamber of Commerce or other tourist agency.

Two historic army divisions maintain museums at Fort Hood: the **1st Cavalry Museum** on Headquarters Avenue and the **2nd Armored Division Museum** on Battalion Avenue. These and the many reconstructed frontier forts in Texas cannot really make the lives of soldiers seem real, but along with humble gun museums and collections of artifacts, they feed the imagination.

Farms and plantations: Texas' first chapter of the **Grange**, an important organization of anti-corporate American farmers that flourished during the Progressive era, was founded at Salado in 1873. The related Farmers' Alliance, which had several million members throughout the country in its most successful days, originated at Lampasas in 1875, about 50 miles (80 km) west of Fort Hood. Together they helped elect the famous Populist, James Stephen Hogg, who was governor of Texas from 1891–95.

Near the I-35 access road at Salado, the antebellum **Robertson Plantation House** is unusually complete with its outbuildings, slave quarters and family cemetery. It was built in 1854 by E.S.C. Robertson, son of Sterling Clack Robertson, who settled 600 families in the Brazos River Basin northwest of Stephen F. Austin's colony.

The steady character, intelligence and diligence with which Austin won the respect of his fellow "Texans" were also displayed by Robertson. One of the

The Hilton at Mountain Home.

202

directors of his "Nashville Company" was Sam Houston, who had already been the Governor of Tennessee and later became both President and Governor of the state of Texas.

The complex, ultimately unsuccessful attempt to turn the settlers into Mexican citizens makes a long and stirring story. The patriarch Moses Austin, father of Stephen, who did not live to see the Anglo-Southerners enter the Promised Land, had wished to give his name to a great port, Austina, to rival New Orleans. Instead, a new capital in the wilderness was named for the Father and Grandfather of Texas.

Nashville, one of the principal settlements of Robertson's colony (now abandoned), was also considered for the capital. If Nashville was the capital of Texas instead of Austin, Robertson would be better known today.

There are a number of interesting cities to the east of I-35 where Central and East Texas merge. **Marlin**, 25 miles (40 km) east of Eddy between Waco and Temple on Texas 7, was settled by Ala-

bama and Tennessee farmers brought to Texas by Sterling Robertson. It was originally "Buck-snort." The Marlin for whom it is named was the first farmer to return after the "Runaway Scrape," when almost the whole population of the rebellious Republic fled before the invading Mexican army and the Indians from which their own army could not protect them. Local artifacts in the **Falls County Historical Museum** at 141 Railroad Street include the gallows from the county jail.

As the style of some of its architecture may suggest, Marlin has been one of the Central Texas spas since 1891 when hot water – not oil, as is often the case elsewhere – was struck in drilling an artesian well. The grand, chateau-like **Highlands Mansion** of 1900 is a reminder of the prosperous times that arrived a considerable while after the Revolution. (It is located east of Texas 6 and Farm Road 147.) Between Marlin and Lott, the land office for Robertson's colony of **Sarahville de Viesca** was located at **Falls of the Brazos** natural

Hamilton's Pool near Austin.

dam. **Fort Milam**, a Texas Ranger outpost, was established nearby.

Reconstruction: Calvert, 41 miles (66 km) southeast of Marlin on Texas 6, is named for Robert Calvert, a descendant of Lord Baltimore and owner of one of the large cotton plantations in the area. The fields here were worked by slaves and, after the Civil War, by black convicts and Chinese and Italian immigrants. The theory was that Northern Europeans were incapable of laboring long in such a climate.

At Calvert, the reconstruction period was punitive and violent in a manner reminiscent of the Deep South. A cage for unreconstructed Confederate sympathizers called a "sky parlor" was placed in a tree or atop a wooden pole where **Virginia Field Park** is now. But the cotton continued to grow: in the early 1870s, Calvert believed it possessed the world's largest cotton gin.

It is said that **Milano**, 15 miles (24 km) southwest of Hearne on Texas 79, owes its name to a Post Office blunder. At the time it applied for a postmark, it was called Milam, in honor of the Texas Revolutionary hero Ben Milam. Apparently there was some confusion in Washington, and authorization was ultimately given to use the misspelling.

A number of Italian immigrants, especially Sicilians, settled close by in the flood-prone Brazos bottomland lying between Hearne and Bryan, where many Italian surnames are still found on country mailboxes.

At the bend in US-190, 18 miles (29 km) southeast of Hearne, **Bryan College Station** has grown together like Temple and Belton. The huge campus of **Texas Agricultural and Mechanical University** is the largest in the United States. There are over 36,000 students, four times as many as in the early 1970s when it became fully co-educational. A&M receives a third of the oil revenue from public lands (endowed before the hidden oil was discovered on them) that has made its rival, the University of Texas in Austin, recipient of the other two-thirds, rich.

Tours of the A&M campus, impressive for its technical and scientific achievements and now seriously considered by bright Texas high school students, can be arranged at the **Information Center** in the **Rudder Tower**. A highlight is the **Carl Metzger Gun Collection** with its famous Colt pistols on the third floor.

If oil had not been found, it is unlikely either UT or A&M would be running after world-class ratings. Between the two, many Texans have warmer feelings for Aggies – trusting, stalwart and stupid as portrayed in the innumerable "Aggie jokes" – than UT "Longhorns," who tend to be more concerned with high style and fashion. In the budget wars between the Austin campus and the state government, politicians, including several colorful governors, have depicted the University of Texas to rural and poor voters as an arrogant, wasteful, rich man's school.

Austin's metro stops: There are two possible routes to Austin, down the Interstate through **Jarrell**, an old Czech community that was a stagecoach stop, or across to Holland and south on State

Left, deer at a local ranch. **Right**, Admiral Nimitz State Historical Park.

95. In fact, 95 can be taken all the way from Temple as a picturesque alternative to I-35. Here, east of the traffic, there are interesting small towns in which to eat or go browsing for antiques, several of them Czech like **Zabickville** east of Holland and Noack.

About 30 miles (48 km) from Belton to **Georgetown**, south of Jarrell, one enters the Austin rapid growth zone, which seems to promise that within a few years now-independent communities like Georgetown will be Austin metro stops. Cities like Georgetown are enjoying a rebuilding period after many years of declining population.

They are being rediscovered, not always by the most working class or conservative city-dweller; and in uncovering their Victorian facades they develop, just like Congress Avenue or Sixth Street in downtown Austin, a solid sense of their history.

A cabin, made of squared logs and hand-hewn limestone, used from the 1850s as a school and a Masonic lodge, was recently removed from its original site – a remote spot – and erected in the park at Austin and West 16th streets in Georgetown.

Best little heifer: The north and south forks of the **San Gabriel River** flow together here. **San Gabriel Park**, on the river east of the Interstate and 1,310-acre (546-hectare) **Lake Georgetown**, are splendid places to have a picnic. Don't forget either that Texas lakes are made for swimming. This one, the Georgetown and Round Rock water supply, is one of the newer lakes. The dam was completed in 1981. There are good-looking late 19th-century buildings in the Courthouse Square, a National Historic District.

Williamson County was originally to be called San Gabriel, but its state senator, "Three-Legged Willie" Williamson, is said to have protested that there were enough saints in Texas already. The upshot of his display of anti-Mexican sentiment was that the county was named for him.

Each of the cities in Williamson County celebrates the founding of the

Left, D'Anis Cemetery, Castroville. Right, Texas has thousands of caves.

county in 1848. With an area of 1,104 sq. miles (2,859 sq. km), it is almost exactly the size of Rhode Island. During the Western Week and Rodeo each June, the little girls parade around the courthouse in homemade cow masks for the Best Little Heifer Contest. The week after the contest, their cute pictures are in the *Williamson County Sun*, published in the square.

Caves and bats: Just off the Interstate (exit 259), is the **Lunar Space Cavern**, discovered in the 1960s when a drill bit being used in the construction of the highway suddenly fell into an empty space. Central Texas is full of caves, usually discovered when an animal falls into them. This one is particularly well-known for its gravity-defying "helicate" formations.

Where there are caves, there must be bats. Georgetown's cave has none, but the Austin-San Antonio area is called "bat heaven" by Dr Merlin Tuttle, the founder and president of Bat Conservation International. Most of the bats in this part of the country are Brazilian or Mexican free-tails. The largest known bat colony in the world is found in the "nursery cave," Bracken Cave near San Antonio, where there are an estimated 200 baby bats per square foot. During World War II, experiments were made with free-tails from Ney Cave with the object of attaching incendiary bombs to them and dropping clusters of approximately 5,000 bats each on Japan.

The springs that one finds here along the Interstate, the caves in Central Texas, and the change in topography – which at times is very noticeable, especially between Austin and San Antonio – are due to the activity of the Balcones Fault Zone that runs alongside I-35 from Mexico up to Oklahoma. To the west, the ground rose up, producing what the Spanish called *Los Balcones* (balconies). The springs, around which early settlements grew from, gush up through fissures in the rock. This important geological formation divides eastern and western Texas.

Sam Bass: In **Round Rock**, 10 miles (16 km) south of Georgetown on Brushy

Slave cemetery at Round Rock.

Creek, they celebrate the founding of the county with an **Old Settlers Week**. The eroded round rock for which the city was named was used to gauge the depth of the water of Brushy Creek, at first called San Francisco Xavier in 1716 by the French explorer and trader Louis Juchereau de Saint Denis. Herds of longhorns being driven down the Chisholm Trail crossed Brushy Creek. **Chisholm Trail Road**, near the shopping mall on the creek west of the highway, actually follows the celebrated trail across it. Some people claim to have seen the ruts worn in the bank by wagon wheels. Recent construction, however, may possibly have wiped them out. Some of the buildings here alongside the Chisholm Trail and the stage route were built as early as the 1850s.

Sam Bass, the legendary train and stage coach robber who claimed never to have killed a man, was ambushed by Texas Rangers in the 100 block of East Main on July 19, 1878. Businesses and condominium blocks are named after the outlaw, who became more famous after he was killed than he had ever been when alive. A cowboy song, of which there are several versions, was supposed to be good for putting cattle to sleep:

Sam Bass came out to Texas, a cowboy for to be.

A kinder hearted feller you seldom ever see.

The Old Round Rock Cemetery is on Sam Bass Road west of the intersection with Old Chisholm Trail. The funny "Dead End" sign has disappeared, but the cemetery, covered with wildflowers in spring, is easy to find. There is an Anglo section with many crooked and cracked Victorian monuments, a more colorful, smaller Mexican section with paper and plastic flowers on the graves, and a slave cemetery with a path winding between handcut headstones where slaves and freedmen are buried. Sam Bass' grave is in the northwest corner between the Mexican and slave cemeteries. The flat granite stone replaces two earlier markers that were chipped away by souvenir hunters, although the nubs of **Austin.**

the previous markers have been placed at each end of the existing grave.

The **Palm House Museum** at 212 East Main is named for a well-known Swedish family. It doubles as the Chamber of Commerce office. The adjoining pharmacy still has the pressed tin ceiling once common in small-town stores but rarely seen now. Before World War II, the swastika was a popular motif on these ceilings.

Vander Clyde, the famous aerialist, was born in Round Rock and lived here much of his life. The opportunity to join a sister trapeze act led him to develop a one-man transvestite show that was very successful in Paris in the 1920s. Clyde made his entrance in an evening dress, completely convincing as a woman, and performed to Wagner and Rimsky-Korsakov. The French artist Jean Cocteau, in whose film *Blood of a Poet* "Barbette" appeared, compared him to the Russian dancer Vaslav Nijinsky: each of them united acting and difficult dancing through the well-disciplined medium of movement.

If it seems remarkable that a Mrs Simpson from Thurber, Texas, became Duchess of Windsor and made a place for herself in the highest fashion ranks, how much more so for a man from Round Rock to have done it. Barbette returned to this suburb of Austin, but sometimes taught younger trapeze artists in Florida.

Nijinsky himself performed in Austin during a World War I tour when several European countries were closed to the Ballets Russes. In the December 1916 Austin newspaper there is an account of him dancing *Les Sylphides* with Lydia Lopokova at Majestic Theater, now known as the Paramount. Nijinsky's *Scheherazade* was not performed in the South because, as the black Golden Slave, he wore what his wife Romola called a "wonderful deep prune color" body makeup, which would have offended sensibilities.

Cruelty to animals: US-79 East is the road to **Taylor**, famous for its barbecue and snake sacking contest. Snake sacking is highly controversial. Have the

snakes been stunned or their mouths sewn up with monofilament? Animal lovers demonstrate outside while the snake handlers, usually covered with bites, say all that preparation would be too much trouble.

AUSTIN: The capital of Texas (population 488,000) is better known in many circles for its boast of being "the live music capital of the world." This reputation is bolstered by a popular, much-syndicated country and western show, *Austin City Limits*, which has an enormous pool of talent from which to draw in the city's many clubs.

As the home of the **University of Texas**, the city melds an air of youthful exuberance with legislative seriousness, but it is primarily a college town with all that that implies. Only a few blocks from the Capitol complex – the heart of state government – renowned **6th Street** reverberates with rock, jazz, blues, country and western and reggae until the early hours.

Austin has for years been growing partly because there was room for it to grow, though this period of over-development is finally coming to an end. Whole series of hilltops on which there were only trees, brush and scrub a few years ago have turned, it seems as if overnight, into neighborhoods of slab-on-grade ranch houses, insensitive to the environment both aesthetically and structurally.

Compared with those elsewhere, costs and profits for developers here are good; Austin land prices are high, but not compared with the prices in New York, Dallas, Phoenix or Los Angeles. But nobody likes traffic, air, water or noise pollution, so city council members often run as development or environmentalist (or "neighborhood") candidates. Running against the developers is a good way to get elected.

Another reason for growth is the unusual number of relatively inexpensive cultural, athletic and educational activities of excellent quality. This aspect of Austin life is important to families, but also to the young people who have always been part of Austin's growth. There

Stephen F. Austin, Amarillo, Capitol and UT Tower on People's Renaissance Market mural.

is a chance here to grow independent of their political ghettos.

Nobody knows whether there will be 750,000 people in Travis County in the next few years, or 2 million, half again or four times the present population. A lot of people are going to get rich(er) while the gap between the "haves" and "have-nots" grows wider. Between the mid-1970s and mid-1980s the strong anti-growth movement hoped to discourage development by refusing to provide roads and utilities. But Austin has grown anyway, faster per capita than many of the other Sunbelt cities.

Walking downtown: Despite the city's sprawl, the downtown area is relatively easy to get around. It is dominated by government buildings, notably the red granite **State Capitol Building.** Limestone is the building material most closely associated with Central Texas, but no Texas limestone strong enough to use for the Capitol could be found. In typically Texas style, the Capitol is just a few feet higher than its model in Washington, DC. It was not completed until 1888, long after General Sam Houston had attempted to establish the state capital elsewhere.

On March 2, 1895, the 49th anniversary of the Battle of San Jacinto, the cornerstone of the State Capitol Building was laid under the supervision of the Grand Officers of the Masons. The Travis Light Artillery fired a 49-gun salute in honor of the event.

Across from the Capitol is the Greek Revival **Governor's Mansion**, built in 1856 by Abner Cook, around which tours are conducted weekday mornings. The tourist information office (closed Monday) is in the Old Land Office building, 11th and Brazos streets, tel: (612) 305-8400. Informative 90-minute walking tours down historic Congress Avenue and along 6th Street leave the Capitol steps at 9am Thursday, Friday and Saturday; also Sunday at 2pm.

Surely one of the most unusual tourist attractions must be the colony of thousands of Mexican freetail bats that congregates under the Congress Avenue bridge over Town Lake, which set off at

aproom at
hiner
rewery.

sunset in search of food. Beside Town Lake (actually the river) on the south side of the bridge is **Zilker Park** with warm springs that offer year-round swimming.

The oldest building in the city is probably the **French Legation**, 802 San Marcos Street east of I-35, a Creole-style mansion built in 1840 by Comte Alphonse Dubois de Saligny, French *chargé d'affaires*, who may never actually have lived in it. It is open Tuesday–Sunday afternoons. Saligny served under Maximilian I, the short-lived French-born emperor of Mexico whose execution in 1867, aged 35, inspired Manet's powerful series of paintings. It is a tradition in Normandy, where Saligny bought a chateau after making himself rich in America, for villagers to "dance on the old count's grave."

The Maximilian Room of Austin's 110-year-old **Driskill Hotel** has mirrors ordered by the tragic Maximilian for his mad Empress Carlotta. The Driskill, whose second owner is said to have won it in a poker game and swapped it five years later for a California vineyard, is in the center of the historic 6th Street block among other Victorian buildings.

Some especially interesting old buildings around town are now museums. The **Austin Museum of Art at Laguna Gloria** (there is also a branch downtown) is located on the banks of Lake Austin on a site chosen by Stephen F. Austin for his own home. The **O. Henry Home**, 409 East 5th Street, was the 1880s residence of the short-story writer William Sydney Porter, where his writing materials and period furniture are displayed. It is open Wednesday–Sunday afternoons, alonh with the 1853 **Neil-Cochran House**, 2310 San Gabriel Street, which is now the Texas home of the grandly-titled National Society of Colonial Dames of America.

Further to the north, at 305 East 44th Street near the airport, is the former home of German-born sculptress **Elizabeth Ney**, who emigrated to the state in 1870 and whose marble busts and statues ordain many European palaces as

Billboard advertising Shiner.

well as the Smithsonian museum. The extensive collection in her studio here can be viewed Wednesday–Saturday afternoons and on Sunday 10am–5pm.

In the marble **Lyndon B. Johnson Library and Museum**, 2313 Red River Street, on the 357-acre (144-hectare) campus of the University of Texas, there is an interesting gift shop with authentic political memorabilia to be found in the museum, which is open daily 9am–5pm except December 25, free of charge. During his presidency (1963-69), Johnson was the recipient of hundreds of gifts from foreign heads of state and most of them seem to be here, along with his 1968 Lincoln limousine. Humanizing his life from boyhood onwards, the exhibitions include a 20-minute multimedia show, as well as a one-hour film of Lady Bird Johnson, who is sometimes regarded with more affection than America's controversial 36th president.

It is commonly, and wrongly, believed that Mrs Johnson is ferried between the LBJ Ranch and her office

LBJ's purported childhood home.

here in a helicopter which lands on the Library roof. For years she has devoted herself to getting the **National Wild Flower Research Center** going on 60 acres (24 hectares) along the Colorado River. About 8 miles (5 km) southwest of Austin at 4801 La Cross Avenue, tel: (512) 492-4200, the Center is open daily except Monday and is a fine place for picnics among the 42 acres (17 hectares) of flowers. There is also a visitor center, a library and "Ralph, the talking lawnmower."

The Hill Country where President Johnson grew up is beautiful, but it was also one of America's poorest regions: another Appalachia. That is, if one means the juniper-covered hills and valleys west and south of Austin where resorts, camps, dude ranches, campers, mobile homes, inner tubes and the little German-American towns are located.

For some, "Hill Country" embraces the flat, fertile land east of here, too – **Shiner**, where Texas' only Texas-owned brewery operates; **Brenham**, where what Texans call the best ice-cream in the world, Blue Bell, is made and **La Grange**, where the "Best Little Whorehouse in Texas" used to stand. (It was moved up to Dallas several years ago.)

An astonishing number of Texas rivers have been dammed for lakes since Lyndon B. Johnson entered Congress. Austin's **High-Land Lakes**, one of which is named **Lake LBJ**, are the places to go to see Texas bluebonnets blooming in the spring.

A steam excursion train runs from Cedar Park City Hall, near US-183 and RM-1431, about 15 miles (24 km) northwest of Austin, through the Hill Country to **Burnet**, on US-281, once a frontier town from whose quarries marble for the Capitol was mined. Weekends only, the 80-year-old *Hill Country Flyer*, tel: (512) 477-8468 for reservations, takes two hours each way through beautiful countryside, allowing a short stopover for shopping. Many visitors stay longer to inspect Burnet's **Fort Croghan Museum, Longhorn Cavern State Park** or take the **Vanishing Texas River Cruise**, a three-hour tour along the Colorado River.

WAXAHACHIE TO WACO

Central Texas is the backyard of Texas, not such a bad thing to be in a state with so many glamorous front yards. Too often Texans and non-Texans, unless headed for lakes or elderly relatives, zoom from Dallas to Austin without exiting the Interstate. Really to understand Texas, leave the causeway between Waxahachie and Waco and "come on around to the backyard."

Waxahachie, located 30 miles (48 km) south of Dallas, is one of the larger city's bedroom communities. Much of the honey in Texas supermarkets comes from Waxahachie, which has been increasingly industrialized. There is a well-marked exit to Waxahachie from Interstate 35 East, the Dallas arm of the Fort Worth-Dallas "Y."

The Gingerbread Trail: The interesting exhibits of photographs and pioneer artifacts in the **Ellis County Museum**, a former Masonic meeting-house on the **Courthouse Square**, are devoted to the history of Waxahachie. (The town's name comes from a Native American expression denoting a cow or buffalo creek.) White settlers arrived in Waxahachie in the 1840s.

Hundreds of late Victorian and early 20th-century houses make Waxahachie justifiably house-proud. Many of these historic homes feature along a route called the "Gingerbread Trail", marked on the free map available from the Visitors' Bureau, 102 YMCA Drive, tel: (972) 937-2390.

The handsome red-brick Greek Revival **Mahoney-Thompson House** at 604 West Main is owned by the museum and specializes in decorative arts such as antique fans, furniture and Bohemian glass. It was built in 1904 at the height of Waxahachie's prosperity along with the **Chautauqua Auditorium**, which is still in use in **Getzendaner Park**. Also of the same period is the ornate Roman Revival **Nicholas P. Sims Library** at 515 West Main with its richly decorated, highly ornate Carrara marble and gold interior.

Waxahachie's best-known building is the 1895 red sandstone and "pink" granite **Ellis County Courthouse** in the imitative Richardson Romanesque style of Texas courthouse architect James Riely Gordon. The courthouse was expensive for the 1890s: it cost $150,000 to construct. An Italian stonecutter who was working on the building is said to have fallen in love with a Waxahachie telegraph operator, Myrtle Frame. Her carved face, which is sometimes described as a "gargoyle," is a recurring exterior motif. The courthouse is one of the most photographed buildings in the state.

Waxahachie has also become a popular film-making location. The 1985 *Peyton Place* remake was filmed here, as were the more recent *Tender Mercies* and *Places in the Heart*. A state agency has successfully promoted movie-making in Texas (the "Third Coast"), where the weather and people are usually accommodating and costs are relatively low. Texas investors are interested in putting money into Texas movies, like

Louis Malle's *Alamo Bay*, released in 1985. And Waxahachie, with its abundant period architecture, is located close to Dallas' already established but hoping-to-grow minor film industry.

Post offices and polkas: Ten miles (16 km) south of Waxahachie on the Interstate is **Forreston**, the oldest town in the area. Another 5 miles (8 km) south, near **Italy**, the Confederates operated a hat factory. Italy was originally called "Houston Creek" because Sam Houston was reported to have camped nearby. Local histories of Texas towns often relate how the Post Office would not issue a postmark unless the name of the town was changed.

After six different names were rejected, settlers wrote back: "Let the post office be nameless, and be damned." Thus the community was Nameless, Texas, from 1880 to 1890, and there is still a Nameless Schoolhouse and Nameless Road. Houston Creek eventually became Italy – a tribute, it is said, for the sunny Central Texas climate. The population of Italy has never exceeded 1,300,

but it received the first fully endowed public library in Texas from S.M. Dunlap, a businessman for whom the **Dunlap Library** is named.

Many of Texas' Czech immigrants settled in this fertile cotton-growing belt. Almost all of them did well as cotton farmers here. Their descendants make up approximately half the population of **Ennis**, on Interstate 45 between Dallas and Houston. Ennis is 20 miles (32 km) northeast of Italy.

Since 1967 Ennis has sponsored the **National Polka Festival** on the first weekend in May, attracting crowds of 30,000 or more. There is an exciting parade of polka bands down the main street, which may be the widest one in Texas. Divided into East and West Main by railroad tracks, it is 340 feet (104 meters) across.

From lakes to fruitcakes: Since 1900, more than 200 lakes have been created in Texas. Lake Bardwell, or the **Bardwell Reservoir**, on Waxahachie Creek 4 miles (7 km) outside Ennis, was built by the US Corps of Engineers in

Left, Ellis County Courthouse appears on the Chautauqua backdrop. Right, Gordon's Ellis County Courthouse.

the early 1960s. Like the other new lakes near **Navarro Mills** and **Mexia**, Lake Bardwell is a popular recreation area with pretty lakeside parks and camping. It is also the water supply for Ennis, Waxahachie and Corsicana. Visitors from out of state – especially New Englanders, whose reservoirs are fenced and carefully patrolled – are often surprised to find Texans fishing, water-skiing and sailing on theirs.

Corsicana, Navarro county seat, is 19 miles (30 km) south of Ennis on I-45 and is named for Corsica, home of the parents of the Texas hero José Antonio Navarro of San Antonio, who signed the Texas Declaration of Independence, helped write the first constitution, and took part in the failed Santa Fe Expedition. The first Texas gusher was not drilled at Corsicana as is commonly believed; however, a 12-year oil boom began in 1894 when the city dug an artesian well and struck oil instead of water. The strike made Corsicana the first oil boomtown in Texas. A current attraction, **Pioneer Village** at 912 West Park Avenue, tel: (902) 654-4846, is made up of reconstructed mid-19th-century log buildings, including an Indian trading post and slave quarters.

Another local product, the "Deluxe" fruitcake from the **Collin Street Bakery** has been exported to almost every country on earth. More than a million pounds (just less than half a million kg) of Texas pecans are baked into these world-famous Corsicana delicacies every year.

A friendly Texas town: Returning to I-35 via State 22 from Corsicana, one arrives at **Milford**. This town, settled in the 1850s, once adopted the good-humored city motto: "The home of 700 friendly people and three or four old grouches." It is nothing more than human nature to leave the freeway in hopes of catching a glimpse of one of the grouches. Milford was named for a ford on Mill Creek, according to *The Handbook of Texas*.

The town of **Hillsboro**, just below the point where I-35 West joins I-35 East from Fort Worth, has been a crossroads

*art of the
Gingerbread
Tour.*

since the 1850s when there was a dirt-floor, elm-pole courthouse here. The hideous limestone **Hill County Courthouse** by W.C. Dodson of Waco, another Victorian courthouse architect, was built in 1889.

Tradition has it that a Comanche chief called Hollow-Hole-in-the-Air died under a tree in the front yard of **Harris House**, the oldest house in Hillsboro. At **Hill Junior College**, there is a **Confederate Research Center** displaying paintings, photographs and documents from the Civil War as well as the uniform worn by Audie L. Murphy, the most decorated American soldier of World War II.

Halfway between Hillsboro and Waco, the small town of **West** has the misfortune from time to time of being confused with the region "West Texas." (So it is called "West, Comma, Texas.") Forty thousand people came here on September 15, 1896, to view the ridiculous staged spectacular of two locomotives of the Missouri, Kansas and Texas Railroad crash into each other. Their throttles tied back to 50 mph (80 kph), the trains exploded on impact, killing two spectators. The agent who dreamed up this reckless stunt was merely fired.

Norwegians and dinosaurs: Twenty miles west of Hillsboro , across the Brazos River, is the region known as the Bosque (Spanish for woods, pronounced like boskey). A number of Norwegians settled here between 1850 and 1875. They fiercely defended their log houses from attacks by the Kiowa and Comanche Indians. Many relics and household items used by these early settlers have been collected for display in the **Bosque Memorial Museum**, Avenue Q in **Clifton**, a small town (population 3,200) also known for its **Texas Safari Wildlife Park**, where many different species can be seen (and sometimes fed) along a scenic seven-mile (11-km) drive. The Nordic heritage is also celebrated with a smorgasbord each November at nearby **Norse** (Farm Road 219 to Farm Road 182).

Northwest of Hillsboro on State 144 is **Glen Rose**, where it is rumored once

Dinosaur Valley State Park.

lived John Wilkes Booth – under the name John St Helen – after he assassinated President Lincoln. Glen Rose is sometimes known as the Petrified City because petrified wood is a popular building material here. Local history is explained in the **Somervell County Museum** at Vernon and Elm streets. Dinosaur traces can be found in the town and in 1,270-acre (514-hectare) **Dinosaur Valley State Park**, 5 miles (8 km) west of Glen Rose. The tracks are easy to find, but there is a steep trail to the river. Long before humans settled in the Bosque River Valley when Central Texas was coastal swampland, dinosaurs left tracks – some of the best preserved examples in the world – in the limestone Paluxy riverbed near Glen Rose. There are no "taildrag marks" in the dinosaurs trackway here – the water was deep enough for the dinosaurs' tails to float – but you can see where the mud oozed up between their toes.

Dinosaur Valley, a rugged ranching area belonging to the Grand Prairie and West Cross Timbers Regions, is one of

the state parks in which part of the official **State Longhorn Herd** is kept. The hundreds of springs here made it a Native American stronghold.

WACO: Until they were driven out, the Waco were a Wichita tribe occupying a site by the 840-mile (1,352-km) long Brazos River in Central Texas, and when the white first settled the area nearly two centuries ago they took **Waco** as the name for their town. First came **Fort Fisher**, then and now a Texas Ranger outpost, but what really brought attention to the town was the construction in 1870 of a massive suspension bridge across the river.

"That bridge was very important," explains local historian Roger Conger. "The Brazos was a veritable iron curtain across the center of Texas. After the Civil War many Southerners were going west. They had to come to Waco to cross the river."

Six bridges span the river within the city today, but the antique suspension bridge (now pedestrian-only) is still the most significant. When the 475-foot (145-meter) bridge supplanted the ferry, it was the longest single-span suspension bridge in America and the second longest in the world. Supported by wire cables and 2.7 million Waco bricks, it was built from the plans of New York's Thomas Roebling, designer of the Brooklyn Bridge. Longhorns and wagon trains bound for the Chisholm Trail traversed it in its earliest days, and until 1889 a toll was charged: "five cents for each loose animal of the cattle kind."

Earliest site: Some of the settlers who followed the Texas Rangers to this beautiful valley on the Brazos in the 1840s lived in log cabins on the site of what is now **Cameron Park** on Rotan Drive. Here are woods, hiking trails, the natural habitat **Zoo** and **Miss Nellie's Pretty Place**, a wild flower preserve that was the home of a former congressman's mother, who donated it to the city.

What the earliest settlement probably looked like can be seen adjoining the riverside Fort Fisher Campground at **The Gov. Bill and Vara Daniel Historic Village**, tel: (254) 755-1160, on the campus of **Baylor University**, the largest Baptist university in the world. Most of the original settlers in this typical cotton town were sharecroppers. The Baylor campus also houses the **Strecker Museum**, devoted to natural history, and the marble-columned **Armstrong Browning Library** with its portraits of – and 4,000 letters written by or to – the Victorian poets Robert and Elizabeth Barret Browning. The library's collection – assembled by Baylor's late professor J.A. Armstrong – is supplemented by 50 lovely stained glass windows depicting verses by the poetic pair.

Between the Baylor campus and US-81 are the **Tourist Information Center**, tel: (254) 750-5996, adjoining the **First Street Cemetery** with its Confederate graves, and other attractions: the **Texas Sports Hall of Fame**, University Parks Drive, tel: (254) 756-1633, where kids can try on helmets of the Houston Oilers or Dallas Cowboys, and the **Texas Ranger Museum & Hall of Fame**, tel: (254) 750-8631. Jim Bowie's knife and the rifle he carried at the Alamo are here, as well as a jewel-studded saddle (which cost $5,800 in 1903), the pistol Pat Garrett used to kill Billy the Kid and enough of the early Rangers' Colt revolvers to equip an army. Each gun weighed more than four pounds (1.8 kg) and had a 9-inch (23-centimeter) barrel.

Six-shooter junction: In its prime, Waco was a rough cowtown. "Next stop, Waco" the train conductors would yell as the train approached. "Get out your six-shooters." The last legal hanging in Texas occurred here in 1923, witnessed by over 4,000 people. In 1955, a Waco television station was the first in the world to broadcast a murder trial.

A more genteel era is reflected by the city's group of 19th-century homes operated from the charmingly gingerbread-style Hoffmann House by the Historic Waco Foundation, 810 South 4th Street, tel: (254) 753-5168, which also hosts the annual Brazos River Festival every April. Two of these Victorian homes can be toured on Saturday and Sunday afternoons. They are the Greek Revival **Earle-Napier-Kinnard House**, 814 South 4th, begun in 1858 but not com-

Left, Texas Ranger Museum. **Right**, Waco suspension bridge.

pleted until 1869; and **Fort House**, 503 South 4th, in which Alabama planter William Aldridge Fort lived with dozens of relatives and slaves in the 1870s. Across the river, at 100 Mill Street, is the Italianate **East Terrace**, shielded by magnificent elm and pecan trees and terraced with brick walls and walks down to the river. Home of pioneer industrialist John Wesley Mann, *circa* 1872, it contains some of the original furniture.

At 1901 North 5th Street, the **Earle-Harrison House**, tel: (254) 753-2032, sitting in the 5-acre (2-hectare) Pape Gardens, is gloriously furnished with paintings, Tiffany glass and sterling silver jugs and goblets. Portraits of General Robert E. Lee abound in some of these old homes, a reminder that Waco's men marched off to support Confederate armies in the Civil War. Six Confederate generals hailed from Waco as did, in modern times, former Texas governor Anne Richards and Madison Cooper Jr, whose 840,000-word novel *Sironia, Texas* – on view in the public library – is said to be the longest ever written.

Among Waco's dozen or more museums is the **Taylor Museum of Waco History**, whose location at 701 Jefferson puts it atop the site of one of the Waco Indian tribe's main villages.

But probably the most unconventional cultural center is the fun-for-the-family **Dr Pepper Museum**, 300 South 5th Street, tel: (254) 757-1024, with its turn-of-the-century soda fountain. Dr Pepper was invented by a local pharmacist in 1885 and the museum covers the entire soft drink industry.

Continuing its journey down to the Gulf of Mexico, the Brazos reflects significant dates in Texas history at many points along its route. Eighty miles (128 km) southeast of Waco, at **Washington-on-the-Brazos**, Texas declared its independence from Mexico in 1836. Then the river was the lifeblood of the fledgling republic, as can be seen in the **Star of the Republic Museum**, whose exhibits include a model of the *Yellow Stone*, the boat that carried the body of Stephen F. Austin, the "Father of Texas," down the river.

Baylor University.

AMARILLO TO LUBBOCK

The Panhandle of Texas is referred to as "West Texas" by the people who live there. The landscape stretches in an unbroken line, with perhaps an occasional pump jack or farmhouse on the horizon. The sunsets can be breathtaking. With nothing to obscure the view, the sky blazes with oranges, yellows and reds and then slowly fades to soft pinks and purples. Driving around at night, you can see the lights of many small towns in all directions. Because of the high altitude, the air is very clear and dry. After the sun sets during the summer months, the clear evenings bring cool breezes.

In the northern Panhandle is **Amarillo** (population 195,000), which means "yellow" in Spanish. In 1887, there was a shipping point here for hauling cattle to market by rail. It is still a major center for cattle distribution; Amarillo claims to have the world's largest private cattle auction. Every year the Amarillo Livestock Auction sells over half a million head. The auctions are mainly held on Monday and Tuesday, but tours are given to visitors daily. Suburban **Old San Jacinto** with its antique and gift stores along a section of historic **Route 66** (now Interstate 40) calls itself "the heart of Amarillo."

Big equine fans will appreciate the **American Quarter Horse Heritage Center and Museum,** on East Interstate 40, where visitors learn why this particular breed was the cowboy's favorite mount. Amarillo is also the headquarters for the Working Ranch Cowboys Association, a rip-roaring group who organize the World Championship Ranch Rodeo held during the month of November.

West of Amarillo on Interstate Highway 40 is one of the area's most celebrated sights: 10 Cadillacs, nose down in an orderly row. **Cadillac Ranch** was conceived by Stanley Marsh, an Amarillo rancher and artist on whose land they are buried.

Preceding pages: bridg over muddy water. Belov Amarillo stockyards.

Visitors to the **Don Harrington Discovery Center** on Streit Drive can enjoy the experience of a 360-degree science and technology theater as well as planetarium shows.

Just south of Amarillo is the town of **Canyon**, where **West Texas A&M University**, founded in 1909, and its **Panhandle-Plains Historical Museum** are located. The largest Texas state museum, one entire wing is devoted to the oil boom years of the Texas Panhandle, displaying 1920s and 1930s equipment and a short feature film. The museum also houses an art collection, geological exhibits and a reconstructed pioneer town of a century ago.

Palo Duro Canyon: Here at Canyon, 20 miles (32 km) south of Amarillo, the flat plains come to a dead halt. What lies ahead is a vast chasm – the **Palo Duro Canyon**. The multicolored canyon – second largest in the US – is 120 miles (193 km) long, 1½–2 miles (2.5–3 km) wide, and has walls as high as 1,120 feet (390 meters). In summertime there are nightly (except Sunday) performances

of the musical drama *Texas*. With a 600-foot (183-meter) canyon wall as a backdrop, a cast of 80 brings to life in song and dance Paul Green's Pulitzer Prize-winning play about the discovery and settling of West Texas.

Geologists say over 90 million years of erosion by creeks and streams, abetted by incessant wind, formed this majestic canyon. *Palo Duro* is Spanish, meaning "hard wood," and refers to the juniper trees found in the area. The Spanish explorer Francisco Vasquez de Coronado is believed to have come upon Palo Duro in 1541 while searching for Quivira, the richest of the mythical Cities of Gold.

Over 300 years later, the canyon became a stronghold of the Comanche Indians led by Chief Quanah Parker, who suffered their final defeat in 1874. They wee surprised by a cavalry force commanded by General Ranald Mackenzie, who drove 1,500 horses and mules out of Palo Duro and slaughtered them. Without their horses, the Native Americans were helpless. The Com-

anches were removed to reservations in Oklahoma.

Today **Palo Duro State Park** comprises more than 15,000 acres (6,000 hectares). A spectacular 10-mile (16 km) drive by car can be made year-round across the canyon floor. Hiking and camping are possible, along with horseback riding in season.

The great ranches: The legendary Charles Goodnight, the first rancher to move into the Panhandle in the 1870s, is closely associated with Palo Duro Canyon and the cattle drives. Goodnight designed the first chuckwagon.

Backed by the British financier John Adair (their cattle were branded with the JA), Goodnight built his herd up to as many as 100,000 head. For a while in the 1880s, theirs was the largest ranch in Texas – more than 700,000 acres (over 283,000 hectares). Then in 1885, the XIT Ranch was established in the far northern Panhandle on 3 million acres (1.2 million hectares) that the State of Texas had traded for the new State Capitol building in Austin.

In order to stock the XIT Ranch, British investors were again brought in. An XIT Reunion is held at **Dalhart** about 80 miles (130 km) north of Amarillo every year in the first full week of August. The amateur rodeo and enormous barbecue attract thousands.

Cowboy Morning on the **Figure 3 Ranch** always draws plenty of guests. It begins with a chuckwagon breakfast on the rim of Palo Duro. Visitors are carried to the campsite in a horse-drawn wagon from Tom Christians' ranch near Claude, on US Highway 287 west of Amarillo. Before returning, time is set aside for exploring the path leading to the canyon floor, for short horseback rides and for visiting with the cowboys, who demonstrate particular skills such as lariat tricks and cattle branding. Another popular attraction is the nightly Old West Show at the **Creekwood Ranch**, which begins with a wagon ride to the campsite where supper is cooked over an open campfire.

Even though the singer Mac Davis claims "happiness is Lubbock, Texas,

Below, view looking west toward Texas Tech from Great Plains. Right, Buddy Holly statue.

BUDDY HOLLY: DON'T FADE AWAY

Charles Hardin Holley, better known as *Buddy Holly*, was born on September 7, 1936. (His name was misspelled on his first recording contract.) Buddy came from a loving, musical family.

As a child he played piano, then accompanied himself with guitar on favorite country songs, particularly those of Hank Williams who, along with Bill Monroe and the Bluegrass Boys, were to influence his singing style.

Rock 'n' roll was being played on radio station KSEL by 1954, but the music was mostly rhythm and blues by black performers. Little Richard, Fats Domino, the Clovers and the Drifters made personal appearances. Early in 1955 KDAV booked Elvis Presley into the Cotton Club, Lubbock's leading country dance hall. Buddy and Elvis became fast and close friends.

In 1955 a recording agent saw Buddy and his group in Lubbock and, soon after, Decca asked him to come to Nashville. *Blue Days, Black Nights* in 1956 was his first release. The song was difficult for reviewers to categorize because it had a country melody with a blues inflection.

In February, 1957, Buddy, Jerry Allison, Niki Sullivan and Larry Welborn made *That'll Be the Day* in Clovis, New Mexico, at Norman Petty's studios. This was the beginning of the Crickets, a name chosen by flipping through an encyclopedia.

In September, 1957, *That'll Be the Day* was Number 1; then *Peggy Sue* became a hit. It is probably better known than any of Buddy's other songs. Its innovative "Holly sound" included steady guitar strumming, rapid accented drumming and his famous "hiccup."

The beautiful *Words of Love* (1957) was Buddy's first experience with overdubbing. He was probably the first rock 'n' roll artist to use vocal and instrumental overdubbing.

Buddy and the Crickets did tours and television appearances. In Australia and Britain they made a lasting impact, notably on both the name and concept of the Beatles. Their records were always more successful in Britain than America.

In April, 1958, *Rave On* was released. Many believe it was the most exciting record the Crickets ever made.

By that summer Buddy was a star. *Not Fade Away, Maybe Baby, It's So Easy* and *Oh Boy!* are all from 1958. He married Maria Santiago the same year.

On February 3, 1959, he was killed, along with singers Ritchie Valens and J.P. Richardson (the "Big Bopper") in an airplane crash near Clear Lake, Iowa.

What rock 'n' roll lost was not just a talented performer, but an artist whose ideas could have profoundly affected the development of American popular music. Buddy was expanding his horizons and wanted to learn and record other styles of music.

He also had visions of a new recording studio in Lubbock to help develop the careers of other West Texas musicians.

Although his dream was cut short, Buddy left a stylistic legacy to generations of musicians. ∎

in my rear-view mirror," most residents of **Lubbock** (population 185,000) would live nowhere else. Later, even Mac concedes at the end of his song that now "happiness is Lubbock, Texas, getting nearer and dearer." Situated at one of the southernmost tips of the Llano Estacado, or "Staked Plains," Lubbock is an oasis of commerce and culture.

Texas Tech University, at 4th Street and Indiana Avenue, is one of Lubbock's main attractions, its full sports agenda enticing enthusiastic crowds. The University's teams are known as Red Raiders and are members of the Southwest Conference.

The University has established the **Texas Tech Museum** and the **Ranching Heritage Center**, a 12-acre (5-hectare) area through which winds a trail past more than 30 buildings (schoolhouse, blacksmith shop, homes, barns, windmills) representing ranching's early days. The museum offers a mixed bag of paintings of the American West along with European art, sculpture, ceramics and some Currier and Ives lithographs. Changing exhibitions narrate the story of the region from prehistoric times through the Spanish explorations and the settling of the region by ranchers and farmers.

The museum, which also contains the **Moody Planetarium**, operates an archaeological site at **Lubbock Lake** that has yielded artifacts and tools from all known cultural groups who once lived in the Southwest – from the elephant-hunters 20,000 years ago to the Comanches of the 19th century. It is believed that at no other site in the New World is such a complete chronological record to be found. Tours are available to visitors on Saturdays and on weekdays (by appointment) during the summer months.

Off University Avenue, three miles south of town, is **Science Spectrum**, a science, nature and technology museum, along with **Omnimax**, a giant domed screen 58 feet (18 meters) in diameter. Both are open daily.

The **Canyon Lakes Project** is a string of five lakes in the **Yellowhouse Canyon**. There are man-made waterfalls,

boat loading ramps, fishing piers, camping and picnicking areas and hike and bike trails. Also in the Yellowhouse Canyon is **Mackenzie State Park**, named for General Ranald Mackenzie, where one of the few remaining colonies of prairie dogs resides. These amusing, squirrel-like creatures provide much entertainment for visitors today, but proved such a pest at one time that farmers did their best to exterminate them. Living in giant underground colonies, their towns covered thousands of square miles under the prairie grass before civilization overtook them.

One might not expect the farmland surrounding Lubbock to include prize-winning vineyards. But the **Llano Estacado Winery**, located 3 miles (5 km) east of US-87 on FM-1585, is one of Texas' largest and most successful wineries. Daily tours and wine tasting are available, tel: (806) 745-2258.

The most famous Lubbockite is **Buddy Holly**, who produced some of the best rock 'n' roll ever recorded. To honor this legend, Lubbock has erected a statue of him in front of the **Civic Center** and begun the **Walk of Fame** nearby honoring musicians from West Texas such as Buddy Holly, Waylon Jennings, Jimmy Dean and Mac Davis. Buddy Holly's grave is in the **City of Lubbock Cemetery** on East 34th Street. Caretakers will direct visitors to the headstone near the entrance. People from all over the world make this pilgrimage to honor Holly.

Fifteen miles southeast of Lubbock, on US-84, is **Post** (population 4,000), a town named for cereal magnate Charles W. Post, who founded it in 1907 after an extended stay in the Kellogg brothers' Battle Creek Sanitarium for his health. Noting that the Kelloggs had devised for their patients food substitutes made from grain, Post blended wheat, bran and molasses to create a coffee substitute called Postum. In the decade beginning in 1902 he spent $60 million to advertise Postum and such other products as Grape Nuts and Post Toasties. Long after his death in 1914, the Postum Cereal Company became General Foods Corporation.

Big steaks fo big eaters, Amarillo.

THE WEST

The people of southern north central Texas call themselves "West" Texans not out of geographical ignorance, but a sense of history and place. After the Civil War their ancestors from Arkansas, Tennessee and other Southern states, knowing no place else to go to begin a new life, headed west where they encountered a foe more relentless than General Sherman: the slow-yielding, tightfisted land itself, ruled by distance, drought and the most ferocious aboriginal army ever to ride horseback. Thus, mile after uncertain mile was conquered by people who were not searching for wealth but a place to survive. They did survive, and left their descendants with the knowledge that anything is possible if one is self-reliant and continues to look to the horizon.

Travel in this relatively featureless landscape can become an agonizingly slow unfolding of geography if you expect to be constantly entertained by the fluff and fanfare of tourist extravaganzas. However, if you adopt the easygoing friendliness of its people and attune yourself to the voices of its heroic past, West Texas will be an unforgettable experience.

Fort Worth to El Paso: West of Fort Worth, where Interstate 20 drops down from rough-cut juniper and oak-covered hills on to the fitful beginning of the plains, are the ruins of **Thurber**, a coal-mining town better suited to northeastern Pennsylvania or the Ruhr Valley than post-frontier Texas. Where 10,000 people from 17 counties lived between 1880 and 1922, there now exist only a tall brick smoke stack, a restaurant-museum, the remains of a great brick factory and a service station. The rest of the town has been sold brick by brick down to the last utility pole. As one looks across the now empty valley to the conical piles of black coal spoil and "red dog" cinders, it is difficult to imagine the wealthy, cosmopolitan city which stood here on the near side of frontier times. Thurber is where the

Metropolitan Opera of New York performed, where Miss Wallis "Wildcat" Warfield, later the Duchess of Windsor, grew up in luxury in one of the mansions along Silk Stocking Road on New York Hill, and where a World War I clothing drive netted no fewer than four dozen mink coats.

In 1895 Thurber was one of the first completely electrified cities in the world. After a long, bitter strike presided over by Texas Rangers, Thurber became the first and perhaps only 100 percent unionized town in America.

The 100 million tons of coal mined at Thurber powered the belching, billowing locomotives of Jay Gould's Texas and Pacific (T&P) Railway as they trundled across the prairie. In 1881 the last 595 miles (958 km) of the T&P main line, parallel to today's I-20, were completed between Fort Worth and Sierra Blanca in a phenomenal 11 months by a crew of 300 hard-drinking Irishmen.

The railroad's role in the rapid demise of the frontier is dramatically demonstrated by the almost simultaneous founding of Abilene, Big Spring, Midland, Odessa and the other major cities of the region as shipping points for cattle. The change from coal to oil-powered locomotives led to the dismantling of Thurber and helped set the stage for the meteoric emergence of **Ranger**, 13 miles (21 km) to the west and the most rip-snorting boomtown of all.

Oil boom doom: Derricks and pump jacks are still in evidence, but the quiet streets of modern Ranger fail to suggest the frenzy of the weeks in 1917 after oil rig McClesky No. 1 blew in with 1,700 barrels a day. At World War I prices, a good well yielded $250,000 a week. The 10 trains that rolled into Ranger every day were filled with speculators, riffraff and ruffians, ambitious men and loose women. The town exploded from a village of 1,000 to a seething city of 40,000 in a matter of months. Streets turned into a sea of mud, traversed on sleds or the backs of men in hip boots. Guests in those days paid luxury hotel rates to sleep in armchairs. The evangelist Billy Sunday went in search of souls to saloons called the Grizzly Bear, the

Blue Moose and Oklahoma, where as many as five people a day met their oil boom doom.

One lease reputedly changed hands three times on a Friday, increasing in value from $150 to $15,000.

Old RIP: A few miles west lies **East-land**, another boomtown gone bust. Today its two principal claims to rather less than universal fame are the postage stamp mosaic mural – depicting the history of the mail service on an epic scale, at the post office – and a "horny toad" named **RIP** (Rest in Peace) who achieved immortality – for a while, anyway.

On display in his miniature coffin in the **Eastland County Courthouse**, RIP resembles a rather flat and very prickly pincushion about the size of a child's hand. This horny toad, in actuality a lizard, achieved fame in 1928 when he was dug out of the courthouse wall after having been placed there along with the cornerstone 31 years before.

Today one approaches **Albany**, northwest of **Cisco**, over the same rolling red plains the cowboys covered on the original trail to Dodge City in the 1870s. Due to overgrazing, however, the lush prairie grasses they found here are gone. There is only the eroded soil and mesquite trees. Although mesquite steals precious moisture from the soil, it puts back nitrogen since it is a leguminous plant. Its beans were ground into a flour by the nomadic Plains Indians, and its wood is considered by many Texans to be without parallel for cooking barbecue. In spite of all its benefits, ranchers hate mesquite like a weed and try to eradicate it. Even so, during droughts when little else survives, cattle eat the honey-sweet beans.

Only in Albany: At first sight, Albany is as unimposing as the mesquite "forests" that surround it, but this prairie town of 2,500 possesses an exceptional collection of 20th-century art displayed in the jail where drunken cowboys and assorted desperados were once detained. The limestone building itself (*circa* 1878) is a good example of frontier architecture, with its decoratively routed

Windmill painted to resemble the Texas flag.

and scored casements and cistern out front. Among the many artists represented in the large permanent collection of the **Old Jail Foundation** are Picasso, Matisse, Giacometti, Marin, Rouault, Henry Moore and Modigliani.

Albany's **Fort Griffin**, 25 miles (40 km) north, stages an outdoor historical pageant called "Fandangle" during the last two weeks in June. The roles of Native Americans, cowboys, buffalo hunters, soldiers, bandits and settlers are sung and acted as they have been for the last 40 years by the descendants of those who originally occupied the Texas frontier. Before leaving Albany, visit the **Ledbetter Picket House Museum**, a restored ranch house with many authentic furnishings.

A similar ranch house served as the commandant's headquarters in the early days of Fort Griffin. Established in 1867, the fort belonged to the outer line of frontier defense. The first line, which swung in a wide arc southwest from Fort Worth to San Antonio, was established in the late 1840s on the edge of Comanche territory. Its line of forts was a buffer between the Plains Indians and white colonies.

From its hilltop, the stone ruins and partially reconstructed wooden remains of the fort look down on what was possibly the roughest, most brawling and iniquitous town in the history of Texas. A century ago when it was a major market for buffalo hides, Fort Griffin was a lawless town with the likes of Pat Garrett, who later won fame by killing Billy the Kid, and Bat Masterson (who was to become Dodge City's famous sheriff) walking its dusty streets. Imagine them at the same bar: bitter, defeated Southern veterans of the Civil War alongside the blue-jacketed conquerors and the "buffalo soldiers," as the Native Americans called freed slaves who were part of the army.

As if they were not enough, add buffalo hunters flush from selling hides plus the professional gamblers and bandits who preyed on them and the bounty hunters who preyed in turn on *them*. The only law was that of the six-shooter.

Horned lizard.

Longhorn cattle and cowboys: Herds of the once threatened longhorn cattle are found in increasing numbers again across the state, but they are particularly accessible to the public at **Fort Griffin State Park**. These descendants of the first cattle brought to the New World by the Spaniards are easy to identify, not only by their extremely long upwardly curving horns but by their white and red spotted hides and thin bodies firmly supported by long hind legs. Their lean meat, the attribute that almost led to the longhorns' extinction, has saved them from oblivion in today's diet-conscious world, where they are herded by weekend cowboys.

Real cowboys still exist, however, and you can find them at the Texas Cowboy Reunion at **Stamford** around the Fourth of July, unquestionably the world's largest and longest-running amateur rodeo.

Farther west, 11 miles (18 km) north of Abilene, is **Fort Phantom Hill**. The very name has the chill of desolation to it. Loneliness still lingers about the tall, solitary chimneys, the empty commissary, guard-house and powder magazine, especially in the dim red light of dusk. From its founding in 1850 to protect the region from hostile Indians, there were frequent desertions from this post where the boredom alternated with Comanche raids. After its abandonment in 1854, the hated fort was burned by one of the withdrawing soldiers. Later it became an overnight stop for mail coaches on the Butterfield trail.

In making your way through the scrub oak and mesquite to Abilene, you will probably see the silver and salmon flash of the scissor-tailed flycatcher. In excited flight the graceful tails, which are twice as long as the bodies, almost seem to flitter like a carnival bird on a stick. This area also has the state's greatest bobwhite quail population.

God's glorious city: Abilene likes to promote its slogan "A Whole Lotta Texas Goin' On", but might more aptly be called the "Glorious City of God." It was almost certainly the subject of **Ranch** Donald Barthelme's short story, *The* **country.**

City of Churches, and it is the home of three religiously affiliated institutions of higher learning – McMurray University, Abilene Christian University and the Southern Baptists' Hardin Simmons. Round-the-clock prayer meetings for rain didn't bring an end to the drought of the early 1950s, but they must have made an impression because the region has been blessed with oil discoveries ever since. Recently, a rig was set up on the **Taylor Court Exposition Center** grounds here just for a demonstration and, of course, it struck oil. Rodeos are held here each spring and fall. **Abilene Zoo** is nearby off State Route 36.

Abilene's **Historical Museum**, 102 Cypress Street, tel: (915) 673-4587, has exhibits relating to Camp Barkeley, the World War II army base and prison camp, whose ruins can still be seen on US-277 south of town. An authentic taste of the Old West is to be had 14 miles (16 km) to the south, where the low, dark juniper-covered hills of the Calahan Divide are broken abruptly at **Buffalo Gap Historic Village**, tel: (915)

572-3365. Buffalo passed through the gap twice each year, leaving behind a permanent trail. Charles Goodnight, the half-Cherokee blazer of the westernmost longhorn trail, described the main herd as being 125 miles (200 km) long and 25 miles (40 km) wide.

A portion of this brown wooly group flowed between these ancient hills. Tonkawa and Comanche Indians camped in the cool shade of the native pecan groves and made arrowheads. Mounds of flint chips and rejected seconds can still be found. Most of the cattle drivers travelling on the Goodnight-Loving Trail to New Mexico and Wyoming brought their herds along this easy route north.

The natural funnel here continued to be a focal point of the region when it was settled by whites in the 1870s. Today, 19 of the original buildings have been restored including the massive limestone courthouse and jail. Besides the century-old architecture and artifacts of frontier days, typical Texas food like barbecue and chicken-fried steak with

onghorns.

gravy are available at several home-style restaurants. The gravestones in the **Buffalo Gap Cemetery** relate the history of the settling of West Texas in a few poignant words. Nearby **Lake Abilene** and **Abilene State Park** complete the tourist picture.

Gypsum deposits: The town of **Sweetwater** just west of Abilene on Interstate 20 was well-named in this area, where many of the streams are tainted with gypsum. Gypsum, otherwise known as Epsom salts, are fine for soaking tired feet but, as a drink, keep one on the run. The rich local gypsum deposits have been put to constructive use in the manufacture of wallboard by two large factories, which can be toured if you make an appointment in advance. A selection of xhibits in the **Pioneer City County Museum** (closed Sunday and Monday) on 3rd Street recall the era of the first arrivals in the region.

One of the few towns in West Texas to predate the coming of the railroad, Sweetwater began in 1877 as a general store for buffalo hunters dug into the banks of Sweetwater Creek. The world's largest rattlesnake roundup is held here during the second weekend in March. It is a bring-em-back-alive affair in which the snakes are milked for their venom and prizes are given for the longest, shortest and heaviest (by the pound) rattlesnakes. A record 14,000 pounds (6,350 kg) were delivered in 1985. If you have ever had a hankering to eat a fried 6-foot-long (2-meter) western diamondback or buy a transparent toilet seat with a rattler coiled in it, here is such an opportunity.

A few moments on the weed-broken tarmac of the **Old Sweetwater Army Airfield** will resurrect memories of the 1940s when hundreds of women received their flight training here before ferrying warplanes across the Atlantic.

Farther west on I-20, past **Colorado City**, is the town of **Big Spring**, a natural oasis occupied by Native Americans as many as 10,000 years ago, when it served as a major rest stop for the tribes on the Comanche War Trail halfway between their home on the High Plains

Pump jacks at Post.

to the north and the white settlements in Texas and Mexico to the south. Since oil was discovered in 1927 it has been a major refining center.

The Native Americans shared its precious water with antelope, buffalo and wild mustangs. The appeal of this ancient oasis is still felt in the cool late afternoon among the trees of **Comanche Trail Park**. Perhaps this is what attracted Joseph Heneage Finch, the seventh Earl of Aylesford, who became one of the area's founding fathers. The **Big Spring State Recreation Area** provides a view of the entire area from a 200-foot (60-meter) mesa within the city limits.

Southbound travelers along US-87 from Big Spring will pass through **San Angelo**, a modern city of lakes and rivers on the edge of the Texas Hill Country. Like San Antonio it has a **River Walk**, winding its way past landscaped gardens, parks and beautiful homes beside the Concho River. There are performances on an outdoor stage where the local symphony plays every Fourth of July. **Fort Concho**, the best preserved of the Indian War stockades, is filled with exhibits from frontier times.

The Permian Basin oil field: At the midway point of the 600-mile (965-km) drive from Fort Worth to El Paso, a mirage of civilization rises out of the endless illusion of water over the highway ahead. The city of **Midland** is dominated by glass and steel towers containing the offices of more than 650 firms dedicated to coaxing crude oil from the bottom of a 250-million-year-old sea now buried tens of thousands of feet below the desert sand.

The **Permian Basin Oil Field** is the second largest in the world, and the price of a barrel of Texas Permian Intermediate Weight Crude is the standard against which the prices of all other US oils are determined.

The nodding pump jacks seem to repeat as they suck at the earth, "fiftydollars, fiftydollars, fiftydollars…" Not only have their rhythms enriched many a rancher, but the University of Texas as well. In the 19th century, having virtu-

etroleum
luseum.

ally no funds to offer the fledgling institution, the state legislature apologetically offered 2.2 million acres (890,000 hectares) of sand and desert scrubland. That these holdings coincide with the outlines of the Permian Basin is a happy coincidence that has bequeathed the University an endowment of approximately 2.5 billion dollars. The science and technology of oil are brilliantly explained in the **Petroleum Museum,** tel: (915) 683-4403, where visitors can inspect antique drilling equipment, stroll along a simulation of the bottom of the sea and buy amusingly oil-related items in the gift shop. The **Museum of the Southwest,** with its collection of art and archaeology, is located in a 65-year-old mansion in spacious grounds.

Midland's other claim to fame is that it is the "Tumbleweed Capital of the World." In the scorching 100°F (38°C) plus days of summer when all else turns brown, legions of prickly green tumbleweeds crowd the roadside, the abandoned fields and the railroad rights-of-way. These tumbleweeds grow up to 8 feet (2.5 meters) tall, awaiting the fall when they break free of the earth to rush pell-mell down the road.

Since Bob Nolan and the Sons of the Pioneers immortalized this common nuisance in the song *Tumbling Tumbleweed,* the plant has become a symbol for the spirit of movement that led to the development of the West Texas frontier, especially in the person of the drifting cowboy.

Midland and **Odessa** share the Midland International Airport, which is home to the **American Air Power Heritage Museum** with its hundreds of thousands of World War II artifacts and veteran, but still operating, wartime aircraft. Also near the airport is the 20-acre (9-hectare) **Water Wonderland** and a stock car racing track.

Just as Midland is the business center of the Permian Basin, Odessa is the home of the oil field worker or "roughneck". *Oil field trash and proud of it,* say bumper stickers often seen on pickup trucks with loaded rifles hung in the back window. No need to search farther for the modern counterpart of the frontier cowboy. Nevertheless, Odessa holds surprises.

For example, the **Globe Theater of the Great Southwest,** a replica of Shakespeare's Globe Theater in London, has a respectable professional repertory company producing the classics year-round. On the grounds of Odessa College is a replica of Stratford's **Anne Hathaway Cottage** housing a Shakespeare Library. For 40 years the Permian Playhouse has presented music, dance and drama. Other Odessa sights are the **White-Pool House** (*circa* 1887), and **The Presidential Museum** with its thousands of exhibits covering the history of US Presidents. Both sites are closed Sunday and Monday.

For a natural wonder, inspect the **Odessa Meteor Crater** just west of town, the nation's second largest, which has a diameter of 500 feet (152 meters). The crater was formed when some 2 million pounds of extraterrestrial iron crashed into the earth at this spot during the last Ice Age.

West of Odessa, the great **Chihuahuan Desert** begins, continuing across the Trans-Pecos region into Mexico. America's most bizarre forest grows along the margin of this desolation. The Havard oak forms a dense, at times almost impenetrable, growth that is easily overlooked because the mature trees are only about 3 feet (1 meter) tall. West Texans call the trees shin oak and the forest the "shinnery."

These plants are marvelously well-adapted to drought, with roots that can reach a depth of 90 feet (27 meters). Even when transplanted to better, moist conditions, the Havard oak remains dwarfed, obviously as suspicious of easy times as the hardy humans who first settled in the region.

The best vantage point for an eyeful of sandy "desertscape" is **Monahans Sandhills State Park,** about 30 minutes west of Odessa on I-20, where naked dunes tower up to 70 feet (21 meters) high and stretch north and south for 200 miles (320 km). Here, where the world is reduced to sand and sky, the **Monahans** soul can expand to consider itself and **Sandhills** where it has been. **State Park.**

THE TRANS-PECOS

The deep rugged canyons of the Pecos River Valley sever Far West Texas from the remaining 85 percent of the state. This Trans-Pecos Region – comprising 30,000 sq. miles (77,700 sq. km) of mostly uninhabited empty space – is bound firmly to New Mexico and Mexico culturally and ecologically. El Paso, its only city, has more in common with Albuquerque, New Mexico or Tucson, Arizona, than with less isolated Texas cities like Dallas and Houston.

Peaks and pines: The starkness of the Chihuahuan Desert landscape is not unrelieved, though. There are thin ribbons of life along the Pecos River and the Rio Grande, or *Rio Bravo* as it is known on the south bank, and in a patchwork of oases nourished by large springs and shallow aquifers. Islands of green rise in the sea of brown: the montane forests and meadows of the high mountains on every horizon, more than 90 of which reach altitudes greater than a mile above sea level.

Six of them soar to over 8,000 feet (2,400 meters), including **Mount Livermore**, which at 8,382 feet (2,555 meters) is the highest peak in the United States east of the Rocky Mountains. In these enclaves of pine, fir, maple and oak there are small populations of elk, black bear, bighorn sheep and mountain lions, the reminders of better, wetter grazing times. There has been a worrying drying trend over the last 100 years and livestock has been allowed to overgraze the land.

The fossil clock: Perhaps nowhere else in the United States can the history of the earth be read so clearly as in dry Far West Texas, where vegetation has not scrawled its graffiti of decay. Nature's first attempts at complex creatures can still be seen in the 600-million-year-old remains of algal colonies in pre-Cambrian limestone near **Allamoore**, 10 miles (16 km) northwest of **Van Horn** at I-10 and Highway 54. Petroglyph tours are conducted from Van Horn, most of whose income is from tourism, with its 20 motels, 18 restaurants, RV parks and gift shops.

Barnacles and corals of both Ordovician and Silurian times, 500 to 400 million years ago when the earth was still covered with water, are found near the highest point of Scenic Drive in El Paso's **Franklin Mountains**. The end of the Paleozoic Era 200 million years ago was typified by warm, shallow seas in which snails and the great shell-bearing ancestors of today's squids abounded. The fossil remains of these Permian period creatures are abundant on the east face of **Leonard Mountain** 9 miles (14 km) north of **Marathon**.

As the clouds move across this desolate land, you may be reminded of the gargantuan pterosaur, whose 51-foot (15.5-meter) reptilian wings cast terrifying shadows on the lesser dinosaurs below. The remains of these cretaceous creatures, the largest animals ever to fly, were found in the Big Bend area in the early 1970s. The unknown still awaits discovery out here where few humans have ever been.

On the face of its mountains, Far West Texas shows the ravaging changes of aeons. The youngest are the Franklin Mountains at El Paso and the **Delaware Mountains** north of **Kent**, which are part of the Rocky Mountain system and still rise at an average rate of more than ¼ inch (0.65 cm) per year. Many of the ranges in the mountain and basin area of Texas were built during the tumultuous Tertiary period about 60 million years ago. This happened when massive uplifting and faulting led to intrusions of molten rock like those in the **Chisos Mountains** of **Big Bend National Park**, and extensive lava flows that created the now weathered **Davis Mountains**. These volcanic formations cover mountains from earlier periods as well as marine sediment and coral reefs. Folding and overthrust faulting have left young rock strata covered by a layer of strata 150 million years older in some places.

Texas' highest and most majestic mountains, the **Guadalupes**, began as a massive coral reef in the Permian world some 250 million years ago. Two periods of uplifting have raised these marine remains to an altitude of over 8,000 feet (2,438 meters) including great 8,749-foot (2,667-meter) **Guadalupe Peak**, the highest point in Texas. Approached from the west on US-62/180, this giant wedge of limestone resembles an enormous ship moving over the desert. The cliffs of **El Capitan Peak** form the prow, 4,800 feet (1,463 meters) above a white sea of salt.

Sparkle in the stone: Rock hounds and gem hunters will not be disappointed with the gifts offered by the naked geology of the Trans-Pecos. An outstanding example is the famous Texas plumed agate, in which red flames and black feather shapes are captured in a translucent white matrix. Plumed agate is most easily found 16 miles (26 km) south of **Alpine**, where opal fillings in lava also occur, and near **Marfa**, the town founded in 1883 by attorney J.M. Dean, who bought land around the railroad station.

Sunburst agate occurs in the vicinity of **Needle Peak** in Brewster County, and blue agate in the Balmorhea area.

Amber, the hard golden resin of prehistoric plants, is occasionally collected from cretaceous coal outcrops along **Terlingua Creek** just west of Big Bend National Park. Large black crystals of augite can be collected in igneous rocks near **Eagle Flat** in Hudspeth County.

The abandoned mercury mines at **Terlingua** offer abundant specimens of cinnabar, which looks much like lipstick smears on the fissured surfaces of igneous rocks. The 27 miles (43 km) of tunnels and shafts, as much as 900 feet (274 meters) deep, have yielded a treasure of rocks, fossils and mineral specimens cast aside by miners intent upon mining only the mercury.

Ore containing the beautiful purple and green crystals of fluorite is mined commercially high in the **Christmas Mountains** just north of Big Bend National Park. Fluorite is also found in the igneous rocks of **Chinati Peak** in nearby Presidio County, and in the Eagle Mountains of Hudspeth County where it also occurs in limestone. Its phosphorescent glow and its fluorescence in ultraviolet **El Capitan.**

248

light make fluorite particularly worth looking for.

Kangaroo rats and mountain lions: After a few hours' exposure to the elements in the Chihuahuan Desert, the smallest sign of life suddenly becomes an object to marvel at and admire. Stoop to search the sand under a greasewood bush south of El Paso or near Salt Flat: you may find the tiny tracks of the kangaroo rat, two hind feet and a trail, but don't expect to see its burrow in the heat of the day. This quintessential desert hermit burrows into a sand dune and pulls the hole in after him, creating a chamber moistened by his breath. The kangaroo rat appears to be able to live without water. It is, in fact, an alchemist, changing the starch of dry seeds, its only diet, into water that it recycles internally.

Another local exotic is the javelina, or peccary, often seen in brushy *arroyos*, or draws. These 30–50 pound (14–22 kg) dark-bristled "pigs" are armed with tusks and musk, but are neither dangerous or even especially unpleasant company. If one of these near-sighted critters "charges" when startled, he is just making a fast getaway. These three-toed cousins of the South American tapir spend most of their waking hours munching the spiny pear cactus.

Tens of thousands of pronghorns roam the high grasslands between 4,000–5,000 feet (1,219–1,524 meters). Although known locally as pronghorn "antelopes," they are not antelope at all but sole members of a family intermediate between deer and cattle. They are faun-colored with black horns, white sides and rumps, and are easily observed because they are curious and confident. They are the fastest mammals native to North America, so they can escape danger quickly. Pronghorns have been timed at 35–45 miles (56–72 km) per hour.

Two species of deer live in the mountain and basin lands of Far West Texas. The eastern white-tailed deer occupies the brush country at lower elevations and the high-mountain pinyon-oak-juniper forests, while the desert mule deer is found in open grassland and desert habitats at intermediate altitudes.

Desert bighorn sheep are rare, fair game only for the nature photographer willing to pack into the high mountains of the **Black Gap** and **Sierra Diablo** state wildlife management areas.

Peregrines and road runners: King of the Air in the southern Trans-Pecos is the endangered peregrine falcon, whose concentration of aeries is the largest in the contiguous 48 states. Peregrines prey on other birds, of which there are more than 350 species in Big Bend Park. The peregrine is usually observed as a dot high in the sky or perched on the edge of its cliff-ledge nest. By folding its 3.75-foot (1.4-meter) wings, it can swoop down on to an unsuspecting mockingbird at over 200 miles (322 km) per hour, with dire consequences.

The comical road runner is another fast, flesh-eating Far West Texas fowl, which runs in a crouched position as though it hasn't started yet, a clever ploy perhaps used to trick lizards or snakes.

Golden eagles soaring on 6½–7½ foot (2–3 meter) wings are frequently seen in winter near the mountains and over the high grasslands of Far West Texas. Adults are uniformly dark underneath, while immature birds show white at the base of the tail and on primary wing feathers. Eagles' wings are held flat while soaring, which distinguishes them from the more abundant vultures, whose wings are tilted upward in soaring flight. The opportunity may present itself to view a golden eagle close up, since many of them come to an ignominious end: when they have eaten so much carrion they cannot lift off quickly and become road-kill themselves.

Survival in dry earth: The flowering plants of the Chihuahuan Desert perform a spectacular, although brief, extravaganza after the spring rains in April and May, but most of the rest of the year they are occupied with vegetative survival. Quite common is the *lechuguilla* plant, a member of the amaryllis family, that is easily recognized by its rosette of succulent bluish-green, spine-tipped leaves about 2 feet (0.67 meter) long and 1.5 inches (4 cm) wide. In true desert plant fashion, it can inflict a painful wound on the unwary.

The yucca species are somewhat similar to agave but are actually members of the lily family. They have narrower, more flexible and less succulent leaves and flower annually. The yuccas have formed a permanent partnership with the pronuba moth, which assures the reproductive survival of both organisms in the hostile desert environment. The moth pollinates a flower, then lays her eggs in the ovary. As the fruit develops, so does the moth larvae, which leave the fruit before damaging the seed. The larvae drop to the ground by a silken thread and burrow beneath the plant to emerge as adult moths during the yucca's next flowering season.

North and west of Van Horn the torrey yucca grows almost to the height of a tree, forming the only "forest" in the desert lowlands. In April this army of "Spanish daggers" topped by meter-long pompoms of large ivory-colored blossoms is unforgettable.

Another plant particularly common on mesas and hillsides is sotol, called "bear grass" for its 4-foot (1.25-meter)

Javelina in Big Bend.

long arching narrow leaves with small claw-like spines along the margins. Its slender, 4–15 foot (1.25–4.5 meter) brush-like flowering stalk may persist for several seasons, serving as convenient perches from which birds can survey their territories.

All of these large plants were important to the Native Americans who inhabited the area, such as the Mescalero Apache (*mescalero* means the "heart" of the agave, which was baked and eaten). Their leaves provided fibre for clothing and utensils, as well as soap, and the thick basal stems were baked in stone-lined fireplaces, of which the scattered remains can be seen. The yuccas, tagged by some people as "desert bananas," have been used as a food source for centuries by the Hopi and Tewas Indians, who grind their seeds for meal. They are a noted home remedy for arthritis and rheumatism and even a source of shampoo.

Greasewood and cactus: Greasewood, or the creosote bush, is – along with cactus – found almost everywhere in the deserts of North America. Its name comes from the thick resin deposited on its small yellowish-green paired leaflets. This diffusely branched shrub is usually only around 3 feet (1 meter) in height, but may grow to 10 feet (3 meters) where there is sufficient water. Greasewood has been used as fuel by the desert cultures for thousands of years. Its wide, even spacing and the general absence of competing species are the result of a special adaptation to the limited availability of water, for greasewood secretes a poison that kills even its own seedlings.

Ocotillo looks like a naked spider on its back. The long, spiny 6–20 foot (2–6 meter) legs protected by stiff spines, are used as living fences by goat raisers. This cautious species puts out leaves only after a rain and discards them as soon as drought returns. The pea family is well represented in the Trans-Pecos by thorny shrubs like the infamous "wait-a-minute bush," or cat claw acacia. Even first encounters elicit the automatic cry of "Wait a minute!" as hikers try to

World's largest road runner at Fort Stockton.

extricate themselves from this vegetable feline's clutches.

The cactus family, that classic form of desert life, originated in the southwestern US and northern Mexico and has attained its greatest diversity there. Although larger members, like the giant saguaro and the organ pipe cactus, are not represented in the Chihuahuan Desert, 106 species of cacti are Texas residents. In fact, the prickly pear apple cactus has become a weed in overgrazed pastures in many parts of Texas.

Instead of having stems and leaves, this plant consists of flat green ovals strung together in complicated erect sequences. The young pads are eaten as a vegetable, and the red fruit makes a refreshing desert dessert if nothing else is available. However, both must be carefully peeled to remove the 4½-inch (11.5-cm) stiff white spines and the not-so-obvious tiny brown barbs.

Pencil cactus looks like a bush of short green cylinders ¼ inch (0.66 cm) in diameter. Beware! They are brittle, and tend to cling to clothing in places where they are detectable only upon sitting down. Cholla, another cactus shrub, 3–12 feet (1–3 meters) high, resembles a string of bumpy sausages. When the fleshy tissue has decayed, the beautiful reticulate vascular system remains and can be used for canes or furniture.

Devil's head cactus is an interesting plant about a foot (31 cm) in diameter, which lurks partially buried, ready to snare a hoof, paw or tennis shoe with its four-pronged spines. On the whole, desert plants are an unfriendly lot best admired from a safe distance.

The few hardy souls: The history of the Trans-Pecos region is a long tale of succeeding cultures doing their best in a bad situation. Toward the end of the last Ice Age about 10,000 years ago big game hunters roamed the area, killing the now extinct giant bison by driving it over cliffs. The oldest buffalo "jump" is at the head of **One Mile Canyon** near **Langtry**.

From about 6000 BC to AD 1000, a semi-nomadic Trans-Pecos people occupied rock overhangs near springs,

Prickly pear cacti.

dined on cactus and mesquite beans, wove baskets and sandals from the fibers of *lechuguilla* and yucca leaves and hunted game with darts launched at high velocity with throwing sticks. The culture asked little of its environment and received 7,000 years' sufferance without having to change. Between AD 800 and 1000, aggressive nomadic hunters eventually displaced it.

Political turmoil among the Pueblos of northern New Mexico in AD 1200 caused the emigration of some of these advanced agricultural people to the flood plains of the Rio Grande near Presidio. This land has been continuously farmed ever since, making it the oldest agricultural land in Texas.

The arrival of the Spaniards in the 1500s, with their slavery and religious intolerance, led to the annihilation of the indigenous tribes. By the 1700s they were replaced by bands of Apache who found fighting the Spaniards in the desert preferable to fighting the Comanche on the plains.

Spain had practically abandoned Far West Texas by the time it became a part of independent Mexico in 1821. As the Anglo frontier moved westward, the fierce mounted Comanche war parties began to prey on wagon trains and Mexican and Anglo settlements along the Comanche War Trail, especially during the late summer and early fall harvest season. To counter these depredations, a line of cavalry forts was established soon after the Republic of Texas joined the United States in 1846.

The best preserved outpost from the tribal wars is old **Fort Davis**, which still stands dramatically with its back to a wall of volcanic rock. At 5,000 feet (1,524 meters) the community is the highest town in Texas and boasts of not possessing a single shopping mall. Named for Jefferson Davis, best known as the President of the Confederate States of America, locally he is remembered as the Secretary of War who brought camels to West Texas.

The area took a tentative step into the modern world when a few Anglo-Americans moved to the Trans-Pecos and be-

Tumbleweeds.

gan to ranch and mine for silver, activities which unfortunately proved to be only marginally productive. This harsh land, where "if it don't bite ya, it'll poke ya with a thorn", remained virtually undisturbed by humans. General Sheridan summed up his impressions by saying if he owned Texas he would "rent it out and live in hell."

Since there is still damned little "law west of the Pecos," Judge Roy Bean's legacy notwithstanding, here in writing is the unwritten code of conduct for these parts:

1. *Never go on a man's land without his permission.*
2. *Don't ask a man how much land he has.*
3. *Never step over a man sleeping on the floor.*
4. *Don't mess with a man's hat.*
5. *Never throw a hat on a bed.*
6. *Never rope another man's cow that wanders onto your land.*
7. *Never take a man's last chaw of tobacco.*

Adherence to these rules allows a man to leave Texas with as many enemies as he came with.

Trans-Pecos Tour: Pecos (population 12,000) makes a logical beginning for a Trans-Pecos Tour if one is crossing the Pecos River from the east by the I-20 bridge. Gourmets should take note: Pecos is to cantaloupe what Smithfield, Virginia, is to ham. The essence of harvest moon and honey condense in the fruit of the well-watered alkaline alluvium surrounding the town.

Downtown Pecos has been preserved and restored to retain the flavor of the 1880s cowboy days for which it was infamous. This was, after all, the site of the first rodeo back in 1883. The boys from the Hashknife outfit challenged boys from other ranches to horse racing, bronc busting and calf-roping contests. The tradition is carried on at the major rodeo held here around the Fourth of July each year.

Marathon, on US-383 to the south, is centrally isolated in a desolate area of interest only to naturalists. Its 1920s **Gage Hotel** has been charmingly reno- **Fort Davis.**

vated and furnished with antiques, Native American artifacts (including altarpieces in some bedrooms) and Mexican furniture in keeping with its role as a desert way-station. Geologists are delighted by the diversity of rocks and minerals in the vicinity. Rugged nature photographers use Marathon as a jumping-off point for trips to **Black Gap Wildlife Management Area**, a mere 55 miles (89 km) away. Though 80 miles (129 km) distant, Big Bend National Park is the next sign of civilization toward the south.

Terlingua (population 25), just west of the park, is now a collection of mostly abandoned stone and adobe ruins, but at the turn of the century it was a prosperous mining town of 2,000 inhabitants where red cinnabar ore was mined and cooked to yield millions of dollars' worth of mercury. Views of the nearby Chisos Mountains in Big Bend Park and multicolored badlands on every side form a surreal backdrop for rock hounds and cactus collectors who can run amuck here. **Farflung Adventures**, tel: (800)

359-4138, offers raft trips of one to nine days' duration on the Rio Grande through narrow 1,500-foot (457-meter) deep canyons or farther down river in challenging rapids.

Watering holes: To escape the desert heat, or just for a good time, enter the bizarre inner world of the **La Kiva Restaurant and Bar**, tel: (915) 371-2250 situated on the banks of Terlingua Creek. Mysterious lights of uncertain source illuminate the walls here, which look like geological formations. Furniture is made from redwood stumps and cowhide. Mysteriously illuminated, as well, are tropical forms of vegetation and the impressive wall-mounted fossil remains of such prehistoric creatures as *Penisaurus erectus*.

The highest waterfall in Texas is located on a private ranch near **Candelaria** northwest of Presidio. **Capote Falls** crashes 160 feet (50 meters) on to the rocks below. Inquire locally about the possibility of a visit. **Shafter** is a ghost town still haunted by prospectors who refuse to give up on an area that pro-

duced most of Texas' silver. Local color is served with the simple Mexican food on the screened porch of **Willis Williams' Shafter House Restaurant**, which overlooks crumbling stone ruins and denuded mountainside areas.

Marfa (population 2,600), a water stop and freight headquarters for the Galveston, Harrisburg and San Antonio railway, was named for a character in Fiodor Dostoevsky's *The Brothers Karamazov* that was being read at the time by the wife of the chief railroad engineer. By 1885, when its impressive courthouse was built, Marfa had a couple of saloons, a hotel and a merchandise store, which also housed the bank, post office and restaurant. Poker bets in the saloons were often made with town lots. Its cool 4,688-foot (1,428-meter) altitude is only one of the reasons visitors come here. Other pursuits include playing golf on the highest golf course in the state, or soaring in sailplanes among the mountains that surround a grassy plateau.

Art town: Several prominent contemporary sculptors have been attracted to Marfa, installing their work in the monumental space of what was formerly **Fort Russell**, the army's last horse-mounted cavalry post. John Chamberlain's crushed-auto-body sculptures and the fluorescent sculptures of Dan Flavin are among the excellent works on display in the fort, but much of the space is occupied by the creations of the New York sculptor Don Judd.

Judd's variously permutated groups of large rectangular concrete structures are rhythmically arranged in an endless progression toward the far horizon. Some 100 aluminum pieces are housed in a glass-walled gun shed.

Sierra Blanca seems to have everything a tourist desires. Dramatic scenery on the doorstep in 6,950-foot (2,118-meter) Sierra Blanca (White Mountain) and "forests" of Spanish dagger yucca plants. It has history: this is where the Chinese railroad workers from the west met the Irish laborers from the east to complete the United States' second transcontinental railroad. Sierra Blanca has interesting architecture, too, in the

nation's only adobe government building still being used today; and it has kitsch, in the shape of a life-sized replica of old **Fort Quitmann**.

Alpine is the largest and most important "city" in the mountain region of Texas, although it has a population of only 5,500. The name Alpine must be considered in perspective. To someone arriving from the broiling flatlands, the town's 4,500-foot (1,372-meter) altitude can seem alpine. It is a popular vacation headquarters for visitors to Big Bend and those who enjoy summer theater productions and museums on the campus of **Sul Ross State University**. A colorful guide to the Big Bend region is available for a small fee from the Big Bend Area Travel Association, PO Box 401, Alpine, TX 79831.

Fort Davis is in the town of Fort Davis, which is in the Davis Mountains, which in turn are in Jeff Davis County. The **Fort Davis National Historical Site** is a window on an important period of America's growth, the mid-1880s. The life of the frontier soldier has been recreated among actual buildings used in the days when he mounted up to escort wagon trains on the Chihuahuan Trail or stage coaches on the Butterfield Overland Mail Route.

A scenic loop through the gentle, weathered slopes of the Davis Mountains can be driven in two hours and is time well-spent. Follow Texas Route 118 north to 166, then stay on 166 until it rejoins Texas 17 south of Fort Davis. From **Wild Rose Pass** on, one has the same view of **Limpia Brook**, as it runs between high cliffs, that the Apache and Comanche raiding parties had as they lay in ambush.

Mount Livermore, the highest peak east of the Rocky Mountains, can be seen from **Madera Canyon**. The eerie domes of the **McDonald Observatory** atop **Mount Locke** deserve a visit. The third largest telescope in the United States is located here along with an 82-inch (210-cm) telescope, the largest anywhere that is available for public viewing. Public use is restricted to the last Wednesday of each month. Written permission is necessary to visit it.

Right, McDonald Observatory.

257

A GUIDE TO TEXAS PARKS

Parks in Texas are as varied as the people and the landscape. There are very large areas, like the massive Big Bend National Park, while at the opposite extreme the most intimate one is probably the grave of Davy Crockett's wife in Acton Cemetery near Granbury in the heart of the Cross Timbers region. Parks planned around lakes and rivers are especially plentiful, testifying to the Texans' love affair with water, historically a rare and even a mystical commodity in much of the state.

Tent and trailer camping, hiking, picnicking, birdwatching, horseback riding, golfing and all manner of zoos are found in parks throughout the Lone Star state. Best of all, Texas parks showcase the natural features of their region, whether they are the moss-laden cypresses of Caddo Lake in deep East Texas, the cliffs of rugged Palo Duro Canyon in the Panhandle or, by contrast, the lonely shell-strewn beaches of Padre Island.

Parks in Texas are numerous. Ten are operated by the National Park Service, more than 120 are state-owned, and there are countless roadside parks. At least one park is found in every Texas town or county and beside every lake. Facilities and standards of maintenance vary, but all these parks exist because of Texans' strong attachment to the outdoors. Many were developed by the Civilian Conservation Corps (CCC), one of Roosevelt's New Deal programs.

National forests: Many Texas parks are built around water. Large lakes are found in many parts of the state. Although mainly for power generation and flood and drought control, they are the basis of some of the best park fun in the Lone Star state. While most lakes are man-made, the parks on Texas rivers are notable for their scenery and natural features. And the many miles of Texas beaches are just plain fun-in-the-sun.

The water-oriented parks in East Texas are justly famous for combining

Preceding pages: Guadalupe Mountains National Park; Sam Houston National Forest. Below, whooping crane at Aransas.

scenery and water sports such as skiing, boating and fishing. Spring and fall are the prettiest times of the year; summertime, as in the Deep South, is hot, humid and bug-ridden. Remember to bring a good insect repellent.

Angelina National Forest, one of the four national forests in Texas, lies on both sides of the **Sam Rayburn Reservoir**, a 115,000-acre (47,000-hectare) lake east of Lufkin, less than 100 miles (160 km) northeast of Houston. This is Texas' largest reservoir and its surrounding recreation areas provide a wide variety of boating, hiking and camping activities in the towering pine forest and along the lake branches. Backpacking and primitive camping are permitted throughout the 5,000-acre (2,023-hectare) Angelina Forest unless otherwise posted by sign.

West of Angelina, the **Davy Crockett National Forest** covers more than 93,000 acres (38,000 hectares) along the Neches River. A second-growth forest, it has made a remarkable comeback since logging stopped in the 1920s. The **4-C Trail**, a scenic 19-mile (31-km) trek, connects **Ratcliff Lake Recreation Area** with the **Neches Bluff Recreation Area**. It is best to travel along it in the fall, winter and spring when the climate is more hospitable and the bugs are less numerous. Primitive camping is allowed along the 4-C Trail, but be suspicious of the water. It is best to either carry your own or to use water purifiers.

Sabine National Forest, the state's largest with 188,000 acres (76,000 hectares), stretches along the Texas side of the 65-mile (105-km) long **Toledo Bend Reservoir** on the Louisiana border near the historic city of **San Augustine** and about 125 miles (200 km) northeast of Houston. It includes a historic battleground where a 47-strong band of Confederate soldiers prevented a Union invasion of Texas.

Five recreational areas here have facilities for all types of hikers, campers, boaters and anglers. Any of them can be used as launching points for exploring the natural and scenic resources of this beautiful East Texas forest, as well as

pursuing the excellent fishing and boating on the reservoir.

Camping, boating, fishing: The smaller lakes that dot East Texas also provide camping, boating and fishing. Catfish, bass and crappie are the major fish, but be sure to have a current fishing license and observe all bag limits. Texas takes its game laws very seriously.

Martin Diego, Jr., State Park on **Steinhagen Lake** is at the northern edge of the **Big Thicket**, 15 miles (24 km) east of Woodville. The trees here are gorgeous in the fall and in addition to water sports, there is a wide variety of interesting birdlife along its trail, including the rare pileated woodpecker.

Lake Livingston State Park, 75 miles (120 km) northeast of Houston, occupies the east shore of the 85,000-acre (34,000-hectare) lake. Ninety-eight species of birds have been spotted along its 4 miles (6 km) of trails.

Just 15 miles (24 km) east is the **Alabama-Coushatta Indian Reservation**, which also has camping facilities. The reservation had its beginning in 1854, when the state legislature gave 1,250 acres (506 hectares) to the Alabamas, who had settled in East Texas 40 years before. Additional land has since been added to the reservation, which is jointly held with the Coushatta tribe. In the summer, the **Indian Village** is open daily, selling traditional handicrafts and featuring dances and a drama based on the origin and history of the Native American tribes.

Farther north, **Caddo Lake State Park** near Marshall, about 170 miles (275 km) east of Dallas, is the essence of East Texas to many people. It is the largest natural lake in the state and elegant Spanish moss drapes its ancient cypress trees. Water-skiing is possible on sections of the lake, but drifting along in a canoe is better suited to its peaceful nature.

About 185 miles (300 km) east of Dallas in the northeast corner of Texas, **Atlanta State Park** sits on the banks of **Lake Wright Patman** in a forest of oak, pine and spring-blooming dogwood. About 140 miles (225 km) northeast of Dallas near the town of

Daingerfield, **Daingerfield State Park** is considered by many people to be the perfect small park. It surrounds a small lake that is often filled with blooming water lilies. Its winding trails reward hikers with glimpses of wildlife, including the red cockaded and the pileated woodpeckers.

Tyler State Park, just north of the city of Tyler and 90 miles (145 km) southeast of Dallas, is a large park with a swimming pool and a good fishing lake. When the dogwood blooms in the spring, Tyler Park is at its best.

Lake Somerville State Park, newer than many parks, lies on the western edge of East Texas near Brenham, 85 miles (135 km) northwest of Houston. The park consists of two units on either side of the lake. They are connected by a 21-mile (34-km) trail, along which are five campgrounds, two of which are especially for equestrians. There are also five parks near the dam that are popular with boaters. On the Brazos River less than 70 miles (110 km) south of Houston, **Brazos Bend State Park** has 3½ miles (5.6 km) of river frontage. The American alligator and hundreds of bird species are stars of the abundant animal and plant communities here, and the migrating waterfowl lure so many visitors to Brazos Bend in the fall that reservations are necessary for its overnight facilities.

Droughts, floods and new lakes: The drought and flood control dam projects of the 1950s and 1960s created a multitude of new lakes in the central and western parts of Texas where, not so long ago, stock tanks were the major bodies of water. There are no pine forests surrounding these lakes, but they often have their own special appeal and their ardent boosters. On the Red River border separating Texas and Oklahoma about 80 miles (130 km) north of Dallas, **Lake Texoma** is popular for sailing and water-skiing. Anglers go after the native Red River white bass, black and striped bass, and the ubiquitous crappie and catfish.

Eisenhower State Park lies on the cliffs above Lake Texoma, with plenty **Fishing in East Texas.**

of room for campers, fishermen and boaters, with even a protected cove for swimmers. There are campgrounds along the lake's 15-mile (24-km) long **Cross Timbers Trail**, which provides beautiful prospects of the lake and valuable insights into the Cross Timbers ecology. Water, however, is not available except in the developed areas and the presence of snakes requires caution.

Five miles (8 km) southeast in **Denison** is the two-story **Eisenhower birthplace**. Water-skiing and scuba diving are popular at **Possum Kingdom State Park**, 100 miles (160 km) west of Fort Worth in the western Cross Timbers. There are 10 miles (16 km) of shoreline around the lake here, shaded by deciduous oaks and the juniper trees that many Texans call "cedar." About 55 miles (89 km) to the southeast is **Lake Mineral Wells State Park**. Sitting in a pretty valley, it has an equestrian trail and small boats for rent. It's a pleasant park, especially in the spring and fall when the trails are most scenic and the fishing is good.

Down the road **Lake Whitney State Park**, 75 miles (120 km) south of Fort Worth, is excellent for water-skiing and bass fishing. Its numerous facilities include an airfield for campers who fly in with the herons and geese. Anglers in search of a good fishing lake with a lot of variety will enjoy **Fairfield Lake State Park**, 90 miles (145 km) southeast of Dallas, noted for large-mouth bass, crappie, catfish, bluegill and drum.

Less crowded: Four parks in North Central Texas, more or less along the Fort Worth-to-Waco corridor, are very pleasant to visit, have good facilities and are not often crowded. **Cleburne State Park**, near the town of the same name and 45 miles (70 km) south of Fort Worth, was built around a small lake by a CCC company that holds a reunion there every Fourth of July. **Meridian State Park**, 70 miles (110 km) southwest of Fort Worth, has a small lake with a hiking trail all the way around.

Mother Neff State Park, 128 miles (206 km) south of Fort Worth, was the first Texas state park. The first 6 acres (2.5 hectares) were donated by Governor Pat Neff's mother. He gave an additional 250 acres (100 hectares) in 1933. Developed by the CCC in the 1930s, it is a fitting tribute to the early park pioneers of the state. **Fort Parker State Park** on **Lake Springfield**, 90 miles (145 km) south of Dallas near Mexia, is large enough for water-skiing and fishing too.

Hill country waterways: Large lakes and cypress-shaded rivers in the Texas Hill Country host a wide array of water activities. There are six large lakes on the lower Colorado River alone (**Lake Buchanan, Inks Lake, Lake LBJ, Lake Marble Falls, Lake Travis** and **Lake Austin**).

The Guadalupe River feeds the large **Canyon Lake** about 40 miles (65 km) southwest of Austin, and six smaller lakes. All of them are dotted with informal camping and fishing areas, and there are well-developed private marinas and resorts along their banks. Inquire at the local baithouses and marinas for the most up-to-date recommendations on campsites and fishing holes.

The Hill Country's most popular lake park is probably **Inks Lake State Park** about 100 miles (160 km) north of San Antonio near Burnet. Water-skiing, scuba diving and fishing are well provided for, and there is also a nine-hole golf course and a 7-mile (11-km) hiking trail. This park has a lot of visitors, and reservations are essential, especially in the busy summer months.

Garner State Park on the Frio River 31 miles (50 km) north of Uvalde, although enlarged, is still crowded, and reservations are necessary year-round for the picturesque cabins. *Frio* means cold in Spanish, and this river usually is. The scenery is at its best when the spring wild flowers make their show, but the river canyon is beautiful any time. One of the best ways to see it is from a rented pedal boat or inner tube.

The **Guadalupe River State Park** is a favorite spot for canoeing, which is a growing sport in Texas. Thirty miles (50 km) north of San Antonio, the park opened in 1983, and its four rapids have excited enthusiasts of all skill levels. The park is one of the most scenic natural areas of the Hill Country, and worth a trip even without a canoe.

Deer, coyotes, raccoons and gray foxes are often spied from the hiking trails, and birders will find golden-cheeked warblers nesting in a stand of Ashe juniper from March to late summer. On the Guadalupe and other rivers in the state, the water levels are unpredictable and subject to rapid rises and falls. Be forewarned: because the run was easy once, there is no guarantee that it will be easy again.

Within an hour's drive north of San Antonio, **Blanco State Park** straddles a mile and a half of the Blanco River, near the old town of the same name. Its small size seems to discourage crowds. First developed by the CCC, the park's main activities are swimming, fishing and watching the river go by.

The diversity of the Hill Country is especially evident at **Pedernales Falls State Park,** about 45 miles (70 km) west of Austin. Along the Pedernales River, there's lush vegetation wherever there's a bit of dirt; above the bank,

armadillos and scrub cedar rule. The Pedernales, like a lot of Texas rivers, floods when it rains, but is otherwise a peaceful stream running over a rock bed into calm pools. Watch out for an occasional treacherous waterfall or whirlpool, especially when the river is rising. The 7-mile (11-km) **Wolf Mountain Trail** is rewarding to skilled backpackers and hardy novices alike.

Lake Brownwood State Park is 22 miles (35 km) west of Brownwood, where the Texas Hill Country becomes West Texas. Its many facilities include picturesquely situated stone cabins. The 7,300-acre (3,000-hectare) lake imposes no limit on boat size.

Keeping cool: Perhaps nowhere in the state are water sports more appreciated than in South Texas, often a pretty dry place. This part of the state can get very hot in the summer, and spring and fall are the most enjoyable seasons for both locals and visitors. **Lake Texana State Park** is well-stocked with catfish, large-mouth bass and striped bass, with early spring being the best time to catch a long **Palo Duro State Park.**

stringer of catfish. Additional campsites are available at the nearby Lavaca-Navidad River Authority's **Brackenridge Campground**.

Although **Lake Corpus Christi State Park** was developed by the CCC in the 1930s, most of its facilities are more modern. Fishing, particularly for the wide variety of catfish, is good in the large lake. Because of its mild climate and proximity to Corpus Christi, 35 miles (55 km) to the south, the park is popular year-round and can become crowded.

Up the Rio Grande near Del Rio, **Amistad National Recreation Area** provides facilities all along the American side of the lake for a number of water sports. Scuba diving is especially good because the water is so clear. Deer hunting (with bow and arrow only) and bird hunting are allowed in certain areas during the season.

One of the largest lakes in Texas, **Falcon Lake**, is also on the US-Mexican border. **Falcon State Park**, 15 miles (24 km) north of the historic border

town of Roma, has comfortable accommodation. Birders here are rewarded with a variety of rare species, including the chachalaca. **Bentsen-Rio Grande Valley State Park**, on the river near Mission, is most popular in the winter when its sub-tropical climate attracts many wintering tourists. Its **Singing Chapparal Nature Trail** interprets the rare birds, animals and plants that can be found in the area.

Hunting and boating: The south is not the only part of Texas where hot summers are tempered by large lakes. Way up in the Panhandle, 35 miles (56 km) east of Amarillo, **Lake Meredith National Recreation Area** cools the arid Llano Estacado. Deer and bird hunting is permitted in certain parts of this park during the season. There is usually a good wind for sailing, but storms are unpredictable and boaters of all types should be very cautious.

Not as heavily developed as Lake Meredith, other West Texas lakes still give welcome recreational relief to many Texans and tourists. **Lake Colorado City State Park**, about halfway between Big Spring and Abilene, and **Lake Arrowhead State Park** near Wichita Falls are both on good-sized lakes and popular with motor boaters and skiers. **Abilene State Park**, about 20 miles (30 km) southwest of town, is just across the road from Lake Abilene, not far from an area once rife with buffalo. The park's campgrounds and swimming pool are set in a historic pecan grove.

At the beach: The beaches of the Gulf of Mexico are the site of some of the state's best developed and most popular parks. **Galveston Island State Park**, on the west end of the island, has well-situated beach campgrounds and picnicking areas. Down the coast is **Mustang Island State Park** with 5½ miles (8.9 km) of Gulf beach. Even with 348 campsites and 100 picnic sites, about half of the beach front is undeveloped. At both parks, reservations are advisable for assured accommodation, especially in the summer.

Padre Island National Seashore, just 14 miles (23 km) south of Mustang Island State Park, is America's largest

ig Bend.

designated national seashore. The facilities and accommodations along its 66-mile (106-km) beach range from every convenience and luxury to none. Probably the prettiest beach in Texas, its sand is white and the beachcombing is good. However, remember that hiking is taxing on the soft beaches, and even the most experienced trekkers should be thoroughly prepared before any extended hike down the island.

In contrast with the crowded beaches of Galveston and Mustang, **Sea Rim State Park**, on the coast near the Louisiana border, is more tranquil. The greater part of the large park is an extensive marsh inhabited by a multitude of alligators, nutria, mink, raccoons and wintering waterfowl.

The most remote beach park has to be **Matagorda Island State Park and Wildlife Management Area**. Accessible only by boat across Aransas Bay, the park has just a few chemical toilets, no electricity and no telephone. Public hunts are occasionally held in the wildlife management area. For more informa-

tion, contact the park headquarters in Port Lavaca prior to a visit.

The Big Bend: There are a number of Texas parks where the outdoor, back-to-nature experience is the major attraction. Texas' Sunbelt growth has made these away-from-the-crowd parks even more inviting. They vary in size, topography, climate, and in plants and animals. Alligators thrive in sections of East Texas, and panthers still prowl in the mountains of Big Bend.

The largest park in the Lone Star state, with more then 700,000 acres (280,000 hectares), is **Big Bend National Park**. It is by many accounts the most beautiful, most varied and most challenging to backpackers and nature lovers of every persuasion. The **Chisos Mountains**, the wide desert, the **Rio Grande River** and the magnificent canyons combine to form a true wilderness, portions of which are still relatively unexplored.

Big Bend is one of those places you have to be going to in order to get there. The closest town is **Alpine**, about 65 **Goliad.**

miles (105 km) northwest of the northernmost tip of the park. From **Fort Stockton** on Interstate 10, take State Highway 385 south through Marathon about 130 miles (210 km) to **Panther Junction**, the park headquarters.

The **Chisos Mountains Lodge** in **The Basin** is open year-round and provides camping and motel accommodations and a full-service dining room. Trailer and tent camping areas are available at The Basin, at **Rio Grande Village** near Boquillas and at **Cottonwood** near Castolon. While there are resortlike facilities at The Basin, the real Big Bend is best seen from its hiking trails or a canoe on the Rio Grande. The National Park Service provides extensive information about the hiking, camping and canoeing options and numerous outfitters in the area specialize in scenic hikes and river trips.

Big Bend is wild country, and should be respected as such. Water can be a problem on either long or short hikes. Dehydration comes on quickly in the dry air, and springs and streams are not reliable for drinking. Always take your own water along with you, and drink some frequently.

Some of the 36 marked hiking trails are easy, others are strenuous and treacherous. Many are interpreted by self-guiding leaflets and trail signs. All can be rewarding for the prepared, sensible hiker who knows his or her limits.

A number of trails take off from near The Basin. During the summer, a hike down the easy, 1½-mile (2.5-km) **Chisos Basin Trail** is guided by a park naturalist. At the overlook about halfway along the trail the major features of the Chisos Basin stand out against the sky: **Emory Peak**, at 7,835 feet (2,400 meters), the highest in the park, **Ward Mountain**, **Carter Peak** and **The Window**, **Vernon Bailey Peak** and **Pulliam Ridge**, **Casa Grande** and **Toll Mountain**. This trail is a good introduction to the park's major features.

Halfway between The Basin and Panther Junction, the **Pine Canyon Trail** explores a wooded canyon for 4½ miles (7.2 km). At trail's end a waterfall pours down the 200-foot (60-meter) cliff after a heavy rain. Just north of The Basin, the moderately difficult 5-mile (8-km) **Lost Mine Trail** follows the north slope of Casa Grande to a point high on the west side of **Lost Mine Peak**, affording beautiful views of the surrounding mountains and canyons. A very difficult trek up Casa Grande Peak (7,500 feet/2,300 meters) takes off from the **Juniper Canyon Overlook** along this trail.

Chimneys Trail, just under 5 miles (8 km), lies southwest of The Basin and leads to a group of high rock outcroppings or "chimneys." Long a landmark in the Big Bend, the southernmost chimney walls contain ancient Native American pictographs.

Two groups of trails into the Chisos lie south of The Basin. The **High Chisos Complex** trails are some of the most beautiful in the park, but they require strenuous hiking and climbing. It's as though the mountains want you to work for the beauty you see. The panorama from the **South Rim Trail** includes Santa Elena Canyon 20 miles (30 km) to the west, Emory Peak to the north, and the mountains in Mexico to the south.

Various trails take off from this one and lead up Emory Peak into **Boot Canyon**, the summer home of the colima warbler, which is found nowhere else in the United States, and along **Blue Creek Trail** and its colorful balanced rocks and pinnacles. While the High Chisos trails are strenuous, they are at least well-marked. The **Outer Mountain Loop** trails, on the other hand, are strenuous and not well-marked. The two series of trails can be combined for a lengthy wilderness expedition. Evidence of old ranches dots the trails, but they're most noted for their varied plant life and spectacular views.

Spectacular canyons: Another popular trailhead is the Rio Grande Village area near the river in the eastern part of the park. A very easy trail, less than half a mile (0.8 km) long, the **Rio Grande Village Nature Trail** interprets several plant habitats, including the lush river flood plain and the arid desert. An overlook at trail's end gives breathtaking views of Mexico, the river, the Chisos Mountains and Boquillas Canyon.

Boquillas, the long canyon in the park, is also accessible along the 1½-mile (2.4-km) **Boquillas Canyon Trail** that leads into the canyon itself.

The huge park has numerous trails scattered throughout. The most spectacular of the Big Bend canyons, **Santa Elena**, can be seen on an easy 2-mile (3.2-km) trail that crosses Terlingua Creek and wanders through the magnificent canyon to the river.

Mariscal Canyon, the most isolated of the three major canyons, is accessible on a strenuous, unshaded 6½-mile (10-km) hike. At the rim, a wide view of the canyon 1,500 feet (460 meters) below rewards the persevering hiker.

Boquillas Canyon is longer than Mariscal, but even gentler. Seventeen miles (27 km) in the canyon and 8 miles (13 km) on the Rio Grande can be a wonderful three-day trip with all the side canyons there are to explore in Texas and Mexico.

Santa Elena Canyon is also 17 miles (27 km) long, but very tricky, especially in high or low water. Eleven miles (18 km) of scenic river precede the canyon entrance. Although quite spectacular, its strong current over hidden rocks can be hazardous. The most dangerous part of the canyon, and the source of its reputation for difficulty, is the rockslide about a mile (1.6 km) beyond the entrance. Running it is always difficult, and downright dangerous at high and low water levels. Portaging the slide is socially acceptable and no blemish whatsoever on anyone's manhood. After the slide, navigation will be more tranquil and boaters can enjoy the colorful canyon walls and explore the jewel-like **Fern Canyon**.

Even from a car the Big Bend visitor can see the wild country. The **River Road** traverses the 51 miles (82 km) between the Boquillas-Rio Grande Village road and **Castolon**. The road can be travelled by most high-clearance vehicles, but its side roads usually require four-wheel-drive. Old ranches and fishing camps occasionally appear along the road, and it passes the ruins of **Mariscal Mine** at the foot of **Mariscal Mountain**. The old mercury mine was developed around the turn of the century and has been inactive since the mid-1920s. The ruins are fun to explore, but beware of open, unmarked mine shafts. Farther west lie the remains of the **Johnson Ranch House**, probably the largest adobe ruin in the park. The road ends at Castolon, a 19th-century farming settlement and early 20th-century US Cavalry and Texas Ranger post.

All in all, Big Bend has facilities and adventures to offer everyone: from resort accommodation to campsites miles and miles from anywhere; from automobile tours to the most rugged climbing trails to river running; from moderate mountain temperatures to hot-as-Texas. But it's still wild country and must be enjoyed on its own terms.

Evergreen forests: Guadalupe Mountains National Park is on the New Mexico-Texas border about 100 miles (160 km) due east of El Paso. The mountains, which range in both states, are probably the largest fossil reef in the world and contain Carlsbad Caverns as well as Texas' highest point, **Guadalupe**

Mission San Francisco de la Espada in San Antonio.

Peak at 8,751 feet (2,700 meters). The landscapes of the park are the most varied in the state.

The Chihuahuan Desert rises to spectacular evergreen forests, likelier to be located in the Colorado mountains than in Texas. The sheer cliffs of **El Capitan** tower 2,000 feet (610 meters). Greasewood and *lechuguilla* give way to lush ferns in the protected canyons. More than 170 species of birds and over 50 different reptiles and amphibians live in the Guadalupe park as well as elk, mule deer, coyotes and a mountain lion and black bear or two.

McKittrick Canyon is one of the highlights of the park. Open by permit, and only during the day, the canyon displays a rare and varied collection of vegetation. High sheltering walls and year-round streams provide a very different climate within the canyon for the ferns, big-tooth maples and little-leaf walnuts that grow there. The marked trail into it is not difficult, but stay on the trail to avoid disturbing the fragile ecological system.

Rugged landscapes also characterize **Palo Duro Canyon State Park** in the Panhandle, spectacular from every angle. Canyons on a smaller scale are the attraction at **Caprock Canyon State Park** about 60 miles (100 km) southeast of Palo Duro.

Central Texas: Central Texas has its share of natural and scenic attractions, too, although the scale is less awesome. **Enchanted Rock State Natural Area**, 18 miles (30 km) north of Fredericksburg, features a billion-year-old granite mountain. Its prominence in the landscape made it a source of Native American ghost tales and a traveler's landmark. While most trails are taxing, one trail to the top of the rock is manageable by most healthy hikers.

A large stand of big-tooth maples about 85 miles (135 km) northwest of San Antonio and 35 miles (55 km) southwest of Kerrville is the focus of **Lost Maples State Natural Area**. One of the few remnants of the large maple forests of a less arid time in Texas, these trees provide glorious color in October. While

Fort Concho
in San Angelo.

most of the trails here are challenging, a short one along the Sabinal River is easy and provides the visitors with a good view of a maple stand. The park is pleasant at all times of year and is particularly popular with birders. Golden and bald eagles can often be seen soaring in the air in the wintertime.

In a relic pine forest less than 30 miles (45 km) east of Austin, **Bastrop State Park** gives another glimpse of an earlier Texas. A rustic park with buildings of native stone and pine, its picturesque cabins were built by the CCC. Reservations for the cabins and campgrounds are necessary year-round.

Palmetto State Park, 60 miles (95 km) east of San Antonio near **Gonzales**, is one of the most attractive little places in the state. Its **Ottine Swamp** is the home of a tropical forest of palmettos (low-growing palms native to Texas) and other exotic flora. Hiking trails show off the plant and animal life and the extensive bird population. Spring and fall are the best times to visit; summer can be humid and stifling.

In East Texas, the **Sam Houston National Forest** offers excellent hiking and camping between Huntsville and Lake Livingston. Its highlight is the **Lone Star Trail**, the longest developed hiking route in the state. The 140 miles (225 km) of trail are a cooperative venture of the US Forest Service and the Houston Sierra Club. **Double Lake Recreation Area** and **Stubblefield Recreation Area** in the forest have extensive camping and picnicking and serve well as trailheads. Camping is permitted along the trail and in designated areas. Hikers must tote their own water in and garbage out. From mid-November until the first of the year, hiking can be dangerous because the hunting season is open.

Some Texas areas are wild and scenic, but not parks *per se*. Still, they provide parklike experiences, although just for the day. A favorite is **Aransas National Wildlife Refuge**, on the San Antonio Bay near Rockport, has a visitors' center and three nature trails for viewing the refuge wildlife, including

Buffalo Springs State Park near Lubbock.

the rare and endangered whooping cranes who winter there. Twenty miles (32 km) of roads through the refuge give glimpses of the many deer, alligators and javelinas, as well as the multitude of other birds who live there year-round. Probably the surest way to see the whoopers is to take the boat that goes out from the **Sea Gun Inn** near Fulton from October to early April. Campgrounds are handy at nearby **Goose Island State Park**.

The **Laguna Atascosa National Wildlife Refuge** is just north of **Port Isabel** on the **Laguna Madre**. When ducks and geese fly south for the winter, this is where many of them come. Camping is not allowed, but there are auto and walking trails. **Santa Ana National Wildlife Refuge**, on the Rio Grande near **McAllen**, has 14 connecting trails through its 200-acre (81-hectare) subtropical forest. It is the northern limit of many Mexican birds' migration. One of the forest's ebony trees may be the oldest and largest in the United States.

Cultural past: A large and growing class of parks protect and display the cultural heritage of the state. The historical and recreational are often combined in these parks, providing fun flavored with a little education.

Dinosaur Valley State Park exhibits the tracks made by the Pleurocelus and Acrocanthosaurus dinosaurs, prehistoric reptiles who walked around this swamp millions of years ago. The interpretive center explains the tracks, and a trail leads right to them. Camping, hiking and picnicking are also provided in this park 60 miles (95 km) southwest of Fort Worth, near **Glen Rose**.

Remnants of prehistoric Texas cultures are preserved in several parks. **Alibates National Monument** in the Panhandle was the source of a particular flint. Close to Del Rio, on the border, is another site with striking evidence of inhabitants 2,000 to 8,000 years ago. These ancient nomadic people painted the walls and ceilings of their cave dwellings with fanciful animals and other images whose meaning is now lost. One pictograph-covered shelter is open to visitors on a guided tour. The

trail leading to it takes stamina, particularly in the summer heat. An award-winning exhibit at the **Seminole Canyon State Historical Park Visitors' Center** interprets the prehistory and history of the park. Campsites with water are available.

Rock art is also found at **Hueco Tanks State Historical Park**, 32 miles (51 km) east of El Paso. Early tribes may have come through the area as early as 10,000 years ago. There is Pueblo rock art dating from AD 1000 and Mescalero Apache images from the 18th century. Water held in the depressions of the rocks made it a popular place in the surrounding desert. The art can be seen on a self-guiding tour. Bird and animal watching is fruitful here, and campsites and picnic areas are available.

Caddoan Mounds State Historic Site, clear across the state in East Texas 30 miles (50 km) west of Nacogdoches, was the home of a group of agricultural Texans from the 8th to the 14th centuries. A sedentary people who may have had some association with the pyramid builders in Mexico, they left behind three large earthen mounds filled with religious and other artifacts. Interpretive exhibits and a self-guided tour explain as much as is known about these ancient people. During summer, archaeological excavations are sometimes conducted at the site, and visitors are invited to watch. Recreational and camping facilities are handy at nearby **Mission Tejas State Historical Park**, 8 miles (13 km) down the road.

Spanish colonial era: The first colonizers of Texas, the Spanish, have left substantial reminders of their presence. The **San Antonio Missions National Historical Park** includes four 18th-century mission churches, a dam and an aqueduct. Primary interpretation is done at **San José Mission**, but the other three, **Concepción, Espada** and **San Juan**, are also open to tourists. All four are still active parishes.

The Spanish mission **Nuestra Señora Espiritu Santo de Zuniga** is the centerpiece of **Goliad State Historic Park**, just south of the historic town of Goliad. The mission was reconstructed by the CCC on the ruins of the 1749 church. The park has a scenic campground on the river and award-winning exhibits in the church and granary. The nearby **Presidio La Bahia** gained notoriety in 1836 when it was the site of Santa Ana's execution of Fannin's men during the Texas Revolution – hence "Remember Goliad!" The old *presidio* has been reconstructed and is open to the public.

Independence: Washington-on-the-Brazos State Historical Park is the site where the Texas Declaration of Independence was proclaimed on March 2, 1836. Although nothing remains of the bustling 1850s town, a replica of Texas' Independence Hall and the home of the Republic's last president have been reconstructed. The **Star of the Republic Museum**, operated by Brenham's Blinn College, sits in the park grounds and has a number of good exhibits about life in early Texas. The park's riverside picnic area is on a bluff above the Brazos, but there are no camping grounds.

Six weeks after the declaration of Texas' Independence, Sam Houston's small band of Texans routed Santa Ana in the marshes of Buffalo Bayou, now commemorated by the **San Jacinto Battleground State Historical Park**. In La Porte, just east of Houston, the San Jacinto Monument rises in the midst of the battleground and houses a museum. The park provides picnic areas, but no campgrounds.

Although the April 1836 battle at San Jacinto established the Texas Republic, it struggled against continued Mexican incursions for the next 10 years. **Monument Hill State Historic Site** in La Grange, 70 miles (115 km) east of Austin, honors the Texans who died in two responses to such attacks, the Dawson and Mier expeditions. The **Kreische Brewery State Historic Site** is contiguous and contains the ruins of a mid-19th-century brewery, at one time the second largest in the state. The sites share a well-developed picnic area and grand views of the Colorado River. No camping is available. **Lajitas.**

Frontier forts: Fortifications of many types are scattered around the state and represent battles of various sorts fought on Texas soil. The most famous, of course, is the **Alamo** in San Antonio, open seven days a week. **Old Fort Parker State Historic Site**, about 35 miles (55 km) east of Waco, commemorates another famous battle of 1836, the Native American attack on Parker's Fort and the subsequent capture of little Cynthia Ann Parker. The "Telling of the Tales" each May vividly recounts the story of this family fort and the lives and deaths of its inhabitants.

The Texas frontier after annexation by the United States in 1845 stretched long and wide and almost unprotected. Settlers in the most remote areas had to create their own defense systems against hostile Native Americans and roving bands of outlaws. **Fort Leaton State Historic Site** on the Rio Grande near present-day Presidio was built by a border trader (some called him a smuggler), Ben Leaton. It was the largest adobe structure in Texas. Now partially restored, it colorfully recaptures this remote Texas frontier life.

The federal government also built forts to cope with Native American threats to the advancing settlers, and a group of fort parks represents the 40-year struggle. **Fort Lancaster State Historic Site**, **Fort Davis National Historic Site** and **Fort McKavett State Historic Site** were all forts built before the Civil War. Fort Lancaster's adobe ruins lie about 70 miles (115 km) east of Fort Stockton, and are interpreted in the visitors' center and via a self-guided tour of the old parade field.

At Fort McKavett, about 40 miles (65 km) northwest of Junction, and Fort Davis, in the Davis Mountains 25 miles (40 km) north of Alpine, little is left of their earliest incarnations, but they have been restored to their post-Civil War state. More forts were built after the war, when Native American hostilities reached their height.

Over 20 buildings at **Fort Concho National Historic Site** in San Angelo are restored. A museum is on the premises but no recreational facilities.

Fort Richardson State Historic Park in Jacksboro, 100 miles (160 km) northwest of Fort Worth, and **Fort Griffin State Historic Park**, 50 miles (80 km) north of Abilene, have been developed with pleasant camping and picnicking adjuncts. Old Fort Griffin is also one home of the official **Texas State Longhorn Herd**. Highlighting visits to any of the forts are the occasional military reenactments: check the individual parks for up-to-date details.

Local heritage: Like the rest of the United States, Texas has become more aware of its cultural heritage over the past 30 years. Almost every city and town has at least one historic house museum that local folks point to with pride. Some are large groupings of houses with a paid staff and long opening hours like **Sam Houston Park** in Huntsville, which has gathered together buildings associated with the Texas hero. Others are smaller, often the work of dedicated volunteers, like **French's Trading Post** in Beaumont, the **Annie Riggs Hotel**, a museum in Fort Stockton, the **Eddleman-McFarland House** in Fort Worth, the **Bishop's Palace** in Galveston, and the **Charles Stillman House** in Brownsville.

The majority of these historic sites and structures date from the 19th century and illustrate life during that era. Four homes in four different parts of the state show the differences and similarities of affluent Victorian Texans. **José Antonio Navarro State Historic Site** depicts more than 20 years in the life of an important San Antonio family headed by the *Tejano* patriot Navarro, a signatory of the Texas Declaration of Independence and framer of the Republic's Constitution.

The **Sam Bell Maxey House State Historic Structure** in Paris, in far northeast Texas, is a large Italianate house containing the furnishings and history of three generations of the politically prominent Maxey family. Samuel was a Confederate general who later served as a US senator. In El Paso, the **Magoffin Home State Historic Site** and the history of its occupants reflect the Territorial style common in the Southwest, and the blending of cultures along the Rio Grande. The **Fulton Mansion State Historic Structure** near Rockport is the restored High Style Victorian mansion of a South Texas cattle baron, with every innovation of the day.

Charming landmarks: Inns in Texas are undergoing a renaissance, as Texas travelers rediscover the charm of these quaint places. Three inns have been incorporated into Texas parks, and are among the most popular stopovers in the state. The **Landmark Inn State Historic Site** in Castroville, 20 miles (30 km) west of San Antonio, is a hotel that evolved as traffic along the Texas frontier grew.

Begun in the 1840s, it was part of a bustling Alsatian commercial complex for the rest of the 19th century. Its old gristmill became Castroville's first electric power plant in the 1920s. The hotel was reopened during World War II. Only eight rooms are available for overnighters; thus the demand is high and reservations are essential. **Indian Lodge** in **Davis Mountains State Park** is an adobe inn built by the CCC. About 35 miles (55 km) northeast of Marfa, it is a favorite stopping place for guests traveling to the Big Bend. Camping is also available in the park. Again, the lodge's rooms are much in demand, therefore reservations should be made as far in advance as possible. Sightseeing and hiking are excellent here, with both the Fort Davis National Historic Site and **McDonald Observatory** situated nearby.

Balmorhea State Park is over the Davis Mountains from Indian Lodge, in the desert about halfway between Fort Stockton and Van Horn. In the 1930s the CCC built one of the largest swimming pools in the world at its **San Solomon Springs**. The pool is more than 30 feet (10 meters) deep in places and covers more than 1½ acres (0.6 hectares). The adobe **San Solomon Courts** were also built by the CCC, but have been modernized.

Some parks defy the usual categories. The **Texas State Railroad Historical Park** runs the 25 miles (40 km) between Highway Department rest area on the River Road.

276

Rusk and Palestine in East Texas and is one of the most popular parks in Texas. The turn-of-the-century rolling stock gives an authentic flavor to the scenic ride along the historic route. The ride takes three hours (round-trip) and there are picnic sites at both ends to round off the journey.

The **Battleship** *Texas* **State Historic Site** is a memorial to Texans who fought in World War II, and is moored at San Jacinto Battleground State Historical Park in La Porte. Commissioned in 1914, it is the only surviving Navy ship that served in both world wars, notably in the Atlantic in D-Day operations off the coast of Normandy in 1944 and in the Pacific at Iwo Jima and Okinawa in 1945. Open to the public seven days a week, the ship features a self-guided tour and many interesting displays about ship life.

Texas has more than 2,000 caves, most of which are located in the limestone and gypsum areas of Central and West Texas. The largest cave in the state is probably **Natural Bridge Caverns** about 15 miles (24 km) west of New Braunfels. Its size and beauty are expressed in the room's names: Pluto's Anteroom. Sherwood Forest, Castle of the White Giants and Hall of the Mountain Kings. It is privately owned and open to the public.

Limestone from the Lower Cretaceous period forms the **Caverns of Sonora**, less than 10 miles (16 km) south of the town of Sonora. With 8 miles (13 km) of passages, it is one of Texas' longest caves. It regularly delights visitors with the variety and delicacy of its formations. Sonora Caverns also operates a campground.

Inner Space Cavern on I-35 between Round Rock and Georgetown is one of Texas' most accessible caves. Its large rooms are unusual in this part of the state, and the tour takes visitors into the most beautiful of them. One of the oldest commercial caves in Texas is **Longhorn Cavern** in the **Longhorn Cavern State Park**, less than 90 miles (145 km) north of San Antonio near Burnet. It has seen a number of uses in the past 100 years but was developed as a tourist cave in 1934 by the Civilian Conservation Corps. Camping is available at Inks Lake State Park 6 miles (10 km) up Park Road 4.

City parks: Texas is also blessed with large metropolitan parks. Often located in the middle of high-rise urban development, they are oases of grass and trees in the rapidly growing Sunbelt cities. Beautiful **Forest Park** in Fort Worth includes the **Fort Worth Zoo**, the **Log Cabin Village** and the **Botanic Gardens**. **Brackenridge Park** in San Antonio has a large zoo and scenic greensward and gardens.

Houston has a number of urban parks, four of which are connected by the **Brazos Bayou Trail: Hermann Park** with its zoo, stables, Museum of Natural Science and planetarium, stands at one end. **Mason Park** is at the other end, and **MacGregor** and **Gus Wortham Parks** are in between. **Fair Park** in Dallas is the site of Texas' annual State Fair in October and contains several museums.

What would those miles and miles of Texas be without the roadside parks that dot the landscape? Many are more utilitarian than scenic, but the following are worth a look: an oasis in South Texas on US-281 between Falfurrias and Rachal; the charming city park on Salado Creek in Salado off I-35; the verdant creekbank park on State 173 near Camp Verde; and the wild flower-covered park (spring and summer) just west of Hye on US-290 near the LBJ parks.

Also worth a stop in the car is the Rio Grande, overlooking a park between Redford and Terlingua with its funky teepees in the Big Bend on FM-170. The park and tourist bureau in Langtry highlight both Judge Roy Bean and the fascinating native desert flora.

There are, of course, many more excellent parks that have not been mentioned here. But the list is also incomplete in that no words or pictures can ever completely capture the beauty and spirit of the Texas landscape like a campout in the East Texas Piney Woods, a hike in McKittrick Canyon, or a float through Santa Elena Canyon on a late fall afternoon.

INSIGHT GUIDES
Travel Tips

Insight Guides portray destinations in depth, providing the complete picture and the top photography

Insight Pocket Guides focus on the best choices for places to see and things to do and include large fold-out maps

Insight Compact Guides' portability makes them the perfect books to carry with you for on-the-spot reference

Three types of guide for all types of travel

INSIGHT GUIDES Different people need different kinds of information. Some want *background information* to help them prepare for the trip. Others seek *personal recommendations* from someone who knows the destination well. And others look for *compactly presented data* for on-the-spot reference. With three carefully designed series, Insight Guides offer readers the perfect choice. Insight Guides will turn your visit into an experience.

The world's largest collection of visual travel guides

Getting Acquainted

Area: 266,874 sq. miles (691,201 sq km).
Capital: Austin.
Highest mountain: Guadalupe Peak, 8,751 feet (2667 m).
Coastline: 367 miles (591 km).
Population: 18.4 million.
Largest city: Houston (population 1.6 million).
Language: English; Spanish minority language.
Time Zones: Central Standard (GMT minus 6); Mountain (GMT minus 7).
Currency: US dollars/cents.
Weights & Measures: Miles and feet; pounds and ounces.
Electricity: 110 volts.
State flower Bluebonnet.
State fish: Guadalupe bass.
International dialing code: (011); Capital, Austin: (512).
Long distance code: US numbers dialed outside the area code called from must be prefaced with a (1).
Local dialing codes: Abilene (915), Amarillo (806), Brownsville (210), Corpus Christi (512), Dallas (214, 972), El Paso (915), Galveston (409), Houston (713), Laredo (210), Lubbock (806), Pecos (915), San Antonio (210), Waco (254). Many businesses have toll-free (no charge) telephone numbers; these are always prefaced with (800) rather than an area code.

Climate

A uniform description of either winter or summer weather in Texas is impossible: while it's snowing in the Panhandle, people wintering on the Gulf Coast may be getting a tan at the beach; Central Texas may be baking in the late summer heat while the maples and aspens turn to fiery shades of red in the Guadalupe Mountains.

Although average temperatures of 30–50°F (around 0–10°C) in winter, 70–90°F (20–30°C) in summer do not

vary greatly around the state, the humidity factor and elevation affect the comfort level considerably. Central Texas, East Texas, the Coastal Prairie and Rio Grande Valley are humid and close to sea level, so it is usually very hot and sticky in the summer, often climbing into the hundreds (38°C) in the months between May and October.

In these areas, it usually does not snow or freeze, although it occasionally does so in a big way. In relatively recent years San Antonio and Austin have been blanketed with snow and ice, with businesses and roads completely closed down for the duration. In the Panhandle and the higher elevations of the Davis Mountains, Guadalupe Mountains and Big Bend area, where fall comes earlier than in the southern part of the state, there is little humidity except snow, which is common in the winters, sometimes causing roads and mountain areas to be closed to the public.

Annual rainfall ranges from 8–12 inches (20–30 cm) in the dry Trans-Pecos region to 52 inches (132 cm) in the wettest parts of the state, such as Houston and far East Texas. The best time for statewide travel is late October–November, March and April, and late May/early June. This will avoid, for the most part, Texas' hottest and coldest temperatures and the heaviest rainfall.

Economy

Beef, cattle and cotton are agricultural mainstays with chemicals, food products, electric equipment, petroleum products, machinery and transportation equipment being the main items manufactured.

Originally heavily dependent on oil and natural gas (Texas produces one-quarter of US oil), the state is now heavily into aircraft, electronics and chemical production. Manufacturing accounts for 15 percent of gross state production. The service area – especially finance, insurance and real estate – accounts for a further 70 percent. The Dallas/Fort Worth area boasts the corporate headquarters of many national companies. An unusually wide range of soil varieties enables farmers to grow almost anything.

Generally, prices in Texas are a bit lower than the US average, largely be-

cause of the overall deflationary state economy. Gasoline, hotels and food are noticeably cheaper than many other parts of the continental United States.

Government

The state's most recent constitution – its fifth – was adopted in 1876. The governor (a four-year term) appoints the secretary of state and the adjutant general, with all other state offices being elective. Both the Texas House of Representatives (150; two-year terms) and the Senate (31 members, four-year terms) meet in the State Capitol in Austin. Texas has 254 counties, more than any other state, each governed by a County Commissioners Court, which sets the county budget and taxes.

Etiquette

The key word here is "relaxed." Openness and natural friendliness rule. Don't be insulted – as new arrivals sometimes surprisingly are – when total strangers smile at you broadly and ask how you are doing as you pass them in the street. You can expect almost everyone with whom you come into contact during the day to ask how you are feeling, where you come from where you are going and, if you prove to be a foreigner, whether you are married, how many children you have, what your job is and why you are here. Or they may just ask how you are "doin'."

This is not inappropriate behavior personally invasive or presumptuous not even an attempt to begin a long intimate conversation. It is a Texas custom, and it is natural friendliness and goodwill that prompts these genial greetings and inquiries from passers by, waiters and salespeople who suddenly become new Texas friends. Don't even be surprised at a congenial slap on the back to emphasize a point, or – particularly in South Texas – a friendly embrace in greeting.

One of the best things about Texas is the lack of dress codes whether on city streets, at the shopping center, at the symphony or theater, or in restaurants. Although some of the more expensive establishments in larger cities like Dallas and Houston require men to wear jackets and ties and women to have on dresses or dress pants, in most restaurants almost any attire is tolerated. However, state regulations require shoes to be worn in eating places, and even most country coffee shops and restaurants hang the sign "No Shirt, No Shoes, No Service" on the door.

In most places where parties wearing jeans and T-shirts happen to be seated next to couples in evening dresses and tuxedos, both groups feel perfectly comfortable. If there is a rule for dress, it may be to wear whatever feels good.

Do not attempt to take your pet into a restaurant with you. This European custom is not followed in most parts of the United States; in fact, health regulations prohibit all animals except seeing-eye dogs in public eating places in Texas.

Ten Facts About Texas

1. The best-known "Texans" who defended the Alamo were actually Tennesseeans: Davy Crockett and Jim Bowie.
2. In 1904, responding to the Post Office's suggested names for their community, the town leaders replied: "Pick your choice" – and Choice (pop. 71) has been the name ever since.
3. John Nance Garner's suggestion that the cactus become Texas' state flower was rejected by the legislature in favor of the bluebonnet. Garner was US vice-president 1933-41.
4. The international border between Texas and Mexico holds the dubious distinction of marking the world's greatest income disparity between adjoining countries.
5. When a community sprang up around a slaughter house and hog rendering plant near Goliad in 1898, its residents defiantly named it Cologne.
6. Three out of America's ten largest cities are in Texas: Dallas, Houston and San Antonio.
7. Every Thanksgiving Johnson City has the Great Turkey Escape, when 100 turkeys too small for the oven are driven through the streets before being fattened up for Christmas.
8. The short tie rope connecting the newborn calf to its mother along the trail was called a "dogie." Hence the phrase: "Get along little dogie."
9. Oddly named Texas communities include Art, Anchor, Bacontown, Black Ankle, Cash, Divot, Sand and Uncertain.
10. The most visited of all presidential libraries is the one devoted to Texas native Lyndon Baines Johnson on the University of Texas campus in Austin.

Planning the Trip

What to Bring

For clothing, natural fabrics such as cotton, linen and wool provide the best comfort in the Texas climate. Go particularly light in summer, but because of the altitude and cool breezes, a sweater can be needed in the evening even then. The midwinters of Central and East Texas, the Coastal Prairie and the Rio Grande Valley usually require only a lightweight coat. In the mountains, High Plains and Panhandle, winters can be so severe that you need layers of warm clothes.

And don't forget your jeans! Texans are very casual dressers and blue jeans away from the office are the norm. They are worn almost any place any time of the day, dressed up or down by changing a shirt, sweater, jacket or accessories. People in Dallas and Houston dress formally for some evening events, but casual pants and dresses for women and shirt-sleeves or tieless shirts and jackets for men are acceptable almost any place you go.

You can buy most anything you need in Texas, but of course it's always a good idea to bring with you any prescription medications and a spare pair of prescription eyeglasses.

Entry Regulations

If entering Texas from another country, you must have a passport with photograph and a visitor's visa. Canadian and Mexican neighbors need only a border pass to enter the United States. For travel to Mexico from Texas, see **On Departure**, p. 283.

Health

Depending upon the country from which you are traveling or through which you have just come, you may need an international vaccination certificate. Many types of over-the-counter medications are readily available, but if you're using prescription medication, it's best to bring along extra. Tap water is fine to drink, but if you're out camping in the more remote parts of some of the state's National Parks or Forests, it is best to bring your own or use purifiers.

Money

American-dollar traveler's checks are a safe currency since they are accepted as cash in most restaurants, hotels and stores, can be exchanged for cash at any bank and will be replaced if lost or stolen. Passports or other photo ID may be requested when cashing traveler's checks. ATM machines are widely available, and major credit cards are accepted most anywhere in the larger cities and towns.

Public Holidays

Banks, federal, state, county and city offices and private businesses often close during public holidays. Many stores remain open during weekends and holidays.

National Holidays
New Year's Day
January 1
Martin Luther King Jr.'s Birthday
January 15
Presidents' Day
Third Monday in February
Easter Sunday
Late March/early April
Memorial Day
Last Monday in May
Independence Day
July 4
Labor Day
First Monday in September
Columbus Day
Second Monday in October
Veteran's Day
November 11
Thanksgiving Day
Fourth Thursday in November
Christmas Day
December 25

State Holidays & Festivals

Confederate Heroes Day
January 19
Mardi Gras
Early February, Galveston
George Washington's Birthday
Third week in February, Laredo
Texas Independence Day
March 2
San Jacinto Day
April 21
Fiesta San Antonio
Third week in April, San Antonio
Polka Festival
First full weekend in May, Ennis
Juneteenth (Emancipation Day)
Week of June 19th, statewide
Lyndon B. Johnson's Birthday
August 27
Oktoberfest
First full weekend in October, Fredericksburg
Texas State Fair
First three weeks in October, Dallas
Wurstfest
First full week of November, New Braunfels
Las Posadas
Second week in December, San Antonio

Getting There
By Air

Air passengers to Texas usually arrive at Dallas–Fort Worth Airport or Houston Intercontinental Airport, although many touch down in El Paso to change planes or take on additional passengers. In addition to these international airports, a network of smaller airports covers the state with flights scheduled to over 30 cities. Connections are easy to arrange, even between different carriers, and there are frequent shuttles between major cities throughout the day. The services of the major airlines such as American, Braniff, Continental, Delta and Eastern are conveniently supplemented by smaller ones such as Southwest, Chaparral, Texas and Muse. European carriers like Air France provide direct flights from Dallas or Houston to Europe. Air fares change frequently, as do schedules and special bargain rates. It is wise to arrange your trip through a travel consultant, who has the most current information. However, all airlines can be contacted directly by telephone for information and reservations. Local or toll-free central numbers can be obtained either from telephone directory assistance (in Texas, dial 1-411) or the *Yellow Pages* of the local telephone directory.

By Train or Bus

Two **Amtrak** lines run through Texas: the *Eagle* from Chicago to San Antonio, with a Dallas to Houston connection; and the *Sunset* from Los Angeles to Miami. The two trains stop at 20 passenger terminals in the state: Alpine, Austin, Beaumont, Cleburne, College Station-Bryan, Corsicana, Dallas, Del Rio, El Paso, Fort Worth, Houston, Longview, Marshall McGregor, San Antonio, Sanderson, San Marcos, Taylor, Temple and Texarkana. Accommodation includes coach and sleeping facilities. There are lounge and dining cars. Outside North America, you can purchase a USA Railpass from travel agencies, which allows unlimited rail travel within specified dates. For reservations and information inside the US, call toll-free numbers (1-800) USA-RAIL or (1-800) 872-7245.

Greyhound buses, (800) 231-2222, connect Texas with the rest of the United States. They accept major credit cards. Buses are air-conditioned and there are restrooms on board. Outside North America, contact your travel agent for an Ameripass, which allows unlimited bus travel within specified dates. Local bus systems serve the downtown and some suburbs of the major cities and towns. Check the Yellow *Pages* under Bus Lines.

By Car

The size and climate of Texas are good reasons to drive since walking between attractions, even in a city, requires more time than most people have for vacations and, much of the year, it is too hot to walk for pleasure. The public transportation systems of San Antonio and Austin are especially efficient. However, Texans rarely take a city bus anywhere when they can use a car. All the major American car hire companies have offices in Texas, and there are some good deals to be had. (*See* **Getting Around**, p. 285.)

US (Interstate) Highways 10, 20, 27, 30, 35, 37, 40 and 45 crisscross Texas, providing direct and relatively hazard-free routes to major cities. For anyone interested in a closer look, however, there are a variety of state highways and back roads (marked on the maps as FM or "Farm to Market," RM or "Ranch to Market," and RR or "Ranch Road") intertwined between all the major cities, smaller communities and even ghost towns. Buy a map and plan a tour, but allow plenty of time to reach your destination since some of these Texas roads get quite winding and pot-holed. Some even become dirt roads.

Be aware, as well, that leaving the main track means fewer gas stations and convenience stores . Even when you travel through a series of small towns, it is possible that after dark or on a holiday many of their gas stations and stores will be closed. However, if you remember to fill the tank and allow plenty of time to get where you're going, especially after dark, these secondary roads may prove the most enjoyable to travel since you'll be able to slow down and enjoy the countryside without having to worry about heavy traffic.

Interstate highways are planned to bypass most towns, and they do get you there fast, but when you are driving from Austin to Dallas or from San Antonio to El Paso, even fast can mean four to ten hours. Along the interstates there are public restrooms and roadside picnic areas as well as food and gasoline.

The Highway Patrol cruises these highways, not just monitoring speed limits but also looking for drivers in trouble. If you have mechanical problems or any other emergency that won't allow you to continue the trip, signal your distress by raising the hood. Motorists are often warned that they are safer staying in the car with the doors locked until a patrol car stops to help, rather than leaving it and attempting to hitchhike. Hitchhiking is not considered safe in the United States, whether you are on the giving or the receiving end. In some places it is illegal.

Specialist Tours

Gray Line tours are available in many Texas towns and cities. For specific information call (800) 950-8285.

Accommodation

In addition to independently-owned hotels and motels in every price range, the many chains operating in Texas even reach into some of its smallest towns. On any budget, you will be able to find a suitable place to spend the night. At the expensive end of the scale there are Sheratons, Hiltons, Marriotts and Hyatt Regencies. More moderately priced choices would be the Holiday Inns, La Quintas and Ramada Inns. Quality Inns, Howard Johnsons and Best Western motels are reasonable; the Motel 6, Days Inn, Rodeway Inn and Travelodge chains are relatively inexpensive. (*See* **Where to Stay**, p. 286.)

On Departure/Traveling On

Many visitors to Texas proceed onwards into or visit Mexico. This can be done at several border points, of which the main ones are El Paso, Eagle Pass, Laredo and Brownsville. For short visits within the border area, no special documents beyond proof of citizenship are required from US citizens; others must carry passports and the appropriate visas if required. If you're traveling deeper into the country or staying for longer than 72 hours, a Mexican tourist card is required. These cards are free from immigration officials at the border and also from Mexican consulates and Mexican government tourist offices. Drivers must obtain automobile permits, valid for 180 days, when venturing beyond the border region. These cost $10 and can be obtained from Mexican immigration officials on production of a tourist card. It is mandatory to obtain Mexican insurance and highly advisable because in the event of an accident vehicles are usually impounded, regardless of fault.

Useful Addresses

The Texas State Travel Guide, published by the Department of Transportation, lists Texas cities with their attractions and is available free from P.O. Box 5062, Austin, TX 78763-5064 or by calling (800) 452-9292. Information on road conditions and routes is also available from the same number.

To request information on standard Texas travel, call or write the Tourism Division, Texas Department of Commerce, P.O. Box 12728, Austin, TX 78711, tel: (800) 452-9292 or (512) 462-9191.

Practical Tips

Business Hours

Offices 8am–5pm Monday–Friday; banks 9-10am–3-4pm Monday–Friday (although most have drive-through sections that stay open longer); retail shops 10-11am–5-6pm Monday–Friday, except in large shopping malls, when hours are extended to 8, 9 or 10pm and weekends. Many museums are closed on Monday.

Tipping

The tip is not included in the check unless you are a group of five or more, when a gratuity of 15 percent may be added to your total. If it has been, it will be noted on the bill; otherwise tips of between 10 and 20 percent are expected. Unless the service is dreadful, you are obligated. Fifteen percent is a good rule of thumb when tipping for any service, including taxi rides and hair cutting and styling, although some Texans have not gotten used to tipping barbers. The owner of a hair salon is usually not tipped. Bellhops and parking attendants expect a dollar, shoeshine dispensers more.

Media

Print

Abilene Reporter News, PO Box 30, TX 79604, tel: (915) 673-4271.
Amarillo Daily News, 900 S. Harrison, TX 79166, tel: (806) 371-8411.
Arlington Citizen Journal, 1111 W. Abram, TX 76013, tel: (817) 548-5400.
Austin American Statesman, PO Box 78767, tel: (512) 445-3500.
Corpus Christi Caller Times, 820 Lower N. Broadway, TX 78469, tel: (512) 884-2011.

Dallas Morning News, 508 Young St, TX 75265, tel: (214) 977-8222.
El Paso Times, Times Plaza, TX 79901, tel: (915) 546-6104.
Fort Worth Star Telegram, 400 W 7th St, TX 76102, tel: (817) 390-7400.
Galveston Daily News, 8522 Teichman Rd, TX 77552, tel: (409) 744-3611.
Houston Post, 4747 Southwest Parkway, TX 77027, tel: (713) 743-3500.
Lubbock Avalanche Journal, PO Box 491, TX 79408, tel: (806) 762-8844.
San Antonio Express News, PO Box 2171, TX 78297, tel: (210) 225-7411.
Waco Tribune-Herald, PO Box 2588, TX 76702, tel: (817) 757-5701.

Broadcast media

There are over 70 television stations and at least 550 AM and FM radio stations in Texas alone. Thanks to cable, satellites or pay television, programs from all over the world can be seen almost any hour of the day or night. The installation of cable in most hotels and motels and many homes means that how a particular station is found depends on where it appears on the cable to which they subscribe. Consult the newspaper for television listings. Radio listings are sometimes given in Sunday supplements of newspapers.

Mail & Telecommunications

The mail system may be the only thing that is constant throughout Texas. First class postage is the same anywhere in Texas or in the United States and bills arrive just as quickly in tiny Cut-and-Shoot as they do in big-city Dallas. Post offices open at 7, 8 or 9am and usually close at 5pm, Monday–Friday. Many of them are open for at least a couple of hours on Saturday mornings, but they are all closed on Sunday. They may also have coin-operated stamp machines that dispense stamps whether the office is open or not. Rates are usually listed nearby. There are also US Post Office Information numbers in the phone book, or you call 411 and ask the operator for the number.

Visitors can receive mail at post offices if it is addressed to them, followed by "General Delivery" and the city name and (very important) zip code. You must pick up this mail in person within a week or two and show personal identification.

Telephone & Fax: To call from city to city in Texas, you must first find out the called area code. The state's vast size requires that it be divided into eight of these 3-digit codes. The proliferation of fax machines and computers within recent years has resulted in more and more areas being hived off into new area codes a a spped quicker than lightening, so don't be surprised if an area code has changed from the one cuurently published.

When calling from one area to another dial "1" before the 3-digit area code and the local 7-digit telephone number. If calling from a pay telephone, you must first insert a coin to connect with the telephone operator.

If you want to pay for the call with coins, a recorded voice will tell you how many to insert. Unless you have a credit card with the telephone company, your only other option is to call your party "collect" (reversing the charges). You will have to give the number you are calling to the telephone operator and identify yourself; the operator will then dial and ask the answering party whether the call will be accepted and paid for.

Directory Assistance calls from pay telephones are free. However, to be connected to some of them you must first insert a coin, but as soon as you are connected with the operator it will be returned to you. To get the information operator dial 411, but to get an information operator in another city, dial 1-(area code of the city)-555-1212.

For local calls from pay telephones which accept coins, insert a coin and dial the 7-digit local telephone number. There is no time limit for local calls.

There are Western Union cablegram offices in most cities. Look in the local telephone directory in the white pages (for major cities, there may be separate books for businesses and residences) under Western Union. Messages and money can be sent over the wires immediately. You must have positive identification, such as a driver's license, to receive money.

The following is a list of local Convention and Visitors Bureaus Free pamphlets can be obtained from all of them, some in foreign languages.

Abilene: 1101 N. 1st Street, TX 79601, tel: (915) 676-2556, fax: (915) 676-1630.
Austin: 201 E 2nd St, TX 78701, tel: (512) 474-5171; fax (512) 404-4383.
Beaumont: 801 Main St, TX 77704, tel: (409) 880-3749 or (800) 392-4401; fax (409) 880-3750.
Corpus Christi: 1201 N. Shoreline Blvd, TX 78403, tel: (512) 881-1888, fax: (512) 888-5627.
Dallas: 1201 Elm Street, TX 75270, tel: (214) 746-6677; fax: (214) 746-6688.
El Paso: 1 Civic Center Plaza, TX 79901, tel: (915) 534-0696; fax: (915) 532-2963.
Fort Worth: 415 Throckmorton St, TX 76102, tel: (817) 336-8791 or (800) 433-5747; fax (817) 336-3282.
Galveston Island: 2106 Seawall Blvd, TX 77550, tel: (409) 763-4311: fax (409) 765-8611.
Houston: 801 Congress Ave, TX 77002, tel: (713) 227-3100; fax (713) 227-6336.
Laredo: 501 San Augustine, TX 78040, tel: (210) 712-1230 or (800) 361-3360; fax (210) 791-7489.
Midland: P.O. Box 1890, TX 79702, tel: (915) 683-3381 or (800) 624-6435; fax (915) 682-9205.
Nacogdoches: 5113 North St, TX 75963, tel: (409) 564-7351; fax (409) 560-3920.
Odessa: 700 N. Grant St, TX 79761, tel: (915) 333-7871; fax (915) 333-7858.
Port Arthur: 3401 Cultural Center, TX 77642, tel: (409) 985-7822; fax (409) 985-5584.
San Antonio: 210 South Alamo, TX 78298, tel: (210) 270-8700 ; fax (210) 270-2782.
San Marcos: PO Box 2310, TX 78666, tel: (512) 393-5900 or (800) 782-7653; fax (512) 393-5912.
South Padre Island: 600 Padre Blvd, TX 78597, tel: (210) 761-6433 or (800) SO-PADRE; fax (210) 893-4266.
Waco: 100 Washington N., TX 76700, tel: (817) 750-5870 or (800) 321-9226; fax (817) 750-5801.

Texas State Board of Tourism, P.O. Box 5064, Austin, TX 78763-5064, tel: (512) 462-9191 or (800) 452-9292.

Current information on hotels, and all kinds of events and cultural activities, can also be found in Texas periodicals. The Texas Highway Department publishes a monthly travel magazine, *Texas Highways*, at a moderate subscription fee (Box 5016, Austin, 78763, tel: (512) 465-7408). *Ultra* and *Texas Monthly* are available on most newsstands.

There are magazines dedicated to a particular city, like *Austin Living*, D *Magazine* (in Dallas) and *Houston City Magazine*. Bookstores display a wide array of books about Texas from the *Texas Almanac* – covering every conceivable subject – to comprehensive bed-and-breakfast listings and bicycling trip guides.

Australia: 1990 S. Post Oak Rd, Houston, TX 77056, tel: (713) 629-9131.
Canada: 750 N. St Paul, Dallas, TX 75201, tel; (214) 922-9806.
Ireland: 1900 W. Loop S., Houston, TX 77027.
United Kingdom: 1000 Lousiana, Houston, TX 77002, tel: (713) 659-6270; Dallas; (214) 637-3600.

Security & Crime

As is the case in large cities all over the world, Dallas, Houston, El Paso, San Antonio, Austin and Corpus Christi have notoriously dangerous areas, especially if one is alone or if it is after dark. Always use common sense and survey your surroundings. Do not walk long distances after dark in strange or deserted parts of town. Keep a watchful eye on your belongings. Do not leave your car unlocked in parking lots, and never leave your children alone. Smaller towns in Texas have much lower crime rates, but use the same precautions everywhere as you would in a big city.

Hotels usually warn you that they will not guarantee the safety of belongings left in your hotel room. If you have any valuables, you may want to lock them in the hotel safe.

Hitchhiking is considered dangerous in Texas and should not be attempted nor should you stop to offer a ride to a hitchhiker. If you have trouble on the road, stay in your car but leave your hood up to alert cruising police cars. Lock the doors.

Medical Services

Due to the large number of cities in Texas, a list of hospitals, doctors, clinics and pharmacies would require far too much space and, in any case, would soon be out of date. Rest assured, though, most cities have 24-hour pharmacies - (often called drugstores) and minor emergency clinics, major emergency rooms at hospitals, and poison control centers. Look in the *Yellow Pages* under these categories or the inside cover of the telephone book. Or, dial 411 for telephone operator assistance.

If you need to call for help, such as an ambulance or the police, many areas of Texas can gain access to the emergency number used in most parts of the country: **911**. A dispatcher will answer your call, provide immediate first aid information if needed, and send help. If in a non-911 area, dial **0** for the telephone operator.

Pests

Because much of Texas is "out of door" (that is, all its small and sprawling cities together occupy only a tiny portion of the state), anyone who spends much time exploring it has a good chance of coming into contact with a Texas spider, scorpion, snake, chigger, mosquito, wasp, fire ant or Portuguese Man-of-War. Avoidance has always been the best strategy against threatening pests. If you are walking in a field, for example, loose clothing discourages ticks and chiggers from finding a tight spot in which to embed themselves. Tall, thick boots usually protect against stinging ground insects and reptiles. Once bitten or stung, however, there are a few procedures which will ease your suffering. The most important thing to do is to find what got you and, if possible, get it (taking the pesky pest with you to a doctor will help determine the correct remedy).

The bite or sting of a **spider**, **ant** or **scorpion** is not usually fatal but it can cause a lot of pain and itching, and the area round it may swell. In most cases, discomfort gradually subsides. If extreme symptoms such as numbness, tingling, shooting pain, high temperature, low blood pressure, abdominal cramps, spasms, breathing difficulty or problems focusing the eyes

occur, see a physician at once. Remember that bringing the insect or reptile with you greatly aids the doctor.

Never bother a **snake**. Most snakes in Texas are not harmful to people and only strike in self-defense. Although *you* know that you are not threatening a snake you did not even notice, just entering its territory and standing too close can agitate it enough to strike. Again, before fleeing in a panic at least try to see what the snake looked like. A positive identification is extremely important for the physician making a treatment decision. **Do not** attempt any first aid treatments such as freezing the limb, tourniquets or the outdated cut-and-suck method. These methods often do no good and sometimes make matters worse. Instead, go to the emergency center of the local hospital.

"Red-on-yellow" is still a reliable way to identify a **coral snake**, but even experienced snake enthusiasts have been fooled in poor light and snatched one up on a country road thinking it was a milk snake. Coral snakes are abundant in Texas and because of their beauty and relatively small size they are frequently picked up by children. Be sure to discourage children from picking up strange animals. Coral snakes and **rattlesnakes** have very different toxins, the toxin of the former attacking the nervous system and the latter primarily affecting the respiratory system and the bite-area tissue by digestion processes. Treatment therefore consists of injecting very different antivenins, which makes identification extremely important. Snakes have control over the amount of venom they excrete when they bite and, in fact, sometimes do not inject any at all. This accounts for varying stories about the results of victims' bites.

Snakes are not quite the omnipresent menace that strangers in Texas fear. They do not loiter around front doors of inhabited houses or slither down city streets. They usually remain in fields or sand dunes and often hide under logs or in holes waiting to hunt at night or early in the morning. Your best bet for seeing one is to keep your eyes peeled for a "roadkill" squashed by a car while trying to make its way across a country road.

Raccoons, **skunks**, **bats** and **squirrels** live in Texas, and you can often

persuade raccoons and squirrels to eat from your hand. This is not wise as all of these animals are potential carriers of rabies, which is easily transmitted to people.

Texans often call **chiggers** "red bugs." There is not much you can do for a chigger bite. A salve from the drugstore may help relieve the itching, but you will just have to wait for it to go away. The same is true of the bite of the **mosquito**, found by the million around the water in low-lying areas.

The **Portuguese Man-of-War** is not a true jellyfish, but it is called that, and hundreds can be found on Padre Island. Washed ashore, their blue balloon-like forms with long tentacles continue to pulsate for a while. If stung by their tentacles, either on shore or in the water where they are harder to avoid than on the sand, you may develop rashes and red welts. A few sensitive victims go into shock or endure fever, cramps and nausea. Some lifeguards treat these stings with meat tenderizer; others wash the area with sodium bicarbonate, boric acid, lemon juice or alcohol. If symptoms are severe, you should see a physician.

Getting Around

There are three airports in Texas classified as international: Dallas-Fort Worth, Houston and San Antonio. The Dallas-Fort Worth International Airport is the world's second-busiest airport and the largest US airport. It is 18 miles (29 km) northeast of Dallas; about 30–45 minutes' driving time from the downtown area.

The Houston Intercontinental Airport is 22 miles (35 km) north of the city via the Eastex Freeway (US-59). Allow 30–35 minutes to get to downtown from the airport, depending on traffic.

The San Antonio International Airport in only 8 miles (12 km) from downtown, which is about 20 minutes by car.

Regular shuttle services are available from all airports. Taxi service is also available, but is usually expensive. Most major hotels provide courtesy shuttle service from the airport to the hotel.

Public Transportation

Bus

Cities, all except the smallest towns, have some form of local bus service at very low rates. Either contact the Chamber of Commerce for listings or call the main office of the bus company listed in the telephone directory. Major cities like Dallas, Austin, San Antonio and Houston offer other forms of bus services well-suited to visitors, such as the Armadillo "trolleys" in Austin and citran in Fort Worth.

Taxi

For intra-city travel, taxis can be a convenient way to get around. However, unlike those in major cities like New York and London, Texas taxis do not cruise around looking for people hailing them from the curb. To get a taxi, you must call the cab company (look under Taxicabs in the *Yellow Pages* of the local telephone directory) and give them your address and destination. A dispatcher then sends a taxi to pick you up. Ask the dispatcher what the rates are, as they vary from the city to city (but not from cab to cab). A 15 percent tip is appreciated by the driver if you are satisfied with the service provided, and especially if you need help with luggage.

Private Transportation

Speed limits for roads and highways are posted on white signs to the right, as are all other driving instruction signs. Some roads are for one-way traffic only and are identified by a black and white sign with an arrow pointing in the permitted direction of travel. At an intersection where each corner has a red stop sign with a smaller sign below it which says "4-Way" or "All-Way," motorists must completely stop and then proceed across the intersection following the order in which they arrived at the stop. The official highway speed limit is 55 miles per hour (89 kph). Although everyone passes you, resist the temptation to acceler-

ate. If caught in a "speed trap" by the Highway Patrol, whose black-and-white cruisers have radar, you will get a speeding ticket that has to be paid in a nearby (or sometimes not so near) town before continuing your trip.

The same advice should be followed when driving through towns and cities. Be sure to notice the white signs warning that, upon entering the town, you will be in a different "Speed Zone Ahead." Be prepared to slow to the lower speed you will soon see posted on upcoming white signs. Some very small Texas towns are notorious for catching and fining drivers who have not quickly slowed down from the highway speed of 55 mph to the in-town 30 mph (48 kph) speed limit. You may not notice the local (variously colored and lettered) police car parked surreptitiously in an alley or behind the Dairy Queen until it is too late.

Pay attention to other drivers flashing their lights at you; probably either an accident or speed trap is ahead (or you may be driving at night without your headlights turned on!). Some Texas motorists ask the gas station attendants if there are Highway Patrol cars ahead but they cannot always be relied on.

Be sure to keep a current driver's license and a certificate proving you have liability insurance with you at all times because you will be required to show them to the law enforcement officer who stops your car for any reason. It is illegal to drive in Texas without both of these items.

A state law requires every passenger in a car to use a seat belt and there are also requirements that small children and babies be secured in youth or infant seats which have been fitted into the car seat.

Although US and Texas laws regarding particular drugs such as marijuana have relaxed somewhat, so that possession of small amounts of certain controlled substances is classified as a misdemeanor requiring the payment of a reasonable fine, it is not recommended that you bring narcotics into Texas or attempt to purchase them while here. Law enforcement officers, if they feel they have "probable cause," can and will, upon stopping you for speeding or any other traffic violation, search your car. Any illegal substances found can be used as evi-

dence against you. Undercover agents may also pose as narcotics dealers. It would be best to stay well away from Texas' increasing efforts to battle its drug traffic.

Car rental: Cars can be rented in most cities. This is usually done at the local airport since much of the rental business is with customers who have arrived by air. Choose the best rate available from one of the side-by-side booths. You must be at least 21 years old to rent a car. Credit cards are accepted, and by several companies they are required. Some agencies expect the car to be returned to them. If you want to drive to another city and fly on from there, be sure to inform the rental agent at the time you arrange the terms. There may be a charge to drop the car at their branch in another city. In any case, make sure one of their offices exists where you eventually want to leave the car.

The major car rental companies all have toll-free (800) numbers and are as follows:

Alamo	327-9633
Avis	831-2847
Budget	527-0700
Dollar	800-4000
Hertz	654-3131
National	227-7386
Thrifty	367-2277

Where to Stay

Hotels

In addition to independently-owned hotels and motels in every price range, the many chains operating in Texas even reach into some of its smallest towns. On any budget, you will be able to find a suitable place to spend the night. At the expensive end of the scale there are Sheratons, Hiltons, Marriotts and Hyatt Regencies. A more moderately priced choice would be the Holiday Inns, La Quintas and Ramada Inns. Quality Inns, Howard Johnsons and Best Western motels are reasonable; the Motel 6, Days Inn, Rodeway Inn and Travelodge chains are relatively inexpensive.

Quaint and historic inns and other lodgings are the specialty of an association called Historic Accommodations of Texas, PO Box 1399, Fredericksburg, TX 78, tel: (800) HAT-8669. A free brochure lists the statewide membership.

Abilene

Antilley Inn, 6550 S. Hwy 83-84, 79606; tel: (915) 695-3330; fax: (915) 695-9872. 52 units, continental breakfast. $
Kiva Inn, 5403 South 1st, 79605; tel: (915) 695-2150 or (800) 592-4466; fax: (915) 698-6742. 183 units, disabled facilities. $

Alpine

The Corner House, 801 E. Avenue E., 79830; tel: (915) 837-7161. Garden with fountain. Home-baked breads. 8 rooms. $
Siesta Country Inn, 1200 E. Holland Ave Hwy 90E, 79830; tel: (915) 837-2503 or (800) 972-2203; fax: (915) 837-9278. Pool, nearby golf, tennis. $

Amarillo

Rodeway Inn Medical Center, 6005 Amarillo Blvd West, 79106; tel: (806) 355-3321, or (800) 228-2000; fax: (806) 358-7689. Pool, 28 units. $
Travelodge West, 2035 Paramount Drive, 79109; tel: (806) 353-3541 or (800) 578-7878; fax: (806) 353-0201. Indoor pool, workout facilities. $

Austin

Austin North Hilton and Towers, 6000 Middle Fiskville, 78752; tel: (512) 451-5757 or (800) 347-0330; fax: (512) 467-7644. Disabled facilities $$
Austin Motel, 1220 S. Congress, 78704, (512) 441-1157; fax: (512) 441-1157. 41 units. Restaurant, whirlpool/spa, laundromat, weekly rates. $
Driskill Hotel, 604 Brazos, 78701, (512) 474-5911 or (800)252-9367; fax: (512) 474-2214. Historic downtown hotel, workout facilities, 77 units. $$$
Doubletree Guest Suites, 303 W. 15th, 78701, (512)478-7000 or (800) 222-8733; fax: (512) 478-5103. Whirlpool/spa, 189 units. $$$
Embassy Suites Downtown, 300 S. Congress Ave, 78704, (512) 469-9000 or (800) 362-2779; fax: (512) 480-9164. Cooked-to-order breakfasts, workout facilities. $$

Four Seasons Hotel, 98 San Jacinto Boulevard, 78701-4039, (512) 478-4500 or (800) 332-3442; fax: (512) 477-0704. 4-star rated hotel and restaurant with outdoor dining overlooking Town Lake, on hike-and-bike trail $$$
The Gardens on Duval Street, 3210 Duval St, 78705, (512)477-9200; fax (512) 477-8602. Rooms in garden setting, central near Univ. of TX. $$
Hyatt Regency on Town Lake, 208 Barton Springs Road, 78704, (512) 477-1234 or (800) 233-1234; fax: (512) 480-2069. Excellent location on Town Lake's hike-and-bike trail. $$$
The Inn on Lake Travis, 1900 American Drive, Lago Vista, 78645, (512) 267-1102, or (800) 252-3040. Tennis, golf, volleyball on 40 acres of lakefront. $$
Lake Austin Spa Resort, 1705 Quinlan Park Road, 78732, (512) 266-2444 or (800) 847-5637; fax: (512) 266-1572. All amenities including handicapped facilities. $$$
McCallum House, 613 West 32nd, 78705, (512) 451-6744; fax: (512) 451-4752. 5 units, private verandas, quiet residential location. $
Radisson Hotel on Town Lake, 111 Cesar Chavez, 78701, (512) 478-9611 or (800) 333-3333; fax: (512) 478-3227. Excellent downtown location on hike & bike trail. $$$
Southard House, 908 Blanco, 78703, (512) 474-4731; fax: (512) 478-5393. 16 rooms in 3 restored houses, very central. $$
Days Inn Austin North, 820 East Anderson Lane, 78722, (512) 835-4311 or (800) 329-7466; fax: (512) 835-1740. Pool, nearby golf. $
Renaissance Stouffer Austin Hotel, 9721 Arboretum Boulevard, 78759, (512) 343-2626 or (800) 468-3571; fax: (512) 346-7953. Restaurant, pool, spa, workout facilities. $$$

Banderas

Chukka Creek Guest Ranch, Tarpley Rd, Route 470, 78003; tel: (210) 460-7859. A/c cabins overlooking the creek, for 1-3 guests. $
Bandera Lodge, 1900 Highway 16 S., tel: (210) 796-3093, fax: (210) 796-3191. Restaurant, pool, nearby golf course $

Comfort

B&B on Cypress Creek, 816 N. Creek Rd, 78013; tel: (210) 995-2479. 2

rooms; wine, cheese & bread upon arrival; creek view. $
Comfort Common, 717 High St, 78013; tel: (210) 995-3030. 8 rooms in historic hotel. Gardens, courtyard, rooms with antiques, charming. $

Corpus Christi

Corpus Christi Fairfield Inn, 5217 Blance Moore Drive; tel: (512) 985-8393; fax: (512) 985-8393. Pool, spa, breakfast included. $
Embassy Suites, 4337 S. Padre Island Dr, tel: (512) 851-1310 or (800) 362-2779; fax: (512) 851-1310. Restaurant, pool, spa, workout facilities. $$
Holiday Inn Emerald Beach, 1102 South Shoreline Blvd, 78401; tel: (512) 883-5731; fax: (512) 883-9079. Restaurant, pool, spa, nearby golf. 368 units. $$
Howard Johnson Hotel, 300 N. Shoreline, 78401; tel: (512) 883-5111 or (800)883-5119; fax: (512) 883-7702. Restaurant, tennis, pool, golf nearby. 173 units. $
Koronado Motel, 3615 Timon Blvd, 78402; tel: (512) 883-4411 or (800) 883-0424. 40 units. Private balconies, one block from bay, walking distance to Texas State Aquarium. $
Best Western Corpus Christi Inn, 2838 S. Padre Island Dr; tel: (512) 854-0005 or (800) 445-9463; fax: (512) 854-2642. 60 units. Restaurant, pool. $
Villa del Sol, 3938 Surfside Blvd, 78402; tel: (512) 883-9748 or (800) 242-3291; fax: (512) 883-7537. 250 units. Whirlpool/spa, kitchenettes. On the beach. $$

Dallas

Aristocrat Hotel, 1933 Main Street, 75201; tel: (214) 741-7700 or (800) 231-4235; fax: (214) 939-3639. 172 units. $$.
Courtyard By Marriott, Love Field, 2383 Stemons Trail, 75220; tel: (214) 352-7676 or (800) 321-2211; fax: (214) 352-4914. 146 units. Whirlpool/spa. $
Embassy Suites, Love Field, 3880 West Northwest Hwy, 75220; tel: (214) 357-4500 or (800) 362-2779; fax: (214) 357-0683. 248 units. $$
Embassy Suites Market Center, 2727 Stemmons Freeway, 75207; tel: (214) 630-5332 or (800) EMBASSY; fax: (214) 631-3025. 244 units. Pool, laundromat. $$$

Fairmont Hotel, 1717 North Akard, 75201; tel: (214) 720-2020 or (800) 527-4727; fax: (214) 720-5269. 600 units. In Arts District. Pool. $$–$$$

Four Seasons Hotel and Resort, 4150 North MacArthur Boulevard, 75038; tel: (972) 717-0700 or 800/332-3442; fax: (972) 717-2550. Raquetball, squash, pools, sauna. $$$

The Grand Kempinski, 15201 Dallas Parkway, 75248; tel: (972) 386-6000 or (800) 426-3135; fax: (214) 701-0342. 527 units. Whirlpool/spa. $$$

Harvey Hotel Dallas, 7815 LBJ Freeway, 75240; tel: (972) 960-7000 or (800) 922-9222; fax: (214) 788-4227. 313 units. Whirlpool/spa, work-out facilities, disabled facilities. $

Wyndham Anatole Hotel, 2201 Stemmons Freeway, 75240; tel: (214) 748-1200 or (800) 996-3426; fax: (214) 761-7242. 1620 units. $$

The Mansion on Turtle Creek, 2821 Turtle Creek Boulevard, 75219; tel: (214) 559-2100 or (800) 527-5432; fax: (214) 528-4187. 141 units. Ranked among world's finest hotels. Famous restaurant. $$$

Quality Hotel Market Center, 2015 Market Center Blvd, 75207; tel: (214) 741-7481 or (800) 421-2555; fax: (214) 747-6191. 224 units. Interpreters, currency exchange, work-out facilities. $

Sheraton Grand at DFW, 4440 W. John Carpenter Fwy, 75261; tel: (972) 929-8400 or (800) 345-5251; fax: (214) 929-0983. Interpreters, whirlpool/spa, work-out facilities. $$

Stoneleigh Hotel & Suites, 2927 Maple, 75201; tel: (214) 871-7111 or (800) 255-9299; fax: (214) 871-9379. 150 units. Interpreters on premises, pool, restaurant. $$$

El Paso & Juárez

Camino Real, 101 S. El Paso, 79901; tel: (915) 534-3000 or (800) 769-4300; fax: (915) 534-3024. 360 units. Historic, highly-rated, health club. $$

Best Western Airport Inn, 7144 Gateway E, 79915; tel: (915) 779-7700; fax: (915) 772-1920. 175 units. Airport shuttle. $

Holiday Inn Park Place, 325 N. Kansas, 79901; tel: (915) 533-8241 or (800) 465-4329; fax: (915) 544-9979. 119 units. Restaurant, pool, free coffee, nearby golf. $

Fiesta Real, ProNaF, Juárez; tel: 1-32-30047. Moderate; 150 units.

Hotel El Presidente, On Avenida Lincoln, Juárez; tel: 1-32-30047. Moderate; 154 units.

Plaza Juárez, Lincoln at Coyoacan, Juárez; tel: 1-32-31310. Moderate; 172 units.

Fort Davis

Limpia Hotel, On the town square, 79734; tel: (915) 426-3237 or (800) 662-5517; fax: (915) 426-2113. 33 units. Restaurant, cocktail lounge.

Old Texas Inn, Main Street, 79734; tel: (915) 426-3118; fax: (915) 426-3879. 6 units. $

Prude Ranch, Highway 118 North, 79734; tel: (915) 426-3202; fax: (915) 426-3502. Old cattle ranch, now dude ranch/mountain resort. Cabins and motel units. Tennis courts. Hot tub. $

Stone Village Motel, Main Street, 79734; tel: (915) 426-3941; fax: (915) 426-3941. 12 units. Close to Fort Davis National Historic Site. Great value. $

Fort Worth

Days Inn Fort Worth West, 8500 I-30 West at Las Vegas Trail, 76108; tel: (817) 246-4961 or (800) 325-2525; fax: (817) 246-0368. Disabled facilities. $

Ramada Downtown, 1701 Commerce St, 76102; tel: (817) 335-7000 or (800) 272-6232; fax: (817) 335-3333. 430 rooms, some with coffeemakers, microwaves, refrigerator. $

Green Oaks Inn, 6901 W. Freeway, 76116; tel: (817) 738-7311 or (800) 433-2174; fax: (817) 377-1308. 284 units. Tennis courts. $

La Quinta Inn West #451, 7888 I-30 West, 76108; tel: (817) 246-5511 or (800) 531-5900; fax: (817) 246-8870. Kitchenettes. 106 units. $

Stockyards Hotel, 109 E. Exchange Ave, 76106; tel: (817) 625-6427 or (800) 423-8471; fax: (817) 624-2571. Near Meacham Field. 52 units. Restaurant, cocktail lounge. $$

Worthington Hotel, 200 Main St, 76102; tel: (817) 870-1000 or (800) 433-5677; fax: (817) 338-9176. Historic downtown hotel, sauna, tennis courts. 504 units. $$$

Fredericksburg

Dietzel Motel, 909 W. Main (Jnct 290W & 87N), 78624; tel: (210) 997-3330. 20 units. $

Gästhaus Schmidt Reservation Service, 231 W. Main, 78624; tel: (210) 997-4712. 114 rooms, all with private bath. They also list 90 different properties for bookings in country homes or in town. $–$$

Galveston

Gaido's Seaside Inn, 3828 Seawall, 77550; tel: (409) 762-9625 or (800) 525-0064; fax: (409) 762-4825. 105 units. Seaview. Tiered flower garden. $

Hilltop Motel, 8828 Seawall Blvd, 77551; tel: (409) 744-4423. 40 units. Gulf view rooms have private balconies. $

Hotel Galvez, 2024 Seawall Blvd, 77550; tel: (409) 765-7721 or (800) 392-4285; fax: (409) 765-5623. 228 units. Historic seafront hotel. Sauna, whirlpool. $$

Day's Inn Galveston, 6107 Broadway, 77551; tel: (409) 740-2491 or (800) 325-2525; fax: (409) 740-2491. 88 units. $

Econo Lodge, 2825 61st St, 77551; tel: (409) 744-7133; fax: (409) 744-7133. 96 units

Harbor View Inn, 928 Ferry Road, 77550; tel: (409) 762-3311; fax: (409) 762-6624. 49 rooms. Close to ferry. $

The Tremont House, 2300 Ship's Mechanic Row, 77550; tel: (409) 763-0300 or (800) 874-2300; fax: (409) 763-1539. 117 units. Historic, near the Strand. $$

Houston

Allen Park Inn, 2121 Allen Parkway, 77019; tel: (713) 521-9321 or (800) 231-6321; fax: (713) 521-9321. 242 units. Interpreters, workout facilities, whirlpool/spa. $

Comfort Inn Brookhollow, 4760 Sherwood Lane, 77092; tel: (713) 686-5525; fax: (713) 686-5365. 46 units. Interpreters, whirlpool/spa. $

Courtyard by Marriott, 3131 West Loop South, 77027; tel: (713) 961-1640 or (800) 321-2211; fax: (713) 439-0989. Whirlpool/spa, workout facilities. $

Days Inn Astrodome, 8686 Kirby Drive, 77054; tel: (713) 748-3221 or (800) 552-0942; fax: (713) 796-2279. 129 units. $

Days Inn Cavalcade, 100 W. Cavalcade, 77009; tel: (713) 869-7121 or (800) 325-2525; fax: (713) 868 5167. 129 units. $

Doubletree at Allen Center, 400 Dallas, 77002; tel: (713) 759-0202 or (800) 772-7666; fax: (713) 759-1166. 341 units. Jogging trails. $$$

Doubletree Hotel at Houston Intercontinental Airport, 15747 John F. Kennedy Blvd, 77032; tel: (713) 442-8000 or (800) 810-8001; fax: (713) 590-8461. 309 units. $$

Fairfield Inn Houston Near the Galleria, 3131 West Loop South, 77027; tel: (713) 961-1690 or (800) 228-2800; fax: (713) 627-8434. 107 units. Whirlpool/spa. $

Grant Motor Inn, 8200 South Main, 77025; tel: (713) 668-8000 or (800) 255-8904; fax: (713) 668-7777. 64 units. Interpreters, spa, reasonable. $

Hobby Airport Hilton, 8181 Airport Blvd, 77061; tel: (713) 645-3000 or (800) 695-2740; fax: (713) 645-2251. 305 units. $$

Hampton Inn I-10, 828 Mercury Dr., 77013; tel: (713) 673-4200 or (800) 426-7866; fax: (713) 674-6913. 89 units. $

Houston Airport Marriott, 18700 Kennedy Blvd, 77032; tel: (713) 443-2310 or (800) 228-9290; fax: (713) 443-5294. 566 units. $

The Houstonian Hotel, 111 North Post Oak Lane, 77024; tel: (713) 680-2626 or (800) 231-2759; fax: (713) 680-2992. 291 units. Tennis, spa. $$$

Hyatt Regency Houston, 1200 Louisiana Street, 77002; tel: (713) 654-1234 or (800) 233-1234; fax: (713) 658-8606. 963 units, downtown location. $$$

La Quinta Inn – 12 locations: **Central, Gessner, Brookhollow, East, Cy Fair, Astrodome, Beltway 8, Greenway Plaza, Intercontinental Airport, West, Wirt, Hobby**; tel: (800) 531-5900. $

Marriott Westloop by the Galleria, 1750 Westloop South, 77027; tel: (713) 960-0111 or (800) 813-3982; fax: (713) 965-9562. 302 units. $

Ritz–Carlton, 1919 Briar Oaks Lane, 77027; tel: (713) 840-7600 or (800) 241-3333; fax: (713) 840-0616. 232 units. Interpreters. $$$

The Sheraton Grand by Houston Galleria, 2525 West Loop South, 77027; tel: (713) 961-3000; fax: (713) 965-0186. 321 units. Interpreters, disabled facilities, whirlpool/spa. $$

The Westin Oaks, 5011 Westheimer, 77056; tel: (713) 960-8100 or (800) 228-3000; fax: (713) 960-6554. 406 units. $$$

Wyndham Warwick, 5701 Main St, 77005; tel: (713) 526-1991 or (800) 996-3426.; fax: (713) 639-4545. 308 units. Disabled facilities, currency exchange. $$

Jefferson

Hotel Jefferson, 124 West Austin St, 75657; tel: (903) 665-2631; fax: (903) 665-2593. 22 units. In historic downtown district. $

Laredo

La Hacienda Motor Hotel, 4914 San Bernardo, 78041; tel: (210) 722-2441; fax: (210) 725-4532. 100 units. Lounge has live *tejano* music Tuesday–Sunday nights. $

Loma Alta Motel, 3915 San Bernardo Ave, 78041; tel: (210) 726-1628; fax: (210) 724-4339. 73 units. Reasonable. Disabled facilities. $

Family Gardens Inn, 5830 San Bernardo, 78041; tel: (210) 723-5300 or (800) 292-4053; fax: (210) 791-8842. 193 units. $

La Posada Hotel, 1000 Zaragoza, 78040; tel: (512) 722-1701; fax: (210) 722-4758. Classic Mexican colonial style. 275 units. Walking distance to international bridge to Nuevo Laredo. $$

Lubbock

Apple Inn, 310 Ave Q, 79415; tel: (806) 763-2861 or (800) 524-3788; fax: (806) 747-1020. 58 units. $

Days Inn Lubbock, 2401 4th St, 79415; tel: (806) 747-7111 or (800) 325-2525; fax: (806) 747-9749. 90 units. $

Lubbock Inn, 3901 19th St, 79408; tel: (806) 792-5181 or (800) 545-8226; fax: (906) 792-1319. 146 units. Cocktail lounge. $

Marathon

The Gage Hotel, Hwy 90 West at Avenue C, Marathon, 79842; tel: (915) 386-4205 or (800) 884-4243; fax: (915) 386-4510. 37 units divided between historic hotel and a newer adobe-style motel across the street. Mexican colonial furnishings and artifacts. Restaurant specializes in Southwestern and Mexican cuisine. $ (hotel); $$ (motel).

Rio-Grande Valley: Harlingen, McAllen & Brownsville

Sun Valley Motor Hotel, 1900 S. 77 Sunshine Strip, Harlingen, 78550; tel: (210) 423-7222; fax: (210) 428-6394. 86 units. $

Motel 6, 224 South US Expressway 77, Harlingen, 78550; tel: (210) 421-4200; fax: (210) 412-8159; 81 units; disabled facilities. $

Holiday Inn Ft. Brown, 1900 East Elizabeth, Brownsville, 78520; tel: (512) 546-2201; fax: (210) 546-0756. Walking distance to Matamoros, interpreters. $

Flamingo Motel, 1741 Central Blvd, Brownsville, 78520; tel: (210) 546-2478; fax: (210) 982-1806. $

La Quinta Inn #705, 55 Sam Perl Blvd, Brownsville, 78520; tel: (210) 546-0381 or (800) 531-5900; fax: (210) 541-5313. Continental breakfast. $

Rancho Viejo Resort and Country Club, US Highway 83 and Rancho Viejo Drive , Brownsville, 78575; tel: (210) 350-4000; fax: (210) 350-9681. Expensive, complete resort. $$$

Casa de Palmas Doubletree Hotel, 101 Main St, McAllen, 78501; tel: (210) 631-1101 or (800) 274-1102; fax: (210) 631-7934. Spanish colonial style inn, 158 units, next door to Mexican consulate. $

Microtel, 700 W. Expressway 83, McAllen, 78501; tel: (210) 687-3700; fax: (210) 630-2727. 102 units, some with microwave and refrigerator. $

Nacogdoches

Econo Lodge, 2020 NW Stallings, 75964; tel: (409) 569-0880; fax: (409) 560-0303. $

Pine Creek Lodge, Rt. 3, Box 1238, 75961; tel: (409) 560-6282; fax: (409) 560-1675. Located in the piney woods on a flowing creek, VCR's in each room, spa. $

New Braunfels

Faust Hotel, 240 S. Seguin, 78130; tel: (210) 620-1530; fax: (210) 620-1530. 62 units, historic landmark, newly renovated. $

Gruene Mansion Inn, 1275 Gruene Road, 78130; tel: (210) 629-2641; fax: (210) 629-7375. Former cotton plantation with 25 rooms scattered in restored barns/sheds with antiques, overlooks Guadalupe River, oldest dancehall in TX next door. $$$

Prince Solms Inn Circa 1898, 295 East San Antonio, 78130; tel: (512) 625-9169 or (800) 625-9169; fax: (210) 625-9169. 10 units furnished with antiques. Fine restaurant, enchanting garden. $$

Schlitterbahn at the Bahn, 305 W. Austin, 78130; tel: (210) 625-2351; fax: (210) 620-4873. 130 units located on the grounds of the 65-acre Schlitterbahn Waterpark. $

Palacios

The Luther Hotel, 408 South Bay Blvd, 77465; tel: (512) 972-2312; fax: (512) 972-3425. Historic antebellum hotel; great views of the bay. $

Port Isabel

Queen Isabel Inn, 300 Garcia St, Port Isabel, 78578; tel: (210) 943-1468 or (800) 943-1468; fax: (210) 943-1468. 7 units, private and quiet. Fully furnished kitchens. Beach gear provided, fishing pier. $$–$$$

Rockport

Ocean View Motel, 1131 South Water St, 78382; tel: (512) 729-3326. 15 units. Fishing pier and picnic area. $

Hunt's Court Motel, 901 South Water St, 78382; tel: (512) 729-2273. 25 units, kitchenettes, waterfront with fishing pier. $

San Antonio

Bullis House Inn/San Antonio, 621 Pierce St, 78208; tel: (210) 233-9426; fax: (210) 299-1479. 7 units. Spacious, fireplaces, VCR, gardens, full kitchen adjacent, near downtown, good value. $

Day's Inn Alamo-Riverwalk, 902 Houston St, 78205; tel: (210) 227-6233 or (800) 325-2525; fax: (210) 228-0901. 81 units. 1 block from Riverwalk and Alamo. $

Executive Guest House Hotel, 12828 US 281 North , 78216; tel: (210) 494-7600 or (800) 362-8700; fax: (210) 545-4314. 124 units. Interpreters, pool/whirlpool/spa, workout facilities; coffeemakers and refrigerators in all rooms. $$

Fairmount Hotel, 401 South Alamo, 78205; tel: (210) 224-8800 or (800) 642-3363; fax: (210) 224-2767. 37 units. Famous restaurant, Polo's, on premises. $$$

La Mansion del Rio, 112 College, 78205; tel: (210) 225-2581 or (800) 531-7208; fax: (210) 226-0389. 337 units. Spanish mission architecture, interpreters, on quiet portion of Paseo del Rio. $$$

Lexington Hotel Suites, 4934 NW Loop 410, 78229; tel: (210) 680-3351 or (800) 267-3605; fax: (210) 228-0663. 207 units. $

Marriott Riverwalk, 711 East Riverwalk, 78205; tel: (512) 223-1000 or (800) 648-4462; fax: (210) 228-0548. Heated pool, saunas. 500 units. Expensive; 500 units. $$$

The Historic Menger Hotel, 204 Alamo Plaza, 78205; tel: (210) 223-4361 or (800) 345-9285; fax: (210) 270-0761. 320 units. Next to the Alamo, spa/fitness center. $$

Hilton Palacio del Rio, 200 South Alamo, 78205; tel: (210) 222-1400 or (800) 445-8667; fax: (210) 270-0761. 481 units. On the riverwalk. Interpreters, currency exchange, work-out facilities. $$$

Radisson Downtown Market Square, 502 W. Durango, 78207; tel: (210) 224-7155 or (800) 288-3927; fax: (210) 734-2451. 250 units. Whirlpool/spa, work-out facilities. $$

Super 8 Motel, 3617 North Pan Am Expressway, 78219; tel: (210) 224-2092 or (800) 800-8000; fax: (210) 637-1033. 93 units. $

Fiesta Texas Super 8 Motel, 5319 Casa Bella & I-10, 78249; tel: (210) 696-6916 or (800) 800-8000; fax: (210) 696-4321. 71 units. $

Sheraton Gunter Hotel 205 East Houston, 78205; tel: (210) 227-3241 or (800) 222-4276; fax: (210) 227-3299. 322 units. Historic. $$–$$$

South Padre Island

Motel 6, 4013 Padre Blvd, South Padre Island, 78597; tel: (210) 761-7911; fax: (210) 761-6339. 52 units. $

Radisson Resort South Padre Island, 300 Garcia St, Port Isabel, 78578; tel: (210) 761-6511 or (800) 333-3333; fax: (210) 761-1602. 185 units, lots of amenities. $$

Van Horn

Best Western Inn of Van Horn, 1705 W. Broadway, 79855; tel: (915) 283-2410 or (800) 367-7589; fax: (915) 283-2143. Restaurant, pool, cocktail lounge. $

Waco

Lexington Inn, 115 Jack Kultgen, 76706; tel: (817) 755-8612 or (800) 537-8483; fax: (817) 755-8612. Near Baylor Univ. Work-out facilities, continental breakfast. $

La Quinta Inn #2511, 1110 S. 9th St, 76706; tel: (817) 752-9741 or (800) 531-5900; fax: (817) 757-1600. $

Waco Hilton, 113 S. University Parks Dr, 76701; tel: (817) 754-8484 or (800) 445-8667; fax: (817) 752-2214. Tennis, whirlpool. $

Bed & Breakfast

Bed and breakfast rates in Texas are very reasonable for the most part. In historic districts or towns, there is not much of a distinction made between "bed and breakfast" and "historic inn", as they are much the same. For information and bookings at many of Texas' B&Bs (but not all), you can contact Bed & Breakfast Texas Style, 4224 W. Red Bird Lane, Dallas, 75237; tel: (800) 899-4538 or (214) 298-8586).

Abilene

Bolin's Prairie House B&B, 508 Mulberry, Abilene, 79601; tel: (800) 673-5855. Historic downtown home, 4 rooms decorated with antiques, full breakfast. $

Amarillo

Country Home B&B, Rt. 1, Box 447, Canyon, 79015; tel: (806) 655-7636 or (800) 664-7636. On 200 acre ranch 20 miles south near Palo Duro Canyon. 60-foot (18-meter) porch, swing. 4 rooms. Full breakfast; featured in Recommended Country Inns. $

Austin

Woodburn House B&B, 4401 Ave D, 78751; tel: (512) 458-4335; fax: (512) 458-4335. Charming Victorian house with wrap-around porches, gourmet breakfasts, fax/computer available. $

Brenham

Ant Street Inn, 107 W. Commerce, 77833; tel: (409) 836-7393; fax: (409) 836-7595. Elegant B&B with stylish, high-ceiling rooms, canopy beds. $$

Dallas

The Rose B&B, 4224 W. Red Bird Lane, 75237; tel: (972) 298-8586; fax: (214) 298-7118. 4 units. Historic, fine antiques. $

Fort Davis

Veranda Country Inn B&B, 210 Court Avenue, 79734; tel: (915) 426-2233; fax: (415) 426-3844. Historic, country adobe architecture. 9 rooms; antique furnishings. Full breakfast. $$

Fredericksburg

Hill Country town of more than 150 B&B-type lodgings.
Fredericksburg Bed &Brew, 243 E. Main, 78624; tel: (210) 997-1646; fax: (210) 997-8026. B&B with Brewpub, biergarten and restaurant. 12 rooms with private bath. Beer samples or credit for breakfast. $

Galveston

Madame Dyer's B&B, 1720 Post Office St, 77550; tel: (409) 765-5692. 3 rooms with private bath, full breakfast. Restored 1889 home, period charm, romantic. $$

Granbury

Dabney House B&B, 106 South Jones, 76048; tel: (817) 579-1260; fax: (817) 579-0426. 4 rooms with private bath, full breakfast. $
Oak Tree Farm B&B, 6415 Carmichael Court, 76049; tel: (800) 326-5595. 5 rooms with private baths. Gourmet breakfast. Country setting, walking trails. $

Houston

McLachlan Farm B&B, 24907 Hardy Road, Spring, 77383; tel: (713) 350-2400 or (800) 382-3988; fax: (713) 355- 3955. 4 rooms. Country seclusion, 1911 farmhouse, nature trails. $
Sara's Bed & Breakfast Inn, 941 Heights Blvd, 77008; tel: (713) 868-1130 or (800) 593-1130; fax: (713) 868.1160. 14 rooms in 1898 Victorian Mansion; VCRs and video library. $–$$

Jefferson

Line Street Guest House, 1105 South Line St, 75657; tel: (903) 665-2592; fax: (903) 665-2593. 4 units. Huge porches, well-kept grounds. $
Pride House, 409 Broadway, 75657; tel: (903) 665-2675 or (800) 894-3526; fax: (903) 665-3901. 10 units. Stately Victorian mansion with princely interiors, luxury. $–$$

New Braunfels

Historic Kuebler-Waldrip Haus & Danville School B&B, 1620 Hueco Springs Loop, 78132; tel: (210) 625-8372, (800) 299-8372. On a ranch, 7 units, full country recreation, close to water recreation. $$–$$$
Karbach Haus B&B, 487 W. San Antonio St, 78130; tel: (210) 625-2131 or (800) 972-5941; fax: (210) 629-0303. 4 spacious rooms with VCR. German-style breakfast. Spa, gardens. $$

Palacios

Moonlight Bay B&B, 506 S. Bay Blvd, 77465; tel: (512) 972-2232; fax: (512) 972-2232. 4 units with indoor/outdoor verandas, bay views, casual elegance, gourmet breakfast. $

Rockport

Blue Heron Inn B&B, 801 Patton St, 78382; tel: (512) 729-7526; fax: (512) 790-9273. Historic home, garden patio for birding, water views, bicycles to use. $

Round Top

Ledbetter B&B, PO Box 212, Ledbetter, 78946; tel: (409) 249-3066 or (800) 240-3066; fax: (409) 249-3330. 22 units. Walking paths, farm animals, volleyball. $$

San Antonio

Beckman Inn & Carriage House, 222 E. Guenther St, 78204; tel: (210) 229-1449 or (800) 945-1449; fax: (210) 229-1061. Full gourmet breakfast. Victorian home in King William's Historic District. Riverwalk/Alamo walking distance. $$
Oge House on the Riverwalk, 209 Washington St, 78204; tel: (210) 223-2353 or (800) 242-2770, fax: (210) 226-5812. An 1857 Antebellum mansion furnished with antiques $$$

Yellow Rose B&B, 229 Madison, 78204; tel: (210) 229-9903 or (800) 950-9903; fax: (210) 229-9903. 5 units with antiques. In King Williams Historic District, walking distance to downtown and riverwalk. $$

San Marcos

Lonesome Dove B&B, 407 Oakwood Loop, 78666; tel: (512) 392-2921; fax: (512) 392-1495. 4 cottages in country setting with full kitchens. Hayrides with campfire dinner and live entertainment every Saturday. $
Crystal River Inn, 326 W. Hopkins, 78666; tel: (512) 396-3739; fax: (512) 353-3248. 12 rooms, gourmet breakfast, antiques, courtyard and rose garden. $

South Padre Island

Moonraker B&B, 107 E. Mariso, South Padre Island, 78597; tel: (210) 761-2206. 3 units 1/2 block from beach, fishing, close to restaurants. $$

Uvalde

Casa de Leona B&B, 1149 Perasall Hwy 140, 78802; tel: (210) 278-8550; fax: (210) 278-8550. Fishing, fountains, antiques, luxurious. $$

Wimberley

Stars at Night B&B, 400 Eagles Nest Dr., Wimberley, 78676; tel: (512) 847-1292. 3 units with hillside view of sunsets from private decks with full kitchens, fireplaces, rising beds. $
Rancho Cama B&B, 2595 Flite Acres Road, 78676. 3 units. Wildlife, river access. $
Homestead B&B, Ranch Road 12 at County Road 316, Wimberley, 78676; tel: (512) 847-8788 or (800) 918-8788. Eight cottages, on swimmable Cypress Creek, decks, hot tub, fireplaces, catered meals. $

Galveston Rentals and Management, 201 Seawall Blvd, Galveston 77550; tel: (409) 765-8600 or (800) 742-5837.
Sand 'N Sea Properties, PO Box 5165, Galveston 77554; tel: (409) 737-2556.
Island Services, tel: (210) 761-2649 or (800) 426-6530.
Padre Rentals, tel: (210) 761-5100 or (800) 292-7518.

Campgrounds

There are more than 200 state-, federal- or private-owned campgrounds throughout Texas.

For information on camping in the national parks, recreation areas, forests and the 20-plus lakes administered by the US Army Corps of Engineers, contact the National Park Service, Southwest Region, PO Box 728, Sante Fe, New Mexico 87504.

Around 70 parks and recreation areas managed by the state permit camping. The Central Reservations number, (512) 389-8900, can be used to make reservations anywhere in the state park system. A handy booklet called *Texas Public Campgrounds* may be obtained free of charge from the Travel and Information Division, State Department of Highways and Transportation, PO Box 5064, Austin, 78763. *RV and Camping Guide to Texas*, the best list of private campgrounds – which comprise about half the total number of campgrounds in Texas – is available free of charge from the Texas Association of Campground Owners, PO Box 14055, Austin 78761; tel: (512) 459-8226. In addition the Texas KOA Kampground Owners Association, 6805 Guadalupe Street, Austin 78752, can provide a list of 18 member campgrounds around the state.

Eating Out

What to Eat

Don't plan on dieting while in Texas: Texans love their food, and a visit here wouldn't be complete without sampling a good portion of it. Tex-Mex food has become synonymous with the state (*see* **Tex-Mex Food**, p. 145), and it's not *all* fire-breathing hot, so even the most wary should give it a try. Another Texas staple is the barbecue, usually huge chunks of beef (sometimes pork and sausage) cooked slowly for hours over special wood such as hickory or mesquite to add the distinctive flavor. Among the celebrated barbecue joints is The Salt Lick at Driftwood, tel: (512) 858-4959, 13 miles (20 km) west of Austin in the Hill Country. The state dish of Texas is chili, and you'll find it in abundance throughout the state. On average, some 15 chili competitions are held each month somewhere in Texas. "Runner-up" to state dish must surely have been chicken-fried steak, an inexpensive steak covered with batter and fried, usually served with gravy and found on most Texas menus. And one musn't forget to try some pecan pie – after all, the pecan tree is the Texas state tree.

Generally, in the big cities you can find almost every type of restaurant, from Thai and nouvelle cuisine, through traditional Texas dishes, to the usual run of nationwide fast-food chains. In the small towns, you've basically got two choices: the local Dairy Queen or some good ol', down-home cookin', "like mama used to make". Experiment and enjoy.

Where to Eat
Austin

Amaya's Taco Village, 5405 N. I-35, Capital Plaza, tel: (512) 458-2531. Mexican, $
Chez Nous, 510 Neches, tel: (512) 473-2413. French, $$
Chuy's, 1728 Barton Spring Rd, tel: (512) 474-4452. Mexican, $
Cisco's Bakery and Coffee Shop, 1511 East 6th Street, tel: (512) 478-2420, Mexican, $
The County Line on the Hill, 6500 West Bee Caves Road, tel: (512) 327-1742, Classic, acclaimed Texas-pit BBQ, $$
East Side Cafe, 2113 Manor Rd, tel: (512) 476-5858, Continental, vegetarian, patio dining, $$
Empanada Parlor, 500 E. 4th St, tel: (512) 480-8902, Vegetarian, pastries, desserts, $

Fonda San Miguel, 2330 West North Loop, tel: (512) 459-4121, Colonial, indoor patio, good ambience, gourmet, interior Mexican, $$$
The Granite Cafe, 2905 San Gabriel St, tel: (512) 472-6483, Southwestern, gourmet, music, $$
Green Mesquite Barbeque & More, 1400 Barton Springs Rd, tel: (512) 479-0485, Good food, live music, $
Hudson's on the Bend, 3509 Ranch Road, 620 (1.5 miles/2 km SW of Mansfield Dam), tel: (512) 266-1369, Classy, continental cuisine/game $$$
Landry's, 600 E. Riverside Dr., tel: (512) 444-1010, Riverfront patio, view of downtown, Passable seafood, $$
Manuel's, 310 Congress, tel: (512) 472-7555, jazz brunch Sunday, Mexican, $$
México Tipico, 1707 East 6th, tel: (512) 472-3222, Mexican, $
Mother's Cafe & Garden, 4215 Duval St, tel: (512) 451-3994, Enclosed garden patio, vegetarian, popular with locals, $
The Old Pecan Street Cafe, 310 E. 6th St, tel: (512) 478-2491, Charming, historic cafe with full menu, $$
Pearl's Oyster Bar, 9033 Research Blvd at Burnet, tel: (512) 339-7444, New Orleans style cuisine, nightly music, $$
El Rinconcito Cucina, 1014 N. Lamar Blvd, tel: (512) 476-5277, South American/Mexican, gourmet, $
Sea Dragon, 8776B Research Blvd, tel: (512) 451-5051, $
Serrano's Cafe & Cantina, 1111 Red River (Symphony Square), tel: (512) 322-9080, Grilled Tex-Mex, patio dining, harpist, $$
Shanghai River, 2700 W. Anderson Lane, tel: (512) 458-9598, Bountiful Chinese buffet, $
Shoreline Grill San Jacinto Center, 98 San Jacinto Blvd, tel: (512) 477-3300, Top-rated steak/seafood restaurant at the Four Seasons Hotel, $$$
Taj Palace, 6700 Middle Fiskville Rd, tel: (512) 452-9959, Close to airport, Indian cuisine, Indian lunch buffet $, ethnic Indian dining $$
Threadgill's, 6416 North Lamar, tel: (512) 451-5440, Texas roadhouse café, Wednesday evening live music, Southern cuisine, Cajun, vegetarian, $
Z-Tejas Grill, 1110 West 6th, tel: (512) 478-5355, Southwestern creative cuisine, $$

La Zona Rosa, 612 West 4th Street, tel: (512) 482-0662, Classic Texas icehouse, cantina, music hall, Mexican, $

Dallas

Alessio's, 4117 Lomo Alto, tel: (214) 521-3585, Italian, $$$

L'Ancestral, 4514 Travis, tel: (214) 528-1081, Beautifully decorated "French country inn"; classic French cuisine, try the escargots and puff pastries, $$$

Baby Doe's Matchless Mine, 3305 Harry Hines Blvd, tel: (214) 871-7310, Multi-level restaurant with steaks/seafood, $$

The Blind Lemon Restaurant, 2805 Main St, tel: (214) 939-0202, Neighborhood hangout, pasta, pizza, burgers, $

Bob's Steak and Chop House, 4300 Lemmon Avenue, tel: (214) 528-9446, Upscale steakhouse, oversized portions, $$$

Bombay Cricket Club, 258 Maple Ave, tel: (214) 871-1333, Northern Indian cuisine, $$$

Cafe Capri, 15107 Addison Rd at Beltline, tel: (214) 960-8686, Stylish atmosphere, excellent seafood, live harpist, $$$

Café Pacific, 24 Highland Park Village, tel: (214) 526-1170, Seafood, $$$

Cappellini's, 3820 Belt Line (suburb of Addison), tel: (214) 488-9494, Area favorite old-world Italian, $$$

Casa Dominguez, 2408 Cedar Springs at Fairmont, tel: (214) 871-9787, Long tradition since 1963, now one of three of this family's establishments, $$

Cenaduria Mexicana, 2013 Greenville Avenue, tel: (214) 827-1494, Original, home-made tasty Mexican, $

Cowboy's, 7331 Gaston, tel: (214) 321-0320, Texas' largest dance floor; pool tables, BBQ, $$

Dakota's, 600 N. Akard, tel: (214) 740-4001, Nationally rated: seafood, wild game, $$$

Del Frisco's Double Eagle Steakhouse, 5251 Spring Valley, tel: (214) 490-9000, Fine steaks, $$$

Dick's Last Resort, Record at Ross, tel: (214) 747-0001, Buckets of ribs, chicken, catfish, crab legs; nightly live music, gospel music Sunday, $

Joe's Crab Shack, 3855 Beltline, tel: (214) 247-1010, Lively scene and crabs, crabs, crabs, $$

Korea House Restaurant, 2598 Royal Lane, tel: (214) 243-0434, Try the tasty yooh hae (steak tartare), $$$

Lone Star Oyster Bar, 3707 Greenville, tel: (214) 827-3013, Cozy pub, topless oysters and cold beer, cheap! $

The Mansion on Turtle Creek, 2821 Turtle Creek Blvd, tel: (214) 526-2121, award-winning American nouvelle, $$$

Martin's Wine Bistro, 3020 Greenville Avenue, tel: (214) 826-0940, Romantic dining, French cuisine, fine wine selections, $$$

Momo's Pasta, 3312 Knox, tel: (214) 521-3009, Good neighborhood Italian restaurant, $

Moon Under Water, 2513 Main St, tel: (214) 741-2537, Varied menu, piano lounge; also live music blues to zydeco, $$

Queen of Sheba, 3527 McKinney at Lemmon, tel: (214) 521-0491, Exotic Ethiopian, $$

Royal Tokyo, 7525 Greenville Avenue, tel: (214) 368-3304, Japanese, $$$

Soul Embassy Cafe, 3840 W. Northwest Hwy., tel: (214) 357-SOUL, Typical southern fare, Sunday "gospel brunch", nightly jazz, $

Stoneleigh P, 2926 Maple Ave, tel: (214) 871-2346, Burgers, snacks, jukebox (large selection), $

Tolbert's Texas Chili Parlor, 350 N. St Paul, tel: (214) 953-1353, Texas regional/hamburgers, $

Trail Dust Steak House, 10841 Composite Drive, tel: (214) 357-3862, Live country music every night, $$

Uncle Julio's, 4125 Lemmon Ave, tel: (214) 520-6620, Local papers call this the best Tex-Mex in town, $

Watel's, 1923 McKinney, tel: (214) 720-0323, French bistro, $$

Galveston

Christie's Beachcomber, 401 Broadway, tel: (409) 762-8648, Popular beach spot, homestyle cooking, buffet, $$

Clary's, 8509 Teichman Rd, off I-45, tel: (409) 740-0771, Longtime family-owned seafood haven, $$$

Fisherman's Wharf, Pier 22 adj. the Elissa, tel: (409) 765-5708, Patio dining overlooking the port, $$

Miller's Landing, Seawall & 19th St, tel: (409) 763-8777, Overlooks the Gulf, seafood, steaks, $$

Ocean Grill Restaurant, 2227 Seawall, tel: (409) 762-7100, On the water, mesquite grilled seafood, $$

The Original Mexican Cafe, 1401 Market, tel: (409) 762-6001, Dispensing Mexican food for 80 years, $

Houston

Annemarie's Old Heidelberg, 1810 Fountainview, tel: (713) 781-3581, German cuisine, piano bar, dancing, romantic, $$$

Athens Bar & Grill, 8037 Clinton Dr., tel: (713) 675-1644, Moussaka, souvlaki, etc., $

Baci-Italian Ristorante, 2443 University, tel: (713) 524-1266, Replicas of famous paintings line the walls of this pasta and seafood place, $$

Barry's Pizza & Italian Diner, 6003 Richmond Avenue, tel: (713) 266-8692, $

Benihana of Tokyo, 9707 Westheimer, tel: (713) 789-4962, also at 3218 Louisiana, tel: (713) 659-8231, $$$

Billy Blues Bar & Grill, 6025 Richmond near Fountainview, tel: (713) 266-9294, 5-story saxophone as landmark, BBQ & live blues, $$

The Bombay Palace, 3901 Westheimer, tel: (713) 960-8472, One of the renowned worldwide chain, $$

The Brownstone, 2736 Virginia, tel: (713) 520-5666, Elegant surroundings, opulently decorated by owner/interior designer, top-notch, $$$

Dave and Buster's, 6010 Richmond Ave, tel: (713) 952-2233, Poolhall and grub, $

Dessert Gallery, 3200 Kirby Drive, tel: (713) 522-9999, Sara Brook's sexy desserts plus furniture as art; open late on weekends, lunch specials, $

Dimassi's, 5064 Richmond, tel: (713) 439-7481, Middle eastern cuisine, part of grocery store, $

Doneraki, 2836 Fulton, tel: (713) 224-2509, Authentic Mexican, live mariachis, $

Golden Room Restaurant, 1209 Montrose Blvd, tel: (713) 524-9614, Tasty Thai food, $

Goode Company Texas BBQ, 5109 Kirby, tel: (713) 522-2530, said to be best barbecue place in the city, $$

The Great Caruso, 1001 Westheimer, tel: (713) 780-4900, Steaks, pasta, vegetarian, $$

Houston This Is It, 207 Gray, tel: (713) 659-1608, Funny name but tasty soulfood, $

Joe's Crab Shack, 601 2nd St (between Houston & Galveston), Kemah, tel: (713) 334-2881, Noisy waiters, funny signs, deck over water, crabs of all kinds, $

Kim Sung, 2001 Jefferson, tel: (713) 222-2461, Vietnamese, $

Kirby Drive Grille, 8111 Kirby Drive, tel: (713) 790-1900, Casual bistro, American food, $

Marina Bar & Grill, 3000 NASA Road, in Nassau Bay Marina, tel: (713) 333-9300, Fresh seafood, grilled steaks, view over water, $$

Maxime's, 3755 Richmond Avenue at Timmons, tel: (713) 877-8899, French cuisine, piano bar, $$$

McGonigel's Mucky Duck, 2425 Norfolk, tel: (713) 528-5999, As Irish as its name, pub grub, $

Ousie's Table, 3939 San Felipe, tel: (713) 528-2264, Cozy ranchhouse with own herb garden, American cuisine, $$

Pappadeaux Seafood Kitchen, 6015 Westheimer, tel: (713) 782-6310, One of four favored local Cajun spots, $$

Rainbow Lodge, No. 1 Birdsall near Memorial Park, tel: (713) 861-6666, Upscale fishing lodge with classy decor, lovely gardens, seafood and wild game, $$$

Rotisserie for Beef & Bird, 2200 Wilcrest, tel: (713) 977-9524, American colonial cuisine, wild game, extensive wine list, $$

Sammy's Lebanese Restaurant, 5825 Richmond, tel: (713) 780-0065, Falafel, tabouli, hummus, $

Vincent's, 2701 W. Dallas, tel: (713) 528-4313, Spit roasted chicken, various meats & seafood, $$

Viva! Healthy Mexican Foods, 2491 S. Braeswood, tel: (713) 666-2491, $

San Antonio

A-1 Barbeque & Lulu's Tin Star Saloon, 1202 W. Commerce, tel: (210) 212-3896, Famous for smoked sausage, $

Asian Kitchen, 1739 SW Loop 410, tel: (210) 675-3117, Chinese restaurant with attached fish market, $

Boudro's, 421 E. Commerce, on the Riverwalk, tel: (210) 224-8484, Ribs, seafood; don't miss the smoked shrimp enchiladas, $$

Cactus Flower Cafe, 711 E. Riverwalk, tel: (210) 224-4555, Tortilla soup, prime rib, sandwiches, $$

County Line, 111 W. Crockett, on the Riverwalk, tel: (210) 229-1941, BBQ, $$

Crumpet's Restaurant & Bakery, 5800 Broadway, tel: (210) 821-5454, Upscale eating, hotel shuttles, $

Fatso's Sports Garden, 1704 Bandera Road, tel: (210) 432-0121, 15 huge TVs for sports fans, volleyball courts, BBQ, $

Fireplace Inn, 13259 Blanco Road, tel: (210) 479-1015, Steak & seafood, $$$

La Fogata, 2427 Vance Jackson, tel: (210) 341-9930, Mexican; nationally recognized among the best, $$

Guenther House, 205 E. Guenther St, tel: (210) 227-1061, Century-old store, restaurant and museum; roof garden, $

Hung Fong, 3624 Broadway, tel: (210) 822-9211, Favorite Chinese location in business 60 years, $

Jailhouse Cafe, 1126 W. Commerce, tel: (210) 224-5001, Varied, many plaudits for the chicken fried steak, $$

Jazz, A Louisiana Kitchen, 2632 Broadway, tel: (210) 473-2520, New Orleans dishes, Cajun stirfry, nightly live jazz, $

Magic Time Machine, 902 NE Loop 410, tel: (210) 828-1470, Theme park restaurant aimed at children, $$

Mama's Cafe, 2442 Nacogdoches, tel: (210) 826-8303, Homestyle food, friendly atmosphere, $

Maverick Cafe, 6868 San Pedro at Oblate, tel: (210) 822-9611, Chinese/Mexican, $

Mi Tierra Cafe & Bakery, 218 Produce Row in Market Square, tel: (210) 225-1262, Colorful, festive time-honored restaurant with bakery, mariachis, $

Michelino's, 521 Riverwalk, tel: (210) 223-2939, Italian country kitchen, pasta, pizza, fabulous desserts, $$

Los Patios, 2015 NE Loop 410 at Starcrest Drive, tel: (210) 655-6171, Tex-Mex & Southwestern in twin garden restaurant by the river, $$

Republic of Texas, 526 Riverwalk at Commerce St Bridge, tel: (210) 226-6256, Enormous steaks, Mexican dishes, margaritas, $$

Rio Rio Cantina, 421 E. Commerce/Riverwalk, tel: (210) 226-8462, Extensive Mex menu; good people-watching, $

Texas Land & Cattle Steakhouse, 60 NE Loop 410 at McCullough, tel: (210) 342-4477, Authentic ranchhouse,

stone fireplaces, covered patio, mesquite grill, $$

Thai Orchid, 9921 I-10 West, tel: (210) 691-8424, Typical Thai, vegetarian-seafood, $

Tokyo Steak House, 9405 San Pedro, tel: (210) 341-4461, Sushi bar, steaks, lobster, $$

Tower of the Americas, 222 Hemisphere Plaza, tel: (210) 223-3101, Spectacular views from the revolving tower; classy food, $$$

El Paso/Juárez

Forti's Mexican Elder, 321 E. Chelsea Place, tel: 772-0066, Steak, seafood and famous chicken *salpicon* , $$

H&H Car Wash & Coffee Shop, 701 E. Yandell Drive, tel: (915) 533-1144, Chorizo burritos or carne picada are the favorites here while you watch the waterworks, $

Kentucky Club, 629 N. Juárez Ave, in Juárez, tel: (52-16) 149 990, Inimitable margaritas, $

Leo's Mexican Food, 5103 Montana Ave, tel: 566-4972, family fare, $

Drinking

For a state with such a robust reputation for living heartily, it may come as a surprise to learn that about one-fifth of the 254 counties choose to be "dry," banning all alcoholic beverages. This rarely presents a problem for would-be drinkers, who merely drive a mile or two to a neighboring county where – drinking-wise – anything goes.

Three of the several brands of beer brewed in the state qualify as "famous" – Pearl, Lone Star and Shiner. Arguments often ensue among the locals as to which is best. Texas wines also have acquired an excellent reputation over the years, and many will be found on menus throughout the state (*see* **The Wine Industry**, p. 68). Tequila may well be the most popular liquor consumed, due to the proximity of Mexico, where it is made and consumed in vast quantities. The tequila-based margarita is probably drunk here in Texas more than anywhere else north of the border. In recent years, the micro-brewery concept has taken hold, with the Belgian-style Celis from Austin having established a statewide reputation. Many "brewpubs" have decent food as well. Some drinking-based establishments to try include:

Bitter End Bistro and Brewpub, 311 Colorado, Austin, tel: (512) 478-2337. **Dick's Last Resort,** 406 Navarro, on the Riverwalk, San Antonio, tel: (210) 224-0026. Rowdy drinking hall with live music; ribs, catfish, chicken, $$ **Howl At The Moon Saloon,** 111 W. Crockett/Riverwalk, San Antonio. Rock and roll singalong and dueling pianos, $$ **Rock Bottom Brewery,** 6111 Richmond Ave, Houston, tel: (713) 974-BREW. In the busiest part of town, $ **Routh Street Brewery & Grill,** 3001 Routh Street, Dallas, tel: (214) 922-8835. Brewpub grub, $$ **The Strand Brewery,** 111 23rd Street, Galveston, tel: (409) 762-0292. Microbrewery with wood-fired pizza oven.

Culture

Dallas/Forth Worth

The Dallas/Fort Worth cultural calendar is crowded with events ranging from the **Shakespeare in the Park** festival, tel: (817) 923-6698, held in Fort Worth's Trinity Park in July and August to the occasional performances by Dallas' **Black Dance Theatre,** tel: (214) 871-2376. The **Morton H. Myerson Symphony Center** in the burgeoning arts district is the home of the **Dallas Symphony Orchestra,** tel: (214) 871-4000, and the **Dallas Opera,** tel: (214) 443-1000, performs between November and February. The **Performing Arts Center** at 5th and Walnut Streets, tel: (214) 205-2780, is the home of the **Garland Civic Theatre** and the **Garland Symphony.**

Other examples of the performing arts include the **Fort Worth/Dallas Ballet,** tel: (817) 763-0207, the **Fort Worth Symphony,** tel: (817) 921-2676, the **Dallas Chamber Orchestra,** tel: (214) 520-2787, the **Greater Dallas Youth Orchestra,** tel: (214) 528-7747, and the **Dallas Children's Theater,** tel: (214) 978-0110. On the lighter side are the regular events staged at the **Starplex Amphitheatre,**

tel: (214) 421-1111, in Dallas' Fair Park and the series of Dallas Summer Musicals, tel: (214) 373-8000, also at Fair Park. A service called **Dallas Artsline,** tel: (214) 522-2659, offers a complete listing of arts events, as do local tourist offices.

Much of Dallas' liveliest nightlife with clubs, bars, theaters and restaurants is centered around **Greenville Avenue,** from the LBJ Freeway down to Ross Avenue, and **Deep Ellum,** the former industrial neighborhood in the 3500 block of Elm just east of the central Expressway. In Fort Worth, head for the stockyards area, where the **White Elephant Saloon** and **Booger Red's Saloon** along E. Exchange Avenue are among the spots offering live entertainment.

Houston

The spectacular **Wortham Theater Center,** completed a decade ago at a cost of $72 million, is home to the **Houston Ballet,** tel: (800) 928-ARTS, and **Houston Grand Opera,** tel: (713) 546-8200 as well as a variety of other activities. Situated northeast of downtown, at the edge of Sam Houston Park, it is the centerpiece of the city's compact Theater District, which also includes the 50-year-old award-winning **Alley Theatre,** tel: (713) 228-8421, which has earned a national reputation for original drama. A couple of blocks away is **Jones Hall,** home to the **Houston Symphony,** tel: (713) 227-ARTS, and the **Society for the Performing Arts,** tel: (713) 227-5134, which presents world-class dance companies, orchestras and solo artists. Broadway shows are regularly presented by **Theatre Under the Stars,** tel: (800) 766-6048, at the downtown Music Hall on Bagby Street.

Rice University has its share of cultural activities with performances by the **Rice Dance Theater** tel: (713) 520-3292, the **Rice Players,** tel: (713) 527-4040, and the **Shepherd School of Music,** tel: (713) 527-4933, and it's well worth making the relatively short trip to Galveston for a performance at the gloriously restored **Grand 1894 Opera House,** tel: (800) 821-1894, whose stage has been graced by everyone from Sarah Bernhardt to the Marx Brothers.

Houston's nightlife is centered upon **Richmond Avenue,** north of the

Southwest Freeway and west of US-610, a short walk from the Galleria. Among the dozens of clubs featuring rock and roll, blues or country and western music, the best known are **Billy Blue's Bar & Grill** and the **Trail Dust Steak House,** both on the Richmond Avenue itself. There are dancehalls in the gay district of **Montrose,** with such lively clubs as **Pacific Street,** tel: (713) 523-0213, and **Heaven,** tel: (713) 521-9123.

San Antonio

Most of the city's best nightlife can be found near the river, with dancing nightly at the **Republic of Texas Nightclub,** 526 River Walk, tel: (210) 226-6256, and rowdy sing-alongs taking place at **Durty Nelly's Irish Pub** in the Hilton Palacio, which claims to hand out one ton of peanuts each week. The **Rivercenter Comedy Club** is a showcase for old and new performers. Off I-35 along Schwertz Parkway is the **Blue Bonnet Cafe,** a 600-seat restaurant and dancehall that features dancing and country western videos shown on a large screen. Half-an-hour's drive away at New Braunfels is century-old **Gruene Hall,** tel: (210) 606-1281, the oldest dance hall in Texas, where Lyle Lovett and Hank Ketchum began their careers.

Austin

In this city of a mere half-million population are more than 100 live music venues, justifying Austin's boast of being "the music capital of America". East 6th Street downtown is the main area, dense with clubs and bars from which music pours virtually all night. For blues try **Catfish Station,** tel: (512) 477-8875, **Joe's Generic Bar,** tel: (512) 480-0171, or **Ego's,** tel: (512) 474-7091, on nearby Congress Ave; rock and pop fill the air at **Babe's,** tel: (512) 473-2262, **Fat Tuesday,** tel: (512) 474-0632, and **Steamboat,** tel: (512) 478-2913; country and western can be found at the **Hang 'Em High Saloon,** tel: (512) 322-0382; variety at the **311 Club,** tel: (512) 477-1630, and **Maggie Mae's,** tel: (512) 478-8541; and jazz at **Jazz on 6th Street,** tel: (512) 479-0474, and **Pete's Peanut Bar & Piano Emporium,** tel: (512) 472-PETE, where customers sing along. These listings, of course, merely scratch the surface of what's available, because music venues are spread all over town. Highly recommended is the veteran **Threadgill's**, tel: (512) 451-5440, where diners share long tables and stomp their feet to a never-ending stream of live country and western groups. The Austin Convention & Visitors Bureau distributes a free folder, *101 Musical Things To Do*, which includes telephone numbers and listings for such seasonal events as Jerry Jeff Walker's annual birthday party, tel: (512) 477-0036, and the summer outdoor concert series in Zilker Park, tel: (512) 499-6700. As befits a college town, Austin is also rich in classical music events, with regular performances by the **Austin Symphony Orchestra**, tel: (512) 474-6064, and the **Austin Chamber Music Center**, tel: (512) 454-7562.

Attractions
Dallas

African-American Museum, 3536 Grand, tel: (214) 565-9026. Open: Monday–Saturday 12–5pm, Sunday 1–5pm. Free.

Arboretum and Botanical Society, 8525 Garland Road (Texas 78), tel: (214) 327-8263. Open: daily 10am–6pm in summer; 10am–5pm in winter. Free.

Biblical Arts Center, 7500 Park Lane. Open: Tuesday–Saturday 10am–5pm, Sunday 1–5pm. Free.

Farmer's Market, Cadiz and Harwood Sts. Open: daily 5am–7pm.

Frontiers of Flight Museum, Cedar Springs at Mockingbird. Open: Monday–Saturday 10am–5pm, Sunday 1–5pm. Admission.

Historical Society, Fair Park, tel: (214) 421-5136. Open: Tuesday–Saturday 9:30am–5:30pm, Sunday 1–5pm. Free.

Horticultural Center, Fair Park Grounds, tel: (214) 428-7476. Seven acres of display gardens. Gardens open daily; visitor's center and conservatory open Tuesday–Saturday 10am–5pm, Sunday 1–5pm. Free.

International Museum of Cultures, 7500 West Camp Wisdom Road, tel: (214) 298-3331. Open: Tuesday–Friday 10am–5pm; Saturday and Sunday 1:30–5pm. Free.

John Neely Bryan Cabin, on Dallas County Historical Plaza at Elm and Market, no phone. Open: daily.

Meadows Museum, in the Owen Art Center at Southern Methodist University, tel: (214) 692-2516. Open: Monday–Saturday 10am–5pm, Sunday 1–5pm, closed Wednesday. Free.

Mesquite Rodeo, 15 miles (24 km) east of Dallas on Loop 635 East in Mesquite, tel: (214) 285-8777. Open: April through October on Friday and Saturday nights. Admission.

Mexican-American Cultural Heritage Center, 2940 Singleton Boulevard, tel: (214) 824-9981. Open: Monday–Friday 9am–5pm. Free.

Museum of African-American Life and Culture, 3837 Simpson-Stuart Road from Interstate Highway 45, tel: (214) 372-8738. Open: Tuesday–Saturday 9.30am–5.30pm; Sunday 1–5pm. Free.

Museum of Art, 1717 North Harwood, tel: (214) 922-1200. Open: Tuesday, Wednesday, Friday–Sunday 11am–4pm, Thursday 11am–9pm. Free.

Native American Cultural Heritage Center, 3635 Greenleaf Street, tel: (214) 631-3920. Open: Monday–Friday 8am–5pm. Free.

Nature Center, 7171 Mountain Creek Pkwy, tel: (214) 296-1955. Open: daily 7am–7pm. Free.

Neiman-Marcus Archive Showcase, Main and Ervay Streets, tel: (214) 573-5780. Open: Monday–Saturday at regular store hours. Free.

Neiman-Marcus Fortnight, Main and Ervay streets, tel: (214) 741-6911. A spectacular store sponsored fair spotlighting a different country each year. Open: every year in October. Call for exact dates. Free.

Old City Park, 1717 Gano Street, tel: (214) 421-5141. Collection of historic buildings of the 1880s. Open: Tuesday–Sunday 10am–4pm. Admission.

Reunion Tower, 300 Reunion Blvd, tel: (214) 712-7145. 50-story tower with observation deck. Open: Monday–Friday 10am–10pm, Saturday and Sunday 9am–midnight. Admission.

The Science Place, Fair Park. **Science Place I** (Southwest Museum of Science and Technology), open: daily 9:30am–5:30pm. Admission. **Science Place II** (includes Planetarium), open: daily 9.30am–5pm. Admission.

The Sixth Floor, 411 Elm St, tel: (214) 653-6666. The John F. Kennedy Memorial in what was once the 6th floor of the Texas School Book Depository. Open: daily 10am–6pm.

Southfork Ranch, in Plano: from US Highway 75 take exit 30 in Plano and drive east 5 miles (8 km) to FM Road 2514, tel: (214) 442-7800. Setting for the television series Dallas. Open: daily. Admission.

State Fair of Texas, Fair Park, tel: (214) 828-2212. Largest state fair in the country. Open: every year in mid-October. Admission.

State Fair Park, Washington St Includes **Age of Steam Museum**, tel: (214) 428-0101; **Science Place and Hall of State**, tel: (214) 653-6666, open daily 9:30am–5:30pm; **Aquarium**, tel: (214) 670-8443, open daily 9am–4:30pm; **Museum of Natural History**, tel: (214) 421-3466, open every Monday–Saturday 9am–5pm, Sunday noon–5pm.

Union Station, 400 South Houston, tel: (214) 653-1101. Amusement and train rides. Always open. Free.

Visitor Center, 1303 Commerce St, tel: (214) 571-1300. Open: Monday–Saturday 8am–5pm, Sunday noon–5pm.

Zoo, 621 East Clarendon, tel: (214) 946-5154. Open: daily 9am–5pm. Admission.

Fort Worth

Amon Carter Museum, 3501 Camp Bowie Blvd, tel: (817) 738-1933. Open: Tuesday–Saturday 10am–5pm, Sunday noon–5pm. Free.

Botanical Garden, 3220 Botanic Garden Drive, tel: (817) 871-7686. Several gardens with varying hours between 8am–7pm. Admission for conservatory, other areas free.

Caravan of Dreams, 312 Houston Street, tel: (817) 877-3000. Primarily a jazz club with some rock and folk. Box office open Monday–Saturday 10am–6pm, Sunday noon–6pm. Admission.

Casa Mañana Playhouse, 3101 West Lancaster, tel: (817) 332-2272. Theatre in the round especially for children. Call for shows. Admission.

Cattle Auction, behind the Livestock Exchange Building on East Exchange near North Main, tel: (817) 625-9175. Call for schedules. Free.

Cattlemen's Museum, 1301 West 7th, tel: (817) 332-7064. Open: Monday–Friday 8am–4:30pm. Free.

Chisholm Trail Roundup, at the Will Rogers Coliseum, 3300 West Lancaster, tel: (817) 336-2491. Open: every year in early June from Friday to Sunday. Admission.

Eddlemen-McFarland House, 1110 Penn Street, tel: (817) 332-5875. Open: Monday–Friday 10am–2pm. Admission.

Heritage Park, North Main at Franklin Street. Ruins of the army post. Always open. Free.

Kimbell Art Museum, 3333 Camp Bowie Blvd on Amon Carter Square, tel: (817) 332-8451. Open: Tuesday–Saturday 10am–5pm, Sunday noon–5pm. Free.

La Buena Vida Vineyards, FM Road 1886 and Highway 199 near Springtown, tel: (817) 237-9463. Open: Monday–Saturday 11am–5pm, Sunday noon–5pm.

Log Cabin Village, University Drive at Log Cabin Village Lane, tel: (817) 926-5881. Open: Monday–Friday 9am–4:30pm. Admission.

Lord's Supper Display, 2500 Ridgmar Plaza. Take the Ridgmar exit from Interstate Highway 30, tel: (817) 737-6251. Open: Monday–Saturday noon–5pm, Sunday 1–5pm. Free.

Museum of Modern Art, 1309 Montgomery, tel: (817) 738-9215. Open: Tuesday–Saturday 10am–5pm, Sunday noon–5pm. Free.

Museum of Science & History, 1501 Montgomery, tel: (817) 732-1613. Open: Monday 9am–5pm, Tuesday–Saturday 9am–8pm, Sunday noon–8pm.

Nature Center and Refuge, 9 miles (14 km) northwest of Fort Worth on Highway 199, tel: (817) 237-1111. Open: Tuesday–Saturday 9am–5pm, Sunday noon–5pm. Free.

Nobel Planetarium/Omni-Theater, 1501 Montgomery, tel: (817) 732-1631. Show times: Monday–Friday 2:30–4:30pm every 1/2 hour, Saturday 11am–4:30pm every 1/2 hour, Sunday 12:30–4:30pm every 1/2 hour. Admission.

Sid Richardson Collection of Western Art, 309 Main Street, tel: (817) 332-6554. Open: Tuesday and Wednesday 10am–5pm, Thursday–Saturday 11am–8pm, Sunday 1–5pm. Free.

Six Flags Over Texas, on the Dallas-Fort Worth Turnpike, tel: (817) 640-8900. Amusement park. Hours vary, depending on time of year. Admission.

Southwestern Exposition and Fat Stock Show and Rodeo, at the Will Rogers Complex at 3300 West Lancaster, tel: (817) 332-7361. Every year in late January and early February. Call for exact dates. Admission.

Southwestern Historical Wax Museum, 601 East Safari Parkway, off I-30 in Grand Prairie, tel: (214) 263-2391. Open: daily 10am–5pm. Admission.

Stockyards Collection and Museum, 131 E. Exchange Ave, tel: (817) 625-5087. Open: Monday–Saturday 10am–5pm. Free.

Stockyards Historic Age Info Center, at 123 E. Exchange Street, tel: (817) 624-4741. Once a rest stop for cowboys riding the Chisholm Trail. Open: Monday–Saturday 9am–6pm, Sunday noon–6pm.

Tarantula Railroad, depots at 2318 Eighth Ave and 140 E. Exchange Ave, tel: (817) 625-7245. Round trips daily. Admission.

Texas Railroad Museum, 5051 James Street, tel: (817) 261-2480. Open: Saturday and Sunday 1–5pm. Free.

Thistle Hill, 1509 Pennsylvania, tel: (817) 336-1212. Open: Monday–Friday 10am–3pm, Sunday 1–4pm. Admission.

Visitors Center, 130 E. Exchange Ave, tel: (817) 336-8791. Open: Monday–Saturday 9am–6pm, Sunday noon–6pm.

Water Gardens, south of the Convention Center downtown between Houston and Commerce Streets. Always open. Free.

Will Rogers Memorial Center, Amon Carter Square, tel: (817) 871-8150.

Zoological Park, 2727 Zoological Park Drive, tel: (817) 870-7050. Open: daily 10am–5pm. Admission.

Houston

American Funeral Service Museum, 415 Barren Springs Dr., tel: (713) 876-3063. Nation's largest collection of funeral service memorabilia. Open: Monday–Saturday 10am–4pm, Sunday noon–4pm. Admission.

Anheuser-Busch Brewery Tour, 775 Gellhorn, tel: (713) 670-1695. Open: Monday–Saturday 9am–4pm.

Arboretum and Nature Center, 4501 Woodway (near Loop 610 in Memorial Park neighborhood), tel: (713) 681-8433. 155-acre (63-ha) native woodlands. Open: daily 8:30am–6pm. Free.

Armand Bayou Nature Center, 8600 Bay Area Boulevard, in Clear Lake, about 25 miles (40 km) southeast of Houston, tel: (713) 474-2551. An 1800-acre (729-hectare) wildlife preserve with hardwood forest, tall grass prairie and bayou ecosystems. Open: Wednesday–Saturday 9am–5pm, Sunday noon–5pm. Free.

Astroworld, 9001 Kirby Drive, off Loop 610, tel: (409) 799-1234. A 75-acre (30-ha) amusement park. Open daily April–Labor Day; Labor Day–November weekends only. Call for admission charges.

Bayou Bend Collection, 1 Westcott Street, tel: (713) 520-2600. 28-room Latin Colonial home and 14 acres of gardens. Gardens open Tuesday–Saturday 10am–5pm, Sunday 1–5pm; collection open Tuesday–Friday 9am–4pm, Saturday 10am–12:45pm. Free.

Burke Baker Planetarium, 1 Hermann Circle Dr., tel: (713) 639-4629. Showtime: Monday–Friday 1, 2, and 3pm, Saturday and Sunday 1–3:30pm every 1/2 hour. Laser Show on weekend eves. Admission.

Center for Photography, 1440 Harold, tel: (713) 529-4755. Open: Saturday and Sunday noon–5pm. Free.

The Children's Museum of Houston, 1500 Benz, tel: (713) 522-1138. Features hands-on exhibits. Tuesday–Saturday 9am–5pm, Sunday noon–5pm. Admission.

Contemporary Arts Museum, 5216 Montrose Blvd, tel: (713) 526-0773. Open: Tuesday–Friday 10am–5pm, Saturday and Sunday noon–5pm. Free.

Fire Museum, Milam and McIlhenny streets, Tuesday–Saturday 10am–4pm. Admission.

Garden Center, 1500 Hermann Drive. Building open Monday–Friday 8am–5pm, gardens open Monday–Friday 8am–8pm (8am–6pm in winter), Saturday and Sunday 10am–8pm (10am–6pm in winter). Free.

Houston Ship Channel, boat tours. No tours in July. Make reservations well in advance and check current tour times.

Japanese Garden, in Hermann Park. Open: daily 10am–6pm. Admission.

Jesse H. Jones Hall for the Performing Arts, 615 Louisiana, downtown, tel: (713) 227-2787 or (409) 237-1439. Home of the **Houston Symphony**, tel: (713) 224-4240; **Houston Grand Opera**, tel: (713) 227-5277; **Houston Ballet**, tel: (713) 225-0271; **Society for the Performing Arts**, tel: (713) 227-1111. Call for schedules and admission.

Lyndon B. Johnson Space Center, about 25 miles (40 km) southeast of Houston on Interstate Highway 45 and then NASA Road 1, tel: (800) 972-0369. Open: Monday–Friday 10am–7pm (10am–5pm in winter), Saturday and Sunday 10am–7pm. Free.

Menil Museum, 1515 Sul Ross. Open: Wednesday–Sunday 11am–7pm. Admission.

Museum of American Architecture and Decorative Arts, on the second floor of Moody Library at Houston Baptist University, 7502 Fondren Road, tel: (713) 774-7661. Open: Tuesday–Thursday 10am–4pm; Sunday 2–4pm. Admission: free.

Museum of Fine Arts, 1001 Bissonnet at Main Street, tel: (713) 639-7300. Open: Tuesday, Wednesday, Friday and Saturday 10am–5pm, Thursday 10am–9pm, Sunday 12:15–6pm. Free.

Museum of Natural Science, 1 Hermann Circle Drive (in Hermann Park), tel: (409) 639-4600. Includes **Burke Baker Planetarium** (see listing), **Cockrell Butterfly Center**, (713) 639-4600, **Lillie and Roy Cullen Gallery of Earth Science**, IMAX Theater, (713) 639-4629, Monday–Saturday 9am–6pm, Sunday noon–6pm. Admission.

Orange Show, 2401 Munger, tel: (409) 926-6368. A labyrinth of indoor and outdoor passages amid whirligigs, antiques, native art and odd mottoes. Open: March–December: Saturday and Sunday noon–5pm, Memorial Day–Labor Day: Monday–Friday 9am–1pm. Admission.

Pioneer Memorial Log House Museum, 1510 Outer Belt Drive, in Hermann Park, tel: (713) 528-9344. Open: on the first Thursday of each month, 1–4pm. Free.

Port of Houston Turning Basin, take Clinton Drive east from US Highway 90, tel: (713) 226-2100. Observation deck open daily 10am–5:30pm.

Railroad Trail Museum, 7390 Mesa Rd Open: March–December 1st and 3rd Sunday 11:30am–4:30pm.

Rice Museum, at Rice University, University Blvd and Stockton Street, tel: (713) 522-0886. Open: Tuesday–Saturday 10am–5pm; Sunday noon–6pm. Free.

Rothko Chapel, 3900 Yupon Street, tel: (713) 524-9839. Open: daily 10am–6pm. Free.

Sam Houston Historical Park, 1100 Bagby, downtown, tel: (713) 655-1912. A collection by the Harris County Heritage Society of seven restored buildings. Open: Monday–Saturday 10am–4pm (last tour at 3pm); Sunday 1–5pm (last tour at 4pm), Call for admission charge.

San Jacinto Battleground State Historical Park, about 21 miles (34 km) east of Houston on Texas Highways 225 and 134. The site of the final battle between the Texas and Mexican armies in 1836. Museum: open daily 9am–6pm; elevator and observation deck: open daily 10am-5:30pm.

San Jacinto Monument, a 570-foot (175-meter) obelisk with highlights of the battle depicted on its sides. Elevator rides to the top: daily 10am–6pm. Admission.

San Jacinto Museum of History, at the base of the Monument, tel: (713) 479-2421. Open: Tuesday–Sunday 9am–6pm. Free.

Sarah Campbell Blaffer Gallery, 114 Fine Arts Building, Univ. of Houston, 4800 Calhoun, tel: (713) 749-1329. Open: Tuesday–Saturday 10am–6pm; Sunday 1–6pm. Free.

Seawall Art Gallery, at Rice University, 6100 South Main Street, tel: (713) 527-8101. Open: Monday–Saturday noon–5pm. Free.

Space Center Houston, NASA Road 1, near Alvin off I-45 South, tel: (800) 972-0369. Open: Monday–Friday 10am–7pm (10am–5pm in winter), Saturday and Sunday 10am–7pm. Admission.

Traders Village, 7979 N. Eldridge, tel: (713) 890-5500. Largest market on Texas Gulf Coast. Open: every Saturday and Sunday. Parking fee.

Underground Tunnels, downtown, beneath over 30 blocks. This maze of underground tunnels may be reached through entrances in major office and bank buildings, shops and restaurants. Maps available at Houston Public Library, 500 McKinney, tel: (713) 224-5441. Open: weekdays only. Free.

Visitor Information Center, 801 Congress St, tel: (800) 231-7799, Monday–Friday 8:30–5.

Visitors' Center for the NASA/Johnson Space Center, Tranquility Park, downtown, bounded by Smith, Walker, Rusk and Bargby streets. Commemorates the landing of Apollo XI on the moon at Tranquility Base. Always open. Free.

WaterWorld, Loop 610 at Kirby Dr., tel: (713) 799-1234. Water-based theme park. Open: weekends in spring and fall; daily in summer, call for admission prices.

Zoological Gardens, 1 Zoo Circle Drive (in Hermann Park), tel: (713) 525-3300,. Open: Tuesday–Sunday 10am–6pm. Admission.

EAST TEXAS
Beaumont

Beaumont Art Museum, 1111 9th Street, tel: (409) 832-3432. Open: Tuesday–Friday 10am–5pm; Saturday and Sunday 2–5pm. Admission: free.

Belle of Beaumont Riverboat, River Front Park off College Street, tel: (409) 832-6064. Various cruises for sightseeing, entertainment or dinner. Call for hours and prices (credit cards accepted).

John J. French Trading Post, 2975 French Road, tel: (409) 898-3267. Open: Tuesday–Saturday 10am–4pm; Sunday 1–4pm, Small admission charge.

Roy. E. Larsen Sandyland Sanctuary, About 25 miles (40 km) north of Beaumont: take US Highway 96 to Silsbee, then Texas Highway 327 west about 2 miles (3.2 km), tel: (409) 385-4135. 2,200 acres (891 ha) on Village Creek. Offers guided hikes and easy one-day canoe trips. Open daily during Daylight Savings Time. Free.

Texarkana

Crystal Springs Beach, About 15 miles (24 km) west of Texarkana, on US Highway 67. A spring-fed lake offers camping, picnicking and boating. Open: summer: daily, 10am–7pm; winter: Saturday and Sunday 10am–7pm. Small admission charge.

Four States Fair and Rodeo, on Four States Fairground in Spring Lake Park, Interstate Highway 30 and Park Road, tel: (214) 793-2941. Every year, the first week in October. Admission charge.

Texarkana Historical Society and Museum, 219 State Line Avenue, tel: (214) 793-4831. Open: Monday–Friday 10am–4pm; Saturday and Sunday noon–3pm. Admission: free.

Longview

Caddo Indian Museum, 701 Hardy (between US Highway 80 and Harrison Road), tel: (214) 759-5739. Open: daily, 9am–6pm. Admission by donation.

Gregg County Historical Museum, 214 North Fredonia, tel: (214) 753-5840. Housed in the restored Everett Building built in early 1900s in the Classical Revival style. Includes the **Amelia Sparkman Belding Heritage Resource Center**. Open: Saturday 10am–4pm. Small admission charge.

Stroh Brewing Company, 1400 West Cotton Street, tel: (214) 753-0371. Tours: Monday–Friday 10am, 11am, 1pm, 2pm and 3pm. Admission: free.

Nacogdoches

Calle del Norte, North Street, Thought to be the oldest public street in the nation. A former center of Caddo Indian settlement.

Hoya Memorial Library and Museum, 211 South Lanana Street, tel: (409) 564-4693. Open: Monday–Saturday 9am–noon and 2–5pm. Free.

Old Nacogdoches University, on Washington Square, tel: (409) 564-0084 or (409) 564-7218. Summer: Monday–Saturday 10am–noon and 2–5pm; Sunday 2–5pm. Admission by donation.

Professional Rodeo Cowboy Association Rodeo, at the Nacogdoches County Exposition Center on West Loop 224. Every year, last week in March. Admission charge.

San Augustine

El Camino Real, *Royal Road* in Spanish, dating from the 1600s, mostly follows Texas Highway 21.

Ezekiel Cullen House, at Congress and Market streets. An 1839 structure. Open: Monday–Saturday 1–5pm.

Mission Nuestra Señora de los Dolores de los Ais, at Mission Hill on FM Road 147. Always open. Free.

Old Town Well, At R.N. Stripling's Drugstore downtown, tel: (409) 275-2262. Open: Monday–Saturday 8am–5pm. Free.

Corpus Christi

Art Museum of South Texas, 1902 North Shoreline Drive, tel: (512) 884-3844. Open: Tuesday–Saturday 10am–5pm. Free.

Bayfest, on Shoreline Boulevard between I-37 and the Convention Center, tel: (512) 887-0868. A three-day arts and crafts fair with ethnic food and music. Open: every year in late September or early October. Call for exact dates and schedules. Free.

Corpus Christi Museum, 1900 North Chaparral Street, tel: (512) 883-2862. Open: Tuesday–Saturday 10am–5pm; Sunday noon–5pm. Free.

King Ranch, on Texas Highway 141, just west of Kingsville, about 35 miles (56 km) southwest of Corpus Christi, tel: (512) 592-6411. 800,000 acres (324,000 ha), it covers much of South Texas and is the largest ranch in the country. Follow the tour around the ranch by the loop (to which visitors are restricted). Tours (daily), 8am–4pm. Free.

Museum of Oriental Cultures, 426 South Staples Street, tel: (512) 883-1303. Open: Tuesday–Saturday 10am–4pm. Small admission charge.

Port of Corpus Christi, access either from Corpus Christi Beach or the Harbor Bridge. This active port, built in 1854, is 45 feet (14 meters) deep. It is the nation's ninth busiest port and you can watch tankers all day carrying oil, grain, farm products and chemicals.

Texas Jazz Festival, Various locations, tel: (512) 854-9634 or 882-5603. A three-day festival drawing many jazz greats from around the country with ongoing performances, workshops, jam sessions and other events. Every year, around the Fourth of July. Call for schedules.

Galveston

1839 Samuel May Williams Home, 3601 Avenue P, tel: (409) 765-1839. Open: Monday–Saturday 10am–4pm; Sunday noon–4pm (extended hours during summer). Admission.

Annual Homes Tour, tel: (409) 765-7834. Tour of 19th- and 20th-century private homes. Every year in May. Call for schedules and ticket prices.

Antique Dollhouse Museum, 1721 Broadway, tel: (409) 762-7289. Open: Tuesday–Saturday 10am–5pm; Sunday 1–5pm; closed in January. Admission.

Arts Center Gallery, 2127 Strand, tel: (409) 763-2403. Open: Monday, Wednesday–Saturday 10am–5pm, Sunday 1–5pm. Free.

Ashton Villa, 2328 Broadway, tel: (409) 762-393. Open: Monday–Friday 10am–4pm; Saturday and Sunday noon–5pm (extended hours in summer). Admission.

Bishop's Palace, 1402 Broadway, tel: (409) 762-2475. 1886 Victorian style mansion. Open: May–September (Memorial Day–Labor Day): daily, 10am–4pm (closed on Tuesday); 1–5pm the rest of the year. Admission.

Blessing of the Fleet, Wharf and 19th Street. Decorated shrimp boats assemble for annual Shrimp Festival. Open: every year, usually the second Sunday after Easter (or the third or fourth Sunday in April). For exact dates and schedule, write to the Galveston Visitors Bureau, 2106 Seawall Blvd, Galveston, 77550. Free.

Bolivar Ferry, leaves from the north end of Ferry Road (Texas Highway 87), tel: (409) 763-2386. Provides access to Point Bolivar for cars and pedestrians via 20-minute ferry ride. Continuous operation. Free.

Center for Transportation and Commerce (Railroad Museum), 123 Rosenberg, tel: (409) 765-5700. Open: daily 10am–5pm. Admission.

County Historical Museum, 2219 Market Street, tel: (409) 766-2340. Open: Monday–Saturday 10am–4pm, Sunday noon–4pm. Free.

David Taylor Classic Car Museum, 1918 Mechanic Street. Open: daily 10am–5pm. Admission.

Elissa, at Pier 22, tel: (409) 763-1877. A restored square-rigged sailing ship built in 1877. Open: daily 10am–5pm (extended hours during Summer). Admission.

Fort Crockett, Seawall Blvd between 45th and 53rd Sts. Defense installation built in 1897.

Grand 1894 Opera House, 2020 Post Office Road, tel: (409) 765-1894. Open: Monday–Saturday 9am–5pm; Sunday noon–5pm. Call for performing arts schedules. Free.

The Great Storm, Pier 21 at north end of 21st Street. 27-minute program on the hour: Sunday–Thursday 11am–6pm, Friday and Saturday 11am–8pm. Award-winning presentation that re-creates the aftermath of the 1900 hurricane that devastated Galveston.

Harbor Tours on the Dixie Queen, from Pier 19, tel: (409) 763-5423. 2-hour tours. Open: daily in summer, 10am, 2pm and 7pm. Admission.

Island State Park, six miles south on FM 3005 at 13 Mile Rd. Open: early June–late August, when outdoor musicals are presented nightly except Sunday. Admission.

Kempner Park, Avenue O at 27th Street. Contains octagonal Gaten

Verein. Popular with local Germans. Open: daily dawn–10pm. Free.

The Lone Star, at Mary Moody Northern Amphitheater in Galveston Island State Park, tel: (409) 737-3440. An annual musical and barbecue, June–August, Tuesday–Sunday 8pm. Call for exact dates and reservations. Admission.

Lone Star Flight Museum, 2002 Terminal Dr. More than two dozen vintage aircraft. Open: daily 10am–5pm. Admission.

Mardi Gras Museum, 2211 Strand. Historic costumes and memorabilia from Galveston's carnivals. Open: Wednesday–Sunday noon–6pm. Admission.

Moody Mansion, Museum and Gardens, 2618 Broadway. Historic home hosting collection of antiques, silver and photographs. Open: Monday–Saturday 10am–4pm, Sunday 1–4:30pm, closed Monday January–March. Admission.

Rainbow Festival, Strand at 21st and 25th streets, tel: (409) 763-6459. Arts and crafts festival coinciding with the annual Blessing of the Fleet. Open: every year in late April. Call for exact dates and schedules. Admission.

Rosenburg Library, 2310 Sealy Avenue, tel: (409) 763-8854. Exhibitions of 19th- and 20th-century history. Open: Monday–Saturday 9am–9pm, Sunday 1–5pm. Free.

Seawolf Park, on Pelican Island (by bridge from 51st Street North), tel: (409) 744-5738. Tours of WWII vintage ships. Open: daily, 6.30am–6.30pm. Admission.

Sweeney-Royston House, 2402 Avenue L, tel: (409) 762-9982. Built in 1800s Victorian style. Open: summer, Tuesday–Saturday 11am–5pm; winter: Tuesday–Saturday 1–5pm. Admission.

Texas Seaport Museum, Pier 21 at North end of Kempner (22nd). Open: daily 10am–5pm. Admission.

Trube House, 1627 Sealy Avenue, tel: (409) 763-5205. Visits by appointment only. Admission.

Visitor Center, Moody Civic Center, Seawall Blvd at 22nd Street.

Beaches: 32 miles (52 km) of open beaches. During winters, cars are not allowed on the beaches; there are parking lots with fees at various beaches. Lifeguards on duty.

Stewart Beach Park, at Seawall Blvd and Broadway, tel: (409) 765-5023. Amusement park. Open daily, dawn–10pm. Parking fee.

R.A. Apffel Park, at the east end of the island, from Seawall Blvd, take the second right turn after Ferry Road, tel: (409) 763-0166. Crabbing, floundering. Open: daily, dawn–10pm. Parking fee.

Galveston County Beach Pocket Park, West Beach is reached from FM Road 3005 and is between 7 Mile Road and 8 Mile Road, tel: (409) 737-1544: Open daily in summer, 9am–9pm. Parking fee.

Galveston Island State Park, West Beach, at 14528 Stewart and 13 Mile Road (from FM Road 3005), tel: (409) 737-1222. Features camping and birding. Open daily: summer, 8am–10pm; winter, 8am–5pm.

Pier fishing: The Gulf is known for excellent fishing, whether from miles off the coast or from any of the piers along the beaches. You must purchase a Texas fishing license (at any of the bait and tackle shops or the piers) and pick up information on size and weight limitations for various fish.

61st Street Fishing Pier, 61st Street and Seawall Blvd, tel: (409) 744-5681. Always open. Admission.

Flagship Fishing Pier, 25th Street and Seawall, tel: (409) 762-2846. Open summer only. Admission.

Gulf Coast Fishing Pier, 90th Street and Seawall, tel: (409) 744-2273. Always open. Admission.

Port Aransas

Deep-Sea Roundup, at the marina, tel: (512) 749-5919. This fishing tournament draws fishing fans from all over to reel in the winning sailfish, marlin, shark, kingfish or other gamefish. Many other events, including water parade, dances and crab racing. Open: Every year in July. For schedules, call the Chamber of Commerce.

Institute of Marine Science, located near the jetty and next to the beach, tel: (512) 749-5919. A graduate research division of The University of Texas at Austin. Tours: Monday–Friday 9am–5pm

Beaches: This, the north end of the Gulf barrier island, is called Mustang

Island. The beach is open at all times and no admission is charged. However, you must buy a Beach Permit, approximately $5 (available almost anywhere: stores, tackle shops, boutiques, the Chamber of Commerce, the police station) in order to park along the beach. Observe speed limits of 15 mph (24 kph). In a conventional car, stay out of soft sand; hard-packed "roads" are the only driving paths permitted. Camping allowed, no charge. If you drive south far enough, you will reach Corpus Christi and the beginning of the Padre Island National Seashore.

Fishing: Considered one of the best places to fish in Texas. Numerous boat chartering companies take small or large parties out into the bay or deep into the Gulf daily. These include the Wharf Cat and the Scat Cat. There are a number of places where boat rental and fishing equipment are available. They are:

Fisherman's Wharf, tel: (512) 749-5760 or 749-5443
The Kingfisher, tel: (512) 749-5597
Port Aransas Boatman, tel: (512) 749-5512
Call for schedules and rates. Jetty-fishing is also very popular. The jetties extend far into the water along the sides of the channel. No admission is charged and you can even rent equipment from bait and tackle shops, including a special "jetty" pole. The **Horace Caldwell Fishing Pier** is always open and has lights for night fishing. All down the beach you will also see people wading in the surf fishing.

San Antonio

The Alamo, Alamo Plaza, tel: (210) 225-1391. Limestone chapel and convent. Museum and Texas History Library. Open: Monday–Saturday 9am–5:30pm, Sunday 10am–5:30pm. Free.

Bexar County Courthouse, Main Plaza, tel: (210) 220-2011. Texas granite and sandstone. Romanesque Revival, built in 1895. Designed by Alfred Giles. Make reservations for tours.

Botanical Center, 555 Funston at North New Braunfels, tel: (210) 821-5115. 33 acres (13 ha), best collection of native plants in Texas. Open: Tuesday–Sunday 9am–6pm. Admission.

Buckhorn Hall of Horns, Hall of Texas History and Wax Museum, Lone Star Brewery, 600 Lone Star, at Mission Road, tel: (210) 270-9400 (information); (210) 270-9465 (reservations). One of the world's finest exhibitions of horns, fins, feathers. Brewery tours available, daily, 9.30am–5pm. Admission.

Carver Community Cultural Center, 226 North Hackberry, tel: (210) 225-6516. Open: Monday–Friday 8:30am–5pm.

Children's Museum, 305 E. Houston, tel: (210) 212-4453. Open: Tuesday–Saturday 9am–6pm, Sunday noon–5pm. Admission.

Cowboy Museum and Gallery, 209 Alamo Plaza, tel: (210) 229-1257. Open: daily 10am–7pm. Admission.

Edward Steves House (Steves Homestead), 509 King William Street, at Johnson, tel: (210) 225-5924. Tours of house provide introduction to King William Street Historic District. Open: daily 10am–4:15pm. Admission.

El Mercado, Santa Rosa and Commerce streets, tel: (210) 207-8600. Typical market from the interior of Mexico. Open: daily 10am–6pm. Free.

Fiesta Texas, off Loop 1604 and I-10, tel: (210) 697-5050. 200-acre (81-ha) theme park highlighting Texan culture and history. Open daily summer, weekends spring and fall, some hours November and December. Call for admission and schedule.

HemisFair Plaza, 92-acre (37-ha) site of 1968 World's Fair bounded by Interstate Highway 35, Alamo, Durango and Market streets, tel: (210) 207-8522. Admission.

Hertzberg Circus Museum, 210 West Market Street, tel: (210) 207-7810. One of the world's best collections of Tom Thumb and other memorabilia. Open: Monday–Saturday 9am–5pm, Sunday 1–5pm. Admission.

IMAX Theater, 803 E. Commerce Street, tel: (210) 225-4629. Call for schedule and reservations. Open: daily at 10am. Admission.

Institute of Texan Cultures, HemisFair Plaza, 801 South Bowie, tel: (210) 458-2300. Twenty-six ethnic and cultural groups featured. Open: Tuesday–Sunday 9am–5pm. Free.

José Antonio Navarro House, 228 South Laredo, tel: (210) 226-4801. Open: Wednesday–Sunday 10am–4pm. Admission.

Justin Boots, North Star Mall, Loop 410 at San Pedro. A 10-ton pair of boots by sculptor Robert Wade. Free.

La Villita, bounded by San Antonio River, Nuevo, South Alamo and South Presa streets, tel: (210) 226-3593. Restored Mexican village. Open: Monday–Saturday 10am–6pm.

Lourdes Grotto Sanctuary, 285 Oblata Drive at Blanco, tel: (210) 342-9864. Copy of the shrine at Lourdes in France. Open: daily 7am–6pm. Free.

Majestic Theater, Majestic Performing Arts Center, 212 East Houston at St Mary's, tel: (210) 226-3333. One of the finest "atmospheric" theatres ever built. Call for performance schedule and admission.

Marion Koogler McNay Art Museum, 6000 New Braunfels Avenue at the Austin Highway, tel: (210) 824-5368. One of the best art museums in Texas. Large collection of 20th-century art. Open: Tuesday–Saturday 10am–5pm, Sunday noon–5pm. Free.

Mexican Cultural Institute, HemisFair Park, tel: (210) 227-0123. Open: Tuesday–Friday 6am–5:30pm, Saturday and Sunday noon–6pm. Free.

Mission Concepción, Nuestra Señora de la Purisima Concepción de Acuña, 807 Mission Road at Mitchell, tel: (210) 534-1540. Oldest unrestored church still in use in America. Open: daily 9am–6pm April– September, daily 8am–5pm October–March. Free.

Mission San Francisco de la Espada, 10040 Espado Road, tel: (210) 627-2021. Founded 1731, completed 1756. Several times restored. Open: daily 9am–6pm April– September, daily 8am–5pm October–March. Free.

Mission San José y San Miguel de Agnayo, 6539 San Jose at Roosevelt, tel: (210) 932-1001. Much of the facade is original, including the famous **rose window**, daily 9am–6pm April– September, daily 8am–5pm October–March. Free.

Mission San Juan Capistrano, 9101 Graf at Ashley, tel: (210) 534-0749. Rubble chapel completed by 1756. Open: daily 9am–6pm April– September, daily 8am–5pm October–March. Free.

Museum of Art, 200 West Jones between Broadway and St Mary's, tel: (210) 820-2111. Six-building complex of converted brewery. Good collection of Texas art, especially furniture. Open: Monday–Saturday 10am–5pm

(Tuesday 9pm), Sunday noon–6pm. Admission.

River Walk (Paseo del Rio), along the San Antonio River downtown, tel: (210) 227-4262. Festivals and holidays celebrated all year. For current schedules, consult local newspapers.

Sea World of Texas, Ray Ellison Drive and Westover Hills Boulevard off Texas 151, 16 miles (25 km) northwest of downtown, tel: (210) 523-3611. Open weekends and some weekdays in spring, daily in summer, and weekends in fall. Call for schedule and admission.

Southern Pacific Railroad Station, 1174 East Commerce at Hoefgen, tel: (210) 223-3226. Restored depot used by Amtrak. Always open.

Southwest Craft Center, 300 Augusta at Navarro, tel: (210) 224-1848. Art gallery, craft instruction. Lunch available in Copper Kitchen. Open: Monday–Saturday 10am–4pm. Free.

Spanish Governor's Palace, 105 Military Plaza, tel: (210) 224-0601. Open: Monday–Saturday 9am–5pm, Sunday 10am–5pm. Admission.

Texas Folklife Festival, tel: (210) 458-2300. Four days in early August. Call for schedule and admission.

Texas Ranger Museum and Texas Pioneer and Trail Drivers Memorial Hall (Pioneer) Museum, 3805 Broadway at Tuleta, tel: (210) 822–9011. Open: May–August daily 10am–5pm, September–April 11am–4pm. Admission.

Texas Transportation Museum, 11731 Wetmore Road, tel: (210) 490-3554. Open: Thursday, Saturday, Sunday 9am–4pm; train and 1920s firetruck rides Sunday 1–3pm. Admission.

Tower of the Americas, HemisFair Plaza, 801 South Bowie , tel: (210) 207-8615. 750-foot (231-meter) tower designed by O'Neil Ford with revolving restaurant. Observation deck: open daily 9am–10pm (till 11pm on Friday and Saturday). Admission.

Trinity University, 715 Stadium Drive near Hildebrand, tel: (210) 736-7011. Campus designed by San Antonio architect O'Neil Ford.

Union Stockyards, 1716 South San Marcos at Pendleton, tel: (210) 223-6331. Oldest active cattle market south of Kansas City. Auctions are held on Monday, Wednesday and Thursday mornings. Open daily 8am–6pm. Free.

United Services Automobile Association (USAA) Building, 9800 Fredericksburg Road near Huebner, tel: (210) 498-2211. Free once-a-week tours of second-largest office building in America – with over 5,000 employees. Reservations necessary.

Visitor Information Center, 317 Alamo Plaza, tel: (210) 270-8748 or (800) 447-3372. Open daily 8:30am–6pm.

Witte Museum of History and Science, 3801 Broadway in Brackenridge Park, tel: (210) 357-1900. Monday–Saturday 10am–5pm (Tuesday 9pm), Sunday noon–5pm. Admission.

Yturri-Edmonds Historic Site, 257 Yellowstone at Mission Road, tel: (210) 534-8237. Early 19th-century adobe house and working mill. Open: Monday–Saturday 10am–4pm, Sunday noon–4pm.

Zoological Gardens and Aquarium, 3903 North St Mary's in Brackenridge Park, tel: (210) 734-7183. Large zoo in abandoned rock quarry is considered one of the best in the US. Open: daily 9:30am–5pm (till 6:30pm April–November). Admission.

BORDER TOWNS
El Paso

Bullfight Museum, in the Del Camino Restaurant, 5001 Alameda (US Highway 80 East), tel: (915) 772-2711. Artifacts associated with bullfighting and toreadors. Open: daily during restaurant hours. Free.

Chamizal National Memorial Museum, 800 South San Marcial, tel: (915) 534-6277. During the first two weeks in March, hosts the Siglo de Oro Drama Festival (free admission), when players from the US, Mexico and Spain perform a classic 18th-century Spanish drama in Spanish (English synopses are presented). Open: daily, 8am–5pm. Free.

Civic Center Plaza, at San Francisco and Santa Fe streets, tel: (915) 534-0600. Center for entertainment, including the El Paso Symphony Orchestra. Open: Monday–Friday 8am–5pm. Free.

El Paso Centennial Museum, at University and Wiggins streets on the campus of the University of Texas at El Paso, tel: (915) 747-5565. Exhibits pertaining to the history of the area. Open: Tuesday–Friday 10am–3pm; Sunday 1.30–5.30pm. Free.

El Paso Museum of Art, 1211 Montana Avenue, tel: (915) 541-4040. Exhibits range from the European masters to pre-Columbian American art. Open: Tuesday–Saturday 10am–5pm; Sunday 1–5pm. Free.

El Paso Museum of History, 12901 Gateway West (on Interstate Highway 10 East, off the exit for the Avenue of the Americas), tel: (915) 858-1928. Exhibits depicting El Paso's history. Open: Tuesday–Sunday 9am–4.45pm. Free.

Fort Bliss Replica Museum, at Pleasonton and Pershing streets, tel: (915) 568-2804 or 568-4518. Replica of the 1800s-adobe Fort Bliss. Open: daily, 9am–4.30pm. Free.

Indian Cliffs Ranch, About 35 miles (56 km) south of El Paso: take Interstate Highway 10 to the Fabens exit, then proceed 4.5 miles (7.3 km) north on FM Road 793, tel: (915) 544-3200. Horseback riding, hayrides, restaurant. Call for reservations and rates.

Magoffin Home State Historic Site, 1120 Magoffin Avenue, tel: (915) 533-5147. Built in the late 1800s in Territorial style. Includes 19th-century Mexican and American Victorian furnishings. Open: daily, 9am–4pm. Small admission charge.

San Elizario Presidio Church, just south of El Paso in the town of San Elizario, tel: (915) 851-2333. Built in late 1700s to protect the Spanish from the Apache. Always open. Free.

Scenic Drive, from downtown, take Stanton Drive to Rim Road and turn right onto Rim, which will become Scenic Drive. From here, you can see three states as well as Mexico. Always open.

Sierra de Cristo Rey, 3 miles (4.8 km) west of El Paso (take the Anapra exit from Interstate 10). A four-mile (6.4-km) long footpath up Mount Cristo Rey takes you to an immense limestone statues of Christ by Urbici Soler that overlooks both Mexico and the US. There is usually a mass pilgrimage up the mountain on the last Sunday in October. Always open.

Socorro Mission, In the town of Socorro on Nevarez Street, just southeast of El Paso, tel: (915) 859-7718. Built in the late 1600s, the beams are believed to have been sculpted by the Piro Indians. A hand-carved wooden statue of Saint Michael stands in the

south sacristy. Open: summer (daily), 9am–9pm; winter (daily), 9am–7pm. Free.

Southwestern International Livestock Show and Rodeo, at the El Paso County Coliseum, 4200 East Paisano, tel: (915) 532-1401. Parade, livestock show auction, bronco riding, calf roping. Every year in February. Call for schedules and admission charge.

Third US Cavalry Regimental Museum, tel: (915) 568-7783 or 568-1922. Military memorabilia of the Third Armored Cavalry Regiment. Open: every Monday–Friday 7.30am–4.30pm. Free.

US Army Air Defense Artillery Museum, Building 5000, tel: (915) 568-5412 or 568-6848. The history of Air Defense Artillery. Open: Wednesday–Sunday 9am–4.30pm. Free.

Wilderness Park Museum, 2000 Trans-Mountain Road, tel: (915) 755-4332. Depicts desert adaptation and nature trail. Open: Tuesday–Sunday 9am–5pm. Free (charge for some exhibits).

Laredo

Falcon State Park, about 80 miles (129 km) south of Laredo on US Highway 83, tel: (512) 848-5327. Birding, fishing, boating, swimming and camping activities available. Open: Monday–Thursday 8am–5pm; Friday–Sunday 8am–9pm, Small admission charge per vehicle.

Nuevo Santander Museum, at Laredo Junior College on Washington Street, tel: (512) 722-8351. Open: Monday–Thursday 9am–4pm; Friday 9am–noon; Sunday 1–5pm. Free.

Republic of the Rio Grande Museum, At San Agustín Plaza on Zaragoza Street, tel: (512) 727-3480. Open: Tuesday–Sunday 10am–5pm. Admission by donation.

San Agustín Church, 215 San Agustín, tel: (512) 722-8164. Always open. Free.

Roma

Ciudad Guerrero, Ciudad Mier, Ciudad Miguel Alem. Three Mexican towns just south of the border, all joined by Mexico Highway 2. Port of entry at Ciudad Guerrero or Ciudad Alem.

Downtown Roma, 15 blocks of historic structures from the 1800s including the Church of Our Lady of Refuge of Sinners, 608 Estrella.

Falcon Reservoir, About 15 miles (24 km) north of Roma, tel: (512) 848-5327. 87,000 acres (35,220 ha). Picnicking, fishing, birding and camping activities are available. Open: summer: Monday–Friday 8am–9pm, Saturday and Sunday 8am–10pm; winter: Monday–Thursday 8am–5pm, Friday–Sunday 8am–9pm. Small admission charge per vehicle.

Port Isabel

Port Isabel Lighthouse State Historical Site, at Maxan and Tarnava streets on Texas Highway 100, tel: (512) 943-1172. Open: daily, 10am–noon and 1–5pm, Small admission charge.

Austin

Arts Warehouse, 300 San Antonio, tel: (512) 473-2505. Studio and exhibition space for local artists.

Celis Brewery, 2431 Forbes Dr., tel: (512) 835-0884. Tours Tuesday–Saturday 2 and 4pm, reservations recommended.

Children's Museum, 1501 W. 5th. Open: Tuesday–Saturday 10am–5pm, Sunday noon–5pm. Admission.

Children's Zoo, 10807 Rawhide Trail, tel: (512) 288-1490. Open: Wednesday, Saturday, Sunday 10am–6pm.

Confederate Reunion, Camp Ben McCullough on Onion Creek near Driftwood, FM Road 1826 south of US Highway 290 West, tel: (512) 472-2596. Dancing, fiddle contests, gospel singing and camping. Every year, around July 4th.

Driskill Hotel, Sixth and Brazos streets. Built by cattle baron Col. Jesse L. Driskill with beautiful corridors and spaces.

Elisabeth Ney Museum, 304 East 44th Street, tel: (512) 458-2255. Restored house and studio of German sculptor who worked in Texas in 1800s. Open: Wednesday–Saturday 10am–5pm, Sunday noon–5pm. Free.

French Legation, 802 San Marcos at East 7th Street, tel: (512) 472-8180. Oldest house in Austin. Museum and creole kitchen. Open: Tuesday–Sunday 1–5pm. Admission.

George Washington Carver Museum, 1165 Angelina, tel: (512) 472-4809. Exhibitions include black history and the interesting culture of Austin and Travis County. Open Tuesday–Thursday 10am–6pm, Friday and Saturday noon–5pm. Free.

Governor's Mansion, Colorado and West 11th streets, tel: (512) 463-5518. Tours: Monday–Friday every 20 minutes between 10am–noon. Call for reservations. Free.

Hill Country Flyer, through the Hill Country from Cedar Park City Hall near US 183 to Burnet, tel: (512)477-8468. Steam excursion train running through the Hill Country. Two hours to Burnet and two hours back, departures Saturday and Sunday at 10am. Admission.

Hippie Hollow, on Lake Travis, take Ranch Road 2222 west to Ranch Road 620. Turn left on RR 620 and then right on Comanche Trail at the yellow flashing light, tel: (512) 266-1644. Nude swimming area. Free.

History Center, 810 Guadalupe at West 9th Street, tel: (512) 499-7480. Open: Monday–Thursday 9am–9pm, Friday and Saturday 9am–6pm, Sunday noon–6pm.

Huntington Art Gallery, 23rd Street and San Jacinto Blvd, tel: (512) 471-7324. Open: Monday–Saturday 9am–5pm, Sunday 1–5pm. Free.

Jourdan Bachman Pioneer Farm, 11418 Sprinkle Cut-Off Road, tel: (512) 837-1215. Open: Monday–Thursday 9:30am–3pm in summer; Monday–Wednesday 9:30am–1pm the rest of the year. Admission.

Laguna Gloria Art Museum, 3809 West 35th Street at the end of Old Bull Creek Road, tel: (512) 458-8181. Open: Tuesday–Saturday 10am–5pm; Thursday 10am–9pm; Sunday 1–5pm. Free.

Lorenzo De Zavala State Archives and Library Building, 1201 Brazos east of State Capitol on Capitol grounds; tel: (512) 475-2445. Open: Monday–Friday 8am–5pm; Genealogy Section and lobby: Monday–Saturday 8am–5pm. Free.

Lyndon B. Johnson Library, 2313 Red River, tel: (512) 916-5136. Museum of LBJ memorabilia. Open: daily 9am–5pm.

Moonlight Towers. Austin's beloved lighting system is a symbol of Austin. 17 towers remain. Contact the Austin Visitor's Center (512) 478-0098) for locations.

Museo del Barrio de Austin, 1619 East 1st Street, tel: (512) 477-5770. Open: Monday–Friday 9am–5pm. Free.

Museum of Art at Laguna Gloria, 3809 W. 35th. Open: Tuesday–Saturday 10am–5pm, Sunday 1–5pm. Admission.

National Wild Flower Research Center, 3 miles (4.8 km) north of Texas Highway 71 off FM Road 973, tel: (512) 929-3600. National clearinghouse for wild flower research. Founded by Lady Bird Johnson. Open: Tuesday–Sunday 9am–6pm.

Neill-Cochran House, 2310 San Gabriel, tel: (512) 478-2335. Limestone rubble Greek Revival house built in 1855. It is now the home of National Society of Colonial Dames if America in Texas. Open: Wednesday–Sunday 2–5pm.

O. Henry Home Museum, 409 East 5th Street, tel: (512) 472-1903. Memorabilia of short story writer. Open: Wednesday–Sunday noon–5pm. Free.

Old Bakery and Emporium, 1006 Congress. Built in 1875–6 as an ice-parlor and bakery. Now run by senior citizens. Open: Monday–Friday 9am–4pm; Saturday 10am–3pm in summer and December.

Old Land Office, 108 East 11th Street, near the southeast corner of the Capitol grounds; occupied by museums: The Daughters of the Confederacy on the first floor, tel: (512) 472-2596; The Daughters of the Republic of Texas on the second floor, tel: (512) 339-1997. Open: Monday–Friday 10am–4pm. Free.

Purple Martin Houses. These pagoda-like houses on 16-foot poles are another symbol of Austin. The purple martin appears in early spring.

Scholz Garten, 1607 San Jacinto near East 17th St, tel: (512) 477-4171. Beer garden popular with politicians, liberals and intellectuals.

St David's Episcopal Church, 304 East 7th. Street at San Jacinto, tel: (512) 472-1196. Oldest Austin church building. Open: daily 8am–5pm.

St Mary's Cathedral, 201 East 10th Street at Brazos, tel: (512) 476-6182. Limestone Gothic Revival Roman Catholic church. Open: daily 6:30am–6pm (visitors are requested not to disturb the noon mass). Free.

Texas Memorial Museum, 2400 Trinity, tel: (512) 471-1604. Historical, archeological and geological collections. Open: Monday–Saturday 9am–5pm, Sunday 1–5pm. Free.

Texas State Capitol, 11th Street and Congress Avenue, tel: (512) 305-8409. Tourist information center on the ground floor. Largest state capitol with an iron dome higher than the US Capitol. Open: Monday–Friday 7am–10pm, Saturday and Sunday 7am–8pm; Tours throughout the day. Free.

Texas State Highway Building, 11th and Brazos streets, tel: (512) 463-8585. Neglected art decor building built in 1933. Open: Monday–Friday 8am–5pm. Free.

Tlawn Academic Center, on the West Mall of the campus, tel: (512) 471-5222. Permanent reconstruction of mystery writer Erle Stanley Gardner's study and J. Frank Dobie collection.

University of Texas at Austin, roughly bounded by Interstate Highway 35, 26th Street, Guadalupe Street, and Martin Luther King Blvd. Including: **Harry Ransom Humanities Research Center**, at the corner of 21st and Guadalupe streets, tel: (512) 471-8944. A Gutenberg Bible, American and Contemporary Latin American art. Open: Monday–Saturday 9am–4:30pm, Thursday 9am–7pm. Free.

Vanishing Texas River Cruise, On RM Road 2341, tel: (512) 756-6986. 3-hour cruise on Lake Buchanan and lower Colorado River. Possibility of bald eagles in winter. Reservations required. Admission.

Visitor Center, 201 E. 2nd St, tel: (512) 478-0098 or (800) 926-2282. Open: Monday–Saturday 8:30am–5pm, Sunday 1–5pm.

Willie N. Festus, rotating steel and fiberglass composite insect on 16-foot (5-meter) pole at 12th and Lamar streets, in front of Terminix Pest Control. Called the Statues of Liberty of Austin, coveted by many a college fraternity.

Willie Nelson's 4th of July Picnic, in South Park Meadows, 9604 South Interstate Highway 35, tel: (512) 282-8320. Several-day festival with top entertainers, local favorites and much beer and food. Make reservations well in advance.

Kerrville

Cowboy Artists of America Museum, 1550 Bandera Highway, tel: (512) 896-2553. Open: Monday–Saturday 9am–5pm; Sunday 1–5pm; closed on Monday during September–May. Call for admission charge.

Kerrville Arts Festival (Texas State Arts & Crafts Fair), at Schreiner College, 3 miles (4.8 km) east of Kerrville on Texas Highway 27, tel: (512) 896-5711. An arts and crafts festival with food and entertainment. Write for more information, and admission charges: Box 1527, Kerrville 78028. Every year on Memorial Day weekend in May: Friday 5–9pm; Saturday 9am–9pm; Sunday 9am–6pm.

Kerrville Folk Festival, At Quiet Valley Ranch, 8 miles (13 km) south of Kerrville on Texas Highway 16, tel: (512) 257-3600 or (800) 842-6156. Features folk and country-western music. Every year on weekends in May, July and September. Call for schedules.

YO Ranch, About 40 miles (64 km) west of Kerrville by Texas Highway 41, tel: (512) 640-3222. A 100-square-mile (259-sq-km) ranch and exotic game preserve. Hunting and photographic expeditions. Guest cabins. Tours start 10am daily with reservations required for entry. Call for admission charge (lunch included).

Stonewall

Lyndon B. Johnson National Historical Park, east of Stonewall on US Highway 290, tel: (512) 644-2241. Includes a replica of the birthplace of President Johnson, the LBJ Ranch itself and the President's grave. For security, tours are permitted only by bus. Tours: daily, 10am–4pm. Free.

Lyndon B. Johnson State Historical Park, 1.5 miles (2.4 km) east of Stonewall on US Highway 290, tel: (512) 644-2252. Includes visitor center, nature trail, picnic sites, swimming pool. Open: summer: daily, 9am–6pm; winter: daily, 8am–5pm.

Stonewall Peach Jamboree, on the rodeo grounds in town. Every year on Father's Day weekend (in June). Contests, dances, games highlight this peach festival.

New Braunfels

Gruene Historic District, about 4 miles (6.4 km) northeast of New Braunfels (off Interstate Highway 35, take FM Road 306 to Hunter Road, turn left). A restored German community.

Gruene Hall, On Gruene Road, tel: (512) 625-9013. The oldest dance hall in Texas, which still operates from Thursday to Sundays. Mostly country and western bands.

Gruene River Company, 1495 Gruene Road, tel: (512) 625-2800. A raft or canoe trip can be arranged down the Guadalupe River.

Guadalupe Valley Winery, At 1720 Hunter Road, tel: (512) 629-2351. Tasting Room and gift shop: Monday–Friday 10am–5pm; Saturday 10am–6pm; Sunday noon–5pm Tours: June–August: Saturday and Sunday noon–5pm; September–May: 3rd Saturday of each month or by appointment for groups of 10 or more.

Lindheimer Home (Museum), 491 Comal Street, tel: (512) 625-7046. Built in 1800s using fachwerk construction, home of internationally known German botanist Ferdinand Jacob Lindheimer who identified many Texas plants. Overlooks Comal River and tubers. Open: May–August: Tuesday–Sunday 2–5pm; September–April: Saturday and Sunday 2–5pm. Small admission charge.

Moyer Texas Champagne, 1941 Interstate Highway 35, tel: (512) 625-5181. Tasting Room: open Monday–Saturday 10am–6pm; Sunday noon–6pm. Tours: Monday–Saturday 10am–5pm. Gift shop.

Natural Bridge Caverns, about 18 miles (29 km) west of New Braunfels by Texas Highway 46 to FM Road 1863 to Natural Bridge Caverns Road, tel: (512) 651-6101. Natural cave formations. Snack bar, gift shop. Open daily at 9am. Tours leave every half-hour throughout the day; length of tour is 1 hr 20 min. Last tour of day leaves at 6pm during June–August and Labor Day weekend. Other months, last tour leaves at 4pm. Admission subject to change.

Schlitterbaun, 400 North Liberty Street, tel: (512) 629-3910. Park opens: May, weekends only; Memorial Day to Labor Day (daily if weather permits), 10am–8pm. Call for admission charge.

Sophienburg Memorial Museum and Archives, 401 West Coll Street, tel: (512) 629-1572. On the site intended for a replica of the family castle of Prince Carl of Solms-Braunfels, who founded New Braunfels. Exhibits and guided tours are also available, Open: Monday–Saturday 10am–5pm; Sunday 1–5pm. Small admission charge.

Wurstfest, at the Wursthalle in Landa Park, tel: (512) 625-2385. A celebration of the Hill Country's German culture. Oompah bands, German food, dancing, historic tours highlight the festival. Every year in October. Call for admission charge.

San Marcos

Aquarena Springs, On Loop 82, tel: (512) 396-8900. An amusement park built around the natural springs at the head of the San Marcos River. Glass-bottomed boats, re-created frontier structures, lodging, unusual underwater theater, herd of swimming pigs. Open: daily: summer, 8am–9pm; winter, 8.30am–6pm; spring, 8.30am–7pm.

Belvin Street Historic District, Six blocks of Victorian houses southwest of downtown. Public tours first weekend in May.

Old Main Building, Southwest Texas State University, tel: (512) 245-2111. When LBJ was a student in the 1920s, most college business was carried out in this building.

Seguin

Los Nogales Museum, South River and East Live Oak streets, south of town square, tel: (512) 379-4277/ 1567. Los Nogales means "walnuts". Pre-Revolutionary stuccoed mud brick building containing museum. **Ralph Castillo Doll's House** next to it and dog-trot house across the street make up instructive Early Texas house group. Visits by appointment. Free.

Sebastapol, 704 Zorn. Not open to the public. Unusual house built in 1851 of concrete with reservoir on roof for air conditioning and Native American sieges.

World's Largest Pecan, northeast corner of Courthouse Square. Sculpture.

Victoria

Fort Saint Louis Site, 13 miles (21 km) south on US Highway 87 to Placedo, then 11 miles (18 km) east on FM Road 616 to Garcitas Creek. Not open to public. Site of La Salle's 1685 settlement.

Victoria Bach Festival, A selection of events take place in various churches throughout the town every year in June. For schedules and venues, call the Victoria Chamber of Commerce, tel: (512) 573-5277.

Victoria Community Concert Series, in University concert hall in May. Prosperous city supports most active community music programs in Texas, bringing top stars (such as Pavarotti, Dame Janet Baker) every year.

Shiner

Spoetzl Brewery, 603 East Brewery, tel: (512) 594-3852. Hospitality room. The only Texas-owned brewery. Shiner beer is brewed with Texas grain and water. The brewery is a popular destination for cycling expeditions from Austin. Make reservations well in advance for groups of 20 or more. Gift shop and Museum open daily except Wednesday and Sunday. Brewery tours Monday–Thursday at 11am. Free.

Helena

Karnes County Courthouse Museum, at Courthouse Square on Texas Highway 80 between Gillett and Karnes City, tel: (512) 780-2868. Museum with exhibits relating to this almost ghost town, near the Chihuahua Trail, which was supposedly ruined by neighboring rancher after his son was killed in a saloon. Open: Tuesday–Saturday 9am–5pm. Free.

Bastrop

Bastrop County Courthouse and Jail, on Town Square, tel: (512) 321-2227. Built in 1800s in Victorian style. Copper-domed clock tower. Open: Monday–Friday 8am–5pm. Free.

Bastrop County Historical Society Museum, 702 Main Street, tel: (512) 321-6177. Open: Saturday 9.30am–5pm; Sunday 1–5pm. Small admission charge.

Bastrop State Park, 1 mile (1.6 km) east of Bastrop on Texas Highway 21, tel: (512) 321-2101. A 2,033-acre (823-ha) forest called the "Lost Pines." Picnicking, golf, swimming and camping (fee). Open: daily, 8am–10pm. Small admission charge per vehicle.

Memorial Medallion Trail, throughout Bastrop, tel: (512) 321-2419. A self-conducted tour of historic buildings. Pick up map at County Courthouse.

Waco

Armstrong-Browning Library, 8th and Speight Streets, Baylor University, tel: (817) 755-3566. Memorabilia of Robert and Elizabeth Browning. Fifty-four stained glass windows each depicting a Browning poem. Open: Monday–Friday 9am–noon, 2–4pm; Saturday 9am–noon. Free.

Art Center, 1300 College Drive, tel: (817) 752-4371. Open: Tuesday–Saturday 10am–5pm, Sunday 1–5pm. Admission.

Cameron Park Zoo, 1600 N. 4th. Open daily 9am–4pm. Admission.

Dr. Pepper Museum, 300 S. 5th, tel: (817) 757-1024. Dr. Pepper soft drink memorabilia. Open: Monday–Saturday 10am–4pm, Sunday noon–4pm. Admission.

Earl-Napier-Kinnard House, 814 South 4th Street, tel: (817) 756-0057. Open: Saturday, Sunday 2–5pm in winter; Thursday–Monday 2–5pm in summer. Admission.

Earle-Harrison House, 1901 North 5th. One of state's finest antebellum Greek Revival homes. Open: Monday–Friday 9–noon, 1–5pm; Saturday, Sunday 1–5pm. Admission.

East Terrace Historic Home, 100 Mill Street, tel: (817) 756-4104. Saturday and Sunday 2–5pm. Admission.

Fort House Museum, 503 S. Fourth, tel: (817) 753-5166. Saturday and Sunday 2–5pm. Admission.

McCulloch House, 407 Columbus Avenue, tel: (817) 753-5166. Open: Saturday and Sunday 2–5pm. Admission.

Strecker Museum, Sid Richardson Science Building, South 4th Street, Baylor University, tel: (817) 755-1110. Indian, geological, biological and anthropological collections. Open: Monday–Saturday 9am–4pm, Sunday 2–5pm. Free.

Taylor Museum of Waco History, 701 Jefferson, tel: (817) 752-4774. Open: Tuesday–Saturday 10am–4pm, Sunday 1–4pm. Admission.

Texas Ranger Hall of Fame and Museum, Interstate Highway 35 at the Brazos River, at Fort Fisher, tel: (817) 754-1433. Open: daily 9am–5pm. Admission.

Texas Sports Hall of Fame, 1108 S. University Parks Drive. Open daily 10am–5pm. Free.

Visitor Center, University Parks Drive off I-35 (exit 335B), tel: (817) 750-8696. Open: daily 8am–5pm.

Waco Suspension Bridge, South 1st Street at Austin Avenue. Always open. Free.

Amarillo

Alibates Flint Quarries National Monument, 32 miles (52 km) northeast of Amarillo. Take Highway 136 northeast for 32 miles (52 km), turn left 1 mile (1.6 km) past Turkey Creek Plant at Alibates Road, tel: (806) 857-3151. Tours: summer (daily), 10am–2pm or by appointment. Free.

Amarillo Art Center, 2200 Van Buren Street, tel: (806) 371-5050. Open: Tuesday, Wednesday and Friday 10am–5pm; Thursday 10am–9pm; closed Monday. Tours by appointment. Free.

Amarillo Livestock Auction and Western Stockyards, South Manhattan at East 3rd, tel: (306) 373-7464. Open: Monday and Tuesday 9am–7pm. Free.

Cadillac Ranch, On Interstate Highway 40 between the Soncy-Helium and Hope exits. Roadside viewing.

Cowboy Morning, At the Figure 3 Ranch, 26 miles (42 km) east of Amarillo near Claude, tel: (806) 374-9812 or (800) 692-1338. A chuckwagon breakfast on a working ranch, followed by hiking, riding, or roping and branding demonstrations. Open: May 15–September only on Saturday at 8am. Reservations necessary. Call for admission charge.

Don Harrington Discovery Center, 200 Streit Drive, tel: (806) 355-9547. Open: Tuesday–Friday 9am–5pm; Night Sky Programs: Saturday and Sunday 1pm; Planetarium Shows: Saturday and Sunday 2pm and 3.30pm. Admission: exhibits free; planetarium, call for charges.

Lake Meredith, 49 miles (79 km) northeast of Amarillo. Take Highway 136 northeast 38 miles (61 km) to Fritch, then east 3 miles (5 km) to Ranch Road 687. Go north 8 miles (13 km) to Sanford Dam, tel: (806) 857-3151. Always open. Free.

Lee and Mary Bivins Home, The Chamber of Commerce, 1000 South Polk at 10th, tel: (806) 374-5238. The Georgian Revival home of early Panhandle cattle baron Lee Bivins and his wife. Open: Monday–Friday 8.30am–5pm. Free.

Lubbock

Buddy Holly's Grave, In the Lubbock Cemetery, East 34th Near Quirt, tel: (806) 762-6411. Open: Monday–Friday 8am–noon and 1–5pm. Free.

Canyon Lakes Project, On University Avenue, downtown. The **Great Yellowhouse Canyon Raft Race** is held every September. Always open. Free.

Llano Estacado Winery, 3.2 miles (5.2 km) east of US Highway 87 on FM Road 1585, P.O. Box 3487, 79452, tel: (806) 745-2258. Tasting room and gift shop: open Monday–Saturday 10am–4pm; Sunday noon–4pm Tours available these hours or by appointment.

Lubbock Lake Archaeological Site, Clovis Road near Indiana in northwest Lubbock, tel: (806) 742-2479. Tours: June–July, Saturday 9am–noon; the rest of the year by appointment only. Free.

MacKenzie State Park, Avenue A near 4th Street. Golf, tennis, picnicking, swimming and camping activities available. Always open. Free.

Moody Planetarium, 4th Street and Indiana, tel: (806) 742-2442. Monday–Friday 2.30pm; Saturday and Sunday 2pm and 3.30pm. Small admission charge.

Pheasant Ridge Winery, 1505 Elkhart Avenue, 79416, tel: (806) 746-6033. Tasting room: tours available by appointment only.

Ranching Heritage Center, 4th Street and Indiana Avenue, tel: (806) 742-2498. Open: Monday–Saturday 10am–5pm (till 8.30pm on Thursday); Sunday 1–5pm. Small admission charge.

South Plains Fair, Avenue A near Broadway on the South Plains Fairground, tel: (806) 744-9557. One of the biggest fairs in the state, held in late September and early October. Small admission charge.

Texas Tech Museum, 4th Street and Indiana Avenue, tel: (806) 742-2490. Open: Monday, Wednesday, Friday and Saturday 9am–4.30pm; Thursday 9am–8.30pm; Sunday 1–4.30pm. Free.

Big Spring

Big Spring Cowboy Reunion and Rodeo, Howard County Fairgrounds on Air Base Road, near intersection of US Highway 80 and Interstate Highway 20 and FM Road 700. Every year in June. Small admission charge.

Big Spring State Recreation Area, from Big Spring, take FM Road 700 west, 1 mile past US Highway 87 to Park Road 8. Picnicking, prairie dog town. Open: daily: summer, 8am–

10pm; winter, 8am–9pm. Small admission charge per vehicle.

Heritage Museum, 510 Scurry, tel: (915) 267-8255. Open: Tuesday–Friday 9am–5pm; Saturday 10am–5pm. Admission by donation.

Pecos

Pecos Rodeo, At Rodeo Arena on US Highway 285, south of the city limits, tel: (915) 445-4442. Every year around the 4th of July. Call for schedules.

West of the Pecos Museum, 120 East 1st, at junction with US Hwy 285, tel: (915) 445-5076. Open Monday–Saturday 9.00am–5pm. Small admission charge.

Fort Davis

Davis Mountains State Park, 4 miles (6.4 km) northwest of Fort Davis on Texas Highway 17 and Texas Highway 118, tel: (915) 426-3337. Open: daily, 8am–10pm, Small admission charge per vehicle for camping.

Fort Davis National Historic Site, on Texas Highway 17, just north of Fort Davis, tel: (915) 426-3225. Open: daily, 8am–5pm.

Marfa

Marfa Lights, an eerie glow seen for centuries in the hills between Marfa and Alpine.

Presidio County Courthouse, on the Town Square, tel: (915) 729-4452. Built in late 1800s in Second Empire style. Open: Monday–Friday 8am–5pm. Free.

Langtry

Judge Roy Bean Visitor Center, on Loop 25, tel: (512) 291-3340. Appointed Justice of the Peace in 1882, Bean held forth at his saloon, the Jersey Lily, named for his idol Lily Langtry, a British actress. Judge Bean was known for dispensing all the law west of the Pecos. Open: daily, 8am–5pm. Free.

Pine Springs

Guadalupe Mountains National Park, on US Highway 62/180, tel: (915) 828-3251. Partially restored fort, established in 1854 as protection against the Apache Indians. The park covers more than 77,000 acres (32,083 ha) and contains 36 mountains over 8,000 feet (2,460 m) high.

Frijole Ranger Station is always open. Vehicles are not permitted in the Park because of its fragile ecosystem, but there are many hiking trails. Handicapped access is now provided. Camping by permit only. Small admission charge per vehicle.

McDonald Observatory, 18 miles (29 km) northwest of Fort Davis on Texas Highway 118, tel: (915) 426-3423. Perched atop 6,800-foot (2,092-meter) Mount Locke, one of the world's largest astronomical research centers. Open: winter: Monday–Saturday 9am–5pm, Sunday 1–5pm; summer: Monday–Saturday 9am–7pm; Sunday 1–7pm. Free.

Activities For Children

For most events, consult *What to Do* guide, but specifically note the following attractions:

Houston's Space Center, 1601 NASA Road, tel: (800) 972-0369, is one of the biggest family attractions with its interactive exhibits, IMAX films about being an astronaut (shown on a screen five storys high), a moon rock display and behind the scenes tour by tram. Open: daily 9am–7pm, 10am–5pm in winter. Another giant screen can be found in the Wortham IMAX Theater at the **Museum of Natural Science**, which also includes a planetarium and a butterfly tropical garden.

Houston has a **Children's Museum** (1500 Binz Street) with hands-on exhibits and mock-ups of ethnic villages. **Six Flags Houston** and its nearby **WaterWorld** are huge theme parks near the Astrodome, the former a 75-acre (30-ha) amusement park with more than 100 rides, and the latter offering body slides and a river for innertube riders.

The **Dallas** area has a variety of amusement parks, including the major **Six Flags Over Texas** and **Wet N' Wild**, a family park with wave pools, water slides, canals and shops. Both of these are in Arlington. The **Sandy Lake Amusement Park** in Carrollton features paddle boats, miniature golf and a giant swimming pool. Go-karts, miniature golf and videos are offered at **Fun Town Amusement Park** at Red Oak, and Sprint-Karts attract young racers at the **Indy Indoor Speedway**, 10323 Harry Hines Blvd, Dallas. There are half a dozen amusement centers,

of which **Virtual World**, 9330 N. Central Expressway, is the most ambitious. Here young adventurers can engage in simulated combat and fly a souped-up hovercraft into the galaxy.

San Antonio has two theme parks: **Sea World of Texas**, 10500 Sea World Drive off Loop 1604, a 250-acre (100-ha) park with killer whales, a shark-infested coral reef and a park with waterslides and exotic birds; and **Six Flags Fiesta Texas**, I-10 West & Loop 1604, with all the familiar rides and attractions. The **Austin** Visitors & Convention Bureau, tel: (800) 926-2282, will send you on request a free brochure, *101 Things for Kids*, containing information and telephone numbers about activities as varied as watching the peacocks in **Mayfield Park**, shopping in a tiny grocery store in the **Children's Museum**, taking a miniature train ride in **Zilker Park** or practicing computer animation at the **Dougherty Arts Center**.

Shopping
What to Buy/Where to Shop

Dallas boasts that it has more shopping centers per capita than any other US city. Not only is it home to the internationally recognized specialty store Neiman-Marcus and the retail giant J.C. Penney, but it is also the site of America's oldest shopping center, **Highland Park Village** (Preston Road at Mockingbird Lane) where Victor Costa, internationally known for copying the designs of Paris couturiers, has a boutique. Avant-garde designer Todd Oldham is a Dallas native. Most of the major names in retailing are represented in Dallas, the latest being Nordstroms in the four-level **Galleria** (LBJ Freeway & Dallas Parkway), with

200 stores in a dramatic glass atrium supplemented by an ice rink and a Westin hotel. Other huge malls include **NorthPark Center** (Northwest Hwy at N. Central Expressway) and **Prestonwood Town Center** (5301 Belt Line Road), which also has an ice rink, along with 160 stores.

Sundance Square, Main & Houston Streets in downtown Fort Worth, is fun to visit with its collection of shops, restaurants, museums set among red brick sidewalks and charming courtyards. Western wear is, of course, a big seller in these parts with 28 shops and restaurants located in renovated hog and sheep pens at **Stockyards Station** (140 E Exchange Ave, Fort Worth) and more western paraphernalia is available in the shops at **Southfork Ranch** (3700 Hogge Rd, Parker), location of the TV-famous Ewing Ranch. Boot fanciers often prefer to go directly to the **Justin Boot Company** Factory Outlet Store in Fort Worth at 717 W. Vickery Blvd, tel: (817) 654-3103.

Factory stores have become a major phenomenon, situated outside almost every big town. Sometimes they are grouped together in malls, each offering different merchandise. Often they stand alone and are enormous. Several chains exist with branches spread over the state. Justin Boots and Cowboy Outfitters, which claims to be the world's largest western store, is headquartered in Justin, but in addition to Fort Worth also has branches in Dallas and Denton – tel: (800) 677-BOOT. A rival, Cavender's Boot City (2019 West S.WE. Loop, Tyler, TX 75701) has stores in Austin, San Antonio, Dallas and Houston. tel: (800) 256-8588 or 256-9190.

Love Field Antique Mall, tel: (214) 357-6500, behind the Mobil station at the entrance to Dallas' Love Field airport, boasts 350 shops in addition to a collection of classic cars. As with everything else there are many different specialties: **The Englishman's Antiques**, 15304 Midway Rd, Dallas, tel: (214) 980-0107, boasts of its vast array of Staffordshire pottery, Welsh dressers and other European furniture. The **Stockyards Antique Mall**, 1332 Main St, Fort Worth, invites you to tour scores of shops in an 1890s hotel.

Antiquing Texas, a comprehensive 48-page tabloid carrying listings and ads for antique dealers across the state, is free if you can find it lying around, but otherwise costs $4 by first-class mail from PO Box 7754, The Woodlands, TX 77387, tel: (713) 364-9540.

There are more than 30 malls in the **Houston** area, a city where shopping is taken very seriously. In the city's southwest section, **Rice Village** was one of the earliest shopping districts and it still draws the crowds today with more than 300 stores ranging from familiar names to fashionable designer boutiques and funky mom-and-pop shops. There are also art and craft galleries and spas. Even bigger is the **Post Oak-Galleria** area uptown, which sports most of the big-name stores – including Neiman-Marcus, Tiffany, Hermes, Marshall Fields, Saks Fifth Ave – and claims to draw 10,000 visitors per day. Three blocks east, the **Highland Village Shopping Center** also features upscale stores. For hard-to-find antiques and arty treasures, check out **The Heights**, whose streets (between 11th and 19th) are lined with Victorian structures and Craftsmen-style bungalows. Western wear is purveyed by **Rick's Ranchwear** (5085 Westheimer) and **Cavender's Boot City**, which has 10 separate locations in Houston alone. tel: (800) 256-9190 for nearest store.

Austin's biggest mall, **Highland Mall**, is at 6001 Airport Blvd, tel: (512) 454-9636, but there are also numerous little specialty shops, such as the **Turquoise Trading Post**, Burnet Road at Koenig, which displays a large selection of Native American jewelry, including Zuni fetishes, Navaho Kachina dolls, medicine wheels and dreamcatchers. The more macabre-minded will enjoy the selection of skulls, hides and trophy mounts available at the **Corner Shoppe**, 5900 Lamar Street. As befits a college town – and state capital – Austin is proud of its literary leanings, pointing out that not only does it house branches of the big bookstore chains such as Borders and Barnes & Noble, but also many independents, among them Congress Avenue Booksellers, Half Price Books – which deals in used books and music – and three stores specializing in African-American literature: Folktales, Just For Us and Mitchie's Fine Black Art Gallery & Bookstore.

Visitors to San Antonio's **North Star** mall (Loop 410 between San Pedro and MacCullough) are invited to begin their browsing with a visit to the information booth to pick up a free shopping bag and a coupon booklet offering discounts at many of the 200 stores. These include such big names as Saks Fifth Avenue, Marshall Field's, Guess, Williams-Sonoma and Gap.

There are other malls, of which the most attractive architecturally is **Rivercenter**, 849 E. Commerce, adjoining the restaurants and IMAX theater in the heart of downtown. **La Villita**, the recreated Mexican village on the site of the original town, and **El Mercado** (514 W. Commerce) both offer specialty shops with Mexican arts and crafts.

Austin

Cadillac Jack Boot Co., 6623 North Lamar Blvd, tel: (512) 452-4428.
Capitol Saddlery, 1614 Lavaca, tel: (512) 478-9309. Leather goods.
Tesoros Trading Company, 209 Congress Avenue, tel: (512) 479-8341.
Texas Custom Boots, 6616 West Highway 290, tel: (512) 892-6321.
Texas Hatters, 5003 Overpass Road, Buda, tel: (512) 441-4287. Clients include Bob Dylan, Willie Nelson and Burt Reynolds.

Brownsville

Tate's, 515 East St Charles, tel: (512) 541-7501. Custom-tailored clothes.

Dallas

Cutter Bill Western World, 5818 Loop 635 (the LBJ Freeway), tel: (214) 239-3742. You can be outfitted here with a custom pair of ostrich skin boots and a 10-gallon hat.
Highland Park Village, at Preston and Mockingbird, tel: (214) 559-2740. The oldest of Dallas' many shopping centers and malls. With boutiques like Courrèges, Kron Chocolatier, Polo/Ralph Lauren, Guy Laroche and the swankiest Sanger Harris in town, Highland Park claims to be Dallas' answer to Los Angeles' Rodeo Drive.
Neiman-Marcus, 1618 Main, tel: (214) 741-6911. There are several Neiman-Marcus stores around town at various shopping malls, but this is the legendary original.

Resistol Hats, 401 Marion Drive in Garland, tel: (214) 494-0511. Here you can get a good western hat for a very reasonable price.

El Paso

The Boo Trader, 10787 Gateway East, tel: (915) 598-6666. Boots by Justin, Nacona, Lucchese and others, and Resistol and Bailey hats.
Champion Boot Company Factory Outlet, 8070 Gateway East, tel: (915) 598-1296.
Cowtown Boot Company, 11401 Gateway West, tel: (915) 593-2929.
Desierto Leather Shop, 1601 Montana, tel: (915) 544-5950.
Hondo Boot Company, 5548 El Paso Drive, El Paso, tel: (915) 778-9841. Mexican-made boots.
Larry Mahan Cowboy Collection, 7661 North Mesa, tel: (915) 833-1193. An outlet for boots inspired by rodeo champion Larry Mahan.
Tony Lama Factory Store, 7156 Gateway East, tel: (915) 772-4327. An outlet for famous Tony Lama boots.

Fort Worth

Justin Boot Company Outlet Store, 717 West Vickery Blvd, tel: (817) 654-3103. Boots, belts, jackets, wallets.
Luskey/Ryon's Western Wear, 2601 North Main Street, tel: (817) 625-2391. Carries Tony Lama and Justin boots, among others.
Williams Western Tailors, 1104 North West 28th Street, tel: (817) 625-2401. This is where the cast of *Dallas* had their shirts made.

Houston

Cutter Bill Western World, 5647 Westheimer, tel: (713) 622-5105. Perhaps the ultimate western store.
Eagle Dancer "The American Indian Store", 159 South Gulf Freeway at FM 518, League City 77573, tel: (713) 332-6028.
The Galleria, 5015 Westheimer, tel: (713) 621-1907. A three-story shopping mall with two hotels, a skating rink, 19 restaurants, 4 movie theaters, and expensive stores such as Neiman-Marcus, Laura Ashley, Gucci, Gumps of San Francisco, Mark Cross, Tiffany & Co., Alfred Dunhill, Cartier and Fred Joiallier of Paris.
Gary's Hats, 312 Louisiana, tel: (713) 227-2996. Could be the largest selection of western hats in Texas. Famous

customers include President Reagan, Roy Rogers, Jimmy Stewart and ZZ Top.

Stelzig's of Texas Western Store, 3123 Post Oak Blvd, tel: (713) 429-7779. Another good western store, even sells saddle blankets.

Paul Wheeler Boot Company, 4115 Willbend, tel: (713) 665-0224. Custom boots which are popular with the Houston oil-rich.

Juárez (Mexico, border)

Centro Commercial ProNaF, off 16 de Setiembre, east of downtown. A government-run center featuring the shop Centro Artesanal, which offers items like Oaxacan pottery.

El Mercado Juárez, near downtown at 16 de Setiembre No. 103. This is the main city market.

Mercado Cuahutenoc, one block off 16 de Setiembre between La Presidencia (City Hall) and Our Lady of Guadalupe Cathedral. A smaller version of El Mercado Juárez.

Matamaros (Mexico, border)

Bazar Mexicana II, 11 Avenida Alvaro Obregón, tel: 011-52-891-23857. Piñatas.

Centro Artesanal, at Avenida Alvaro Obregón and Iturbid, next to the El Presidente Hotel, tel: 011-52-891-20384. Features Michoacán and Oaxacan pottery and *huipiles* from Yucatan. Prices are fixed by the Government; no bargaining here.

Mary's, 26 Avenida Alvaro Obregón, tel: 011-52-891-22431. Papier-mâché animals, ceramics, woven goods.

Mercado Juárez, Matamoros and Nueve streets. This is the main market.

Myrta's Dress Shop, 23 Avenida Alvaro Obregón, tel: 011-52-891-22369. Dresses, silver jewelry.

Nocona

Nocona Boot Company, US Highway 82, Nocona, about 100 miles (161 km) north of Fort Worth, tel: (817) 825-3321. One of the four big bootmaking companies in Texas, Nocona boots were first made in 1879 by H.J. Justin. Call the factory before visiting.

Nuevo Laredo (Mexico, border)

El Mercado, 300 Guerrero. This is the main marketplace.

Marti's, 2933 Victoria and Guerrero, tel: 011-52-871-23137. Famous for first-quality Mexican crafts.

San Antonio

El Rio Gallery, 504 Riverwalk, tel: (512) 222-9380.

Frost Brothers, 217 East Houston, tel: (512) 226-7131. San Antonio's version of Neiman-Marcus. Also located at various shopping malls.

Joske's, at Alamo Plaza and Commerce, tel: (512) 227-4343. San Antonio's most popular department store. Also located at various shopping malls.

Kallison's Farm and Ranch Supply, 1025 Nogalitos, tel: (512) 222-8411. Texas' equivalent of a New England general store. Ranch and farm supplies.

La Tienda, 123 Alamo Plaza, tel: (512) 222-1588. Mexican imports.

Lucchese Boot Co., 4001 Broadway, tel: (512) 828-9419. Founded in 1883 by Italian immigrant Sam Lucchese, has had clients such as the late John Wayne and Lyndon Johnson.

Market Square, 514 West Commerce, tel: (512) 299-8600. Mexican imports at the El Mercado building. Also restaurants, art galleries and bars.

Clothing Chart

This table compares American, Continental and British clothing sizes. It's always advisable to try clothes on before buying as sizes can vary.

Women's Dresses/Suits

American	Continental	British
6	38/34N	8/30
8	40/36N	10/32
10	42/38N	12/34
12	44/40N	14/36
14	46/42N	16/38
16	48/44N	18/40

Women's Shoes

American	Continental	British
4.5	36	3
5.5	37	4
6.5	38	5
7.5	40	6
8.5	41	7
9.5	42	8
10.5	43	9

Men's Suits

American	Continental	British
34	44	34
–	46	36
38	48	38
–	50	40
42	52	42
–	54	44
46	56	46

Men's Shirts

American	Continental	British
14.0	36	14.0
14.5	37	14.5
15.0	38	15.5
15.5	39	15.5
16.0	40	16.0
16.5	41	16.5
17.0	42	17.0

Men's Shoes

American	Continental	British
6.5	–	6
7.5	40	7
8.5	41	8
9.5	42	9
10.5	43	10
11.5	44	11

Armchair Travel

Movies/Videos

Many of the state's major towns and cities have established their own Film Commissions, as the state has grown increasingly popular with moviemakers. Almost everybody has seen a movie with Texas as its main location. If not, here are a few to see:

Giant (Elizabeth Taylor, Rock Hudson, James Dean), shot at Marfa in the Trans-Pecos region in 1956.

The Last Picture Show, a Peter Bogdanovich film written by Texan Larry McMurtry.

The Alamo, 1960.

The Best Little Whorehouse in Texas, 1982.

Big Country, 1982, starring Charlton Heston, Gregory Peck, Burl Ives and Jean Simmons.

Honeysuckle Rose, 1980, with Willie Nelson.

Texasville, 1990, another Bogdanovich film.

Paris, Texas, a 1984 Wim Wenders film.

The Trip to Bountiful, 1985.

The Positively True Adventure of the Allegedly Texas Cheerleading Mom, a Michael Ritchie film from 1993.

Bonnie & Clyde, 1967, starring Warren Beatty and Faye Dunaway.

Born on the Fourth of July, a 1989 Oliver Stone film starring Tom Cruise.

Blood Simple, a 1984 Coen brothers film.

Urban Cowboy, which proved to be the (temporary) downfall of John Travolta in 1980.

Discography

The following are considered to be among the best of recorded Texas music (*see also* **Musical Traditions**, p. 72):

Buddy Holly, *Buddy Holly: From The Original Master Tapes* (MCA)

Lightning Hopkins, *Texas Blues* (Arhoolie)

Blind Lemon Jefferson, *King of the Country Blues* (Yazoo)

Willie Nelson, *Red-Headed Stranger* (Columbia)

Roy Orbison, *The Legends: Roy Orbison* (CBS Special Products)

Big Mama Thornton, *Hound Dog: The Peacock Records* (MCA)

Stevie Ray Vaughan & Double Trouble, *Couldn't Stand the Weather* (Epic)

T-Bone Walker, *The Complete Imperial Recordings* (EMI)

Various artists, *Tejano Roots/Raices Tejanas* (Arhoolie)

Various artists, *Texas Music Vols. 1, 2 & 3* (Rhino)

Further Reading

Books
General

1001 Texas Place Names by Fred Tarpley (University of Texas Press, 1988)

Backroads of Texas by Ed Syers (Gulf Publishing, 1988)

The Best of the Old West by Ron Butler (Texas Monthly Press, 1983)

Cattle Kings of Texas by C.K. Douglas (Cecil Baugh, Dallas, 1939)

The Chisholm Trail by Wayne Gard (University of Oklahoma Press, 1954)

Cow People by J. Frank Dobie (Little, Brown & Co., 1964)

The Cowboy Encyclopedia by Richard W. Slatta (ABC-CLIO, 1994)

Encyclopedia of the American West, eds. Charles Phillips & Alan Axelrod (Simon & Schuster, 1996)

A Guide to the Lone Star State, WPA guide; Revised edition ed by Harry Hansen (Hastings House, 1970)

How Come It's Called That? by Virginia Madison & Hallie Stillwell (October House, 1958)

Journey Through Texas by Frederick Law Olmsted (1860: republished 1969 by Burt Franklin, NY)

Life on the King Ranch by Frank Goodwyn (Texas A & M University Press, 1993)

The Longhorns by J. Frank Dobie (Bramhall House, 1961)

A New Handbook of Texas (Texas State Historical Association, 1996)

The Texas Coast by Robert R. Rafferty (Texas Monthly Press, 1986)

Texas Wines & Wineries by Frank Giordano (Texas Monthly Press, 1984)

They Called Them Greasers by Arnoldo De Leon (University of Texas Press, 1983)

Where Texas meets the Sea by Brian Wooley (Pressworks, Dallas, 1985)

History & Current Affairs

A Personal Country by A.C. Greene (Texas A & M Press, 1979)

Austin: Old and New: A Map Guide to the Heart of the City (Treaty Oak Press, 1984)

Cowboy Culture. A Saga of Five Centuries by David Dary Avon, 1982)

Early Times in Texas by J.C. Duval (Stock-Vaughn Co., 1892)

The Galveston That Was by Howard Barnstone (MacMillan, 1966)

The German Texans by Glen E. Lich (Institute of Texas Cultures, 1981)

The Handbook of Waco and McLennan County, Texas, ed. Dayton Kelley (Texian Press, 1972)

Historic Austin: A Collection of Walking/Driving Tours (Heritage Society, 1981)

Houston: A History by David G. McComb (Univ. of Texas Press, 1981)

The Illustrated History of America's Great Department Stores by Robert Hendrickson (Stein & Day, 1979)

Lone Star: A History of Texas & the Texans by T. R Fehrenback (Collier Books, 1968)

North Toward Home by Willie Morris (Delta, 1976)

People & Places in the Texas Past by June Rayfield Welch (GLA Press, 1974)

Sam Houston's Texas pictures & text by Sue Flanagan (University of Texas Press, 1964)

San Antonio. A Historical and Pictorial Guide by Charles Ramsdall (University of Texas Press, 1976)

Texas: 1876, ed. Robert S. Gray. (Cordovan Press, 1974)

Texas: A Bicentennial History by Joe B. Frantz (W.W. Norton & Co., 1976)

The Texas Almanac (Dallas Morning News)

The Years of Lyndon Johnson: The Path to Power by Robert A. Caro (Vintage, 1983)

Art & Architecture

Center: A Journal for Architecture in America (Center for the Study of American Architecture).

Harwell Hamilton Harris by Lisa Germany Austin, (Center for American Architecture, 1985)

Talking with Texas Writers, by Patrick Bennett, (Texas A & M Press, 1980)

Texas Catalog: Historic American Buildings Survey by Paul Goeldner (Trinity University Press, 1974)

Texas Museums: A Guide-book. by *Ron & Paula Tyler* (University of Texas Press, 1983)

Natural History

The Explorer's Texas: The Lands and Waters by Del Weniger (Eakin 1984)

A Field Guide to the Birds of Texas by Roger Tory Peterson (Houghton Mifflin Company, 1963)

The Guadalupe Mountains of Texas by Alan Tennant (University of Texas Press, 1980)

Roadside Geology of Texas by Robert
  Sheldon (Mountain Press, 1979)
Texas Weather by George W. Bomar
  (University of Texas Press, 1983)
Wildflowers of Texas : A Field Guide
  by Geyata Ajilvsgi (Shearer Publish-
  ing, 1984)

Other Insight Guides

The 200 titles in the acclaimed *Insight
Guide* series cover every continent,
with a great many books covering major cities and regions in the US.

There are also over 100 *Pocket
Guides*, designed to assist the traveler
with a limited amount of time to spend
in a destination. The carefully planned
one-day itineraries written by a local
resident make a location easily accessible, and each book contains an easy-
to-use full-size pull-out map.

In addition, more than 80 *Compact
Guides* offer the traveler a highly portable encyclopedic travel guide packed
with carefully cross-referenced text,
photographs and maps.

Other *Insight Guides* that highlight
destinations in this region are:

Insight Guide: Crossing America. By
documenting travels across two trans-
American routes, our writers and photographers have created a realistic
portrait of the places, peoples and history of the USA.

Insight Guide: New Orleans. Founded
by the French, conquered by the Spanish, this colorful city lies to the north
of the Caribbean Sea. We bring to life
the home of jazz and the wonderful
Mardi Gras.

Insight Guide: The Rockies. This dramatic land of sweeping vistas, mountain passes, abundant wildlife and
whitewater rivers is a visual feast for
the intrepid traveler.

Index

S